FUNDAMENTALS OF AUDITING

Dr. Risha Khandelwal

TAP

Toronto Academic Press

FUNDAMENTALS OF AUDITING

Dr. Risha Khandelwal

Toronto Academic Press
4164 Lakeshore Road
Burlington ON L7L 1A4
Canada
www.tap-books.com

Email: orders@arclereducation.com

ISBN: 978-1-77956-311-8

Toronto Academic Press publishes wide variety of books and eBooks. For more information about Toronto Academic Press and its products, visit our website at www.tap-books.com.

ABOUT THE AUTHOR

Dr. Risha Khandelwal has expertise in finance and global business as an academician and researcher. She has been teaching and conducting research for more than six years. She has held positions at JECRC University in Jaipur and GL A University in Mathura. She received the UGC fellowship after passing the NET-JRF. She has written case studies, book chapters, and research papers that have been indexed by Google Scholar and SCOPUS. She is proficient in utilizing econometrics to analyze secondary data. She is currently a freelancer, helping academics with their research projects.

Table of Contents

List of Figures

List of Table

PREFACE

As the global economy transitions towards a knowledge-based paradigm, technology is increasingly essential across various sectors. Industry 4.0, characterized by advancements in data analytics, blockchain, artificial intelligence (AI), and other technologies, is reshaping traditional practices in industries from manufacturing to business operations. Within the accounting profession, these technological innovations are poised to bring about significant changes, particularly in auditing practices.

The evolution of Industry 4.0 in auditing initially began with the electronic processing of data, marking a pivotal shift towards the use of technology in accounting processes. General Electric's pioneering use of computers in accounting in 1954 represented a seminal moment, despite initially limited accessibility among accountants. Subsequent advancements led to the development of smaller, more affordable computers, facilitating broader adoption and training in electronic data processing within accounting firms.

By 1968, the introduction of Generalized Audit Software (GAS) marked a milestone in audit technology, enabling auditors to automate and streamline data analysis and verification processes. This software framework was instrumental in enhancing audit efficiency and accuracy, laying the groundwork for further technological integration in auditing practices.

Today, the accounting profession is increasingly embracing technological advancements to enhance audit processes. AI, blockchain, and big data analytics offer capabilities that promise unparalleled speed, accuracy, and depth in audit procedures. These technologies enable auditors to analyze vast amounts of data rapidly, identify patterns, detect anomalies, and provide valuable insights that support informed decision-making by organizations.

However, while the benefits of technological integration in auditing are substantial, there are challenges that warrant careful consideration. Issues such as job displacement due to automation, complexities in error tracing within automated systems, and cybersecurity risks underscore the need for a cautious approach in adopting and implementing new technologies in auditing practices.

This book explores these recent technological developments in audit work, providing insights into how AI, blockchain, and data analytics are revolutionizing audit methodologies. It aims to equip accounting professionals, educators, students, and policymakers with a comprehensive understanding of the opportunities and challenges presented by Industry 4.0 in auditing, emphasizing the importance of balancing technological innovation with ethical and practical considerations within the evolving landscape of the accounting profession.

Content/Structure of the Book

The book is structured into ten comprehensive chapters, each addressing essential aspects of auditing practices and principles.

Chapter 1 serves as an Introduction to auditing, providing a foundational understanding of the purpose, scope, and importance of auditing in ensuring financial integrity and accountability.

In Chapter 2, the effective approaches to auditing are explored, detailing methodologies and techniques that auditors use to gather evidence, assess risks, and evaluate internal controls.

Chapter 3 examines into effective audit strategies, emphasizing the planning, execution, and supervision of audits to achieve reliable and objective audit outcomes.

Audit reporting is the focus of Chapter 4, discussing the preparation and communication of audit findings and recommendations to stakeholders, highlighting the importance of clarity, transparency, and accountability.

Internal audit practices are examined in Chapter 5, covering the role of internal auditors in evaluating organizational processes, systems, and controls to enhance efficiency and compliance.

Chapter 6 addresses audit procedures of government organizations, including government audit and audit of local bodies, which focus on specific areas of concern or regulatory requirements.

Depreciation, a critical accounting concept, is discussed in Chapter 7, exploring methods of calculating and recording depreciation expenses to reflect the gradual wear and tear of assets over time.

Chapter 8 focuses on professionalism in auditing, discussing ethical considerations, professional standards, and the responsibilities of auditors in upholding integrity and independence.

Finally, Chapter 9 covers the journalization of transactions, detailing the recording of financial transactions in journals as a fundamental step in the auditing and accounting process.

Through these 9 chapters, this book provides a comprehensive overview of auditing principles, practices, and techniques, equipping readers with the knowledge and skills necessary for effective auditing in various organizational contexts.

Audience

This book is tailored for a diverse audience ranging from students and professionals in accounting and auditing to practitioners in business management and regulatory compliance. It serves as an essential resource for undergraduate and graduate students studying auditing, providing a comprehensive foundation in auditing principles, practices, and methodologies. For aspiring auditors, the book offers theoretical insights and practical applications necessary to understand the auditing process, including risk assessment, evidence gathering, and reporting standards.

Professionals in accounting and auditing fields will find the book invaluable for enhancing their knowledge and skills in conducting audits, ensuring compliance with auditing standards, and improving audit quality within their organizations. The detailed discussions on audit planning, execution, and reporting provide practitioners with practical guidelines to navigate complex auditing challenges effectively.

Additionally, business managers and executives benefit from the book's insights into how auditing contributes to organizational governance, risk management, and internal control assessment. It highlights the strategic importance of auditing in enhancing transparency, accountability, and trust among stakeholders, thereby supporting informed decision-making and sustainable business practices.

Regulatory authorities and policymakers also find relevance in the book's exploration of legal frameworks and regulatory requirements shaping auditing practices. It offers a critical perspective on compliance issues and the evolving role of auditors in ensuring financial integrity and corporate governance standards.

Overall, this book caters to a broad audience seeking to deepen their understanding of auditing principles, enhance professional competencies, and navigate the dynamic landscape of auditing in today's global business environment. Whether used as a textbook in academic settings or as a reference guide in professional practice, the book equips its readers with essential knowledge and skills to excel in auditing roles and contribute to organizational success through rigorous audit practices and ethical standards.

Learning Features

- Start-of-chapter learning objectives
- Key terms in each chapter
- Summary Points at the end of each chapter
- Review Questions at the end of each chapter
- Case Studies and Activities in each chapter for solving real problems
- References at the end of each chapter

CHAPTER 1

Comprehension to Auditing

LEARNING OBJECTIVES

After studying this chapter, you will be able to:

- Understand the meaning and importance of auditing;
- Discuss the process and challenges of auditing in a computerized environment;
- Describe accounting concepts that are relevant to auditing practices;
- Gain knowledge about the roles and responsibilities of an audit committee; and
- Define and explain information systems (IS) auditing standards.

KEY TERMS FROM THIS CHAPTER

Accounting system
Borrower company
Financial statements
Audit department
Decision-making process
Material error

INTRODUCTION

An audit involves an auditor looking over several books of accounts and physically checking inventory to ensure that all departments are adhering to the established procedure for recording transactions. It is carried out in order to verify the accuracy of the financial statements that the company provides. External audits of privately held businesses can be very beneficial in eliminating any prejudice regarding the financial health of the organization. Audits search for statements on any given object that contain what is known as a material error. They can assist in empowering stakeholders to make better, more informed decisions about the subject of the audit by giving them a sense of accuracy regarding the subject's current state. When audits are carried out by outside parties, the opinion regarding the subject of the audit—a company's books, the organization as a whole, or a system—can be open and truthful without having an impact on regular working relationships.

The majority of businesses undergo an audit once a year, but even larger businesses may undergo audits on a monthly basis. Because there are strong incentives for companies to purposefully falsify financial information in an effort to commit fraud, some are legally required to conduct audits. Auditors are a resource that some publicly traded companies use to assess the efficacy of internal controls on financial reports.

Every society's economic decisions must be based on the information available at the time of the decision. For instance, a bank's decision to lend money to a company depends on a number of factors, including the company's financial statements, past financial relationships with the company, and other considerations. Reliability of the information used in the decision-making process is necessary if decisions are to be in line with the decision makers' intentions. Inaccurate information can lead to resource inefficiencies that are detrimental to both society and the decision makers themselves. Assume for the purposes of this lending decision example that the borrower company is ultimately unable to repay the loan, and the barfly obtains the loan based on false financial statements. Consequently, the bank has suffered a loss on both principal and interest. Additionally, the money was taken away from another business that could have made good use of it. The probability of decision makers receiving inaccurate information rises with the complexity of society. This is due to a number of factors, including the existence of intricate exchange transactions, the remoteness of the information, and the volume of data. The decision-maker needs to devise a strategy for ensuring that the information is sufficiently reliable in order to overcome the issue of untrustworthy information. He must do this by balancing the anticipated benefits of obtaining more trustworthy information against the cost. Engaging independent third parties to conduct an audit or other form of verification is a popular method for obtaining such trustworthy data. Afterwards, the audited data is utilized in the decision-making process with the understanding that it is fairly accurate, impartial, and comprehensive.

1.1. IMPLICATION OF AUDITING

Therefore, auditing is the process of having an impartial, credentialed individual look over the company's books of accounts and vouchers to verify their accuracy. The precise procedures followed in a financial, operational, or compliance audit make up the auditing process. The procedures could change based on the business and the kind of audit services that the owners of the company asked an outside accounting firm to provide. The majority of businesses perform annual financial audits; operational and compliance audits are typically carried out as needed. Three fundamental steps are typically involved in the auditing process: planning, fieldwork, and reporting.

If the business fails the initial audit process, a follow-up step might be required. Planning is usually the auditing process's initial step. Typically, it starts with management of the business consulting with auditors to determine what kind of audit services the business needs. Internal controls, banks, fixed asset, and full financial engagements are examples of typical audits. Because each audit may involve varying degrees of auditor involvement, audit fees are frequently also discussed at this point. Higher levels of audit services typically cost more because they take more time and effort from auditors. Normally, the auditing process advances to the fieldwork phase after the audit engagement services are selected.

The auditors' practical examination of financial and operational data takes place during the fieldwork phase of the auditing process. The type of audit and the quantity of errors discovered during the fieldwork phase determine the field's breadth and depth. Auditors take a sample of the company's financial or operational data and compare it with the accounting or operational policies of the organization. When there are notable deviations or malfunctions, auditors usually choose to select a second sample to check for additional errors. In the event that additional errors are found, auditors typically label the company's entire information-related process as unsuccessful. Auditors frequently simply note the number of deviations or failures discovered in the information if the second sample is error-free. In most cases, auditors start the reporting portion of the auditing process after the fieldwork is finished. During the reporting stage of the auditing process, the auditors typically speak with management of the company to discuss their findings. In this meeting, management has the opportunity to refute any conclusions and ask the auditors to go over items discovered in the fieldwork phase again. In order to fulfill their documentation requirements, auditors may ask management for more information during this meeting. Auditors typically draft the final audit report, which can be distributed to external stakeholders, after company management and the auditors have approved the initial audit report.

Remedial audits are carried out on companies that do not receive a passing audit score during the follow-up stage of the auditing process. Acceptable audit scores are typically assigned to each department within the operations of large or publicly traded companies. Remedial audits are merely an extension of the process, so it is not uncommon for auditors to routinely demand smaller businesses conduct them.

ICAI Auditing Standards

The Standards on Auditing (SAs) are a comprehensive set of auditing standards established by the Institute of Chartered Accountants of India (ICAI). These guidelines are in line with the International Standards on Auditing (ISAs) and offer a framework for conducting audits in India. The planning, risk assessment, audit evidence, and reporting phases of the auditing process are all covered by the ICAI's auditing standards. They seek to improve the audit process's quality, consistency, and transparency in order to increase the financial statements' dependability. Important standards include SA 315—which concentrates on detecting and evaluating the risks of material misstatement—and SA 200, which describes the fundamentals and obligations of auditors. The standards (SA 500 series) also address the use of external confirmations, documentation requirements, and internal control evaluation. They also provide guidance to auditors on how to handle unique situations, like group financial statement audits (SA 600 series), and how to express an opinion on the financial statements (SA 700 series). All chartered accountants conducting audits in India must adhere to these standards, which are updated on a regular basis to take into account modifications to the business landscape, legal requirements, and international best practices.

IFRS Auditing Standards

The International Accounting Standards Board (the Board) created and maintains the International Financial Reporting Standards (IFRS Standards), a single set of auditing guidelines that are meant to be applied consistently throughout developed, emerging, and developing economies.

Components of IFRS Standards

You can prepare interim financial statements in accordance with IFRS Standards by incorporating illustrative disclosures and using a companion disclosure checklist. They consist of two parts and are compliance-focused:

- Illustrative disclosures based on a hypothetical multinational corporation that show one potential format for financial statements prepared under IFRS; and
- Complementary disclosure checklist: lists the disclosures needed for audit services.

For its members, the IFRS offers auditing standards. This encourages consistency and quality among the participants.

Checklist for Audit of Financial Statements under IFRS:

1. Make sure you abide by all agreements—including operating, leasing, and debt agreements—both new and old, as well as any amendments passed throughout the year. These agreements will be examined by your auditor as part of the fieldwork audit procedures, and they will be used to create the IFRS footnotes for your financial statements.
2. Reconcile all of the bookkeeping accounts, such as cash, inventory, accounts payable, receivable, and accrued costs. Preparing financial statements starts with this reconciliation. It's possible that

you'll need expert auditing services with prior IFRS experience.

3. All related party transactions, such as purchases, leases, and sales, should be gathered and assembled in detail. The IFRS mandates full financial accounting documentation during auditing.
4. Ascertain that you adhere to the rules and standards for IFRS auditing. Consistency in your internal audits: incorporate the capitalization policy.
5. Adjust equity accounts to reflect modifications to existing agreements or the addition of new ones. These accounts, which are a component of the financial transactions in the fiscal year, are required by the IFRS Act for the financial statements.
6. Make sure everything on the IFRS checklist is ready before the audit. The items vary based on the kind and scale of the business. Make sure the schedules for Property, Plant, and Equipment (PP and E) are current. Make sure all of the assets you bought and sold during the fiscal year are included in your PP&E summary with their dates, amounts, and thorough descriptions.

1.1.1. Objectives of Auditing

The main objectives of auditing are:

A. Primary Objectives

The Primary objectives of auditing are as below:

- *Fairness of Statements:* Assessing the fairness of statements is the goal of auditing. Following an audit, the financial statements can present a true and fair picture. It is not feasible to provide 100% accuracy due to the limitations of financial statements; therefore, an effort is made to present a fair picture of financial statements.
- *Prescribed Laws:* The audit's goal is to confirm that the financial statements were prepared in accordance with the applicable laws. Numerous laws regulate the operations of numerous businesses. The auditor can say whether or not the final accounts were prepared in accordance with the laws as prescribed.
- *Accounting Policies:* Examining the accounting policies is the goal of auditing. When creating accounting records, adherence to the accounting policies is required. A more efficient accounting system can yield superior outcomes. Regarding accounting practices that serve the interests of business, the auditor is qualified to provide an opinion.
- *Independent Opinion:* The audit's objective is to provide an unbiased opinion. The auditor needs to do his job with integrity. Managers and other people must not have any influence over him. High ethical standards are necessary for independent reporting.

B. Secondary Objectives

The Secondary objectives of auditing are as given:

- **Detection of Errors:** The goal of auditing is to find the mistakes. The auditor has tools at his disposal to identify mistakes in the accounting records. It is management's responsibility to prevent mistakes.

Error detection and correction are aided by the independent audit work.

- *Detection of Frauds*: Finding frauds is the aim of auditing. Fraud detection is the responsibility of the management. An audit may find the different kinds of fraud. For the benefit of the owners, the management may take action to rectify the negative effects of frauds.
- *Prevention of Errors*: The auditing process's aim is errors. Errors can be avoided by implementing efficient internal controls. Employee negligence or a heavy workload can also contribute to mistakes. Every employee shouldn't have to shoulder more work than necessary. A junior employee's work should be reviewed by a senior employee.
- *Prevention of Frauds*: Preventing fraud is the goal of auditing. In accounting, it encompasses record-keeping manipulation or alteration, asset misappropriation, leaving out the effects of transactions from records or documents, documenting transactions without providing sufficient context, and improper application of accounting rules. An efficient internal check is a helpful tool in the fight against fraud.

C. Special Objectives

The Special objectives of auditing are:

- *Management Audit*: A management audit's objectives are to evaluate performance, examine organizational structure, and recommend the best course of action. It is a voluntary audit that has the ability to check policies by going through management functions.
- *Tax Audit*: To appease the tax officers is the goal of auditing. To ascertain the income, the can be performed. Tax audits can be used by partnership firms and sole proprietors to resolve their tax disputes.
- *Social Audit*: Measuring the business's social performance is the goal of the social audit. The preservation of the environment is a concern for society. The business performance of the society can be examined by the social audit.
- *Propriety Audit*: An integrity audit's goal is to look into how money is being used. Utilizing resources economically and in the best interests of business is a requirement. Every rupee that is spent for the good of business needs to have a reason. The audit can identify prudent financial management.
- *Cost Audit*: Verifying the accuracy of cost accounts is the goal of a cost audit. The management was required to maintain books and other records in accordance with the cost objectives. The management can increase operational efficiency with the aid of the cost audit.
- *Operations*: The goal of an operations audit is to stop resource abuse. It's included in the social audit. When allocating funds, management needs to exercise caution. To get the best results at the lowest possible cost, resources must be used wisely.
- *Bid Offer*: Finding the true value of the business forbid offer is the audit's main goal. Sales are then based on the net tangible asset

value. On the basis of such price, the bidders may submit their bids. The audited accounts are used as a reference to make decisions.

- *Purchase Consideration*: The audit's goal is to ascertain a company's purchase price. The value of the assets and liabilities is determined by the audited accounts. Both buyers and sellers learn what a business is truly worth. They could agree to combine or merge their businesses.
- *Loan*: A loan could be the audit's goal. The management has the option to speak with lenders and banks. The source of funding for the bankers is audited accounts. The loan facility is legally required to have audited accounts.
- *Admission*: The purpose of the audit may be an admission of a partner. The audited accounts can provide information to new as well as old partners. They can decide terms and conditions for admission. The value of assets and liabilities is agreed upon.
- *Profits*: The purpose of audit may be checking variations in profits. The fluctuation in profits can be analyzed by an expert auditor. The file of business depends on reasonable profits.

1.1.2 Significance of the Audit in an Organization

To enhance the caliber and safety of your goods and services as well as to establish a consistent and dependable workflow, audits are crucial for your company. Some audits are required by law, such as privacy audits for companies that handle personal data or financial audits for publicly traded companies. Nevertheless, audits are still beneficial even if your company is exempt from that requirement.

Although auditing reduces risk in companies and enterprises, the very concept of auditing makes people shudder. Nevertheless, many businesses use optimal auditing as a tool to assess business performance and enhance their management, procedures, and policies. Typically, auditing is a component of a function that looks at the financial, operational, and accounting records to see if the business or company is abiding by accounting principles, applicable laws, and governance standards.

Here are three roles of auditing that are less popular yet very crucial.

Audit Promotes A Sound System Of Internal Control:

The internal operations of an organization can be monitored through an audit. Furthermore, from the standpoint of business process and documentation, an effective internal working process is a collection of preventive, strategic, and directing control techniques that arises from the company's dedication to good governance.

Auditing Helps In Detecting Fraud In Timely Manner

If appropriate auditing procedures were followed, many of the recent disasters could have been avoided. As a tool, auditing highlights problems and other warning signs that might point to atypical work. An expert auditor could find significant misbehavior by looking through the financial and operational records of the business. The clues might be concealed as fictitious money transfers, competing interests between company executives, or resource mismanagement.

Audit Protects The Reputation Of The Company:

In the end, the combination of the two aforementioned functional benefits of auditing contributes to enhancing the company's reputation by acting as a barrier against declining operations and finances. In order to enhance the company's reputation in the eyes of its clients, government agencies, investors, and other stakeholders, the signature of an established and independent auditor is highly significant.

1.1.3 Statutory Requirements of the Auditing

The word "statutory" indicates that a statute has mandated the audit. A statute is a law or rule that is passed by the related government's legislative branch. Federal, state, and local governments are among the entities that have the authority to enact laws. A statute in business also refers to any regulation that the board of directors or executive committee of the company establishes.

An audit is a review of the documents that a company, government agency, or individual has on file. Usually, this entails looking over different financial records or other data. An organization's records pertaining to income or profit, investment returns, expenses, and other items may be reviewed during a financial audit. A combined ratio is also computed using a number of these items.

Finding out whether money was handled correctly and whether all necessary filings and records are accurate are frequently the goals of a financial audit. The auditing body informs the parties involved in the audit at the outset of what documents are needed for the investigation. In order for the auditors to conduct their analysis, the company they are auditing collects and provides the information they are asked to. If errors are discovered, the proper sanctions might be implemented. Being the target of a statutory audit does not always indicate malfeasance. Rather, it is frequently a formality meant to ensure that different records are regularly examined by a qualified third party, thereby aiding in the prevention of activities like the misappropriation of funds. This also holds true for other kinds of audits.

Use and workflow

Every municipality may be required by state law to participate in an annual statutory audit. This might mean going over every account and financial transaction and releasing the audit findings to the general public. Holding the local government responsible for how it uses tax payer money is the goal. Numerous government agencies take part in audits on a regular basis. This makes it easier to verify that money given out by a bigger government body, like the federal or state governments, has been spent sensibly and in compliance with any applicable laws or regulations. Foreign governments frequently demand access to the findings of a statutory audit, which is another common occurrence for multinational corporations. Consider XYZ Corp. as an example, which is headquartered in the US but has branches and conducts regular business in Europe. In some European nations, it might be legally necessary for those business units to undergo a statutory audit.

1.1.4 Who can be an Auditor?

A qualified individual with the responsibility of reviewing an organization's financial statements, confirming their accuracy, and confirming compliance with relevant accounting rules and guidelines is known as an auditor. In India, a member of the Institute of Chartered Accountants of India (ICAI) and a Chartered Accountant (CA) with a current Certificate of Practice (COP) are prerequisites for becoming an auditor. Any person, partnership firm, or limited liability partnership (LLP) that satisfies certain requirements may be appointed as an auditor under the Companies Act of 2013. Individual auditors must be well-versed in auditing procedures and free from any disqualifying conditions, such as being indebted to the company, owning stock or interests in the entity under audit, or having certain relatives in executive roles at the business.

If all of the partners operating under the firm's name are certified chartered accountants, an audit firm—a partnership or an LLP—may also be designated as an auditor. The company must also abide by the ICAI's guidelines for audit quality and ethics. Furthermore, if the firm or any of its partners are in a conflict of interest with respect to the company that is being audited, or if they are otherwise disqualified under the Companies Act, they cannot be appointed. Throughout the audit process, an auditor—whether an individual or a firm—must remain impartial and independent. They cannot be related to the client in any way that would make it more difficult for them to render an unbiased decision.

The Companies Act of 2013 expressly prohibits certain individuals from being appointed as auditors. These consist of corporate entities, company officers or workers, and people or businesses whose dealings with the company could affect their independence. In addition, those who have been found guilty of fraud within a certain time frame or who are partners or relatives of the company's directors or employees are not eligible. Furthermore, it is against the law for an individual or organization to take on the role of company auditor if they have any direct or indirect substantial financial or commercial interests in the company, any of its subsidiaries, or its holding company.

Normally, at the company's annual general meeting (AGM), the shareholders appoint the auditor. The Board of Directors may choose to designate the auditor in specific circumstances, such as the first auditor following incorporation or in the event of a casual vacancy. Unless they are reappointed, the auditor's term of office normally runs until the end of the following AGM. The Companies Act prohibits auditors from working for the same company for more than ten years in a row for listed companies and some other categories, encouraging auditor rotation to improve audit quality and independence.

In the end, an auditor's job is to do their work in compliance with the ICAI's Standards on Auditing in order to give a reasonable assurance that the financial statements are free from material misstatement, whether from fraud or error. They play a critical role in preserving the honesty and openness of financial reporting, protecting stakeholder interests, and fostering investor confidence in the capital markets.

1.1.5. Types of Auditing

In general, an audit is an investigation of an existing system, report, or entity. There are a number of types of audits that can be conducted, including the following:

Compliance audit

A compliance audit is a comprehensive analysis of an organization's adherence to legal mandates. Audit reports evaluate the thoroughness and resilience of the risk management procedures, security policies, user access controls, and compliance planning throughout a compliance audit. Whether an organization is a public or private enterprise, the types of data it handles, and whether it transfers or keeps sensitive financial information are all factors that influence the specific topics covered in a compliance audit. A compliance audit is a formal review of an organization's operations and procedures that focuses primarily on an entity's compliance with internal rules, regulations, policies, decisions, and procedures. An audit report will address the effectiveness of user access controls, security policies, risk management protocols, and compliance plans.

Internal system audit

Internal audits assess an organization's corporate governance, accounting procedures, and internal controls. These audits support timely and accurate data collection and financial reporting in addition to ensuring compliance with laws and regulations.

Businesses that employ internal auditors do so to support their management teams. Additionally, by spotting issues and fixing mistakes before an external audit finds them, these audits give management the resources they need to achieve operational efficiency.

It is only fitting that Internal Audit's operations be overseen by the CEO or Board of Directors via its Audit Committee, given that Internal Audit is accountable to upper management. For internal audit to be a reliable source of information for leadership, its members need to be impartial and free from internal politics. Working with management, Internal Audit reviews control activities over important systems and processes in a methodical manner under the direction of the Audit Committee.

Internal audits are the term used to describe the reviews carried out by internal audit. An internal audit can be used to evaluate how well a process is being carried out or how well an organization is performing in comparison to various guidelines, policies, metrics, or laws. A company's internal controls for accounting, corporate governance, financial reporting, and IT general controls may be examined as part of these audits. Evaluation of the efficacy and efficiency of crucial business processes, like supply chain management, may also be a part of internal audits. Internal auditors are those who work in the internal audit department. Internal auditors can work across the board for a company or focus on specific areas of expertise.

Surveillance audit

The ISCC EU and ISCC CORSIA certified economic operators are subject to the surveillance audit requirements; ISCC PLUS is exempt from these requirements. These requirements also apply to economic operators certified under ISCC EU and ISCC PLUS for surveillance audits. Six months following any economic operator's first (initial) certification in a high-risk supply chain, the certification body is required to perform mandatory surveillance audits. Economic operators who gather, process, store, or trade materials run a high risk even though they might be able to receive additional incentives in certain EU Member States (e.g. double-counting), such as products based on waste and residues or waste and residues. For traders and collection sites handling residues as well as waste (e.g. utilized vegetable or cooking oil) as well as virgin oils. Three months following the first (initial) certification (covering the first mass balance period), a surveillance audit is required for palm oil and rapeseed oil. Following the same risk-based methodology, this surveillance audit will be carried out in addition to the one that must occur six months following the initial certification. Audits of surveillance must always take place on the property. Traceability requirements should be the primary focus of the surveillance audits, e.g. the examination of mass balances and delivery documentation.

1.1.6 Difference between Internal and External Audit

There are several key differences between external and internal audits.

1. The degree of independence is where things differ first. While we, as an independent third party, conduct external audits, the company's own staff or the internal audit department works with our assistance to conduct internal audits. Accordingly, an external audit offers a more objective evaluation of the financial data and business operations of a company, whereas an internal audit is typically more subjective—but that's where we come in. We make sure a business cannot use the audit to further their own objectives.
2. The extent of the evaluation is another distinction between internal and external audits. External audits typically cover a set time period, like a year, and are concentrated on financial data and documentation. Conversely, internal audits concentrate on the overall operations and procedures of the business and can address a broad range of subjects, including technology and systems, human resources, compliance, and risk management.
3. The degree of detail in the assessment is the third distinction between internal and external audits. Since external audits are mandated to reassure stakeholders that the company's financial statements are accurate and compliant with applicable laws and regulations, they are typically more thorough and in-depth than internal audits. Conversely, internal audits concentrate more on locating possible hazards and areas where the business's operations can be strengthened.

Although they are sometimes mixed up or misinterpreted, internal and external audits have distinct functions. An organization's financial data and records are independently evaluated by external auditors, whereas its operations and procedures are examined by internal auditors. While both kinds of audits are crucial for guaranteeing the integrity and correctness of a business's financial data and operations, their scopes and levels of detail in their evaluations differ. It is imperative that organizations comprehend the distinctions between internal and external audits and leverage both forms of audits to enhance their financial reporting and overall functioning.

1.1.7. Classification of Audit

Audit may be classified into two categories mainly:

- According to organizational structure of a business; and
- From practical point of view.

A. According to Organizational Structure of a Business:

1. **Statutory Audit:** Certain private institutions also have their accounts audited by certified auditors (Quadackers, Groot, & Wright, 2014). Because an audit is not mandated by law, it is referred to as a private audit. These institutions can be of three different kinds, which are as follows:

i. **Company Audit:** The owner has the sole authority to appoint an auditor in the event of a proprietary concern. The terms specified in the agreement will govern his rights, responsibilities, and type of work. So that he can be held accountable for any allegations of negligence, this auditor needs to receive explicit written instructions from his client outlining what needs to be done and how to proceed. By presenting the agreement, he can defend himself against such accusations.

ii. **Audit of Trusts:** Generally, trusts are established for the benefit of the defenseless and vulnerable, such as widows and children, who are not qualified to view or comprehend the accounts of these trusts. As a result, the trustees are charged with keeping track of the assets and accounts. However, in a great deal of instances, the trustees either keep no records at all or, if they do, the records are frequently false. Certain provisions are occasionally included in the trust deed for the appointment of auditors to verify the trusts' financial statements in order to prevent such a circumstance. Public Trust Acts have been passed in a few Indian states, requiring certified auditors to conduct a mandatory audit of trust accounts.

iii. *Audit of Other Institutions*: There are other corporate bodies such as electricity and gas companies which has been formed under their respective statutes. There is another set of public bodies in the name of public corporations,

2. **Private Audit:** The institutions which are private in character also get their accounts audited by some qualified auditors. As such an audit is not required by statute, it is known as private audit. There may be three types of such institutions which are as follows:

i. *Audit of the Accounts of Sole Trader*: The appointment of an auditor in case of a proprietary concern rests absolutely on the proprietor. His rights, duties and nature of work will depend upon the terms given in the agreement. Such an auditor must get clear instruction in writing by his client as to what he has to do and how he has to proceed so that he can be held responsible for any charge of negligence and by producing the agreement, he can protect himself against such a charge.

ii. *Audit of the Accounts of Partnership Firms*: In case of a partnership firm, the auditor is appointed by agreement between the partners. His rights, duties and liabilities are also defined by mutual agreement and can be subjected to modification.

iii. *Audit of the Accounts of Other Individuals and Institutions*: There are other individuals, e.g., rent collectors, estate managers, etc., who have large income and huge expenditure. The qualified auditors are appointed by these individuals in order to verify various accounts prepared by the accountants.

3. **Government Audit:** The government conducts audits of its various offices and departments through a distinct department known as the accounts and audit department. The Comptroller and Auditor General are in charge of this department and is supported by a variety of officials at different ranks. There is no statute defining the responsibilities and liabilities of these auditors. They cannot be appointed auditors for matters of public concern since they are not public auditors. They operate in accordance with departmental policies and procedures because they are designed for use by government departments.
4. **Internal Audit:** Certain business establishments, due to their organizational structure, designate auditors who are tasked with conducting a continuous and routine examination of their financial records. Internal auditors are those who perform audits on a permanent basis. In addition to auditing the accounts, these auditors must report on ways to make the internal control system more effective and efficient as well as ways to improve the accounting system. They are not obligated to submit their reports in the same way as external auditors because they are not appointed as public auditors or external auditors. Internal auditing, to put it briefly, is the annual review of a company's books of accounts carried out by paid employees known as internal auditors (Quinn, 2002). Internal auditing has a slightly different scope. It has a stronger connection to managerial responsibilities than accounting tasks.

1.1.8. Roles and Responsibilities in Auditing

In order to achieve these objectives, several persons and/or groups interact and affect the audit process.

- **Taxpayers:** The books and records of the taxpayers form the foundation of the entire audit process. Important details regarding tax liability may also be found in the written and verbal declarations of the taxpayers. For the taxpayers to comply in the future, they must be aware of the law.
- **Auditors:** The auditor might be the only person with access to the taxpayer's records, can conduct in-person interviews, watch how taxes are reported, and can provide the taxpayer with information. As a result, the auditor bears main accountability for accomplishing the above-discussed general audit objectives. Auditors are expected to adhere to the Auditing Standards as outlined in this manual and are regarded as professionals. The auditor must communicate his requirements to the taxpayer, the supervisor, and/or the bureau chief.

  Auditors must gather the facts.

  - What does the business do?
  - How does the business do it?
  - How does it relate to taxation?
  - Document findings.
  - Keep the taxpayer informed.

- **Supervisors:** The auditor might be the only person with access to the taxpayer's records, can conduct in-person interviews, watch how taxes are reported, and can provide the taxpayer with information. As a result, the auditor bears main accountability for accomplishing the above-discussed general audit objectives. Auditors are expected to adhere to the Auditing Standards as outlined in this manual and are regarded as professionals. The auditor must communicate his requirements to the taxpayer, the supervisor, and/or the bureau chief.
- **Bureau Chiefs:** The heads of the audit bureaus oversee the bureaus' operations. To achieve the Division's goals, goal-setting at the bureau/district level is the responsibility of the Audit Bureau Chiefs. Bureau Chiefs are in charge of guiding unit supervisors in achieving team objectives while making the most economical and effective use of departmental resources. In order to ensure that the audit section operates as efficiently as possible, bureau chiefs are also in charge of developing audit tools. This includes training, updating manuals, and determining and disseminating technical and policy information by taking part in Core.
- **Core:** The Deputy Director of Audit, audit bureau chiefs, and audit managers make up Core, whose job it is to decide on audit policies and procedures and find solutions to audit problems so that audits are carried out and finished fairly across the division. Core takes into account additional variables, like upcoming laws or court cases involving tax-related matters. Core is also in charge of creating the audit policy.
- **Audit Technical Support Services (ATSS):** ATSS reports to the Deputy Director-Audit. ATSS's main functions are audit review and assessment, quality control, technical advice, statistical reports, and the provision of feedback to management on individual, section, and division training issues.
- **Protest Office:** The Protest Office handles taxpayer protests of audit assessments as well as protests of other enforcement activities and reports to the Legal Services Bureau. Protest personnel can review, rework, verify taxability, and look at legal issues involved.
- **Legal Services Bureau:** The Legal Services Bureau is a legal resource for Audit. Legal Services assists the Audit & Compliance Division by providing legal advice regarding audit policy and resolving questions related to the interpretation and application of tax law. This office also supports the actions of the Department in hearings.
- **Deputy Director-Audit:** The Deputy Director-Audit is ultimately responsible for program level performance standards for the CRS, CIT, PIT, Oil and Gas, Miscellaneous, and Fuel taxes. The Deputy Director is knowledgeable about the tax programs and aware of audit activities. The Deputy Director – Audit supervises the Audit Bureau Chiefs and leads Core.
- **Director's Office:** The overall objectives for Division activity are set by the Director's Office of the

Audit and Compliance Division. The efficiency of the audit sections in achieving the fundamental audit objectives is a concern shared by the Director and Deputy Director-Audit. In addition to ensuring that the work of the Audit Section is valuable and efficient, the Director works as a liaison with the Cabinet Secretary's Office in tandem with the Deputy Director-Audit.

- **Secretary's Office:** The Secretary's Office is responsible for interaction with the Legislature in the creation of tax statutes, promulgating necessary regulations, and writing rulings.
- **Administrative Services Division:** This division affects audits through overseeing the audit budget and through development of the systems which capture audit data.
- **Returns Processing Division:** This division affects audits by processing self-assessments and payments.

1.1.9. Measurement Criteria

To determine whether the basic audit objectives are being met, certain measurement criteria are applied to the audit results. Those measurement criteria can be categorized as follows:

- **Quantity:** The number of audits conducted is significant mainly because effective enforcement of the tax laws requires a minimum level of "audit coverage." The percentage of all taxpayers that are subject to an audit in a given year is known as audit coverage. The Division can monitor its audit coverage targets by keeping tabs on the quantity of audits it completes annually.
- **Dollars:** The amount of money assessed matters because it aids in identifying the taxpayers who have misapplied or underpaid the greatest amount of taxes. Any tax agency's audit coverage is typically less than 5%, so it is imperative that the taxpayers chosen for audit are those who have underreported to the greatest extent. We can assess if we are meeting our audit revenue targets by tracking the money collected from audits over time.
- **Quality:** In general, the quantity and kind of review comments that supervisors and the ATSS generate, the quantity and kind of protests that are received, and the percentage of collection recovery on audit assessments can all be used to gauge the quality. We ensure that resources are used effectively, educate taxpayers, and maintain a high collectability rate by encouraging high quality standards.
- **Compliance:** This is the most difficult criterion to apply. It has to do with the affect of the audit effort on the entire taxpayer population. It is presumed that the more audit coverage achieved, the greater the incentive for taxpayers to correctly self-assess. Also, it is presumed that targeting specific industries with reporting issues will assure greater compliance within those industries.

1.1.10. The Audit Process

Tax audits generally have four stages:

1. **Pre-Audit Research:** Assessing whether the audit assignment

satisfies the initial selection criteria and determining the optimal audit approach in advance are the goals of pre-audit research and audit planning. Pre-audit research will differ depending on the tax program, but it will always involve talking with the audit supervisor, reviewing Department records, and getting in touch with the taxpayer initially. The findings of this kind of research should be utilized by the auditor to plan the audit's methodology and timetable. In-depth office research should cut down on fieldwork time and help the auditor by highlighting any anomalies that require further examination.

2. **Investigation / Fieldwork:** An exit interview usually follows an initial interview conducted at the taxpayer's place of business, which is followed by fieldwork. Nonetheless, the auditor may also conduct an investigation in the office.

   The initial interview ought to be seen as a chance to learn things that will help you improve the efficacy and efficiency of the audit. To ensure that the data collected is accurate, the auditor should talk with the taxpayer about the auditing process. But if the taxpayer is evasive, the auditor ought to exercise judgment. Auditors should collaborate with taxpayers to obtain the records and information they request, even though they may ask for specific records containing the required information from them. During the exit interview, the auditor should discuss the audit's findings, offer draft work papers, notify the taxpayer of any missing documentation, outline the available remedies, and teach them how to accurately evaluate themselves.

3. **Audit Documentation (Write Up):** Throughout the entire process, the audit is being documented. In order to precisely identify audit exceptions, auditors record—or document—their findings and conclusions throughout the interview and investigative processes. The draft work papers and narratives are arranged and edited into a final report during the write-up stage. The permanent work paper file, which serves as the supporting documentation for an assessment, is created during this process. It is not prudent or feasible to record every detail of the audit processes that are carried out. To decide what data is required to support the noted exceptions and what is not, the auditor must exercise judgment. There may be minimum information requirements in audit policies. Supervisors are able to clarify that prerequisite.

4. **Review:** The review procedure guarantees that audit procedures are uniform amongst the districts and that the audits fulfill the Division's quality standards. All audits have to go through three main reviews: the ATSS review, the supervisor review (if needed to confirm that quality standards are met), and the self/peer review. The purpose of the auditor/peer review is to confirm that the reviewer has carefully examined the work as indicated on the Quality Assurance Evaluation Form (QAEF). In order to make sure that proper procedures

are followed, work papers are properly documented, the appropriate statutes are used, and narratives are well documented, the supervisor thoroughly reviews the audit at each phase. Compliance with audit policy and tax law is the main focus of ATSS review. This review also attests to the audit's inclusion of all the data required to support it in the event of a protest. Lastly, the purpose of the ATSS review is to evaluate the adequacy of the supervisor, peer, and auditor review processes.

1.1.11. Advantages and Inherent Limitations of Auditing

- **Advantages of Auditing**: Auditing has several advantages which are given as follows:
    1. It detects errors and frauds with suggestions for their prevention.
    2. To avoid such mistakes being committed the accounts are kept up-to-date.
    3. The parties feel confident of the audit report because it was done by an independent person or body.
    4. Accounts as audited stand authentic.
    5. The auditors are competent persons in the fields of accounts and financial laws so can render advice to management.
    6. In case of joint stock companies, the director has no chance of taking undue advantages.
    7. Auditing accounts facilitates settlement among partners.
- **Limitations of Auditing:** It should be evident at this point that the purpose of a financial statement audit is to give the auditor the ability to provide an opinion on the financial statements. Actually, determining the true and fair picture of an enterprise's financial situation and operating performance is aided by the auditor's opinion. It is important to highlight that the AAS-2 subtly states that the auditor's opinion does not guarantee the enterprise's future viability or the effectiveness or efficiency with which management has handled the enterprise's affairs. Furthermore, there are a few inherent limitations with the auditing process, i.e. a constraint that is unsurmountable regardless of the scope and nature of an audit process. It is critical to comprehend these inherent audit limitations because doing so will only serve to clarify the audit's overall goals.

The Inherent Limitations Are:

- First and foremost, the work of an auditor requires the use of judgment. For instance, it involves determining the scope of audit procedures and determining whether the management's estimates and judgment were reasonable in preparing the financial statements. Furthermore, the auditor can only reach reasonable conclusions based on a large portion of the evidence at his disposal. The audit evidence that an auditor gathers is typically more persuasive than conclusive. The auditor's opinion is limited due to these factors. Thus, it is rare to achieve complete certainty in auditing. It's also possible that some significant financial informational misstatements brought on by fraud or error, if any, go undetected.

- An efficient internal control system is typically necessary for the audit process as a whole. Furthermore, it is abundantly obvious that there is always a chance that an internal control system won't function exactly as intended. Without a doubt, internal control systems have some intrinsic flaws. Any internal control system may not be able to stop management fraud or fraud involving employee collusion. Certain management levels may have the authority to override controls; for instance, they may instruct subordinates to record transactions inaccurately or conceal them, or they may suppress information about transactions. The inherent limitations of an audit are also influenced by these inherent limitations of the internal control system.

Generally following are the Limitations of auditing:

i. *Non-Detection of Errors/Frauds*: Auditor may not be able to detect certain frauds which are committed with mala fide intentions.

ii. *Dependence on Explanation by Others*: Auditor has to depend on the explanation and information given by the responsible officers of the company. Audit report is affected adversely if the explanation and information prove to be false.

iii. *Dependence on Opinions of Others*: Auditor has to rely on the views or opinions given by different experts viz Lawyers, Solicitors, Engineers, Architects etc. he cannot be an expert in all the fields

iv. *Conflict with Others*: Auditor may have differences of opinion with the accountants, management, engineers etc. In such a case personal judgement plays an important role. It differs from person to person.

v. *Effect of Inflation*: Financial statements may not disclose true picture even after audit due to inflationary trends.

vi. *Corrupt Practices to Influence the Auditors*: The management may use corrupt practices to influence the auditors and get a favorable report about the state of affairs of the organization.

vii. *No Assurance*: Auditor cannot give any assurance about future profitability and prospects of the company.

viii. *Inherent Limitations of the Financial Statements*: Financial statements do not reflect current values of the assets and liabilities. Many items are based on personal judgement of the owners. Certain non-monetary facts cannot be measured. Audited statements due to these limitations cannot exhibit true position.

ix. *Detailed Checking Not Possible*: Auditor cannot check each and every transaction. He may be required to do test checking.

1.2. AUDITS IN COMPUTERIZED ENVIRONMENT

While it also poses technological risks, information technology aids in the reduction and improved management of business risks. Because of their unique qualities, computerized information systems need a variety of controls. Business risks are managed by application controls, and technology risks are managed by general IS controls. The goals of the audit function remain the same whether information is maintained manually or through computerized means, despite the differences in controls. The methods and instruments used may vary. New audit techniques have been produced as a result of modifications to control and audit instruments and procedures. The technology is mapped onto the internal controls. It is important to comprehend these controls and their mapping as tools for testing and assessing these controls. For the auditor to function well in a computerized setting, they must pick up new skills.

These new skills are categorized in three broad areas:

- First, understanding of computer concepts and system design;
- Second, understanding the functioning of Accounting Information System (AIS), an ability to identify new risks and understand how the internal controls are mapped on to the computers to manage technology and business risks; and
- Third, knowledge of use of computers in audit.

Acquisition of these skills has also opened up new areas of practice for auditors like Information system audit, security consultancy, web assurance, etc. (Bailey & Jensen, 1977).

1.2.1. Accounting Information Systems in Computerized Environment

Accounting records are stored in computer files in an electronic environment. There are three types of computer files: master, parameter, and transaction files. This classification is based on the necessity, frequency of updating, and necessary level of security, not on the kinds of records. Utilizing the tools offered by the operating system, database, and application software, file and record security is put into practice. Transaction-processing systems are becoming more and more important in supporting business operations as a result of the growing use of information systems. Furthermore, a

TPS is frequently AIS. Three components make up every transaction processing system: input, processing, and output. Since information technology operates under the GIGO principle, authorized, accurate, and complete input is required.

The input is automated to accomplish this. These days, a wide range of devices are available to automate a TPS's input procedure. Batch processing and online processing are the two forms of TPS. Every system has a different implementation of documents, controls, and security.

COBIT (Control Objectives for Information Technology) is an internal control framework established by ISACA for an information system. COBIT can be applied to the Accounting Information System. To apply the COBIT framework an organization should:

- Define the information system architecture;
- Frame security policies;
- Conduct technology risk assessment;
- Take steps to manage technology risks like;
- Designing appropriate audit trails;
- Providing systems, software security;
- Having a business continuity plan;
- Managing IS resources like data, applications and facilities;
- Periodically assessing the adequacy of internal controls; and
- Obtaining independent assurance for the information system.

The functioning of typical sales, purchase and pay roll accounting system in a computerized environment. In particular, we focus on the inputs required, application control, processing, reports generated, exception reports, files used and standing data used.

1.2.2. Impact of IT on Economics of Auditing

IT's effect on auditing's nature and finances. The economics of auditing have evolved along with the new practice areas and the IT skills that auditors now possess. IFAC has released a number of pertinent standards for computerized auditing over the last thirty years. These standards address topics such as standalone computers, database systems, online information systems, risk assessment in a computerized environment, etc. A few guidelines published for the manual environment also apply in this situation. AICPA and ISACA have released standards addressing different aspects of IS auditing. Information technology also affects work papers, reporting, audit documentation, etc. The skills and knowledge of traditional auditing, information systems, business and technology risks, IT impacts auditing, audit planning, audit risk, audit tools and techniques, etc. are all integrated into computerized auditing. Overall audit risks can now be managed and decreased since risk detection can now be regulated with the use of computer-assisted tools and procedures.

This preliminary review is the first step in the risk-based audit approach. Risk assessment comes next. Under the audit approach, auditing is done either through or around computers, depending on how intensely information technology is used. The next stage is to evaluate application and general IS controls after the approach has been chosen. The information systems are used to create reports, gather and analyze evidence, and assess controls using CAATs.

1.2.3. Concept of Security

Information security resources are susceptible to a range of technological risks, resulting in losses related to money, productivity, and intangible assets. In actuality, resources like data are the organization's material and monetary assets. A control structure known as security is put in place to ensure the availability, confidentiality, and integrity of data, application systems, and other resources. Information security can be implemented effectively by adhering to a few principles. These include: Accountability, which refers to the organization's clear distribution of roles, responsibilities, and accountability; Raising security awareness within the company; integrated security efforts; Cost-effective information security implementation; Regular evaluation of security requirements; and Timely security implementation. Application controls and general IS controls are used together to implement information security. Implementing security policies, procedures, and standards; utilizing systems software to implement security; creating a business continuity plan; and conducting information systems audits are examples of general IS controls.

In addition, a number of other control mechanisms are also employed in their implementation, such as the formulation and execution of security policies; environmental, physical, logical, and administrative controls; physical controls, such as locks and keys, biometric controls, and environmental controls; logical controls, such as access controls imposed by database management systems, operating systems, and utility software through sign-on procedures, audit trails, etc.; administrative controls, such as duties separation, security policies, protocols, and standards; disaster recovery and business continuity plans; information systems audit, etc.

1.2.4. IS Management

Information systems auditing is the process of gathering and analyzing data to ascertain whether information systems protect resources, uphold data integrity, successfully accomplish organizational objectives, and minimize risks. Data integrity is what all manual audits and IS audits have in common. Every kind of audit (information audit) needs to assess the accuracy of the data. Because IS audits are focused on efficacy and efficiency, they also incorporate aspects of management and proprietary auditing. IS audit assesses the role of IS management. There are five IS resources, per COBIT. Facilities, data, people, technology, and application systems. Like any other management function, the IS management function can be broken down into four stages:

- Management (which is equivalent for planning and organization)
- Implementation and Deployment
- Directing and Controls
- Audit and Monitoring

The most crucial tasks and safeguards for every resource at every stage of information systems management. We also go over the kinds of things an IS auditor would like to look over for each resource at each phase. All things considered, it is important to remember that the systems audit, which examines the controls applied to the system through the use of systems software, is the central component of IS auditing. Acquisition of skills, not knowledge, is required for systems auditing.

1.2.5. Availability of Information Systems

Three things are served by security: integrity, availability, and confidentiality.

Access controls guarantee availability and confidentiality; backup plans and business continuity processes guarantee availability. Availability risk is a significant risk associated with technology. The necessity for a disaster recovery plan is acute due to the growing integration of business processes with information systems, which are subject to technological risks. A disaster recovery plan places different IS resources in place in case such a disaster ever occurs, even though insurance can compensate for the loss of resources. It is a corrective control as a result. Business impact analysis is the first step in a business continuity plan, which also includes risk evolution and outage loss estimates. Disaster recovery resources are deployed based on outage costs. Disaster recovery resources cannot be implemented for all types of disasters due to cost/benefit considerations. These are set up for important applications and probable disasters. Financial auditors can also gain insight into the risks and significance of application by looking at the estimates and priorities set for the disaster recovery plans. This may also be taken into consideration when organizing an audit in a computerized setting.

1.2.6. Access Control

The operating system and the database are the two fundamental pieces of software used in all information systems. Both are capable of managing who has access to the apps and data. Whereas the database manages access at the record and field levels, the operating system manages access at the directory and file levels. This section covers the operating systems' security implementation capabilities. The access control features of database and operating systems are used to implement application controls. An interface between the application controls and the general IS controls is offered by both. Controlling who has access to the data, applications, and other resources is essential to ensuring data integrity.

All users must get just-minimum access which has two aspects to it:

- First, only authorized users should have access; and
- Second, access should not be unrestricted even for authorized users.

The basis for access should be need. All operating systems provide two different kinds of facilities for this: authorization and authentication. Only authorized users are able to access the systems thanks to authentication. Only minimal access to the files and directory is permitted with authorization. Systems administration is a tool available in all operating systems to handle these two facilities. Learning about the authorization, authentication, and system administration features associated with these facilities should be the auditors' first task after switching to the new operating system. Thankfully, the majority of operating systems share similar features, which speeds up the learning process.

1.2.7. Database Management

Data independence and data sharing are two crucial features that databases offer. Data independence refers to data being stored independently of applications, while data sharing refers to users and applications sharing data. These characteristics facilitate the implementation of information systems while also raising security concerns. Databases come with features like data dictionaries and database administrators who help with database implementation. Additionally, a database management system offers tools to address the issues of data independence and sharing. Every database has the tools necessary to set up authorization systems and sign-on processes (user identification and authentication). Adhering to the just-minimum-access rule is necessary to preserve data integrity. Application controls and the audit train are implemented using the database facilities. It is necessary to routinely backup the data files. According to the IT Act, electronic records are subject to the same record retention regulations as paper records. Standards for database systems used in accounting information systems have been released by the IFAC, and the Reserve Bank of India has also mandated record retention guidelines for banks. The most widely used RDBMS in the world, including in India, is Oracle, which offers tools for implementing access controls via authorization and sign-on processes. The implementation of authorization involves assigning roles to users, creating roles, and granting privileges to objects.

1.2.8. Application Controls and Their Functioning

Different kinds of application controls and their operations are discussed. Organizations encounter two categories of operational risks: business risks and technology risks. Technology risks can be managed and minimized by standard Information Systems (IS) controls, while business risks are managed by application controls. However, it's challenging to clearly separate the two, as application controls operate on the infrastructure provided by general IS controls. The main goal of application controls is maintaining data accuracy. This is achieved through ensuring the accuracy of input, processing, and output. Application controls primarily focus on audit objects. The goal of any audit is to confirm the claims made in the financial statements. By evaluating application controls, all seven types of claims made in a financial statement can be verified. COBIT has extensively covered application controls in all stages of information systems governance.

Application controls can be categorized as: Input validation, Input authorization, Input verification for completeness, and Input validation for accuracy. Controls over stored data integrity, controls over consistency of stored data, and checks for completeness and accuracy of stored data also fall under this category. Controls over data processing completeness and accuracy, restricted access to resources and data, and protection of output confidentiality and integrity are additional categories. These controls are essentially programmed procedures, and their efficiency can be evaluated through ongoing audits or substantive audits using general auditing software.

1.2.9. Evaluation of Business Risks

The job of a financial auditor is to evaluate business risks. By putting application controls in place, business risks are managed and controlled. Thus, a financial auditor's main responsibility is to assess application controls in order to minimize control risk. The garbage-in-garbage-out principle is adhered to by computers. Therefore, it is preferable to have application controls reviewed for compliance. Application controls are program procedures, so once they adhere to the company's internal control policies, they will continue to do so unless modified. Nonetheless, compliance testing is challenging, indirect, and demands more money, time, and resources—just like in the manual environment. Thus, substantive testing is carried out in the majority of cases. Only the most important systems are subjected to compliance testing. Evaluating the claims made in the financial statement is the goal of substantive testing, or any testing for that matter. That is, if the true and fair picture is shown in the financial statement. The auditor must design his audit to employ such tools and techniques, as to lower the detection risks, since he has little control over inherent risks and control risks. Here, computer-assisted methods and tools are helpful, but more importantly, a general toolkit that offers the means to carry out substantive testing.

In the category of general audit software, ACL is the industry leader. The software gives auditors the tools they need to assess each of the seven categories of claims included in financial statements. In addition to giving users the ability to comprehend the data and files, it also provides the ability to create work papers that are essential for any audit assignment. ACL Software offers tools to understand the quantitative features of the data as well as the qualitative features of the data. It also offers facilities for carrying out substantive testing. To enable both, the analytical procedures and substantive testing at the transaction level, it has utility facilities like indexing, sorting, joining, setting relation, creating output files, exporting files, extracting files, etc. The ability to create a command log is a great feature of ACL. This helps with work papers, enhances the quality of the audit, and maintains an eye on the auditor. Default log files are included with every ACL document. It can also be used to test the controls that have been put in place on the system, such as the operating system's and database's security features. As a result, it can support systems audits as well.

1.3. ACCOUNTING CONCEPT RELEVANT TO AUDITING

Establishing guidelines for the notion of materiality and how it relates to audit risk is the aim of this standard. When performing an audit, the auditor should take materiality and its connection to audit risk into account.

Information is considered significant if it is false (i.e., omission, or inaccurate statement) may have an impact on users' economic decisions made based on the financial data. Materiality is determined by the item's size and nature, evaluated in light of the specifics surrounding its misstatement. Consequently, materiality serves as a cut-off point or threshold rather than being a fundamental qualitative attribute that is necessary for the information to be valuable.

To allow the auditor to provide an opinion on financial information prepared in accordance with accepted accounting standards and practices as well as any applicable legal requirements, is the main goal of an audit of that financial information, the evaluation of professional judgment's materiality.

The notion of materiality acknowledges that certain issues, either separately or collectively, bear some weight in the true and fair disclosure of financial data in compliance, both concerning individual account balances and transaction classes as well as the level of financial data as a whole. Other factors that could impact materiality include relationships and balances on individual accounts as well as legal and regulatory requirements, non-compliance with which could have a big impact on the financial data. Depending on the subject of the audit, various levels of materiality may arise from this process.

The quantity and quality of misstatements must be taken into account, even though the auditor typically sets an acceptable materiality threshold to identify quantitatively material misstatements. A poor or inaccurate description of an accounting policy, when it is likely that the description would mislead a user of the financial statements, is an example of a qualitative misstatement. The quantity and quality of misstatements must be taken into account, even though the auditor typically sets an acceptable materiality threshold to identify quantitatively material misstatements. A poor or inaccurate description of an accounting policy, when it is likely that the description would mislead a user of the financial statements, is an example of a qualitative misstatement.

- Materiality should be considered by the auditor when;
- Determining the nature, timing and extent of audit procedures; and
- Evaluating the effect of misstatements.

1.3.1. Going Concern

- The purpose of this Auditing and Assurance standard (AAS) is to establish standards on the auditor's responsibilities in the audit of financial statements regarding the appropriateness of the going concern assumption as a basis for the financial statements.
- When planning and performing audit procedures and in evaluating the results thereof, the auditor should consider the appropriateness of the going concern assumption underlying the preparation of the financial statements.
- The auditor's report helps establish the credibility of the financial statements. However, the auditor's report is not a guarantee as to the future viability of the entity.
- In the absence of information to the contrary, financial statements are prepared with the assumption that an entity will continue as a going concern for the foreseeable future, which is typically a period of time not to exceed one year after the balance sheet date. As a result, assets and liabilities are documented during regular business operations. The entity might not be able to realize its assets at the recorded amounts if this assumption is incorrect, and the amounts and maturity dates of its liabilities might also change. Consequently, it might be necessary to make adjustments to the financial statement's asset and liability amounts and classifications.

Appropriateness of the Going Concern Assumption:

- The auditor should consider the risk that the going concern assumption may no longer be appropriate.
- Information from the financial statements or other sources may indicate a risk that the company's ability to continue as a going concern may be in doubt. The following is a list of examples of these indicators that the auditor would take into account. The existence of one or more does not always indicate that the going concern assumption needs to be questioned, nor is this listing exhaustive.

1.3.2. Corporate Ethics and Accountability

The ability of people impacted by a corporation to hold corporations accountable for their actions is known as corporate accountability. This idea necessitates significant modifications to the legal system that businesses are subject to. These include giving directors additional legal responsibilities to address social and environmental issues in addition to their current financial responsibilities, and giving local communities the ability to sue for damages when they have suffered because of a director's breach of their obligations. The corporate accountability "movement" holds that businesses should be "held to account," suggesting enforceability, rather than encouraging them to voluntarily provide an account of their operations and impacts to improve their social and environmental performance. Compared to proponents of corporate social responsibility, this is a more radical stance. NGOs and regional partners have waged numerous campaigns against corporations on a variety of issues throughout the years.

Instead, the term "corporate accountability" is frequently used to describe more forceful or binding methods of influencing corporate behavior. The phrase "corporate responsibility" is frequently used to refer to voluntary methods, even when those methods are backed by incentives derived from the market. Corporate accountability generally suggests that pressure from external social and political actors affects the actions of the company. These players have a variety of options for tactics, such as using the legal system to compel the application of social norms. One reason why ethics should be taken into account in the workplace is demonstrated by a survey conducted by Management Today and KPMG Forensic Accounting, which included over 800 directors, managers, and partners:

- More than 2 out of 3 say that everyone lies to their boss on occasion.
- Less than half consider the people at the top to be strong ethical role models.
- Over 20% felt it was okay to surf the net for pleasure during work time.
- Around 25% would not say that favoring friends or family in awarding contracts was totally unacceptable.
- Some 7% agreed it was okay to artificially inflate profits so long as no money was stolen.
- Only 1 in 5 were prepared to say that charging personal entertainment to expenses was totally unacceptable— (less than 15% for board directors).
- People over 40, those in financial positions and those in the public sector take a more judgmental approach to ethical behavior.
- A dishonest member of staff may receive a clean reference from 3 in 10 managers.
- Reasons for not reporting a fraud include alienate myself, none of my business, jeopardize my job, everybody's doing it, and it is fair game.
- Nearly 10% of board directors say it is acceptable to massage their profit figures as long as no money is stolen.
- **Ethical Codes**: There are many different codes that have been developed to suit various organizations. These codes cover items such as conduct, gifts, objectivity, and honesty.
- **The Nolan Principles:** This is a set of standards that cover people in public life, be they ministers, civil servants or people working in the wider public sector. The short but powerful set of seven principles can be used as the basis for developing a more detailed code for public sector organizations. There are seven standards in the Nolan code:

i. *Selflessness:* Holders of public office should take decisions solely in terms of the public interest. They should not do so in order to gain financial or other material benefits for themselves, their family or their friends.

ii. *Integrity:* Holders of public office should not place themselves under any financial or other obligation to outside individuals or organizations that might influence them in the performance of their duties.

iii. *Objectivity:* In carrying out public business, including making public appointments, awarding contracts or recommending individuals for reward or benefits, holders of public office should make their choices on merit.

iv. *Accountability:* Holders of public office are accountable for their decisions and action to the public and must submit themselves to whatever scrutiny is appropriate to their office.

v. *Openness:* Holders of public office should be as open as possible about all the decisions and actions that they take. They should give reasons for their decisions and restrict information only when the wider public interest clearly demands.

vi. *Honesty*: Holders of public office have a duty to declare any private interests relating to their public interests and to take any steps to resolve any conflicts arising in a way that protects the public interest.

vii. **Leadership:** Holders of public office should promote and support these principles by leadership and example.

- **Ethical Reporting:** The growth in Social, Ethical and Environmental (SEE) reporting has resulted in a code prepared by the Association of British Insurers on this topic, and extracts include that the board:
- Takes regular account of the significance of SEE issues.
- Identifies significant risks and opportunities arising from SEE issues.
- Has adequate information and directors are trained in SEE issues.
- Should ensure effective systems are in place to manage significant SEE risks.

1.4. AUDIT COMMITTEE

Within a company, an audit committee is a specialized governing body. The audit committee receives reports from internal and external auditors. The committee is in charge of giving the auditors guidance, oversight, and assistance while they perform their duties. An audit is a thorough examination of a company's financial dealings and operational procedures. The audit committee's four primary responsibilities are to choose the audit firm, mentor the auditors, evaluate the audit report, and report the audit's findings to the board of directors of the business. The committee operates independently of the regular governing boards to guarantee an impartial and equitable audit review. A mandatory requirement for all publicly traded companies is to release annual audited financial statements. The audit committee alone is in charge of choosing an audit firm. It needs to specify the range of tasks, the kinds of audits that will be carried out, and how frequently they will occur. A request for proposals for audit services is the usual procedure. Companies that are interested reply with their degree of experience, offering, and cost. After compiling a short list and conducting interviews, the committee makes the decision. Reviewing randomly selected transaction details is called a financial audit. Assuring the accuracy of the values reported on the financial statements is the aim of the audit. To establish the reader's level of confidence in the numbers and to make sure that standard business procedures are being followed, every item that was chosen is thoroughly examined. There are numerous other kinds of audits that can be carried out. To make sure that standard business procedures are being followed, a systems or operational audit is conducted. Transactions are chosen at random, and the department in charge must submit proof that they followed the right procedures by way of supporting documentation. An audit report offers a high-level overview of the auditor's conclusions followed by a thorough report on the transactions examined, the level of compliance, and any issues the auditor found. This report is given to the audit committee, who then has the chance to ask the auditors questions regarding their conclusions and any reservations they may have had. The committee prepares a report for the company's governing body following each audit. Their feedback and recommendations for priorities are included in this report. The list of flaws that must be fixed before the next audit is conducted is determined by combining the two reports.

1.4.1. Role of the Audit Committee

An audit committee will be established by the main board to perform those duties that the board decides should be properly allocated to this specialist forum.

The role of the audit committee may therefore incorporate some the following components:

- *The External Audit Process:* To review the external audit process and make recommendations to the board where appropriate.

- *The Final Accounts:* To consider the annual accounts and the external audit report that attaches to these accounts.
- *Systems of Internal Control:* To consider the adequacy of systems of internal controls. The current move to require directors to report on their systems of internal control means that this is starting to assume a higher profile.
- *Internal Audit:* Involvement in the appointment of the internal auditors and ensuring that the internal audit function operates to professional standards performs well and discharges its responsibilities under the audit plan and strategy.
- *Risk Management:* The audit committee will ensure that there is an effective system of risk management within the organization and that this system supports the controls which, in turn, provide a reasonable expectation of achieving organizational objectives.
- *Compliance and Propriety:* An oversight of systems and procedures is in place to ensure compliance with regulations, policies, laws and procedures and the organization's code of conduct. Also ensure that the organization is able to prevent, detect and respond to fraud and allegations of fraud.
- *Financial Management:* To consider the finances and expenditure of the organization and ensure that there is a good financial reporting and budgeting system in place and that this feeds properly into the process for preparing the annual accounts.
- *Special Investigations:* The audit committee may request special investigation from the internal audit, compliance officer, external auditor and external specialists where there is a need to probe into sensitive problems that fall within its remit.

1.4.2. Corporate Governance Committee

The set of guidelines and practices that an organization will employ to manage its day-to-day operations is known as corporate governance. People with financial stakes in the organization are protected thanks to this governance. An organization's management group as defined by its corporate governance is expanded upon by a corporate governance committee. Since shareholders own the company, publicly traded companies frequently use governance. The goal of corporate governance and its committees is to provide these people with eyes and ears inside the company. A continuous corporate governance committee that oversees other committees is frequently established by organizations. The executive governance committee is the name of this umbrella organization. This committee is composed of a number of positions held by directors and executive managers, though senior operational managers may also hold positions within it. Other committees, including development, building, audit, and compensation committees, are frequently formed by the executive committee.

The goal of a development corporate governance committee is to identify new avenues for the company's expansion and growth. To guarantee that they have a diverse range of experience and knowledge, this committee will consist of people from a variety of positions or roles within the organization. This committee is beneficial to organizations because it frequently offers a new perspective on growing the business or operations. A building committee will concentrate on overseeing a large organization's real estate. Many businesses will establish a subsidiary corporation to hold the company's real estate and buildings for legal reasons. Given that a company's assets usually consist largely of buildings and other facilities, the purview of this corporate governance committee is more internal in nature. Since that most organizations are able to depreciate their buildings or facilities for tax purposes, accounting may also play a significant role in this group. A crucial component of corporate governance, particularly for firms that are publicly traded, is the audit committee. Throughout their existence, publicly traded companies are typically required to submit to multiple financial audits. There are internal and external audits. Internal audits are a common tool used by managers and business owners to assess operations and make decisions. The purpose of external audits is to give shareholders access to financial health information. The audit committee is in charge of organizing the audit procedure and making sure the business complies with current legal requirements. Committees on compensation examine the funds disbursed to top executives. These people frequently receive generous benefit packages that may include bonuses, stock, or other advantages. The committee responsible for compensation will review the job descriptions to ascertain whether the salaries and benefits offered align with industry norms.

1.5. IS AUDITING STANDARDS

Information systems (IS) auditing is a specialized field, and the expertise required to conduct these audits necessitates standards unique to IS auditing. Promoting globally applicable standards is one of the objectives of the Information Systems Audit and Control Association (ISACA) in order to realize its mission. One of the main ways that ISACA has contributed professionally to the audit community is through the creation and utilization of the IS Auditing Standards.

The framework for the IS Auditing Standards provides multiple levels of guidance:

Standards define mandatory requirements for IS auditing and reporting. They inform:

- IS auditors of the minimum level of acceptable performance required to meet the professional responsibilities set out in the ISACA Code of Professional Ethics for IS auditors
- Management and other interested parties of the profession's expectations concerning the work of practitioners
- Holders of the Certified Information Systems Auditor (CISA) designation of requirements. Failure to comply with these standards may result in an investigation into the CISA holder's conduct by the ISACA Board of Directors or appropriate ISACA committee and, ultimately, in disciplinary action.

When deciding how to implement the standards, the IS auditor should take them into account, apply professional judgment when doing so, and be ready to defend any deviations. The IS Auditing Guidelines aim to offer additional guidance on adhering to the IS Auditing Standards. Examples of procedures that an IS auditor might adhere to during an audit engagement are provided by procedures. The procedure documents do not establish requirements; instead, they offer guidance on how to carry out IS auditing work while adhering to the standards. The IS Auditing Procedures aim to furnish additional details regarding adherence to the IS Auditing Standards. Resources ought to be consulted for advice on best practices. According to the COBIT Framework, management is in charge of protecting all of the company's assets. In order to fulfill this obligation and meet its goals, management needs to set up a sufficient internal control framework. A comprehensive set of controls and control methods are offered by COBIT for the information systems management environment. Based on the selection of particular COBIT IT processes and the taking into account of COBIT information criteria, the most pertinent content from COBIT that is applicable to the scope of the specific audit is chosen. The following are arranged according to the IT management process using the COBIT Framework. Because COBIT is designed to be used by IS auditors, business and IT management, and others, it facilitates the communication of best practices, the understanding of business objectives, and the formulation of recommendations based on a widely accepted standard reference. COBIT consists of:

- *Control Objectives:* High-level and detailed generic statements of minimum good control.
- *Control Practices:* Practical rationales and "how to implement" guidance for the control objectives.
- *Audit Guidelines:* Guidance for each control area on how to obtain an understanding, evaluate each control, assess compliance and substantiate the risk of controls not being met.
- *Management Guidelines:* Guidance on how to assess and improve IT process performance, using maturity models, metrics and critical success factors. It provides a management-oriented framework for continuous and proactive control self-assessment specifically focused on:
- *Performance Measurement:* How well is the IT function supporting business requirements? Management Guidelines can be used to support self-assessment workshops, and they also can be used to support the implementation by management of continuous monitoring and improvement procedures as part of an IT governance scheme.
- *IT Control Profiling:* What IT processes are important? What are the critical success factors for control?
- *Awareness:* What are the risks of not achieving the objectives?
- *Benchmarking:* In order to assess IT performance in business terms, Management Guidelines provides example metrics. What are others doing? How can results be measured and compared?

The primary objective indicators pinpoint and quantify the results of IT procedures, while the primary performance indicators evaluate the processes' effectiveness by gauging the factors that facilitate them. Capability assessments and benchmarking are made possible by maturity models and maturity attributes, which aid management in measuring control capability, identifying control gaps, and formulating improvement plans.

1.5.1. Code of Professional Ethics

The Information Systems Audit and Control Association (ISACA) sets forth this Code of Professional Ethics to guide the professional and personal conduct of members of the Association and/or its certification holders.

Members and ISACA Certification holders shall:

- Support the implementation of, and encourage compliance with, appropriate standards, procedures and controls for information systems.
- Perform their duties with due diligence and professional care, in accordance with professional standards and best practices.
- Serve in the interest of stakeholders in a lawful and honest manner, while maintaining high standards of conduct and character, and not engage in acts discreditable to the profession.
- Maintain the privacy and confidentiality of information obtained in the course of their duties unless legal authority requires disclosure. Such information shall

not be used for personal benefit or released to inappropriate parties.

- Maintain competency in their respective fields and agree to undertake only those activities, which they can reasonably expect to complete with professional competence.
- Inform appropriate parties of the results of work performed; revealing all significant facts known to them.
- Support the professional education of stakeholders in enhancing their understanding of information systems security and control.
- Failure to comply with this Code of Professional Ethics can result in an investigation into a member's or certification holder's conduct and, ultimately, in disciplinary measures.

CASE STUDY

OLD WORLD PIZZA COMPANY (OWP) BROKER AUDIT

Company profile

OWP is the leading branded frozen pizza manufacturer in the United States and Canada

2009 Revenue 2009- $800 million. Estimated Trade Marketing budget- $100 million

- Distribution Channel: Grocery, Mass and Club
- Utilizes an on-line Trade Marketing and Promotion planning and budgeting system
- Employs single Broker with National reach charged with the responsibility to research and resolve Deductions
- Ultimate responsibility for Deduction management and resolution place in the OWP Customer Financial Services group (Credit and Collection)

Business Situation

There were several strategic business reasons OWP wanted to initiate these Broker Audits. They include the following:

- OWP wanted to ensure their Finance and Sales policies and procedures were being consistently followed. They wanted to create accurate accounting for promotions, monitor spending and make sure that it was not excessive or wasteful.
- Create 'bulletproof' documentation of 'bill-back' spending through the Deduction Clearing process to satisfy their Internal Auditors and SOX requirement. At the same time ensure that Marketing had accurate spending information, coded correctly to each promotion, to be able to evaluate the effectiveness of the promotions.
- Because OWP used asset-based financing it was imperative that A/R contained no receivables subject to recourse. Valid deductions needed to be identified and cleared faster while all invalid deductions needed to be properly supported, charged back and collected as fast as possible.
- OWP also wanted to be sure that the Broker was collecting the maximum possible amount of invalid deductions. Not clearing deductions for the sake of clean reporting and meeting time lines. It was also expected that Broker Audits would significantly improve Broker responsiveness to the Credit, Customer Service and Accounts Receivable functions.

Technical Situation

A detailed evaluation of OWP's recent past and current technical situation uncovered the following technical challenges during the evaluation of its policies, procedures and broker execution:

- Originally used JD Edwards and Seibel but both were configured in a less than optimum manner. The configuration problems continued to plague OWP until OWP switched to Gelco from Seibel and ultimately from JDE to SAP.
- OWP relied on single national brokerage to represent them from a sales and deduction resolution standpoint. From an efficiency standpoint the Broker implemented an imaging system which enabled them to stop maintaining paper files. This operational change was implemented without consultation with OWP.
- Also adding to the challenges and leading to a feeling of uneasiness on the part of OWP were 1) the acquisition of the Gelco system by Adesso and 2) the purchase by OWP of a new operating company, Idaho Frozen Potato Company, which previously had used a different broker.

Solution

IAB's solution for OWP was a fully managed annually recurring Broker Audit of the 'Hub' processing offices. Special focus was placed on offices which did not track with the others in regard to deduction resolution statistics.

- The first step in Implementation was to determine the scale of the Audit Program. IAB along with the OWP chose the largest Brokers offices for the first year, along with selected, problem Broker offices, as well as the Broker offices responsible for a handful of problem customers. Next we determine the frequency of audit program, which was three per month based on how many offices we have to cover in the year.
- The audit program and goals are then communicated to the selected Brokers Work with Sales and Notify the Broker force of the audit program Settled deductions data is generated and report of open deductions pending resolution is included when determining the appropriate sample size to request.
- The sample request was always created and submitted prior to the audit, with several 'surprise' deductions requested and reviewed during the actual audit. Worksheets were set up and completed with as much detail from the Event Planner prior to the audit with space to record findings. Previous audit points were re- addressed.
- Again, working with OWP, IAB determined what needed to be audited to ensure the strategic business reasons were addressed and the goals of the program were meet. This included the following: IAB reviews compliance with established policies and procedures; specifically reviewing open and closed deductions and payments to customers by checks verifying that valid deductions are not claimed multiple times.

The steps necessary to create and conduct this Broker Audit program were not complicated. The program was divided into three phases, 1) program planning, 2) audit execution and 3) reporting and corrective actions.

- Phase 1 was organized and managed by IAB with significant involvement of OWP Finance and Sales administration.
- Phase 2 was handled completely by IAB working with the Brokers.
- Phase 3 includes minimal involvement by OWP. IAB completely handled the reporting and corrective action follow-up with Broker and as necessary involves the OWP Regional Sales management, Sales administration and Finance.

Resources from OWP used to conduct the audit include OWP Sales and Finance policies; Event Planners and Budgets for the period to be audited; the Audit sample pulled for auditing from Settled Deductions, Settled Post Audit Deductions, Open Deductions and Accounts Payable checks when made payable to Customers. Resources required from the Broker for onsite audits include:

- A suitable work space
- Documentation maintained (files, paper or imaged, expected to contain)
- Contracts
- Proofs of Performance
- Customer claims or invoice
- Customer remittance
- Original invoice, Sales histories
- Broker sign-off / authorizations / approvals
- Comments / emails regarding exceptions

Benefits

Establish clear understanding of and compliance with Your Company's Finance and Sales policies and procedures. Never assume that your Broker knows your companies Deduction Resolution Policies and Procedures. Broker Audits are an effective 'template' for on-going communications. They significantly improve Broker responsiveness to the Credit, Customer Service and the Accounts Receivable functions. Specific significant benefits include:

- Created 'bulletproof' documentation of Deals, Promotions, and Sales Agreements, as well as valid 'bill-back' spending through the Deduction Clearing process. Imaging systems are the leading edge when it comes to documentation, but without your companies clearly spelled out requirements its value is questionable. More than ever complete consistent documentation is the key to protecting your company from invalid deductions and is clearly an area where a Broker should be held responsible.

- Cleared deductions faster while denying all invalid claims. Today it's all about balances, how to keep your deduction balances low. Broker Audits help you accomplish this in 3 ways. (i) Clear valid deductions faster with better staffing, better documentation, and better communication; (ii) Collect invalid deductions faster by proving your case faster with detailed documentation. (iii) Reduce incoming deductions, by NOT being a target for retailers who take the path of least resistance when it comes to deductions.
- Satisfied internal auditors and SOX requirement. Documentation of Trade Marketing Spending through deductions is just as important as documentation of payments made by check through A/P. In addition, faster resolution of both valid and invalid deductions provides a more accurate picture of Accounts Receivable and Sales Revenue.
- Created metrics to measure the effectiveness of the various Broker locations through the use of a Broker Scorecard. This enables year-on-year tracking of improved performance, meaningful management reporting and corrective action follow-up based on detailed accurate statistical reporting.

ACTIVITY

ANALYZING AUDIT FINDINGS

- **Objective:** To familiarize students with the process of auditing and interpreting audit findings. Provide students with a sample audit report. This could be a report from a recent audit conducted in a company, government agency, or nonprofit organization. Divide the class into small groups (3-4 students per group). Assign each group a section of the audit report to analyze (e.g., findings, recommendations, management responses).
- **Assessment**: Evaluate student participation in group discussions and the quality of their analysis based on the criteria provided. Encourage critical thinking and application of auditing principles throughout the activity.

SUMMARY

- Audit is the examination or inspection of various books of accounts by an auditor followed by physical checking of inventory to make sure that all departments are following documented system of recording transactions.
- Audits performed by outside parties on private companies can be extremely helpful in removing any bias when it comes to the state of a company's financials.
- The auditing process is the specific steps used in a financial, operational or compliance audit. The steps may vary depending on the company and the type of audit services company owners requested from an external accounting firm.
- The purpose of auditing is to detect frauds. The management is responsible for the detection of frauds. The various types of fraud may be detected by an audit. The management can take steps to correct the wrong effects of frauds for the benefit of owners.
- The purpose of management audit is to assess the performing, review the organizational structure and suggest the best course of action. It is a voluntary audit and an audit (It can go through management functions to check the policies.
- Supervisors are responsible for monitoring workloads, evaluating individual auditor performance, and reviewing each part of the audit to the extent necessary to assure that the final package meets division quality standards. Supervisors are also responsible for the productivity of their sections.
- The amount of dollars assessed is important because it helps to target the taxpayers who have underpaid or misallocated the largest amount of taxes. Since audit coverage for any tax agency is generally less than 5%, it is crucial the taxpayers selected for audit are the ones responsible for the largest amounts of under-reporting.
- Information technology helps in the mitigation and better control of business risks, and at the same time brings along technology risks. Computerized information systems have special characteristics, which require different types of controls.
- In the computerized environment accounting records are kept in computer files, which are of three types, namely master file, parameter file and transaction file. This classification is not based on the types of records but on the basis of need and frequency of updation and level of security required.
- Information security resources are vulnerable to various types of technology risks and are subject to financial, productivity and intangible losses. Resources like data actually represent the physical and financial assets of the organization.
- Information systems audit is a process to collect and evaluate evidence to determine whether the information systems safeguard assets, maintain data integrity, achieve organizational goals effectively and consume resources efficiently.
- Corporate governance is the framework of policies and procedures an organization will use to run its business operations. This governance ensures protection for individuals who are financially vested in the organization.

- The specialized nature of information systems (IS) auditing and the skills necessary to perform such audits require standards that apply specifically to IS auditing. One of the goals of the Information Systems Audit and Control Association (ISACA) is to advance globally applicable standards to meet its vision.

REVIEW QUESTIONS

1. How can accountancy and auditing be distinguished from each other?
2. What are the roles and responsibilities in auditing?
3. How do accounting information systems function in a computerized environment?
4. What are the principles of corporate ethics and accountability?
5. What is the role of the audit committee?
6. How does the corporate governance committee function?

REFERENCES

1. Abbott, L. J., Gunny, K., & Pollard, T. (2017). The impact of litigation risk on auditor pricing behavior: Evidence from reverse mergers. *Contemporary Accounting Research, 34*(2), 1103–1127. https://doi.org/10.1111/1911-3846.12215
2. Abbott, L. J., Parker, S., & Peters, G. F. (2010). Serving two masters: The association between audit committee internal audit oversight and internal audit activities. *Accounting Horizons, 24*(1), 1–24. https://doi.org/10.2308/acch.2010.24.1.1.
3. Bailey, A. D. Jr. (2014). Perspectives on the Public Company Accounting Oversight Board (PCAOB) 2004-2005. *Accounting Horizons, 28*(4), 889–899. https://doi.org/10.2308/acch-50736.
4. Bailey, A. D. Jr., & Jensen, D. L. (1977). A note on the interface between compliance and substantive tests. *Journal of Accounting Research, 15*(2), 293–299. https://doi.org/10.2307/2490492.
5. Quadackers, L., Groot, T., & Wright, A. (2014). Auditors' professional skepticism: Neutrality versus presumptive doubt. *Contemporary Accounting Research, 31*(3), 639–657. https://doi.org/10.1111/1911-3846.12038.
6. Quinn, L. R. (2002). Tension? *Strategic Finance, 84*(2), 29–35.

CHAPTER

2 Effective Approach of Auditing

LEARNING OBJECTIVES

After studying this chapter, you will be able to:

- Understand overview of audit approach;
- Know about internal audit activity planning;
- Identify the risk-based control and audit;
- Discuss on audit sampling; and
- Describe value for money audit.

KEY TERMS FROM THIS CHAPTER

Accounting firm
Balance sheet
Financial performance
Financial reporting system
Generally accepted accounting principles (GAAP)
Audit methodology
External audits
Financial position
Professional standardsr

INTRODUCTION

The impact of a client's operating environment, management information and financial performance, and the efficacy of the client's internal controls are all taken into consideration by the Audit Approach risk analysis methodology. It is predicated on an extensive, current comprehension of the business and sector of the client, acquired via an exhaustive examination of the internal and external operating environments. It lets us create an audit program with the best possible mix of tests that are tailored to the specific needs of each client. It also offers a standard procedure for creating and recording the audit program's foundation. We can schedule our work to be commensurate with the risk of a material error in particular accounts and transactions thanks to the Audit Approach. This serves as the foundation for organizing the minimal amount of work required to reduce audit risk in each domain to a minimum. Because of this, each audit process has a distinct goal that is connected to the unique circumstances of the company; nothing is routine and thus might not be required. By using this strategy, we can more evenly distribute our audit work throughout the year and prevent both over and under-auditing.

Professional standards demand that we take audit risk and materiality into account when determining the scope, timing, and nature of our audit procedures as well as when assessing their outcomes. During the first planning stage, there are two levels at which materiality is determined: planning materiality, which is the overall level related to the accounts taken as a whole, and tolerable error, which is the level of a specific balance or class of transactions. The risk that an auditor might unintentionally neglect to update their opinion on materially misstated accounts is known as audit risk. In order to assist us in creating an audit plan that will yield enough data for us to assess whether the accounts are materially misstated, we address materiality and audit risk on an overall basis.

The risks that: A material error will not be prevented or detected on time by the system of internal control, risk; A material error not detected by the system of internal control, detection risk; and Variables in a company's internal or external operating environment will result in a material error, inherent risk; are multiplied at the account balance or class of transactions level to form audit risk. The methodology offered by the Audit Approach allows us to connect these risk concepts to materiality and to the type, scope, and timing of our audit processes.

2.1. OVERVIEW AND STAGES OF AUDIT APPROACH

A specific set of steps or procedures known as audit methodology is employed to evaluate the financial and operational risk of a business. Both internal and external audits can be used to examine particular data pertaining to various business operations. Audits typically check the validity and accuracy of financial data. Nonetheless, some audits concentrate on non-financial factors. Typically, a preliminary risk assessment starts with a management interview. The scope and depth of the audit methodology are typically decided upon at this meeting because company management typically shares the highest risk areas of the business.

Following the meeting, auditors typically gather their notes and draft a formal agreement defining the audit's parameters. Modifications to the auditing process might necessitate adding a new section to the original written contract. Auditors usually start the planning phase after finishing the initial risk assessment stage. Auditors are introduced to every business area they will be auditing during the planning stage of the audit methodology. During this phase of the audit, walkthroughs are frequently used to acquaint auditors with company personnel and their distinct duties. The original audit scope agreement may be amended to include any additional vulnerabilities found by the auditors. The auditors are typically introduced to department managers by company management, which gives them the freedom to conduct interviews without undue influence. This preserves the audit methodology's integrity. After auditors have completed their audit planning assessment, the testing phase usually starts.

The most important part of the audit methodology process is the testing phase. In order to identify any infractions of internal operational standards or the generally accepted accounting principles (GAAP), auditors actively review financial data or business procedures. Typically, auditors take a sample from large data sets and conduct independent testing on it. If there are too many errors in the first test sample, the audit methodology might ask auditors to check more data or just label the first sample as flawed or against company policy. After testing is finished, auditors and management usually have a farewell meeting. The final stage of the audit process is represented by the exit meeting. During this meeting, company management and auditors can go over the audit findings and talk about any significant infractions or malfunctions that were found during the testing stage. After the audit exit meeting, formal audit opinions are typically filed within a week. In the exit meeting, companies have the option to contest audit findings if they are deemed minor or inconsequential in relation to their overall business operations. If too many violations were found during the first audit, audit methodologies may require companies to conduct a second audit.

2.1.1. Audit Approach: Four Types of Audit Approaches

The strategies or tactics auditors employ when performing audit assignments are known as audit approaches. Using an audit approach, internal and external auditors carry out their work in different ways according to the scope, nature of the client's business, audit risks, and nature of the engagement. It's crucial to choose the appropriate audit methodology. It can assist auditors in enhancing the efficacy and efficiency of their audits. The appropriate audit strategy may also enable auditors to concentrate on the appropriate areas and expend less energy on the low-risk areas. Various audit firms may employ distinct audit methodologies to carry out their audits. The most common strategy is the risk-based approach. This is due to the possibility that this strategy will enable auditors to focus on the most important areas of concern and reduce audit risk. Internal and external auditors typically employ four fundamental audit approaches. The four main auditing techniques are as follows:

- **Substantive Procedures Audit Approach:** When internal controls over financial reporting or the financial reporting system are unreliable, this strategy is typically used. Internal control over financial reporting by the entity will not be tested by auditors. They will concentrate on the significant or large transactions before moving on to the substantive testing. This method, also known as the "vouching approach," entails auditors choosing a large number of transactions and then determining whether or not those transactions have sufficient and trustworthy supporting documentation. Additionally, auditors will verify that accounting recognition and classifications adhere to the framework and accounting standard used in the preparation of the audit financial statements. This approach's drawback is that it necessitates testing a high volume of transactions, which will require more audit resources than others. Additionally, this strategy has the advantage of assisting auditors in reducing risks that internal control over financial reporting was unable to identify.
- **Balance Sheet Audit Approach:** The idea behind the balance sheet audit approach is that auditors assume that if the account balances on the balance sheet are accurately recorded, the income statements' accounting transactions will follow suit. With this strategy, the auditor will concentrate their testing on high-value balance sheet items and pay less attention to transactions in the income statements. Using this method, auditors determined that a transaction in the income statements is unlikely to be materially misstated if the items or accounting balance in the statement of financial position are accurate. Within balance sheet items, the primary financial assertions are existence, valuation, obligation, and right. Furthermore, if these claims are true, then it is very likely that the claims that they relate to are true as well. For instance, if it is verified that the assets' existence, valuation, and rights are accurately recorded in the balance sheet for both periods. Less is altered than depreciation in the event of inaccurate recording.

- **System Based Approach:** Substantial-based approach and system-based approach are not the same. The auditor does not rely on the client's internal control over financial reporting when using the substantive based approach, thus they do not conduct testing. They proceed to attest to each significant transaction in stat. However, using the system-based audit approach, auditors first ascertain from the entity's management team that a robust internal control system is in place. However, auditors must fully comprehend the client's internal control over financial reporting before relying on the system or internal control. Auditors must then test and validate those internal controls after they have completed their understanding of them. This is to make sure they are robust enough to generate accurate financial reports. Although the volume of transactions is not as high as with the substantive approach, auditors must still conduct substantive testing if they determine that internal control over financial reporting is robust.
- **Risk-Based Audit Approach:** The approach that you have likely heard about and used the most is the risk-based audit approach. The three main tenets of the risks-based approach are meeting the objectives, reducing audit risks, and requiring less work. This is the reason why auditors employ this strategy the most. The main way a risks-based approach works is by comprehending the environments, internal controls, and business of the client. The next step for auditors is to evaluate the potential risk areas and material misstatements in the financial statements. Following the identification of the risk areas, the auditors will develop their program and resources to identify potential risks. By doing this, auditors can test areas with lower risks while still meeting the goal with less time spent testing them.

2.1.2. Develop an Audit Approach

An accounting firm's set of procedures or actions when examining a client's financial data is known as an audit methodology. Because every client operates differently, each methodology is usually unique. Planning, fieldwork, reporting, and follow-up are the four steps involved in developing an audit methodology. To completely develop a practical methodology, auditors need to complete a few different tasks at each step. After a business signs the engagement letter with a client, a large portion of the work is completed. After the client first signs with an accounting firm, planning takes place. Auditors conduct management team interviews and create an audit schedule and plan. There is an initial scope included in the audit methodology. To decide how to finish fieldwork, auditors examine information from other sources, including current data and audit reports from the past. Due to increased audit risk, accounting firms may decide not to continue working with companies that have a history of financial difficulties.

Most audit work is completed by auditors during fieldwork. The sample size, testing procedures, and internal controls that auditors must examine are all outlined in the audit methodology. This process includes risk analysis as well. Auditors develop a fundamental evaluation of the risks that are present in the client's business operations. When risk is identified in the early phases of fieldwork, auditors can talk about how to handle these areas and adjust the audit process to guarantee a thorough audit of the client's data.

An audit's reporting phase marks the start of the process's conclusion. Generally, the audit methodology describes the preliminary matrix that the auditors create for their customer. A brief report on audit findings and the items' material impact on financial information are included in the matrix. Before releasing a formal audit report, auditors are usually required by the methodology to discuss a draft matrix with the client. If the client can demonstrate that the findings are not problems, auditors may reconsider some of their conclusions. The last step in an audit methodology is an audit follow-up. A second audit is required to make sure there are no issues with the current financial information if a client receives a qualified or adverse audit opinion. According to the audit methodology, all areas that failed the first audit must be tested again when the auditors return to the client for a remedial audit. Auditors retest updated data to make sure the client adjusted accounting procedures to fix earlier mistakes. The remedial audit usually employs the same methodology, albeit one that is less rigorous.

2.1.3 Assessment of Compliance Risk

A systematic process for identifying, assessing, and prioritizing legal and regulatory risks that could endanger the company is called a compliance risk assessment. It makes it possible for the company to focus vital resources on the biggest risks and areas without enough controls. A process for compliance risk assessment assists in identifying possible hazards that might draw regulatory attention, result in legal action, or result in fines. It is a means of promoting ongoing development and a component of a larger risk management plan.

Here's why you need to conduct a compliance risk assessment:

- This approach takes a proactive stance in handling compliance risks and guarantees the establishment of a strong corporate compliance program. The evaluation aids in detecting shortcomings in the present risk management and compliance procedures.
- Compliance risk assessments increase stakeholder participation and contribute to the development of a security-conscious and compliant culture. In the long run, the assessments improve cost-effectiveness and spare organizations from the financial strain caused by data breaches.

Businesses can find and address instances that, if ignored, could make them non-compliant by using compliance risk assessment. Organizations must match compliance requirements with their current cybersecurity policies, procedures, and controls in order to conduct compliance risk assessments. It finds holes and suggests plans for filling them in order to keep an efficient compliance posture.

2.1.4 Development of Audit Plan

A successful audit is based on careful planning. When carried out correctly, it is an essential initial step in the audit process that aids auditors in conducting effective audits, guaranteeing standard compliance, and reducing risk. Given the ever-increasing complexity and shifting risks that businesses face in today's environment, this is especially crucial. However, audit planning is not a straightforward, box-checking procedure. A number of things need to be taken into account, including the client's operations, internal control system, and business environment, as well as the engagement's timing.

Developing an audit plan typically involves several key steps, which include:

1. **Gain knowledge of the client**

It is important to have a clear understanding of the client when developing an effective audit plan. This involves knowing the following:

- The client's legal structure, ownership, governance, and related parties;
- The client's industry, regulatory, and other external factors;
- Their business model;
- The objectives and strategies and related business risks; and
- The measurement and assessment of the entity's financial performance.

Along with understanding reporting deadlines and the nature of communications with management and those responsible for governance, the auditor must also be aware of any reporting requirements outlined in contracts or statutes. In an audit involving an ongoing client, a significant portion of this paperwork can be carried over from the prior year, with a focus on any modifications that might have happened lately.

2. **Understand the system of internal controls**

It is imperative that the audit team comprehends, assesses, and records the internal control system elements pertinent to the audit for the entity. It is imperative to acknowledge and specify the information sources consulted and the steps taken to achieve comprehension.

3. **Determine materiality**

Establish materiality levels so that you can concentrate on areas that could have the biggest impact on the financial statements. This is a step in developing the audit's overarching plan. Based on the financial statement user's perceptions of the specific items, the auditor also evaluates whether lower materiality amounts are appropriate for specific classes of transactions, account balances, or disclosures in this step.

4. **Conduct risk assessment**

When making a risk assessment, audit teams take the following actions:

- Identify significant audit areas;
- Document the risks of material misstatement affecting the relevant assertions for each significant audit area (including fraud risks or other significant risks);
- Assess those risks;
- Select an audit approach that is appropriately tailored to respond to the assessed level of risk; and
- Document the linkage of the assessed risks to the audit procedures that respond to those risks.

When performing risk assessments, a number of factors are taken into account. The significance of reported amounts, the outcomes of preliminary analytical processes, data gathered about the entity and its surroundings (including its internal control system), the assessment of fraud, conversations within the engagement team, and the outcomes of engagement acceptance or continuation procedures are some examples of these factors. It is imperative to take into account additional assignments completed on behalf of the organization, as well as any additional resources offering data pertinent to recognizing and evaluating hazards.

5. **Establish audit strategy**

As was previously mentioned, creating an audit plan entails creating an audit strategy. The scope, timing, and nature of the audit procedures are described in the audit strategy. These choices take into account the auditor's intentions to gather information about the operational efficacy of internal control.

6. **Allocate resources**

It is crucial to assign audit team members according to their qualifications and experience in order to support the delivery of an efficient audit. This covers staff management and supervision.

7. **Document**

Create a documented audit plan that guides the audit team and describes the intended audit procedures.

2.1.5 Details of Documents to be collected

A comprehensive review of an organization's financial records, procedures, and activities is conducted during an audit to guarantee their correctness, comprehensiveness, and adherence to local, state, and federal laws. For a thorough audit to be conducted and to provide evidence for the auditor's opinion on the financial statements, a multitude of documents are needed. Internal control records, legal documents, financial records, and external confirmations are just a few categories into which these records can be broadly divided.

Financial records, which comprise the main financial statements like the cash flow statement, income statement, balance sheet, and statement of changes in equity, are the cornerstone of the auditing process. A thorough record of all financial transactions that took place during the period under review is provided by the general ledger, which the auditor also requires. To verify particular balances and transactions, subsidiary ledgers like accounts payable and receivable are also required. To confirm cash balances and make sure all cash transactions have been accurately recorded, bank statements and reconciliation documents are essential. In-depth schedules, such as depreciation plans, inventory valuations, and aging analyses for creditors and debtors, that reconcile the financial statements with the supporting documentation will also be required by the auditor.

Knowing the entity's legal and regulatory surroundings and making sure that applicable laws are being followed require knowledge of legal documents. Articles of association, memorandum of association, board meeting minutes, and shareholder resolutions are among these documents that the company has. Their purpose is to assist the auditor in determining if the organization's actions align with its governance framework and legal obligations. Copies of all agreements, leases, contracts, and loan documentation are also needed to confirm the terms and conditions under which the business functions and to evaluate the accuracy and completeness of the disclosures made in the relevant financial statements. To verify that employee-related costs, liabilities, and obligations are accurate, employment contracts, payroll records, and benefit plans are required.

An entity's internal control systems are essential for both preventing and detecting errors or fraud, and records of internal controls are needed to assess how well they are working. Compliance papers, risk management guidelines, control protocols, and internal audit reports are a few examples of these records. Additionally, the auditor must examine documentation of assignment segregation within the company, authorizations, approvals, and reconciliations. Auditor comprehension of the control activities and their sufficiency is further enhanced by process documentation, such as flowcharts and narratives that depict the entity's internal control environment. Entities that mainly rely on computerized systems for financial reporting should pay special attention to records of information technology controls, such as user access logs, change management protocols, and cybersecurity practices.

In order to confirm the legitimacy and correctness of specific balances and transactions, external confirmations are official documents that are obtained straight from outside sources. To confirm account balances, loan terms, and any contingent liabilities, for instance, auditors frequently ask banks for confirmations. Similar to this, letters of confirmation can be forwarded to suppliers to confirm accounts payable balances or to customers to confirm accounts receivable amounts. Additional forms of verifications can be made with custodians or brokers for stock ownership, fund managers for investment holdings, or insurers for insurance coverage. The findings and conclusions of the auditor are bolstered by these independent and trustworthy confirmations.

Documents pertaining to taxes are also essential to the audit process. These consist of tax assessments, income tax returns, letters to the authorities, and records of tax planning techniques. These records assist auditors in confirming the accuracy and compliance with applicable tax laws of the tax provisions and liabilities shown in the financial statements. To make sure that these responsibilities are appropriately accounted for, additional paperwork pertaining to indirect taxes, such as GST or VAT returns, excise duties, and import/export duties, might be needed.

Documents that are essential for auditing also include management representations. These are official declarations from the entity's management attesting to the completeness and accuracy of the data supplied to the auditors. A management representation letter usually addresses a number of topics, including compliance with applicable laws and regulations, the disclosure of all pertinent information, and the recognition and measurement of assets and liabilities. This letter protects the auditor in the event that a material misstatement or omission is later found and provides extra proof for the financial statements. Lastly, in order to assess any ongoing legal disputes, claims, or compliance issues that might materially affect the financial statements, correspondence and communication records with regulatory bodies, legal counsel, and other external actors might be required. This includes any compliance reports that are turned in to regulatory agencies, letters or notices from regulatory bodies, and information about current or prospective legal actions. These records assist the auditor in determining whether the financial statements' potential liabilities and contingencies have been appropriately disclosed or provided for.

2.1.6 Identification of Compliance Gap

In order to get off to a good start with compliance, you must first assess your current circumstances. It significantly affects how quickly businesses reach the audit-ready stage and benefit from certification. Compliance gap analysis is viewed by chief compliance officers as a directing tool for their compliance initiatives. By carrying out a comprehensive gap analysis, you can find out exactly what aspects of your security posture are strong and weak. Additionally, it is an exercise that helps you develop better strategies to strengthen your security posture and directly indicates the compliance maturity of your organization.

The process of identifying areas where an organization's practices, policies, and procedures don't comply with the necessary standards, laws, or regulations that apply to its operations is known as compliance gap identification in auditing. A number of factors, such as insufficient internal controls, out-of-date policies, a lack of knowledge or training, modifications to legal requirements, or deliberate disrespect for compliance standards, can result in compliance gaps. Finding these gaps is an essential component of an audit because it lets companies know where they run the risk of legal trouble, financial trouble, or damage to their reputation. It also enables them to take corrective action to bring their compliance up to date.

Auditors use a methodical approach to find compliance gaps, which starts with a comprehension of the regulatory landscape in which the company functions. Examining pertinent laws, rules, industry standards, and internal policies that the company must follow are all part of this process. The auditor looks into whether the company has procedures in place, like compliance monitoring systems, recurring policy reviews, or designated compliance officers, to keep abreast of modifications to these requirements. The lack of such mechanisms poses a serious compliance risk in and of itself, putting the company at danger of inadvertently breaking any new or updated regulations.

The organization's internal controls and procedures must be thoroughly evaluated as the next step. Auditors assess how well the internal control framework is planned and executed to stop, identify, and address non-compliance. They evaluate if crucial procedures like financial reporting, data security, anti-corruption efforts, environmental regulations, and employee rights have sufficient controls in place. Auditors search for particular flaws that could result in a company's non-compliance with internal policies or applicable laws, such as inadequate documentation, weak access controls, lack of segregation of duties, or ineffective oversight functions. A compliance gap could be indicated by any departure from best practices or established procedures.

In order to ascertain whether transactions, records, and procedures adhere to pertinent laws and regulations, auditors also carry out thorough tests of them. This entails confirming whether the company is keeping accurate and comprehensive records, submitting timely and accurate tax returns, abiding by labor laws, following health and safety guidelines, and obeying laws protecting the environment. Auditors might, for instance, check payroll records to make sure wage laws are being followed, look over contracts to make sure contractual obligations are being met, or evaluate procurement procedures to make sure anti-bribery and anti-corruption standards are being followed. Potential compliance gaps are highlighted by any discrepancies or instances of non-compliance found during these tests.

Assessing the success of the company's compliance culture and training initiatives is a crucial step in finding compliance gaps. Auditors evaluate if there is a strong compliance culture within the company, meaning that staff members are conscious of their responsibilities and the repercussions of breaking the law at all levels. This entails going over the company's ethics guidelines, compliance manuals, code of conduct, and frequency and quality of employee training. A significant compliance gap that can expose the organization to significant risks is a weak compliance culture, which can be indicated by inadequate training, a lack of awareness, or insufficient communication about compliance expectations. In order to learn more about management's and employees' perspectives on and methods for addressing compliance, auditors also hold conversations with them. To find out if there are any areas where employees are unsure about compliance requirements or where they think there might be gaps, they may conduct surveys or interviews. These exchanges can reveal possible non-compliance areas, like conflicts of interest, ethical questions, or insufficient whistleblower reporting procedures, that may not be immediately apparent from documents or records.

Additionally, data analytics and other audit tools are used by auditors to find trends or abnormalities that might point to compliance gaps. Unusual transaction patterns, frequent modifications, or recurrent control failures, for example, could indicate compliance framework weaknesses. In order to find areas where the organization might not be meeting expected compliance standards, auditors can also compare the organization's practices to best practices or industry benchmarks. After finding compliance gaps, auditors evaluate each one's possible consequences and seriousness, taking into account things like the possibility of fines from the authorities, monetary losses, business interruptions, or reputational harm. The audit report usually includes recommendations for corrective measures to close the gaps as well as a record of the findings. To guarantee ongoing compliance, auditors might advise bolstering internal controls, revising policies, improving staff training, or putting in place more reliable monitoring systems.

2.1.7 Audit Report and Communication

A key component of any successful audit is efficient reporting and communication. It allows the organization to enhance its operations and procedures in addition to assisting in ensuring that the audit's goals are met. The effective distribution of audit findings, conclusions, and recommendations to the pertinent stakeholders is a component of audit reporting and communication. Ensuring that communication is lucid, succinct, and comprehensible to all stakeholders is imperative. The audit report serves as the principal means of communication for auditors to convey to the audited organization's management the audit findings, conclusions, and recommendations. The report ought to be factual, impartial, and offer a fair assessment of the audit's conclusions. Along with identifying nonconformity areas, the report should also highlight areas that could use improvement. The report ought to be organized so that it is simple to read and comprehend.

Here are some key points to consider when communicating audit findings:

1. Be clear and concise: Technical jargon should not be used in the report; instead, straightforward, understandable language should be used. Steer clear of using lengthy words, acronyms, and abbreviations that could confuse the reader.

2. Provide evidence: The audit findings should be supported by evidence in the report. This contains particular instances, records, and information from the audit.
3. Identify areas of nonconformity: The report must specify the nonconformity areas and offer a concise justification for the problem. The pertinent section of the standard that was not met should also be included in the report.
4. Provide recommendations: The report should provide recommendations for corrective action to address the nonconformity. The recommendations should be practical and actionable.
5. Follow up: In order to address the nonconformity, the report ought to offer suggestions for corrective action. The suggestions ought to be doable and realistic.

The successful completion of any audit depends on efficient communication and reporting. Making sure that all parties involved can understand the communication is the auditor's responsibility. The report must identify nonconformity areas, offer recommendations, cite evidence to support audit findings, and monitor the implementation of the suggested corrective actions.

2.1.8 Follow Up and Monitoring

You must be fully aware of the audit's goals and parameters before you can begin tracking down and keeping an eye on the actions taken. These are the standards that establish the scope, motivation, and methodology of your audits. They also assist you in assigning priorities to the audit tasks, establishing due dates and assigning roles, and tracking developments and results. The audit plan or report should contain the objectives and scope of the audit, which should be shared with all pertinent parties.

Track the audit actions and status

Tracking the audit actions and status on a regular and methodical basis is the next step. To do this, you can use a variety of tools and techniques, including software applications, databases, dashboards, and spreadsheets. The primary objective of tracking is to document every audit action's specifics, including the audit action's description, owner, completion date, due date, supporting documentation, and verification. Monitoring the status of each audit action—whether it's pending, ongoing, finished, or past due—is another benefit of tracking.

Communicate the audit results and feedback

Another important step is to communicate the audit results and feedback to the stakeholders involved in the audit process. This includes the auditee, the auditor, the management, and the customers. Communication can be done through various channels and formats, such as meetings, emails, reports, presentations, or newsletters. The main purpose of communication is to share the audit findings, recommendations, actions, and outcomes, as well as to acknowledge the achievements, challenges, and lessons learned.

Verify the audit actions and outcomes

Informing the parties involved in the audit process of the audit's findings and comments is a crucial next step. This covers the management, the customers, the auditee, and the auditor. There are many different ways and platforms for communication, including emails, reports, presentations, newsletters, and meetings. The primary goal of communication is to acknowledge accomplishments, obstacles faced, and lessons learned while also disseminating audit findings, recommendations, actions, and results.

Review and improve the audit process

The final but equally important step is to evaluate and enhance the auditing procedure itself. This entails assessing the audit process's advantages and disadvantages, figuring out what works and where it needs to be improved, and putting the improvements and adjustments into action. To do this, you can use a variety of instruments and techniques, including audits, checklists, surveys, and feedback forms. Making sure the audit process is efficient, effective, and in line with the organization's standards and goals is the major goal of reviewing and improving it.

Follow up and monitor the audit actions

Not only is it a good idea to monitor and track the execution of audit actions, but many quality standards and regulations also demand it. It assists you in making sure that your company complies with the demands and specifications of your stakeholders, consumers, and government authorities. It also aids in enhancing the effectiveness, standing, and competitiveness of your company. You can confidently and successfully monitor the implementation of audit actions by following the steps described in this article.

2.2. INTERNAL AUDIT ACTIVITY PLANNING

The results of the enterprise risk assessment or the risk assessment exercise serve as the foundation for developing the IA Plan. Other projects or processes may be chosen to be included in the IA Plan in addition to the business processes that were discovered during the risk assessment exercise. These internal audit projects could be named by the audit committee or management of the organization through specific requests, depending on what they deem to be important issues, follow-up reviews related to previous internal audit projects, and any additional areas of concern that are approved by the audit committee to be added to the IA Plan over time.

Inputs to the internal audit planning could typically include a combination of the following:

- Outcomes of a risk assessment (enterprise and process risk), including key risks and associated internal controls.
- Requirements from management and/or audit committee.
- Industry information.
- Results from external audits and reviews.
- Previous internal audit results.

An extensive list of audit projects for possible inclusion in the IA Plan may result from a relatively high number of process and/or strategic risks when using an enterprise risk assessment to develop the plan. When scoping audit projects to be included in the IA Plan, internal auditors use professional judgment to take into account the findings of risk assessments, process analyses, and other data. Even after the audit committee approves it, the internal audit plan is dynamic by nature and may need to be modified as the organization's business is impacted by a variety of internal and external environmental factors that change over time. As a result, industry standard procedure calls for creating a comprehensive internal audit plan for a period of 12 months that is subject to at least an annual update, along with a strategic plan for two to three years. The audit engagement teams should keep an eye on the approved IA Plan's applicability and recommend any updates that are needed to take the organization's changing risk profile into account. Formally revisiting the enterprise risk assessment and the ensuing internal audit projects on a yearly basis is another way to carry out the IA Plan maintenance process. Many companies set up a quarterly process, usually in conjunction with quarterly audit committee meetings, to review internal audit progress for the quarter, talk about important issues found, and assess changes to the IA Plan that are suggested for the remaining portion of the year. In any event, open channels of communication should be kept open and accessible between important internal audit stakeholders when situations arise that call for decision-making in regular audit committee meetings, regardless of the precise timing and format of the update process.

- **Enterprise Risk Assessment:** Risk assessments are carried out during the audit planning phase of risk-based internal auditing. Risk assessment is required as part of the planning process for the IA activity (macro level) in order to identify, measure, and prioritize risks. This will allow attention to be directed toward the areas that are most vulnerable to higher-risk scenarios. The most important audit areas are determined by the auditors through the use of risk assessment in the micro-level planning of individual audit engagements. Based on this identification, the auditors create a work program that "tests the most important controls, or to test the controls at greater depth or with more thoroughness". According to certain organizations' methodologies, the macro-level risk assessment is also known as "enterprise risk assessment." Strategic risks pertaining to the goals and strategies of the entire organization are recognized and evaluated in an enterprise risk assessment. Important procedures that reduce strategic risks are also noted. Stated differently, the enterprise risk assessment informs the creation of the internal audit plan and centers on the strategic risk profile of the organization "as is."

Interviews with management personnel are frequently conducted as part of the risk assessment processes in order to gather information about the organization's vision and strategies, important business processes and their goals, key risks that affect the realization of the organization's vision, strategy, and/or goals, the impact and likelihood of those risks on the organization, and management's evaluation of the efficacy of the controls and processes the business has put in place to manage those risks. Any process that is linked to and controls a strategic risk to the goals of the organization is considered significant. Generally speaking, the business processes that are part of the internal audit plan are those that the company has set up to handle the biggest risks to the company. If available, data from the previous internal audit as well as business and industry expertise are additional inputs for the enterprise risk assessment.

The identified risks are then ranked according to the pre-defined criteria. Information is collected on management's perceptions regarding:

- *Gross Risk*: The significant risks to the organization's objectives that must be managed well to support the achievement of those objectives, regardless of the effectiveness of the processes and controls implemented to address those risks.
- *Residual Risk*: The remaining level of risk to the organization's objectives once the effects of existing business processes and controls are considered.

The areas and business processes to be audited are determined and prioritized based on the perceived risk (either gross/inherent or residual/exposure). Process level risk analysis is a useful tool for scoping specific internal audit engagements. It can be used as part of the enterprise risk assessment to better understand a business unit or important process. Alternatively, it can be used as part of internal audit execution. For instance, the organization's financial reporting process might have been classified as a high-risk area following the completion of the enterprise risk assessment. It might be required to conduct additional risk analysis at the process level in order to better understand which areas of the financial reporting process are at higher risk. The narrative description of the process with flowcharts, strategic risks the process is associated with, process level risks and established internal controls, and the process risk matrix—which illustrates the relationship between the impact and likelihood of occurrence of the identified process risks and their relative significance—are common documentation elements for process risk analysis.

- **Internal Audit Engagement Execution:** Internal audit engagement execution, which includes creating an engagement plan, a work program, and test procedures, is done after the IA Plan is approved. This process's internal audit activities are carried out in accordance with the knowledge obtained from enterprise risk assessment, internal audit planning, and, if applicable, process risk analysis. According to the audit methodology, internal auditors concentrate on offering the organization opportunities for performance improvement and findings during this stage of the audit cycle. The internal audit execution phase typically involves the following tasks, in the following order of completion:
  - Process Risk Analysis
  - Develop Work Program
  - Execute Work Program
  - Document Test Results & Evidence
  - Report Results i.e., Identified Issues
- **Process Risk Analysis:** In order to create an effective and efficient work program that concentrates work efforts on important areas of the business process, a process risk analysis is carried out at the start of the execution phase. The amount of work completed during the enterprise risk assessment determines how much work is done for the process risk analysis. The risk assessment used to plan the IA activity will be more generic and likely to concentrate on major risks at the strategic level if it is created without some sort of process-level analysis. In that case, more effort will be needed to create a work program that is both successful and efficient during the planning and scoping phases of each engagement. An essential tool for figuring out the extent of an internal audit engagement is a process risk analysis. This is often carried out via interviews and discussions, much like the enterprise risk assessment. Process owners and control owners are common examples of people with familiarity with the process with whom these interviews and discussions are usually conducted. Workflows are often used to give a brief description of the process risk analysis. The analysis will serve as the foundation for determining the scope of each audit task. Internal auditors examine the process's management in comparison to industry best practices when

conducting process risk analysis, e.g, regulatory requirements, industry standards and guidelines, and other information on published leading practices. The practice that helps the organization achieve its strategic objectives within the parameters of its procedures and structure will ultimately be the one that is appropriate for the organization.

- **Development of Work Program:** The work program creates test procedures that are implemented to help internal auditors evaluate whether internal controls put in place to reduce risks are in place within the organization and how effective they are. The risks and controls related to the activity under review should be known to internal auditors in order to develop the work program for the audit engagement. Since this comprehension will aid in identifying the testing's primary focus areas. The work program's main objective is to test internal controls related to the hazards that have been prioritized. However, testing internal controls might not be required if it is discovered that the control's design is flawed or that it is not functioning.

There are generally two types of internal audit procedures:

- Tests of design are associated with the internal control design and is primarily performed during the process risk analysis.
- Tests of effectiveness confirm whether key internal controls identified during process risk analysis are in existence and are operating effectively as intended.

- **Work Program Execution and Documentation:** The work papers should be cited in all test procedures. Internal auditors are expected to properly and sufficiently document work papers with traceability as part of the internal auditing practice. In particular, test evidence needs to be properly documented in the work papers so that someone else reading it can reach the same conclusions. Work papers should also have the preparer's and reviewer's signatures on them. Lastly, there ought to be a direct correlation between the test procedures and the audit engagement plan's defined scope.
- **Reporting:** The results of an internal audit activity are communicated through an audit report. It is crucial that the work papers sufficiently and unambiguously support the reported results in the report. The conclusions in the work papers and the internal audit report should line up with the supporting documentation. When fully implemented, reporting under the risk-based internal audit methodology gives management information about any areas that are found to have unacceptable residual risk or that can be improved in order to manage process and strategic risks more successfully.
- **Documentation Traceability:** There should be a clear connection between the audit objectives, the audited unit's objectives, and the organization's strategies and objectives, as the audit cycle's emphasis on traceability across various documents underscores. "Related to the risks faced by the auditable unit in its effort to meet

its established objectives" should be the audit objective. Since risks are only important in relation to the organization's strategic objectives, a successful risk-based audit plan should begin with these goals. The work program's audit tests are then created to gather enough data to support the audit objectives.

2.2.1. Objectives of Internal Audit Reports

Reports on internal audits have three primary purposes: i.e. to elicit action from management and their support for it. But before internal auditors document the audit results and notify and persuade management of these findings, management will not take any action.

Within these three objectives the report overall serves the following functions:

- To assure management that risks are well controlled;
- To alter (inform) them to areas where this is not the case and there are defined risk exposures;
- To advise (and convince) them on steps to improve risk management strategies;
- To support action plans prepared by the management.

Internal auditors should make sure that their reports are balanced to meet these objectives. Otherwise, all the efforts and extensive resources used to conduct an engagement are put to waste.

2.2.2. Readers of Internal Audit Reports

An internal audit report has many different user groups, each with a specific need. When writing a report, internal auditor should consider such users and make sure that a single report is balanced to meet each group's demands.

In LGA for example, internal audit reports have the following groups of users:

1. In the audited unit (heads of departments/unit, and process owners):
   - This group are more interested to see what needs to be done for them to improve and meet their operating objectives and targets.
   - In this case, they are likely to read all detailed explanation of the finding (on what is wrong) and auditor's recommendations to correct.
2. Executives and directors (e.g., DED and Audit Committee, and Council):
   - More interested on issues of overall governance and effectiveness of risk management.
   - They need auditor's assurance/ opinion if the audited unit will likely meet its objectives as intended by the executive, and whether laws and regulations are complied with.
   - They are more likely to read the executive summary of the report to get an overview, and go into specific details if the issue is of more relevance.
3. External auditors (and external stakeholders e.g., RAS, IAG, PMO-RALG etc.):
   - They have variety of needs, depending on the issue that moment.
   - But external auditors mostly likely to use internal audit reports as an assessment tool to see how much

reliance they can make on internal auditor, and or take on board some of the internal audit findings.

- Other may be more interested in seeing the quality of reporting etc.

2.2.3. Types of Internal Audit Reports

Internal audit reports can be grouped into the following main types:

- *Engagement Reports*: Reports on results of individual assurance audit assignments.
- *Periodic Reports*: Quarterly audit reports that provide an overview of the internal audit unit's audit and non-audit operations for the given period (quarter) i.e. It is an overview of all the non-audit activities completed during the quarter as well as the individual engagement reports. The Internal Audit Unit's (IAU) annual report provides an overview of the audit services or activities that were performed during the year. It is created using quarterly reports as a basis.
- *Special Audit Reports*: Report on management's special audit arrangements and other special investigations. They must, however, be customized to fit the unique terms of reference that gave rise to these particular assignments.

2.3. RISK BASED CONTROL AND AUDIT

The internal control framework, which includes the risk management framework and the internal audit framework, differentiates among three levels of control:

- Internal control, whether preventive or reactive, is used in the framework of risk management and is the responsibility of management, or risk owners. Its goal is to prevent or lessen the effects associated with the occurrence of risks.
- "Compliance" level: this level oversees risk assessment and control procedures and makes sure they align with organizational objectives (risk management unit); it also helps and monitors risk-owners' actual implementation of risk management.
- By assessing the effectiveness of internal controls, procedures, and management as well as the risk management system, "risk-based audit" guarantees the efficient use of audit resources to evaluate the management of risks associated with an organization's actions. As a result, internal audit tracks and displays the advancement of implementing audit recommendations and enhancements within the audited domain.

The Risk Based Audit (RBA) objectives are as follows:

- *Assurance for the Risk Management Strategy*: To ascertain the extent to which all line managers review the risks/controls within the scope of their own responsibility; to evaluate the adequacy of risk management policy and strategy for achieving their objectives;
- *Assurance for Management of Risks/Controls*: To encompass all the key risks as well as enough of the other risks to support confidence in the overall opinion reached; to evaluate the adequacy of the risk management processes designed to constrain residual risk to the risk appetite;
- *Assurance for the Adequacy of the Review/Assurance Process*: Quality assured to engender confidence in the review process; to identify limitations in the evidence provided, or limitations to the depth/scope of the reviews undertaken; to identify gaps in control and/or over control, and provide opportunities for continuous improvement; to support preparation of internal audit summary report to the risk committee/chief statistician.

The RBA management cycle is carried out through the following six steps:

i. *Object*: Procedures, processes and internal service charters, risks selected according to priorities but: risks within risk appetite, risks not requiring audit in the short term, risks otherwise audited, tolerable risks.

ii. *Audit Plan*: Internal audits to be carried out in the short term are managed according to an annual plan that is endorsed by the board, and shared with the organizational divisions involved. Such a plan shows, with reference to any action:

- The audit lifespan,
- The team composition,
- The accountabilities,
- The audit tasks (according to procedures, contractual requirements, etc.),
- The documents required,
- The lead times.

The annual plan is prepared for a single year on the basis of the strategic plan, according to risk assessment. Therefore, audit planning takes into account the results of previous audit studies, as well as management assessment of current levels of risk related to specific organizational programs.

iii. *Audit Run-Up*: Audit run up consisting of some actions that are preliminary to actual audit, such as:

- Formal assignment of duties;
- Definition of the activity plan;
- Identification of documents needed to define the audit range of reference and intervention;
- Communication on audit start;
- Kick-off meeting with the staff involved.

iv. *Audit Implementation:* Actual audit, consisting of:

- Operational meetings;
- Preliminary assessment of criticalities;
- Check of suitability and accordance with the risk management or quality system; and
- Drawing up recommendations and possible mitigation actions.

Risk managers can evaluate the efficacy of controls for each risk with the help of audits. One could evaluate whether the controls are sufficient to lower the risk level (i.e., to lower the risk from extremely high to medium or low), or if more measures or treatments are needed.

v. *Reporting*: Auditing ends with a meeting for sharing the main results obtained. An audit report is drafted that contains:

- Its findings,
- The actions performed,
- The criticalities found, and suggestions proposed,
- Possible action plan, in cooperation with the unit/division involved.

Some of the treatment strategies suggested during this process will be appropriate for inclusion in the internal audit plan (feed-back). Proposals for additional treatment strategies to lower the level of risk will emerge after the assessment of the control effectiveness for each risk. The purpose of the follow-up is to verify that any comments or suggestions have actually been implemented in terms of response actions.

2.3.1. Need a Risk Based Assessment Framework (RBAF)

The environment in which transfer payment programs operate is complex and full of interconnections, including those resulting from authorities, various risk drivers, governance requirements, and global expectations. Each of these elements has an impact on how the program is designed and carried out. Risk-Based Audit Frameworks can help managers function in this complex environment more economically and effectively by doing the following:

- Enhancing managers' and employees' understanding and communication of risk and related mitigation options;
- Strengthening accountability for achieving objectives and stewardship over public funds;
- Facilitating managers' achievement of government-wide requirements for solid risk management; providing a basis upon which to create contingency plans;
- Helping to secure funding for new or renewed programs; and
- Enhancing information for decision-making.

2.3.2. Development and Implementation of the RBAF

The key parties that should be involved in the development and implementation of an RBAF are as follows:

- Program managers are primarily in charge of making sure that the RBAF accurately and thoroughly analyzes potential risks to the attainment of goals and includes strategies for monitoring, mitigating, and reporting those risks at a reasonable cost;
- Internal Audit and program personnel who could lead the preparation of the RBAF's Internal Auditing section and offer professional guidance and technical assistance in risk identification, assessment, and monitoring;
- Assessment personnel who may offer insight and experience in identifying areas where RMAFs and RBAFs may overlap as well as in situations where RMAFs and RBAFs are being combined; and.
- TBS Program and Center of Excellence for Internal Audit analysts, who can offer guidance during their preparation, have been assigned responsibilities and possess knowledge of the program's and the RBAF's requirements, respectively. As collaborators, interested parties and delivery partners/co-delivers may also be involved.

2.3.3. Planning and Preparing an RBAF

The level of included in an RBAF document will vary according to the nature, complexity and sensitivity of the programs. In planning and developing the level of information and effort required to prepare the RBAF, consideration should be given to the following:

- Uncomplicated programs with low materiality and a straightforward accountability and risk management environment would require a less detailed and resource intensive RBAF;
- High priority and complex programs with significant materiality (relative to the overall departmental budget) and a diversified and complex environment would require a more detailed RBAF and a larger investment of time and effort;
- The breadth and complexity of the program's RMAF could be used as a guidepost for RBAF development; and

- Meaningful information should be provided in each section of the RBAF. The next sections of this document will guide the reader through the components of an RBAF and the steps involved in their development.

2.3.4. Risk of Fraud and Error in Audit

The following events may increase the risk of fraud or error:

- Internal Control Faults: Weaknesses in the design of internal control system and non-compliance with laid down control procedures, e.g., a single person being responsible for receipt of all pasts/ mails and marking it the relevant sections or two persons responsible for receipt of all posts/ mails but the same is not followed in the practice.
- Doubts about the integrity or competence of the management, e.g., domination by one person, high rate of employee turnover, and frequent change of legal counsels of Auditors, significant and prolonged understaffing of the accounts department, etc.
- Unusual pressures within the entity, e.g., industry is doing well but the Company's performance is poor, heavy dependence on a single line of product, inadequate working capital, need to show more profit to support the share market price, etc.
- Unusual transactions e.g., transactions with related parties, excessive payment for certain services to lawyers, etc.
- Problems in obtaining sufficient and appropriate audit evidence, e.g., inadequate documentation significant differences between the figures as per accounting records and confirmation received from third parties etc.

2.3.5. Auditor's Duties and Responsibilities in Respect of Fraud

An auditor's main goal is to provide a judgment on the financial statements. However, the risk of material misstatements in the financial statements due to fraud or error must be taken into account by the auditor while performing the audit. The purpose of an audit carried out in compliance with widely accepted auditing standards is to reasonably assure that there are no material misstatements in the financial statements as a whole, whether as a result of fraud or error. Although conducting an audit may serve as a deterrent, fraud and error cannot be prevented by the auditor, and they cannot be held accountable for it. Since the auditor bases their opinion on the idea of obtaining reasonable assurance, they cannot guarantee that material misstatements—whether the result of fraud or error—will be found during an audit. Thus, the following does not, by itself, prove that there was a material misstatement of the financial statement due to fraud or error.

- Failure to obtain reasonable assurance,
- Inadequate planning, performance or judgment,
- Absence of professional competence and due care, or,
- Failure to comply with auditing standards generally accepted

This is especially true for some types of deliberate misstatements, as auditing processes might not be able to find an intentional misstatement that is covered up by cooperation between one or more management personnel. Those in charge of governance, staff members, outside parties, or situations involving forged paperwork. The suitability of the auditor's reports based on the outcomes of these procedures and the appropriateness of the audit procedures carried out under the given circumstances determine whether the auditor has conducted an audit in compliance with generally accepted auditing standards. The auditor should plan for and account for the possibility of material misstatements of the financial information due to fraud or error when conducting his examination. He ought to ask the management if there has been any fraud or serious mistake, which has taken place during the reporting period, and adjust his auditing processes as needed. The auditor should take into account the possible impact of the suspected fraud and error on the financial information if the circumstances point to their possible existence. Before voicing his opinion, he should take into account the pertinent laws and regulations if he is unable to find proof. Additionally, the auditor must promptly notify the relevant management level of the misstatement and take into account any requirement to report the change in governance. Before disclosing the financial data or before ending the engagement, he might also seek legal counsel. In the event that the auditor's modified procedures reveal the fraud's existence, the auditor should ensure that the fraud's impact is accurately reflected in the financial data or that the error is fixed. In order to properly frame his report, the auditor should also take into account the consequences of the errors and frauds. If there is a substantial fraud, the financial statement should disclose it. His audit report ought to contain a suitable disclosure in the event that insufficient is made.

2.4. AUDIT SAMPLING

The application of an audit procedure to a subset of the items in an account balance or transaction class is known as audit sampling. Every unit in the sample should have an equal chance of being chosen based on the sampling strategy used. The purpose of this is to assess a particular facet of the data. When population sizes are large, audit sampling is necessary because it would be extremely inefficient to look at the entire population. This Auditing and Assurance Standard (AAS) aims to set guidelines for the planning, selection, and assessment of an audit sample as well as the analysis of the sample's outcomes. Both statistical sampling techniques are covered by this AAS in the same way. When used correctly, either approach can yield adequate audit evidence.

The auditor must plan and choose an audit sample, conduct audit procedures on it, and assess sample results when employing statistical or non-statistical sampling techniques in order to produce enough relevant audit evidence. "Audit sampling" is the process of applying audit procedures to less than 100% of the items in an account balance regarding a particular feature of the items chosen to help form or form a conclusion about the population.

It's critical to understand that some testing methods do not fit the definition of sampling. Sampling is not used in tests that are run on all 100 items in a population. Likewise, since the items were not chosen from the entire population on a basis that was expected to be representative, applying audit procedures to all items within a population that have a particular characteristic (for example, all items over a certain amount) does not qualify as audit sampling with regard to the population examined or the population as a whole. These items might suggest a feature of the remaining subset of the population, but they wouldn't always serve as the foundation for a reliable inference about that subset.

There are multiple ways to engage in audit sampling, including the following:

- *Block Sampling*: A consecutive series of items are selected for review. Though this approach may be efficient, there is a risk that a block of items will not reflect the characteristics of the entire population.
- *Haphazard Sampling*: There is no structured approach to how items are selected. However, the person doing the selections will probably skew the selections (even if inadvertently), so the selections are not truly random.
- *Personal Judgment*: The auditor uses her own judgment to select items, perhaps favoring items that have larger monetary values or which appear to have a higher level of risk associated with them.
- *Random Sampling*: A random number generator is used to make selections. This approach is the most theoretically correct, but can require more time to make selections.

- Stratified sampling. The auditor splits the population into different sections (such as high value and low value) and then selects from each section.
- *Systematic Sampling*: Selections are taken from the population at fixed intervals, such as every 20th item. This tends to be a relatively efficient sampling technique.

2.4.1. Factors in Determining Sample Size- Sampling Risk

When determining the sample size, the auditor should consider sampling risk, the tolerable error, and the expected error.

1. **Sampling Risk:** The risk associated with sampling is the potential for the auditor's conclusion, drawn from a sample, to differ from the conclusion reached if the entire population underwent the same audit process. Sample risk is a concern for the auditor in both substantive procedure and control tests.

- Tests of Control
  - *Risk of Under Reliance*: The risk that, although the sample result dose not support the auditor's assessment of control risk, the actual compliance rate would support such an assessment.
  - *Risk of Over Reliance*: The risk that, although the sample result supports the auditor's assessment of control risk, the actual compliance rate would not support such as an assessment.
- Substantive Procedures
  - *Risk of Incorrect Rejection*: The risk that, although the sample results the supports the conclusion that a recorded account balance or class of transactions is materially misstated, in fact it is not materially misstated.
  - *Risk of Incorrect Acceptance*: The risk that, although the sample result supports the conclusion that a recorded account balance or class or transactions is not materially misstated.

Because they typically result in more work being done by the auditor or the entity to prove that the initial conclusions were incorrect, the risks of under reliance and incorrect rejection have an impact on audit efficiency. Compared to the risks of under reliance or incorrect rejection, the risks of overreliance and incorrect acceptance have a greater potential to compromise the effectiveness of the audit and result in an incorrect opinion on the financial statements. The amount of sampling risk that the auditor is ready to take on based on the sample's findings influences the sample size. The larger the sample size that is required, the less risk the auditor is willing to take.

2. **Tolerable Error:** Tolerated error is the highest amount of error in the population that an auditor would be willing to accept and still determine that the audit objective has been met by the sample's results. For substantive procedures, acceptable error is tied to the auditor's determination of materiality and is taken into account during the planning phase. A larger sample size will be required the smaller the tolerable error. Based on the initial evaluation of control risk, the auditor would be willing to accept

the highest rate of deviation from a recommended control procedure in tests of control, which is known as the tolerable error. When all audit procedures are taken into account, the auditor can conclude, with reasonable assurance, that the financial statements are not materially misstated. In substantive procedures, the tolerable error is the maximum monetary error in an account balance or class of transactions that the auditor would be willing to accept.

3. **Expected Error:** In order to determine that the actual error in the population is not greater than the planned tolerable error, the auditor must typically analyze a larger sample size when error is expected in the population than when it is not expected. When it is anticipated that the population will be error-free, smaller sample sizes are justified. The auditor would take into account factors like error levels found in prior audits, modifications to the entity's procedures, and information gleaned from other procedures when estimating the expected error in a population.

2.4.2. Evaluation of Sample Results

On each sample item, those audit procedures that are appropriate to the particular audit objective, the auditor should:

- **Analysis of Errors in the Sample:** The auditor must first ascertain whether the item in question is, in fact, an error before delving into the analysis of the errors found in the sample. The auditor will have used the audit objectives to define what constitutes an error when creating the sample. For instance, a mis posting between customer accounts has no effect on the overall amount of accounts receivable in a substantive procedure pertaining to the recording of accounts receivable. Therefore, even though it might have an impact on other audit sections like the evaluation of dubious accounts, it might be appropriate to regard this as an error when assessing the sample results of this specific procedure. If the auditor is unable to obtain the expected audit evidence for a particular sample item, they may still be able to obtain adequate audit evidence by executing alternative procedures. For instance, by examining later payments from the customer, the auditor might be able to gather sufficient appropriate suit evidence that the receivable is legitimate if a positive account receivable confirmation has been equated and no response has been received. The item would be considered erroneous if the auditor is unable or unwilling to carry out adequate alternative procedures, or if the procedures carried out do not allow the auditor to obtain adequate audit evidence. The auditor would also take into account the errors' qualitative aspects. These consist of the type of error, its root cause, and any potential repercussions for the error on subsequent audit phases. The auditor may find that, upon examining the errors found, a number of them share a characteristic, such as a transaction type, location, product line, or time frame. Under such conditions, the auditor may elect to determine which items in the population share the characteristic, creating a subpopulation, and expand audit protocols in this domain. After that, the auditor would conduct a different analysis depending on the items looked at for every subpopulation.

- **Projection of Errors:** The population from which the sample was drawn is shown the error results of the sample by the auditor. There are multiple appropriate ways to project error results. But in every scenario, the projection technique must match the sampling unit selection technique exactly. The auditor must consider the qualitative aspects of the errors discovered when projecting error results. Following the division of the population into subpopulations, each subpopulation's error projection is completed independently, and the results are aggregated.
- **Reassessing Sampling Risk:** The auditor must take into account the possibility that population errors could be greater than the allowable error.

  In order to do this, the auditor considers the outcomes of other audit procedures pertinent to the particular control or financial statement assertion and compares the projected population error to the allowable error. In the case of substantive procedures, the projected population error utilized for this comparison is net of the entity's adjustments. The auditor reevaluates the sampling risk when the projected error surpasses allowable error, and if that risk is deemed unacceptable, they may contemplate extending the audit procedure or implementing alternative audit procedures.

2.4.3. Test Checking

In audit, test checking entails examining a small number of randomly chosen transactions from a large set of transactions. To put it simply, when tests are being checked, a sample of entries from each class are chosen, examined, and if they are found to be correct, the remaining entries are also assumed to be correct. Test checking is a commonly used alternative to detailed checking, which is typically unnecessary from an economic perspective.

- **Adoption of Test Checking Methods by Auditors:** Depending on the specifics of each case, the auditor's judgment and discretion are the only factors that determine whether or not to use testing methods. Test checking should be used and done carefully and intelligently to avoid potentially harmful outcomes. Nonetheless, the effectiveness of test checking is largely dependent on the internal check system in place as well as the auditor's intelligence.
- **Safeguards for the Application of Test Checking:** While applying test checks the auditor should take the following precautions:
- As far as possible sample transactions should be selected from every book.
- The selection of transactions should be so distributed that the work of almost all the clerks of the client is checked.
- The items should be selected at random.

- As fraudulent manipulations are common during the first and last months of the period under audit, the entries made during these periods should be checked thoroughly.
- In the selection of entries and accounts for applying test checks, care should be taken to check the different portions of the work at each audit.
- Cash book and pass book should be checked thoroughly.
- The auditor should select the transactions on his own. He should not consult the staff of the client while selecting the transactions.

If the auditor exercises the above safeguards with care and caution, the results are bound to be encouraging and satisfactory.

- **Advantages of Test Checking**: Test checking enjoys the following advantages:
  - It saves time and energy.
  - If the selection of transactions is done intelligently, test checking is useful and purposeful.
  - The volume of work is reduced. So the auditor can carry on many audit simultaneously.
  - It helps the auditor to arrive at a definite conclusion in regard to the true and fair view of the state of affairs of the concern.
  - It helps in reducing the cost of audit.
- **Disadvantages of Test Checking:-** Test checking suffers from the following disadvantages:
  - It is not possible to detect all the errors and fraud.
  - The clerks of the client may become careless because they know that their work will not be checked in detail.
  - Under test checking, although the auditor checks the whole of the work through test checking, suspicion and doubt will remain in his mind.
  - It is of no use if proper and effective systems of internal checks and controls are not being adopted in business.
  - It is not suitable for small business concerns.

2.4.4. Routine Checking

Routine checking is the process of verifying the arithmetical accuracy of accounting records and determining whether the regular bookkeeping mechanism has been applied correctly by looking over entries as they appear in the books of account. Routine checking, which includes checking casts, subcasts, carry forward of balances, other calculations, posting in ledgers, balancing ledgers, and transferring ledger balances to the trial balance, is the process by which auditors review common records and books. The auditor only needs to identify simple frauds and clerical errors. An auditor should perform more than just routine checks in order to identify all significant errors and frauds.

It involves a stereotyped work including the checking of:

- Posting from books of original entry to ledger accounts,
- Castings or totaling of journals and ledgers,

Balancing of ledger accounts,

- Carry forwards,

- Drawing up of the trial balance, and
- Preparation, casting and balancing of final accounts.

Objectives of Routine Checking:

- *Arithmetical Accuracy:* The goal of routine checking is to verify that the books of accounts are accurate in their math. Books that are error-free can be useful in determining what is true and equitable about business matters.
- *Corrects Posting:* The goal of regular checks is to verify that posts are accurate. The books are created by client staff. The head of management is in charge of accurately recording and posting entries.
- *No Alteration:* The goal of routine checks is to ensure that client staff members haven't altered any figures. Accounting personnel have a moral obligation to avoid manipulating data. Changing the numbers is not possible due to routine checking.

Essentials of Routine Checking:

- *Sub-Casts*: Sub-cast is a part of routine checking. Sub-total possible in account matters. The sub-cast must be correct.
- *Casts*: Cast is a part of routine checking. Total in journal and ledger account should be examined for accurate results.
- *Carry Forward*: Carry forward is a part of routine checking. The balance of one page can be transferred to the next page.
- *Posting*: Posting is a part of routine checking. The entries are posted to the ledger accounts. Posting must be properly examined.
- *Balancing*: Balancing is a part of routine checking. Taking the difference of debit and credit in the account is called balancing.
- *Carry Down*: The amount in an account can be transferred to next page. The carry down is part of routine checking.
- *Transfer*: Transfer is a part of routine checking. The amount in one account can be transferred to another account.

Auditor's Duties in Routine Checking: It should be kept in mind that because this kind of work does not fully substantiate the transactions and does not go behind the entries appearing in the books, it can never establish the accuracy of the accounts in every way. As a result, routine checking is typically not thought to be a crucial component of audit work, particularly in cases where self-balancing ledgers are kept up to date and a trial balance has been properly agreed upon. Routine checking, however, should not be disregarded by auditors as it can be useful in identifying small errors. He needs to be especially careful about the chance that audit clerks will find this kind of work boring and skip it or neglect it.

The current accounting and internal checking systems should be used to determine the extent to which routine checking is permitted. All castings, postings, etc., in the case of a small business where there is essentially no internal check and a low volume of transactions ought to be confirmed. However, in the event that the business is sizable, with a high volume of transactions and a reasonably dependable internal control system, it might be adequate to perform test checks or selective checking, i.e. thorough examination of specific transactions that have been carefully chosen. However, regardless of the type and effectiveness of the internal checking system, an auditor should always remember that test checks are completed entirely at his own responsibility and that he will always be liable for any error that may go undetected.

- **Routine Checking of Particular Books:** When it comes to routinely checking the various books of accounts, an auditor may, within the parameters of detailed checking that he determines after considering all the pertinent factors mentioned above, adopt the following procedure: Cash Book. For a small business, the full volume of castings and postings should be checked; however, for a large undertaking that uses the self-balancing system, only postings to nominal or private ledgers and a portion of those to personal ledgers may be verified. The totals of the debtors' and creditors' ledger columns should be verified with the total debtors' and total creditors' accounts, and cross-totals of different columns should be compared with grand totals when the cash book has analysis columns.
- *Petty Cash Book*: It is important to carefully review the general cashier's receipts and the posting of analysis column totals to both personal and impersonal ledger accounts. It is necessary to check a percentage of the different analysis columns in addition to the castings and cross-castings of the total column.
- *Sales, Purchase and Returns Inward and Outward Books*: Verification is necessary for posting totals to total accounts and impersonal ledgers, as well as for part of postings to personal ledger accounts. A portion of the computations and the castings need to be verified. A portion of the analysis columns must be cast, with the cross-casts agreed upon with the total columns, in cases where distinct analysis columns are offered for departmental accounts or as part of a self-balancing system.
- *Bills Receivable and Payable Books*: Verification is necessary for posting totals to total accounts and impersonal ledgers, as well as for part of postings to personal ledger accounts. A portion of the computations and the castings need to be verified. A portion of the analysis columns must be cast, with the cross-casts agreed upon with the total columns, in cases where distinct analysis columns are offered for departmental accounts or as part of a self-balancing system.
- *Journal Proper*: Since this book documents various significant transactions, e.g., opening and closing entries, adjustments, depreciation, and provision for bad debts, among other things, it is preferable to carry out a thorough examination of the castings and postings.
- *Debtors' and Creditors' Ledgers*: Although postings to these ledgers will have already been examined during the examination of subsidiary books, it is still advisable to scan the accounts again in order to identify any unpicked items. Depending on the size of the company, all or some of the castings should be confirmed. Individual ledger account balances

should be confirmed, and a detailed review of the balances for every ledger should be conducted. The total of each list should be compared to the corresponding total or adjustment account in the general ledger in cases where the self-balancing system is in use.

- *Impersonal or General Ledger*: Postings would have previously been examined during the examination of subsidiary books, but the accounts must now be carefully examined to identify any unchecked items, if any. Carefully inspecting castings and balancing is recommended.
- *Miscellaneous Books*: A thorough examination of computations, castings, and entries in certain significant memorandum books, such as postage books, wage sheets and salary books, stock ledgers, etc., is recommended for auditors, based on any potential internal checks that may be in place, the precise scope of the detailed inspection.

Routine Checking of Final Accounts:

- *Trial balance and Difference in Books:* The balances of individual accounts in the general ledger and the totals of the schedules taken from the debtors' and creditors' ledgers should be compared to the corresponding entries in the trial balance after all subsidiary books and ledgers have been checked. The trial balance casting should also be confirmed. Generally speaking, an auditor shouldn't begin work until the books of accounts are finished and a trial balance has been prepared and approved. Nevertheless, there are situations where a trial balance may not agree despite the best efforts of the clients' staff and the audited accounts are urgently needed. In these situations, the auditor may choose to pass over the discrepancy for the time being and permit it to be shown in the balance sheet as a difference-in-books or suspense account if he is confident that a strong internal control system is in place that makes it difficult for any major error to remain undetected and that the difference in the trial balance is tiny due to small errors. An auditor may conduct a thorough examination along these lines until the reasons for the discrepancy are determined, though, if there is even the slightest uncertainty regarding the type and severity of the errors contributing to the difference:
- If the self-balancing system is in use, check the trial balance of the particular ledger which shows a difference.
- Check the castings of debit and' credit columns of the trial balance.
- As a short-cut method, halve the amount of difference and see if any identical sum has been put in a wrong column.
- Compare each figure of the trial balance with the respective ledger balance.
- Check castings and balancing of each ledger account.
- If all the aforesaid measures taken step by step fail, all entries and postings should be checked in details until the cause of the difference is discovered.

It should, however, be remembered that it is no part of an auditor's duty either to prepare a trial balance or to reconcile a difference therein and that if he is ever asked to do so he would act as an accountant and not as an auditor.

- *Profit and Loss Account*: The profit and loss account should, whenever feasible, be split up into a few standard and easily accessible sections, namely, accounts for manufacturing, trading, profit and loss, and profit and loss appropriation, depending on the type of business, the needs of the owners, and any applicable legal requirements. It is ideal for every section of the profit and loss account to be structured to provide the most comprehensive information possible and to make it easier to compare different categories of income and expenses to those from prior years. It is best to group expenses into standard categories for this purpose, e.g., financial expenses; establishment, management, or administrative expenses; manufacturing, productive, or direct expenses; maintenance, and depreciation; selling and distribution expenses, etc.

  Naturally, it should be understood that an auditor cannot mandate that a company adopt a specific type of profit and loss account unless mandated by law; however, he should take care to ensure that the account discloses the correct financial result. He is also expected to ensure that all applicable legal requirements are met in relation to this account. The Steam Packet Company of Royal Mail case unequivocally demonstrated that an auditor faces the possibility of being accused of carelessness if he fails to notify shareholders of any unusual item included in the profit and loss account. Last but not least, it is preferable that whichever format is chosen, it be used annually and consistently.

- *Balance Sheet:* In order to present a true and fair picture of a company's financial situation, a balance sheet should display all assets and liabilities under appropriately categorized headings in addition to accounting for them at their correct values. A balance sheet's contents and the arrangement of its assets and liabilities are subject to no hard and fast rules, with the exception of those outlined in the Companies Act and the Insurance and Banking Regulation Acts and the Electricity Act. One of the auditor's responsibilities is to ensure that, whichever approach is chosen for marshalling assets and liabilities, it is applied consistently and uniformly each year. It is important to remember that a balance sheet is more than just a statement of assets and liabilities, as is sometimes mistakenly believed. It also includes other items that aren't strictly speaking considered assets and summarizes all balances found in books of accounts, including the balance of the profit and loss account., deferred revenue expenditure, debit balance of profit and loss account, etc. If the balance sheet presents a "true and fair view" of the business's situation, it should be mentioned in the auditor's report on the accounts of the company.

- *Simplified Presentation of Accounts:* The working results and financial state of affairs of industrial and business undertakings as set out in their final accounts, particularly the published accounts of companies, are of interest to many other classes of people in the modern world, where the social outlook of business activities is becoming increasingly important. These people do not only include owners or shareholders. g. including holders of debentures, potential investors, taxing authorities, creditors, clients, banks and financial institutions, workers and labor unions, investment consultants, stock and share brokers, economists, lawmakers, and various government agencies involved in the regulation of economic activity. Many of the aforementioned individuals find the accounts too technical to comprehend, with the exception of experts. In addition, the vocabulary of financial and accounting terms is growing, as is the application of new accounting techniques. Therefore, the final accounts that are released in the required format rarely fulfill the intended purpose, i.e., to present a "true and fair" picture of a company's financial standing. In recent years, the aforementioned consideration has led to the realization that accounts must be presented in a clear, understandable, and non-technical manner that highlights the main stages of activity within a given period in the form of profit and loss statements, illustrated charts, graphs, and diagrams, as well as condensed explanatory balance sheets. This approach is gaining popularity, especially among progressive organization managers who wish to update all stakeholders on their accomplishments, future plans, and activities. Where applicable, half-yearly unaudited (estimated) financial results must be released in newspapers in accordance with stock exchange regulations.

The following special factors may, however, be borne in mind with regard to simplified presentation of accounts:

- This is supplementary and not alternative to final accounts in statutory and standard forms.
- The supplementary information should be in simple, non-technical language and be easily reconcilable with the statutory accounts.
- Such information need not be audited.

1. **Advantages of Routine Checking**

- *Accuracy:* Regular verification ensures that accounting records and books are accurate. Subtotals, totals, posting for cast and carry forward, balancing, and transfer are all indicated as accurate.
- *Frauds:* By checking the books of accounts, frauds can be found and addressed. The head of management is accountable for identifying instances of fraud. With this tool, the management can fulfill its obligations.
- *Posting Verification:* By performing this check, is able to confirm the postings made in the ledger. An accurate posting can present financial statements in a true and equitable manner. Through it, the management is able to verify postings.

- *No Change in Figures:* This verification helps to rule out any figure tampering. This checking will help the management fulfill its obligation because the staff is unable to change the numbers.
- *Final Checking:* The benefit of this check is the reduction in final checking labor. Since routine checking has already accomplished the majority of the work, the final checking can be done earlier.

2. Disadvantages of Routine Checking

- *No Care*: The work of this checking is given, to the junior worker. They are doing not contemplate it as vital matter. So the expected results can't be created for audit purpose.
- *Fraud*: The demerit of this checking is that planned frauds don't seem to be disclosed. The responsibility of fraud lies on the pinnacle of management. The audited accounts could fail to supply true and truthful read.
- *Errors*: The demerit of this checking is that errors of principle are not disclosed. The responsibility of errors can be placed on the head of the management. The audited accounts may fail to provide true and fair view.
- *Monotony*: The work of this checking is boring and time consuming. The clerks go on checking the totals and sub-totals and balances. It does not improve the performance of employee rather it brings monotony.

3. Routine Checking Versus Test Checking

- *Fraud*: In routine checking frauds are easily checked. In case of test checking pre-planned frauds cannot be checked.
- *Errors*: The errors may exist in books of accounts in case of test checking. There are no errors in routine checking.
- *Cost:* There is less cost in test checking due to less work. In routine checking there is more work so there is more cost.
- *Time*: Routine checking requires more time for completion of work. Test checking can be completed in less time.
- *Useful*: Test checking is useful for auditor to complete many audits during one year. Routine checking is useful to complete few audits in one year.
- *Part*: Test checking is a part of audit sampling. Routine checking is a part of vouching.
- *Report*: Audit report shows true and fair view in case of routine checking. The report may not show true and fair view in test checking due to undiscovered errors and frauds.

2.5. VALUE FOR MONEY AUDIT

Due to the apparent challenges in measuring the performance of non-profit organizations (NPOs), particularly in the public sector, value for money auditing, also known as performance auditing, has become more and more popular. In contrast to the private sector, NPOs have prioritized service delivery over shareholder value and the accountability of funds entrusted to them. Stakeholders want to get the most value for their money when these NPOs spend it on their behalf.

1. **Accountability**: The main problem with value for money in local government areas (LGAs) is that public monies allocated to them should be used as efficiently and effectively as possible, and those in charge of spending them should be held responsible for their economical, efficient, and effective management. One of the reasons for the discussions surrounding accountability in LGAs (as well as other public sector organizations) is the fact that data regarding the objectives and outcomes of public spending comes from a range of different sources:

- Example: The public is the primary recipient of spending decisions, which are carried out by LGAs and officials in other public services. The central government and the treasury make the major decisions regarding funds and allocations in LGAs. Due to this division, it is frequently challenging to find out how public funds are spent and the outcomes of that spending that are accepted by all of the LGA stakeholders (e.g., politicians, local government representatives, auditors, and the general public). The VFM-audit is now a component of the effort to resolve these disputes and get better Value for Money.

2. **VFM Dimensions:** In the concept of value for money audit there are two dimensions that auditors need to understand:

a. *The Project Dimension:* This considers performance issues relating to the implementation of the project or system to be audited. The main focus, as indicated in Figure 2.1, is how the project moves from the commitment to the achievement of this outcome.

The following are the project dimension:

- *Commitment:* Set the management to set objectives and define the purpose of the project or intervention (i.e., objectives and intentions);
- *Economy:* Funds/resources assigned to procure inputs;
- Efficiency: Inputs are put in the production process by undertaking the planned activity to produced outputs;

- *Effectiveness:* Outputs (in terms of goods and services) are put into use to cause the outcome and meet the intended objective set at the commitment stage; and
- *Cross Cutting:* Compliance with laws and regulations.

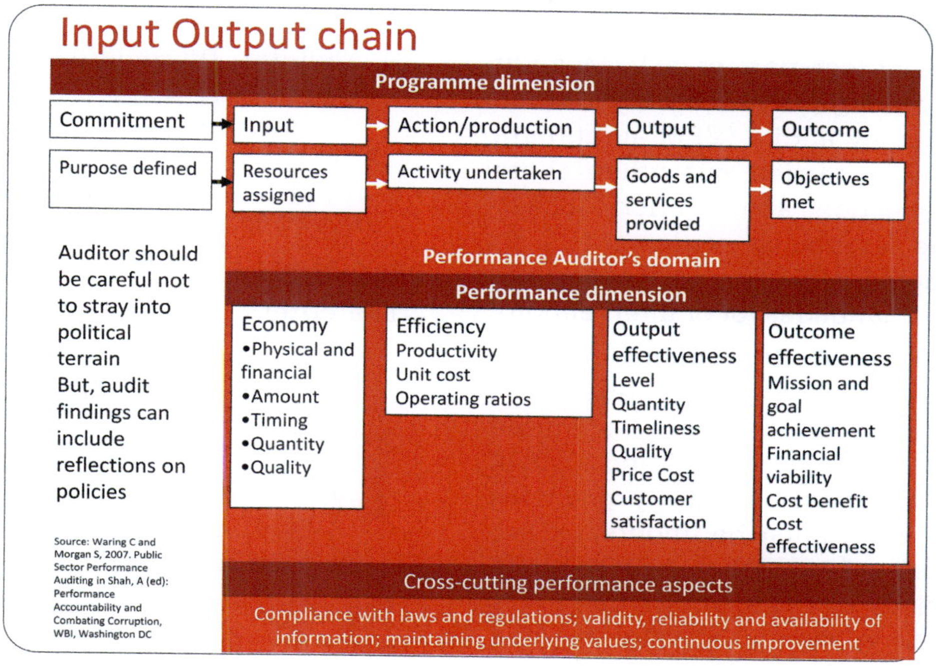

Figure 2.1. *Dimensions in value for money audit.*

Source: https://image.slidesharecdn.com/deckonconsultancytrainingandauditsv0-180802091620/75/Deck-on-consultancy-training-and-audits-v0-1-24-2048.jpg.

When a VFM auditor is called in to evaluate the performance of the project or intervention, his/her concern will be aligned with those of the project dimensions but this time in examining how the project management as secured value for money at each component of the VFM chain i.e.:

- *Commitment:* What the objectives/ intentions of the project (but limits this evaluation as to not question political issues that led to the project);
- *Economy:* How the project use their funds to procure inputs (e.g., Staff time, and other resources)? The main issues would be on amount, timing, price, quantity and quality of resources procured;
- *Efficiency:* How inputs are used to produce outputs (goods & services)? Question the input/output in terms of wastage, timeliness, quantity, quality, and customer satisfaction;
- *Effectiveness:* How the outputs produce outcomes (i.e., effects on users)? Main issue would be are the original intentions/objectives met? Mission and goals achieved? Financially viable?
- *Cross-Cutting Aspects:* Like any other audit, here the main concern is how did the project managers, in their implementation, complied with other governance issues and laws and regulations, standards, values, and best practices.

2.5.1. Planning a Value for Money Audit

- **Identify Audit Concern or Issue with Value for Money (VFM) Audit:** The hardest part of a VFM audit is defining the objectives. Value for money audits (VFM audits) are typically carried out when there are questions about performance or value for money settlements (i.e., economy, efficacy, or efficiency of a particular endeavor or intervention).
- **Develop Audit Questions:** As opposed to financial audits, VFM audits typically have a single main "audit question" and a small number of supplementary questions (i.e., what must be understood) or theories (i.e., what needs to be verified? The VFM audit's objectives are to respond to, validate, and draw conclusions regarding these queries. The audit questions serve as the basis for all data evaluation, analysis, and evidence collection.

The questions/objectives that are set should give a clear direction for the audit such that:

- They define the area to be audited (e.g., Political objectives, grants, government reforms, government services, etc.);
- Has to define what is to be examined i.e. deviations related to three E's (Economy, Efficiency, Effectiveness); and
- Could also include the causes (of deviations) and consequences.

- **Setting the Audit Criteria:** The audit criteria specify the standards by which the subject of the audit, project, undertaking, services, program, or operation will be evaluated (e.g., laws, regulations, set goals, professional norms, public perception, etc. The audit criteria should be complete, unbiased, fair, useful, and of a qualitative or quantitative nature. It's critical to understand the nature of the audit criteria that were selected; they could be normative, specific, or more general in scope.

The criteria may reflect:

- What should be according to laws, regulations or objectives;
- What is expected, according to sound principles and best practice; and
- What could be (given better conditions)?

The nature of the audit and the audit questions determines the relevance and the type of suitable criteria. The following are possible sources of criteria:

- The law and regulations;
- Standards developed by recognized professional organizations;
- LGA Reports on Plans and Priorities and Performance Reports;
- Generally accepted good practice;
- Standards established by the audited organization; and
- Measures created especially for the audit, drawing on previous LGA work as well as standards and practices from other organizations engaged in comparable activities or from criteria modified for use in similar engagements.
- **VFM Audit Approaches**: In formulating the audit methodology, involves the following key considerations:

- Define how to get the information you need;
- Define how to analyze the collected information;
- Where can we get the data we need – sources?
- How do we collect the data? (Document, data registers, interviews, questionnaire, observations, pictures, etc.
- Again, the audit questions set in section above are the major determinant of the audit approach.

There are generally two approaches in conducting a VFM Audit:

1. *Auditing Results Directly*

a. This type of audit focuses on assessing the results achieved in relation to those intended.

b. The audit does not initially examine the details of the methods or processes but looks at the outputs or outcomes themselves.

c. The approach is particularly appropriate where there are suitable criteria available to measure the quality, quantity and cost of the outputs.

d. The types of problems that may be identified include:

e. Services that are not in accord with the program mandate;

f. Unit costs that exceed departmental standards, or costs of comparable activities in other sections of the government or in outside organizations, and

g. Goods or services that do not meet standards of quality or quantity.

2. *Auditing the Control Systems*

a. This approach is designed to determine if the organization has adequate control systems to provide reasonable assurance that the intended results are achieved.

b. This approach focuses initially on systems and controls and later proceeds to the assessment of the output and outcome of the project.

c. Normally, only high-risk components of the system would be reviewed in depth. Controls are chosen for audit on the basis of their significance to the achievement of key results.

2.5.2. Fieldwork in VFM Audit

The fieldwork stage of a VFM audit is when auditors go out and gather relevant and substantial evidence to back up the audit's conclusions and findings. The purpose of the fieldwork is to gather information that will address the audit questions formulated in the planning phase. Utilizing the auditor's dimensions outlined in Figure 2.1 above, the auditors will gather data on each of the VFM components in accordance with the predetermined criteria, i.e., the three Es and cross-cutting problem:

- *Economy:* How the project use their funds to procure inputs (e.g., Staff time, and other resources). The main issues would be on amount, timing, price, quantity and quality of resources procured.
- *Efficiency:* How inputs are used to produce outputs (goods and services). Question the input/output in terms of wastage, timeliness, quantity, quality, and customer satisfaction.
- *Effectiveness:* How the outputs produce outcomes (i.e., effects on users). Main issue would be are the original intentions/objectives met? Mission and goals achieved? Financially viable?

- *Cross-Cutting Aspects:* Like any other audit, here the main concern is how did the project managers, in their implementation, complied with other governance issues and laws and regulations, standards, values and best practices.

2.5.3. Developing an Audit Findings in VFM

The difference between the current situation and the criterion is the VFM finding, just like in any other kind of audit. Findings are circumstances that the auditor observed while on the job and that will be utilized to address audit-related queries. When the criterion is contrasted with the current circumstances, the audit finding takes place.

As seen in Figure 2.2, an audit finding is produced by gathering data comparing the current situation (what is) to the predetermined standard (what should be). The audit finding is a comparison of the two (particularly a discrepancy between the criterion and the condition).

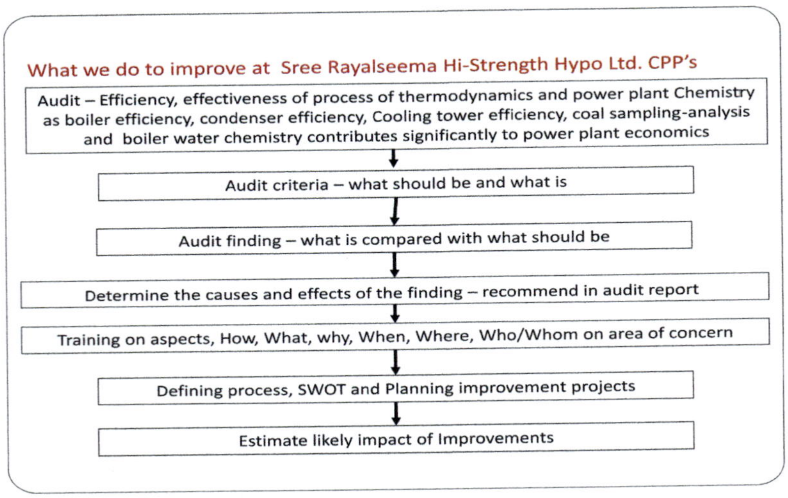

Figure 2.2. *Process of identifying findings and developing recommendations.*

Source: https://image.slidesharecdn.com/deckonconsultancytrainingandaud itsv0-180802091620/75/Deck-on-consultancy-training-and-audits-v0-1-9-2048.jpg.

2.5.4. Structure of VFM Report

An audit report for VFM lacks a set format. The objectives, nature, scope, and time period of the audit, as well as any limitations; The professional standards used; A description of the program or activity that was audited, including management's responsibilities; The criteria used and any disagreement with management regarding their suitability; The observations made; The recommendations made to guide corrective action; Management comments (if provided), including planned action in response to the audit and any differences of opinion; and The conclusions reached against each audit objective, however, must all be made extremely clear to the readers of a VFM audit report.

CASE STUDY

AUDITING AND CONSULTING WITH AN ASSOCIATION TO NAVIGATE FINANCIAL CHALLENGES

Problem

When the accounting firm that had worked with a $20 million association for several years stopped responding to calls about an upcoming audit and questions about ownership of a new building, the association's chief executive officer was in a dilemma. With an upcoming Board meeting and the deadline for an annual report looming, and with no audit scheduled, he called Gelman, Rosenberg and Freedman with whom he had worked in the past.

Action

Despite a busy schedule, Gelman, Rosenberg and Freedman assembled a team to perform the fieldwork and help the association meet its goal of completing the audit in time for the Board meeting and annual report deadline.

When the association formally went out to bid for new auditors the following year, Gelman, Rosenberg & Freedman was selected. In addition to the firm's responsiveness the prior year, GRF also had decades of experience working with nonprofits.

During the next several years, Gelman, Rosenberg and Freedman's accounting specialists not only worked with the chief executive officer and chief operating officer on the annual audit, but also assisted with other operational concerns.

Gelman, Rosenberg and Freedman consulted with the association to improve procurement policies, advised on alternative investments and helped train staff to better understand unrelated business income tax. When the association expressed concerns about management of the building it had just purchased, Gelman, Rosenberg and Freedman evaluated the management company and identified problems related to a lack of monthly reconciliations and the absence of some supporting schedules. The findings validated the earlier uncertainty and the association subsequently moved to hire a new management company.

Finally, association management wanted to ensure it was sufficiently protected against fraud and, separately, respond to staff complaints about a lack of timely reimbursement. After investigating these issues, Gelman, Rosenberg and Freedman established that the association's internal controls were sufficient to protect against evidence of past attempts at fraud and that it was a lack of clear documentation by staff, and not weaknesses in accounting processes, that had led to reimbursement delays.

Solution

Gelman, Rosenberg and Freedman established from the beginning that it could respond effectively to the satisfaction of the association. From the client's need for a quick but thorough audit, to working closely with executive management on several operational and growth areas, Gelman, Rosenberg and Freedman demonstrated its expertise as a valuable professional services partner that helped maximize the success of its client.

ACTIVITY

Prepare a project report on the role of audit committees in enhancing corporate governance and audit quality. Evaluate the responsibilities, composition, and effectiveness of audit committees in overseeing financial reporting integrity and internal control frameworks. Discuss the impact of regulatory requirements (e.g., SOX Act) on audit committee practices and their contributions to mitigating financial risks and enhancing transparency.

SUMMARY

- The Audit Approach is a risk analysis methodology that focuses on the combined impact of the environment in which a client operates, the client's management information and financial results, and the effectiveness of the client's internal controls.
- Audit methodology is a particular set of processes or procedures used to assess a company's financial and business risk. Internal and external audits may be used to review specific information relating to different operations of a company.
- An audit methodology is the series of tasks or activities an accounting firm goes through when reviewing a client's financial information. Each methodology is typically different due to the differences in client operations.
- The IA Plan is developed based on the outcomes of the risk assessment exercise or the enterprise risk assessment. In addition to the business processes identified during the risk assessment exercise, other processes/projects may be selected for inclusion in the IA Plan.
- Risk-based internal auditing involves performing risk assessments in the audit planning stages. In planning for the IA activity (macro level), risk assessment shall be performed to identify, measure, and prioritize risks so that focus is placed on the areas that are threaten by higher degree of risks.

- A process risk analysis performed at the beginning of the execution phase is aimed to serve as a risk-based scoping exercise for the development of an effective and efficient work program which focuses work efforts on key areas to the business process.
- The primary objective of an auditor is to express an opinion on the financial statements. However, the auditor while conducting the audit is required to consider the risk of material misstatements in the financial statements resulting from fraud or error.
- Audit sampling is the use of an audit procedure on a selection of the items within an account balance or class of transactions. The sampling method used should yield an equal probability that each unit in the sample could be selected.
- If the auditor expects error to be present in the population, a larger sample than when no error is expected ordinarily needs to be examined to conclude that the actual error in the population is not greater than the planned tolerable error.
- Test checking in Audit means checking a few transactions selected at random from a large number of transactions. In simple words in test checking a representative number of entries of each class is selected and checked and, if they are found correct, the remaining entries are also taken to be correct.
- Value for money audit (also known as performance audit) has gained popularity in non for profit organizations (NPOs), especially in the public sector due to the apparent difficulties in measuring the performance of these organizations.

REVIEW QUESTIONS

1. Define the internal audit engagement execution.
2. Discuss about development and implementation of the RBAF.
3. Write the risk of fraud and error in audit.
4. Describe the advantages and disadvantage of routine checking.
5. Evaluate the planning a value for money audit.
6. What is an audit report? Mention types of internal audit reports.
7. Discuss the key issues lead to the need of value for money in LGAs.

REFERENCES

1. Azuma, N. (2003). The role of the supreme audit institutions in NPM: International trend. Government Auditing Review, Board of Audit of Japan, 85–106.
2. Azuma, N. (2004). Performance measurement of supreme audit institutions. Government Auditing Review, Board of Audit of Japan, 65–94.
3. Azuma, N. (2005). The role of the supreme audit institutions in new public management (NPM): The trend of continental countries. Government Auditing Review, Board of Audit of Japan, 69–84.

4. Behn, R. D. (2001). Rethinking Democratic Accountability. Brookings Institution Press.
5. Bowerman, M., & Humphrey, C. (2002). Limiting the scope of central government audit: A constitutional problem or a sensible solution? In V. Montesinos & J. M. Vela (Eds.), Innovations in Governmental Accounting (pp. 331–341). Kluwer Academic Publishers.
6. Bowerman, M., Helen, R., & Humphrey, C. (2000). In search of the audit society: Some evidence from health care, police, and schools. International Journal of Auditing, 4, 71–100. https://doi.org/10.1046/j.1099-1123.2000.00018.x.
7. Chelimsky, E. (2007). On fulfilling the accountability purpose in audit and evaluation: Integrating politics and public involvement. In Auditing for Social Change: A strategy for Citizen Engagement in Public Sector Accountability (pp. 115–142). United Nations, Department of Economic and Social Affairs.

CHAPTER

3

Strategies for Successful Audit

LEARNING OBJECTIVES

After studying this chapter, you will be able to:

- Understand the principles of risk-based strategic planning in auditing;
- Demonstrate knowledge of managing performance within an audit context;
- Analyze the outsourcing approach in auditing practices; and
- Develop effective interviewing skills relevant to auditing procedures.

KEY TERMS FROM THIS CHAPTER

Audit management	Audit service
Business risk	Taxpayer
Customer services	Financial experts
Transaction cycle	Internal Revenue Service (IRS)

INTRODUCTION

An audit strategy can be a plan for conducting an audit internally or a strategy for managing an audit conducted by an outside organization, like a tax bureau. Planning, research, and organization can all help to speed up and improve the efficiency of the process in both situations. There are numerous approaches to audit strategy; in more complicated situations, a number of financial experts advise enlisting the services of a certified accountant or consultant who can make sure that all legal requirements are fulfilled throughout the procedure. An audit strategy functions as the fundamental guide for a company's actions in the event that it chooses to conduct an internal audit. The audit strategy specifies objectives for the audit to meet in addition to logistical issues like when the audit will take place, whether internal accountants or an outside expert will conduct it, and how long the procedure will take. For example, one of a financial institution's main objectives could be to determine how susceptible they are to fraud or misappropriation of funds, or whether adjustments to staffing and customer services have resulted in a notable increase in expenses. Estimates of the cost of the auditing process may also be included in the audit plan.

An internal audit's primary goal is to find waste and high-risk areas; if it is successful, it will provide a precise report on the department's risk tolerance and how funds are being used. Developing a sound audit strategy with specific objectives can help guarantee that the information required to develop and carry out effective solutions to any issues is obtained. An audit can also assist in determining whether the objectives of a plan that was recently implemented by a department to increase efficiency are being met. An audit strategy aids in organizing and directing the frequently challenging process of being audited by a tax authority, such as the Internal Revenue Service (IRS) in the United States. The audit strategy will center on providing clear evidence of this fact if an individual or business is audited even though they have filed and paid all of their taxes correctly. When an error, fraud, or lack of funding has resulted in tax issues, an audit plan will typically concentrate on coming up with a fair resolution. Organizing all pertinent documents that will be required is the first step in any audit strategy, regardless of the reasons for the audit. The majority of audits start with a notification outlining the precise issues at hand, so the taxpayer being audited will have a good idea of the kinds of documents that will be required. Determining whether a business or taxpayer will manage the audit on their own or hire a tax attorney is also crucial. In order to reduce the likelihood of contradictory statements, some strategies also advise selecting a single person to speak with the IRS agent if managing the audit without legal assistance.

3.1 SPECIFIC TECHNIQUES AND SKILLS NEEDED FOR THE SUCCESSFUL AUDIT

An impartial, unbiased examination of a business's finances and operations is called an audit. A variety of hard and soft skills are used by auditors to give businesses the best recommendations and solutions. Acquiring knowledge about those abilities and how to develop them can help you have a prosperous auditor career. This article covers the responsibilities of an auditor, defines auditing skills, gives examples of these skills, and offers advice on how to effectively highlight these skills on a job application.

3.1.1 Auditing Skills

An individual can acquire or possess auditing skills to help them carry out auditing tasks accurately and competently. In order to detect any inconsistencies in the reports and improve the organization of financial documents, audit scrutiny necessitates a wide range of knowledge, strong analytical abilities, outstanding interpersonal skills, and the capacity for close attention to detail. Using their expertise in accounting, auditors can evaluate the effectiveness and fairness of an organization's internal controls, management goals, compliance with legal requirements, and accounting procedures.

Here are some examples of skills that auditors often use:

Communication skills

In order to keep an organization's financial records up to date, auditors frequently interact with clients and work in tandem with other departments. To ensure that the recipient understands the message, effective communication is essential to accomplishing this. Being a great listener is also crucial in order to comprehend the speaker's viewpoint and adjust your criticism appropriately.

Financial skills

Before beginning an audit, an auditor must have the technical know-how to prepare and arrange financial statements and the ability to expertly manage a company's financial records. In order to do this, the auditor may pick up a lot of knowledge about the client's company and the sector in which it works. Knowing how a business in that sector normally makes money and spends money, which accounts are used to record those transactions, and what could happen to those accounts could be useful.

Analytical skills

The capacity to see past the obvious and a logical, methodical approach to problem-solving are prerequisites for being analytical. This is important for auditing because it makes error detection faster. Strong analytical abilities enable auditors to promptly pinpoint procedures that need attention and offer suggestions for improvement. The auditor can identify problems and their root causes, decide on or suggest a course of action, and assess the possibility and possible consequences of financial statement errors when they possess analytical skills.

Attention to detail

Being meticulous is one of the most important abilities for an auditor. All of the data that is provided, including any odd trends or patterns, may be examined by an auditor.

It is crucial that they take note of any patterns, customs, or irregularities they come across. They might overlook a possible fraud scheme if they choose not to investigate these anomalies.

Deadline adherence

Timeliness has a direct correlation with auditing. This makes it crucial to have the ability to manage all tasks that aid in meeting deadlines.

Due to the unique structures and requirements of each organization, deadlines may vary. The deadlines in every organization differ. A competent auditor can meet deadlines without sacrificing the caliber of their work.

Business acumen

Companies are flourishing when they take a dynamic approach. Knowing the business models outside of the routine audit checks can be very helpful in these situations. Auditors can learn this skill gradually or through a great deal of experience and practice. While working with an organization and getting to know its complexities, auditors acquire this skill. Additionally, they can learn it by staying current with the shifting trends in the industry.

Initiative driven

Most businesses welcome proactive, accountable, and initiative-driven auditors. Deep knowledge and enthusiasm are necessary for this work, which ignites a person's zeal for taking initiative. Being an initiative-driven thinker and having a passion for learning can make an auditor better.

Collaboration

Auditors frequently collaborate with teams, obtaining information from various business divisions and incorporating it into the documentation. Because of this, it's critical to coordinate departments and gather the necessary data. Efficient workflow can be achieved through teams maintaining a balanced work ethic. In order to produce error-free reports and offer recommendations, auditing also necessitates an understanding of the roles and procedures of various departments.

Critical thinking

Critical thinking abilities are necessary for professionals performing audits. This ability can assist auditors in finding more effective solutions to particular or challenging issues. Audit professionals can succeed by eliminating biases and having a fundamental understanding of the various perspectives to enable a critical and impartial perspective.

Organization

Professionals who handle financial data benefit from being able to organize their documents. It also aids in time management and gets rid of redundant tasks in the workflow. Additionally, having good organizational abilities makes them seem credible to shareholders or corporate executives with whom they may deal during an audit.

3.1.2 Improve Audit Skills

Below are a few ways to improve your audit skills and become a better professional:

1. **Learn consistently.** Maintaining current knowledge of industry news, regulations, and financial developments, along with keeping up with the latest developments in the field, can help you grow as an auditor.
2. **Practise active listening.** While conducting audits, paying close attention to the speaker can help you become a better communicator, grasp their viewpoint, and build cordial and productive working relationships.
3. **Join a programme.** By attending and participating in seminars, workshops, and other similar events, you can gain knowledge from others› experiences as well as exposure to various methods for conducting audits more effectively.
4. **Enhance your perspective.** Instead of looking at each step separately, you can approach auditing more objectively and draw conclusions that can be put into practice by viewing it as a process that consists of multiple steps.

3.1.3 Audit Skills In The Workplace

Audit work can sometimes be challenging and complex. Possessing the requisite skills can help you overcome unique challenges during your job and succeed as an auditor. Here are a few ways an auditor can use their skills to benefit a company:

- Ensuring adherence to the industry-related rules and regulations
- Checking if financial statements comply with the regulations
- Conducting background checks on potential employees
- Compiling information for better decision making about expenses
- Reviewing information security procedures
- Suggesting changes in policy for overall organisational growth

3.1.4 Ways to Highlight Audit Skills

There are moments when audit work is difficult and complicated. Having the necessary abilities can help you succeed as an auditor by enabling you to overcome particular obstacles at work. Here are some examples of how an auditor's abilities can help a business:

On the resume

Put your relevant skills in a skills section of your resume so that you can do the job well. When discussing your experience with auditing software, be sure to include any other accomplishments that demonstrate your proficiency and how they can help the company. In the education section of your resume, you have the option to emphasize any relevant coursework you completed. To make sure hiring managers can easily see your license and certification details, you can include them separately. This will increase the likelihood that they will consider you for the position.

In the cover letter

Provide a brief summary of any prior auditing experience you may have had in your cover letter, along with your accomplishments in the workplace, whether you worked for a small or large company. If you don't have any experience, talk about any relevant courses you've taken or volunteer work you've done that will make you a more effective auditor. In your application, highlight your dedication to precision and correctness and describe how these attributes qualify you for the position.

During an interview

Spend some time reading the job description to determine what particular abilities the company is seeking in a candidate. Consider instances in the past where you have applied these abilities. Putting these examples on paper and getting them ready is a good idea because hiring managers might inquire about them. To avoid misunderstandings and improve your chances of getting hired, try practicing expressing your auditing expertise and pertinent experience in a clear and succinct manner.

3.1.5 What Does An Auditor Do?

A business's financial department relies on auditing to perform a variety of necessary tasks, such as recording transactions, keeping track of transactions, and assisting management and executives in adhering to current business laws. A few more duties of an editor are as follows:

- Analysing the financial reports and records of an organisation
- Preparing and maintaining the balance sheets and other documents
- Identifying the loopholes for improvement in the current system
- Finding the levels of financial risks involved
- Protecting the company from defying the laws
- Reviewing the existing structure and making recommendations

An auditor may take on additional responsibilities to guarantee accurate record-keeping. Industry to industry may differ in this, but the fundamental duties always stay the same. A bachelor's or master's degree in finance, accounting, commerce, or a similar discipline is necessary to work as an auditor. Depending on the role, seniority, and business models, organizations may have different hiring standards for people with specialized auditing skills.

3.1.6 Technique for Auditing Skills

To put it simply, the instruments used to carry out the audit are called auditing techniques.

The strategies used by the auditor to verify the accounts are known as auditing techniques. "Any technique used by auditors to uncover problems in established process and controls as well as determine deviations from actual accounting and controls established by a business or organization" is the definition of an auditing technique. Following are the important techniques of audit.

Examination of books of accounts

The basic technique of an auditor is to examine the books of accounts. The examination is conducted to verify the accuracy of data.

Vouching

It refers to the examination of the original documentary evidence supporting the transaction.

Examples for vouchers are invoices, bills, receipts, debit and credit notes, etc.

Inquiry

The auditor makes inquires and collects information from persons inside and outside the organization to check the correctness of the recorded data.

Sampling

Sampling refers to selecting and checking a few items from the whole accounting information.

Confirmation

The auditor contacts debtors, creditors, officials, etc and collects information which helps him to confirm the transactions.

Compliance test

These tests are employed by the auditor to check the effectiveness of the internal control system prevailing in the organization.

Financial system analysis

To determine the relationship between two accounting figures, financial statements like the balance sheet and profit and loss account are reanalyzed. Ratio analysis is a common tool used by auditors to evaluate a company's profitability, solvency, and liquidity.

Computer techniques

The auditor may use techniques such as audit software, test packing, mapping, etc to test the accuracy of accounting data.

Observation

The auditor relies on personal observation and witnesses the physical stock taking conducted at the end of the year.

Expert opinion

The auditor contacts experts like engineers, lawyers, etc to gather their Opinion about the business. He also depends on the internal auditors for completing his work.

3.2. RISK-BASED STRATEGIC PLANNING

A Chief Audit Executive (CAE) may wish to create a formal audit strategy for a variety of reasons, and internal audit strategies begin with well-defined objectives. Setting resources in the direction of approved goals creates the conditions for success. The elements shown in the figure have an impact on the process of establishing precise audit objectives (Figure 3.1). Since audit objectives are a product of shifting forces at play, there is no one correct way to define them. Although this seems simple, there isn't always a clear understanding of the goals. An opportunity to reach consensus regarding the key differences between the roles of audit and management. Numerous factors influence the final model that is chosen. These include the opinions of the CAE, the demands of management, and the nature of the workforce.

Figure 3.1. *Setting audit objectives.*

Source: https://d3i71xaburhd42.cloudfront.net/b332fb5b95d8a06b1b210dcca2334a4701b84a15/203-Figure8.1-1.png.

3.2.1. The Corporate Risk Strategy

The corporate assessment of business risk is a fundamental component of audit strategy. This determines the control requirements of an organization. A risk survey entails the following and requires discussion with middle management:

- Defining the audit unit.
- A comparison of the relative risks that come with each unit.
- Studying the kinds of issues that units tend to draw.
- Risk classification for resources that are then allocated through an audit plan.

1. **Risk Assessment**: A methodology that takes into account the fact that various activities are linked to varying kinds and degrees of risk should be developed. "The CAE should establish risk-based plans to determine the priorities of the internal audit activity, consistent with the organization's goals," states the IIA Performance Standard 2010 clearly. Although there isn't a universal recipe, we must make sure that:

The methodology is accepted by the organization.

- It is applied to the audit universe in a consistent fashion.
- It is based on the corporate risk assessment and ongoing operational risk reviews.
- The organization would have to be broken down into auditable units and one approach in Brink's

Modern Internal Auditing: It suggests three options for identifying audit units:

- By function accounting, purchasing payroll
- By transaction cycle cash receipts, production
- By geography

Management Participation: A further aspect of audit strategy relates to the need to involve management in the process. Management participation includes:

- Explaining that audit operates to a risk-based strategy.
- Ensuring that this strategy is based primarily on addressing organizational risk and control needs.
- Publicizing the link between risk and resource allocation.
- Keeping management informed as to changes to the existing strategies.
- Securing avenues whereby relevant information may be imparted to and from management.
- Clarifying the agreed cut-off points between management and internal audit's roles.
- Retaining a degree of independence that gives audit the final say in strategy and planning

2. **Successful Strategic Implementation**: Getting auditors to collaborate proactively to move the audit service in the right direction is known as strategic development. For any strategy to be successful, there must be a unifying purpose. The CAE may create a chain, as shown in figure that symbolizes the flow necessary for effective strategic implementation. Recognizing this is crucial for audit management because it is predicated on strong leadership that permeates the audit function with a compelling message (Figure 3.2).

Figure 3.2 *Successful strategic flow.*

Source: https://d3i71xaburhd42.cloudfront.net/b332fb5b95d8a06b1b210dcca2334a4701b84a15/204-Figure8.2-1.png.

3.2.2. Managing Performance

When conducting an audit where staffing is included in the work's terms of reference, audit would typically advise staff appraisal as a management control. Therefore, one could contend that this method should be used by auditors to manage the internal audit function. Staff appraisal programs, however, rely on how they are formulated and put into practice to determine whether they are a positive or negative incentive. The idea behind staff appraisals is to motivate employees by outlining expectations and then gauging their progress toward meeting those goals. Positive actions that can be taken in cases where performance is below expectations are the other advantage. Career development programs, which can also be used to guide employee activities and guarantee proper advancement in order to retain competent employees and improve underperforming ones, are supported by appraisal schemes. There is a basic diagram in Figure 3.3 that can help explain this.

Separating performance evaluation from the processes for handling unacceptable subpar performance and specific issues is an alternative method of approaching the appraisal process. The latter would be used in situations where performance flaws are evident and cannot be resolved by conventional training and development initiatives. The organization's ability to differentiate between various management techniques for addressing a range of performance-related issues is the basis for the figure. Therefore, the disciplinary procedure is used to address any procedure violations by the auditor. When an employee is frequently absent from work, the frequent sickness policy kicks in; when an employee performs poorly, special measures are taken that could lead to the auditor's termination. The performance appraisal system can be run in a positive manner at all times in this way. Specific staffing issues are managed by different, independent agreements that are not related to performance reviews. The auditor will receive extra attention; this won't wait for or depend on the program for performance appraisals. By doing this, issues of this nature can be expedited before they become unmanageable. The appraisal scheme may carry on in a positive manner in the interim. The terms "quality, excellence, growth, performance, and advancement" might all help to foster a positive atmosphere. The counterargument is that before any performance reviews can be scheduled, this supportive atmosphere needs to be established. Regardless of one's perspective, it is imperative that auditors receive positive appraisals.

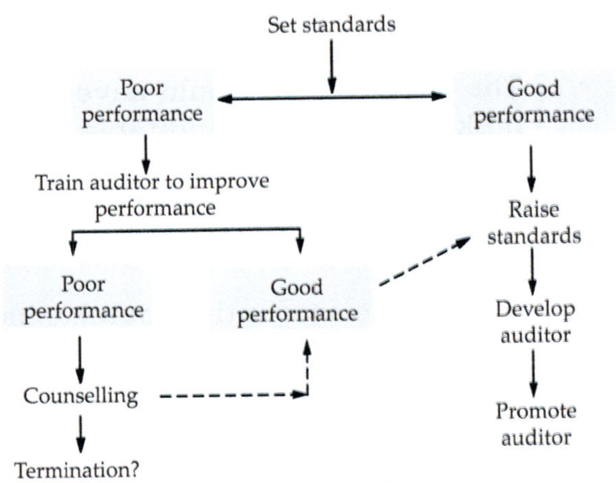

Figure 3.3. *The auditor appraisal process.*

Source: https://d3i71xaburhd42.cloudfront.net/b332fb5b95d8a06b1b210dcca2334a4701b84a15/205-Figure8.3-1.png.

This in turn depends on:

- Keeping the accent on praise.
- Not using the appraisal scheme to criticize but using it to develop.
- Using performance appraisal to engender good communications and listening skills.

- Seeking to promote a win/win environment where all sides gain.

Every auditor can have their performance goals based on the quarterly or annual plans. This will depend on finishing specified audits, adhering to spending plans, executing unique tasks like the audit manual, and reaching a target proportion of chargeable to non-chargeable hours. When departmental or organizational targets are the source of these targets, hierarchies may be created to allow goals to cascade down in a form of management by achievement. The following is a list of some examples of specific performance goals for teams and units:

- Absenteeism rate.
- Amount of alteration as a result of management review.
- Currency of time-monitoring information.
- Currency of timesheets submitted and authorized.
- Degree to which auditors keep within the budget hours for each audit.
- Extent of audit automation.
- Extent to which audit objectives have been met.
- Extent to which desks are kept clear.
- Extent to which developmental plans have been achieved.
- Extent to which files hold all relevant information.
- Extent to which follow-up audits find that recommendations from previous reports have been implemented.
- Extent to which the annual and quarterly plan has been achieved.
- Extent to which work plan has been completed.
- Level of absences from work.
- Level of audits within time budget.
- Level of complaints.
- Level of compliance with the audit manual.
- Level of draft reports requiring rewrites.
- Level of involvement of auditee in the audit terms of reference.
- Level of managerial agreement to audit risk criteria.
- Level of positive comments from clients via satisfaction questionnaire.
- Level of problems found during work reviews.
- Level of recoverable hours to non-recoverable hours charged in the period.
- Level of satisfaction from the clients.
- Level of staff grievances against management.
- Level of suggestions from audit staff to audit management.
- Number of aborted audits.
- Number of audit reports issued.
- Number of auditors passing professional exams.
- Number of audits completed on time.
- Number of audits delegated by the audit manager.
- Number of improvements to the audit manual.
- Number of recommendations agreed.
- Rate of production of audit products.

- Regularity of group and departmental meetings.
- Staff turnover.
- The percentage of recoverable hours charged.
- The percentage of staff with poor timekeeping.
- Time taken by auditors to get access to audit management.
- Time taken to find specific files.
- Time taken to issue audit reports after completion of the audit.
- Time taken to respond to management requests for assistance.

Productivity can be defined as follows: inputs are produced through a process that is appropriately controlled. Setting standards for the output based on the specified level of inputs is one way to gauge how effective this control is.

These standards turn into targets, and productivity can be evaluated based on how well these targets have been met as long as systems for measuring the work have been put in place. Productivity factors are one aspect of a system that career development uses to gauge how an auditor is progressing. Performance measures are one method of doing this. This allows audit management to evaluate an auditor's performance based on both more objective and quantitative criteria. The limitations of productivity measures must always be understood. Although they may seem scientific, they are really based on underlying, subjective principles that have been approved by management. The only true benefit is that, when implemented methodically, they might encourage a certain level of uniformity among employees. By showing some of the goals we are trying to help employees achieve, they may also give development plans some direction. The SMART test model that is commonly used for target setting is derived from the following model, with some modifications.

- S: Specific
- M: Measurable
- A: Achievable
- R: Results oriented
- T: Time based
- **Dealing with Typical Problems**: While inefficiency should be controlled and kept to acceptable levels, perfection is unachievable. Creating plans to address issues in internal audit is the responsibility of audit management. Disregarding substandard procedures and failing to request pertinent control data are actions that hinder the provision of quality services. Common issues include the following:
- Excess hours charged.
- Inadequate working papers.
- No follow-up procedure.
- Low pay.
- Inadequate audit manual.
- Poor planning.
- Inadequate supervision.
- Lack of continuing professional education.
- No career development.
- Reporting delays.
- Lack of professionalism.
- Financial emphasis.
- Performing line functions.
- No defined approach.

3.2.3. The Audit Manual

The subject of audit manuals supports professional standards for implementing the chosen audit strategy and touches on several related topics, such as standardization, protocols, limiting creativity, and audit approaches. As stated in Brink's Modern Internal Auditing, "Audits must be managed, and the best tool for audit management is an audit manual." An internal audit manual serves as a company-wide reference for the audit's contents, outlining how each step should be handled and providing an overview of some models that support this crucial method.

- **The Role of the Audit Manual**: Before thinking about suitable models, it is important to define the audit manual's purpose and goals. A variety of sources have been taken into consideration because publications about performance and internal auditing practices are relevant to the subject. The necessity to document information is addressed in IIA Practice Advisory 2330-1, which states that the CAE "should establish working paper policies for the various types of engagements performed." Standardized engagement working papers, like audit programs and questionnaires, can increase an engagement's effectiveness and make it easier to assign engagement work. "A device that involves the accumulation and dissemination of all those documents, guidance, direction, and instructions issued by audit management that affect the way the audit service is delivered is what we mean when we define the audit manual," says our team. The auditor can obtain guidance by using the manual as a channel. The material that is currently available offers feedback from a wide range of sources and will shed light on the numerous concerns related to the creation and application of audit manuals.

Manuals fulfill the following roles:

- Defining standards and methods of work.
- Communicating this to auditors.
- Establishing a base from which to measure the expected standards of performance.
- **Standardized Forms:** The idea of standardized documentation and the audit manual's related function are one problem. It should be made clear that our definition of audit manuals is as a managerial tool for guiding auditors before we discuss standard forms. This indicates that the formal standards that must be met include standardized procedures. The use of ad hoc forms for documentation standards without manual coordination will inevitably result in inconsistencies and inefficiencies. There is a wealth of information available regarding the benefits of standardization, and the following aspects stand out:
- The most well-known standardized processes are internal control questionnaires and audit programs, which are created by numerous audit departments.
- Flowcharts ought to adhere to a standard format that is applied uniformly across the audit division.
- Report writing can have a "house style," and standardization promotes consistency.
- Standardization may cause auditors to focus more on the real goals of the task at hand and less on format and procedure.

- If the audit objectives are not kept in mind, standardization can serve as a crucial control over each audit assignment that prevents people from wandering aimlessly.

After developing a model audit manual, we have come to the conclusion that the audit manual should be the conduit for all efforts aimed at standardizing procedures. This could be the greatest advantage of allocating resources for the creation of an extensive and current handbook. Having standardized procedures that can be automated and a formal means of putting these procedures into practice are crucial for the advancement of an audit automation strategy (i.e., an audit guidebook).

- **Audit Approach and Methodology:** Because auditing can be done in a variety of ways in practice, we are concerned that the manual projects the audit personality or the voice of the director of auditing. Due to their recognition of this problem, the IIA standards have formulated their requirements in a manner that has two main implications. First, it is accepted that there will always be variations in audit techniques and methods; second, it is insufficient to merely state that a particular set of standards is being followed. In order to be implemented across the audit department, the precise audit philosophy needs to be decided upon and documented. We are heading toward the idea that both seasoned and inexperienced auditors require clear instructions on how to perform the specific audit role. The audit manual is the best tool for documenting the agreed-upon solution in this regard. Every audit department needs to provide a specific product that comes from the agreement reached between the organization and audit. An approach that has been carefully considered can help develop the capacity to participate in less structured activities and transition between projects without restriction. Though not from the generalized set of audit procedures, this may be outlined in the audit manual.

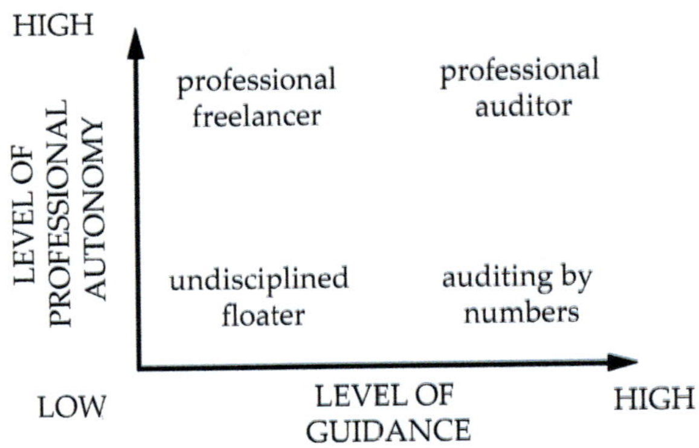

Figure 3.4. *Autonomy versus control.*

Source: https://d3i71xaburhd42.cloudfront.net/b332fb5b95d8a06b1b210dcca2334a4701b84a15/210-Figure8.4-1.png.

- **Impact on Creativity:** The level of guidance and standardization that a thorough audit manual offers and the auditor's professional autonomy seem to be at odds with one another. For audit productivity to be increased, both are necessary. This conflict is similar to the age-old issue of managing control and autonomy—autonomy being the capacity to succeed or fail. Uncertainty about what constitutes successful performance hinders auditors' ability to perform, and bureaucratic constraints make it difficult to make significant progress. This inherent conflict must be acknowledged in audit manuals. The need to preserve professional autonomy and the manual's fundamental goals of offering guidance throughout the audit function are incompatible. Standardized audit procedures impose greater restrictions on the auditor's efforts the more guidance they provide. The conflicting forces of autonomy and control must be balanced (Figure 3.4).

The relationship between these two key factors is outlined in the model in the figure. We need to get to a place where auditors maintain their creative and professional flair while focusing their efforts as directed by the chief internal auditor, in accordance with the current audit strategy and organizational culture.

By developing the "professional auditor," we would be able to move closer to the target position, which is depicted in the figure's far right corner.

- Ensure that more comprehensive guidance is only provided where it is required.
- Leave general reference material outside the main audit manual.
- Indicate whether a particular procedure is optional.
- Explain why a procedure has been selected.
- Allow departures as long as they are documented and justified.
- Encourage all auditors to participate in improving the manual and consider rotating the task of maintaining it.
- Do not appoint an auditor until the approach and standards are explained and he/she can work within them.
- Where a requirement in the manual has been overridden consider whether an amendment is required.
- Ensure that auditors who refuse to perform to the requirements of the manual are moved out of the audit department.
- Test each section that is drafted to ensure that it is not unnecessarily cumbersome and bureaucratic.
- Watch out for auditors who appear demotivated and investigate underlying reasons.
- Ensure that there is a continuous program to search for and amend all faults.
- **Structuring the Audit Manual:** As with other features of a manual the structure and content depend on the particular circumstances, although it is possible to set out a four-tier model for structuring the manual in Figure 3.5.

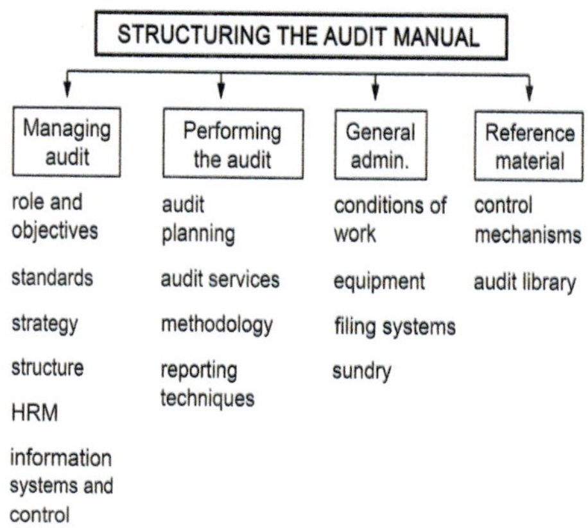

Figure 3.5. *Structuring the manual.*

Source: https://d3i71xaburhd42.cloudfront.net/b332fb5b95d8a06b1b210dcca2334a4701b84a15/211-Figure8.5-1.png.

- It is generally better to have a few main sections as with the model in figure so as to generate some degree of form and structure.

- Keep basic reference material outside the audit manual.
- Maintain an extensive up-to-date audit library and cross-reference this to the audit manual.
- Ensure that all the topics mentioned in figure are fully dealt with in the manual so as to promote a complete and worthwhile document.

3.3. DELEGATING AUDIT WORK

More junior employees should be assigned tasks by audit management. This has the potential to be a very effective strategy for both improving general productivity and training auditors. Delegation has advantages and disadvantages, and it must be understood and managed. The delegation process entails granting permission to carry out specific duties. Management is still ultimately in charge and is answerable for the result. The Figure 3.6 depicts one perspective on delegation.

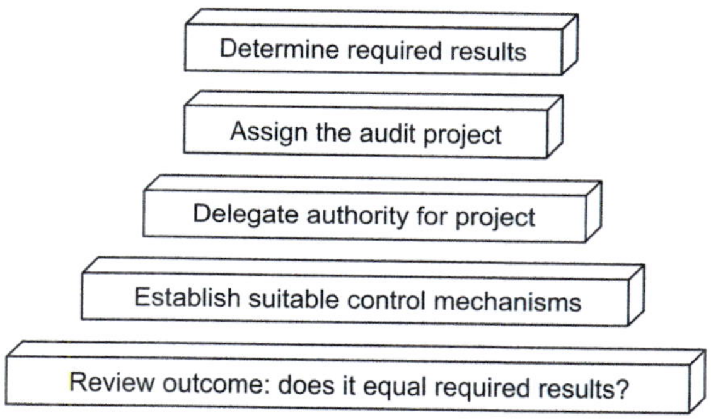

Figure 3.6. *The delegation process.*

Source: https://d3i71xaburhd42.cloudfront.net/b332fb5b95d8a06b1b210dcca2334a4701b84a15/211-Figure8.6-1.png.

- **Delegation in Internal Audit:** We distinguish between practical and technical delegation. When it comes to technical delegation, the CAE is ultimately in charge of the internal audit department's operations. Likewise, audit managers are accountable for the actions of the employees under their supervision. Through delegation, auditors can carry out their daily tasks without hindrance, working within audit plans that assign specific responsibilities to each internal auditor. When duties that are typically assigned to managers are assigned to auditors in addition to or instead of their regular workload, this is referred to as restricted delegation. These additional, more difficult jobs and projects need to be closely monitored. An illustration would be the audit manual, whose upkeep falls under the purview of the CAE but could be delegated to a more seasoned auditor.

Other examples are:

- Audit Brochures: Marketing logos and web-based material

- The Annual Report: Client presentations
- Special Projects: Internal reviews of audit files
- Quality Assurance Programs: The audit charter
- Auditing Standards: Staff training and development

Delegation does not mean renunciation of accountability. Delegation must be done carefully and the CAE must be involved in issues that significantly affect the audit services. This covers delicate subjects including private audit marketing plans, controlling the audit budget, disciplining auditors, the audit committee, significant grievances against auditors, and audit strategy reviews. Benefits include the positive impact on employees and completing tasks. Principal advantages include:

- Auditors may be able to do a better job than their managers.
- Auditors themselves learn to delegate.
- New ideas may be generated.
- It acts as a communication device between managers and staff.
- It promotes trust across the internal audit department.

Management is forced by delegation to establish precise goals and boundaries. Senior auditors might put in hours working on a mysterious project with no tangible results. The audit manager is motivated to clearly define and convey the goals through delegation. It must be predicated on mutual trust between individuals, each with unique needs. Allowing errors is a necessary part of relinquishing some managerial power on the audit manager. Supervisors ought to recognize better performance when employees take on more challenging tasks. Better performance is stimulated by delegation because it creates opportunities. When more demands lead to stress and impair the auditor's capacity to meet the challenge, issues arise. It is preferable to put in the extra work to advance the auditor's career development, which is why an internal promotion policy may be helpful. Benefits have to be genuine.

3.3.1. Audit Information Systems

The computer has a significant impact on auditing tasks. Impacts can be seen in the audit field, in the way audit work is carried out, or in the way audit itself makes use of computers to increase efficiency. Information technology (IT) should be continuously explored by management as a means of enhancing the audit service. This could entail hiring computer staff to advance IT expertise within the division. To guarantee that effective information systems (Figure 3.7) are created to support the overall audit strategy, an information systems strategy should be developed.

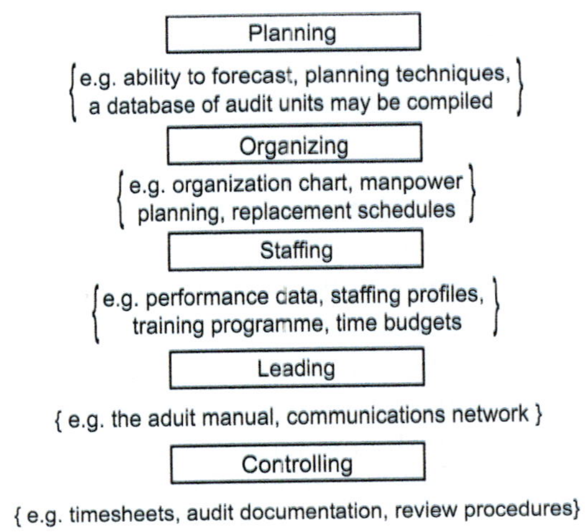

Figure 3.7. *Impact of information.*

Source: https://d3i71xaburhd42.cloudfront.net/b332fb5b95d8a06b1b210dcca2334a4701b84a15/213-Figure8.7-1.png.

In order to give auditors confidence when utilizing automated systems, the strategy should also focus on enhancing general computer literacy. This could open up the door to a career in computer auditing, wherein one could eventually pick up advanced computing abilities. Accessible public networks, like the Internet, provide an almost infinite repository of reference data. One possible addition to the audit library over time would be the development of internal information databases. To be honest, it is hard to see how an audit department could make systems-based auditing a top priority without creating a database of the available control mechanisms. The PC laptops can create direct information links between the auditor and the audit office by sending files to the audit manager for review. The independent contractor auditor, whose credo is "Have laptop, will travel," can then be promoted. Moreover, time-tracking systems have the ability to integrate with planning and control systems and track audit hours. They can also be utilized as an accounting and billing system.

- **Time Monitoring Systems:** The majority of internal audit units will likely have time management systems, which are crucial information-based systems. This should make it possible for audit management to get reports on staff performance on a regular basis. It will be put to use in order to support various performance targets that should have been established for audit teams as well as auditors. They ought to address every specific information requirement that arises from the audit time management (Figure 3.8 & 3.9). This will include both specially requested items and periodic reports. The time frame, types of work, auditors, audit groups, and the audit unit as a whole should all be covered in the reports. It should therefore report on:
- Time spent on audits.
- Audits over budget.
- Non-recoverable time charged (such as training).
- Breakdown between assurance work and consultancy engagements.
- Audits that should have been completed.

The inputs of a suitable time monitoring system may be illustrated in Figure 3.8:

- The various roles of time management information should be duly recognized and catered for here we would expect any such systems to cover the following functions:
- A method of charging time to specific audit jobs.
- A way of identifying variances from planned to actual hours though incorporating budgeted hours to each chargeable job.
- A method of charging clients for work carried out and generating the supporting schedules and covering invoice if needs be. Accordingly, it is important to identify a client for each job that is set up on the system.
- A method of establishing the status of each job. The messages may be used in any good system to compile a form of database of audit jobs, which will provide summary information. This may range from terms of reference, assigned auditor, special features, stage indicators (say planning, field work or reporting) and so on.

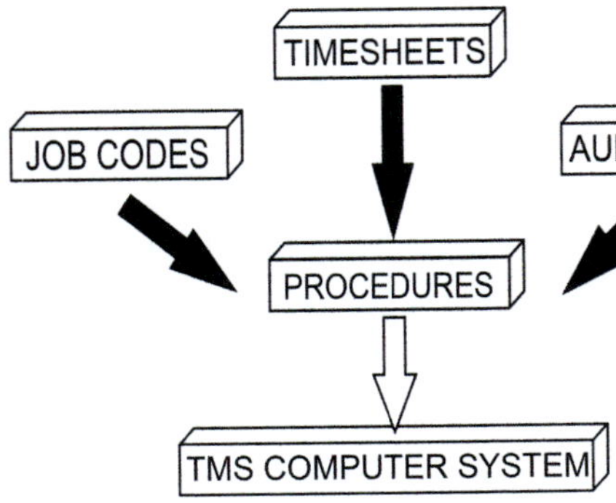

Figure 3.8. *Time monitoring system inputs.*

Source: https://d3i71xaburhd42.cloudfront.net/b332fb5b95d8a06b1b210dcca2334a4701b84a15/214-Figure8.8-1.png.

Usually, the time management system consists of a computer program that tracks and reports auditors' work hours. For the system to function, three key elements have to be added. This contains the job coding (as well as the clients), the scheduled hours, and the auditor's weekly timesheet. Therefore, purchasing and installing a time management system on a computer or network is not enough. Before a suitable reporting system can be put online and be of any use to audit management, the underlying procedures need to be thoroughly considered and addressed. Expanding on the previous point, time management tasks should also be resourced as legitimate systems development projects. In this case, the work is given to the audit administration officer in addition to being given a high profile and the status of an official computer project.

To this end, for larger audit units, we may designate the following key officers:

- A systems controller
- A systems manager
- The data owner

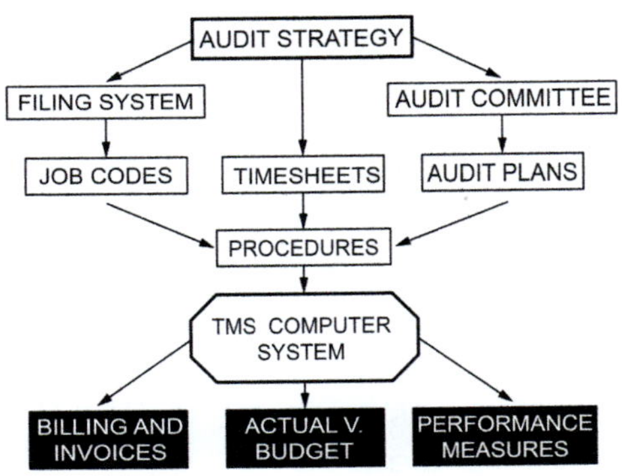

Figure 3.9. *The audit time monitoring system.*

Source: https://d3i71xaburhd42.cloudfront.net/b332fb5b95d8a06b1b210dcca2334a4701b84a15/215-Figure8.9-1.png.

Codify the work according to the reporting structure that was chosen. The audit committee might be of a different opinion. We can obtain reports in this way that organically fit into our quarterly, annual, and monthly reporting frameworks.

Avoid letting auditors set up unique codes for minor tasks that could overload the system. To document these one-time tasks, a general code of "advice and information" may be utilized. We might establish a deadline and mandate that jobs that are, say, shorter than one or two days must adhere to this code. If this strategy is used, timesheets must accurately document all work details and be kept on file in case the client has any questions later. Following this line it is as well to have small number of fixed codes for non-recoverable time such as annual leave, training, sickness and so on. Have strict rules on who can set up codes and budget hours. This should be restricted to senior staff.

Activity reports should be checked by the audit managers on a regular basis. We may set out an example of a coding structure where systems and investigations work has been separated.

Supervisors depend on the increasing application of information technology, which entails increased computerization. This also applies to the internal audit division, and in accordance with company policies, appropriate standards need to be used to control these developments. Automation is a given, and the audit department needs to maintain the same standard of controls over the departments it examines.

3.3.2. The Internal Audit Function

Where internal auditing has not previously been required, legislation and/or internal pressures may cause this to change. Proposals for improved corporate governance may elevate the issue of secure control systems to the level of an organizational concern that needs to be resolved by creating an audit committee. Studies have indicated that the audit committee will eventually become more focused on internal audit, even if its primary focus is on external audit. We discuss the common scenario in which a newly established internal audit function needs to be established. Concerns consist of:

- *The Audit Charter:* This sets out the role and objectives of internal audit and is at the core of the delivery of audit services.
- *Audit Standards:* The CAE has to decide on two types of standards before the new audit function can be developed professional and operational standards.
- *The Code of Conduct:* Another consideration when setting up a new audit service is whether to set standards of conduct before recruiting staff.
- *Recruitment and Selection:* It is essential that the 'rounded person' is acquired with a whole package of attributes. Training can only go so far, and we are not talking only about formal qualifications and experience.
- *Training:* A training budget is essential for the newly formed internal audit unit.
- *The Business Risk Assessment:* This is an important part of the development of a new audit function.
- *Information Systems (IS) Audit:* One matter that should be high on the agenda for the CAE when

designing the new internal audit service relates to IS audit.

- *Fraud Work:* There is a need to define a clear policy on the detection and investigation of fraud and irregularities.
- *Business Planning:* The new CAE should devise and publish a business plan that covers the internal audit unit.
- *Assurance and Consulting Services:* One question to be tackled early on in the life of the newly formed unit is related to the type of services that will be provided by internal audit. It is incumbent upon the CAE to decide the best way to discharge the audit role and which services will be provided and to which degree. It is possible to break down the audit role into two:
- *Risk-Based Assurance-Based Audit of all Services:* financial, operational, strategic and automated systems. Consultancy projects requested by management into regularity, compliance, VFM, management development and others.
- *Budgets:* While the CAE must seek to negotiate an adequate budget, there is little scope to secure extensive funding at the outset. The launch of the new service. The new service must be introduced to the organization. All the well-known devices that this entails should be applied.
- *The Audit Manual:* Most of the matters mentioned will be documented the audit manual and there is nothing wrong with allowing this document to grow as the audit unit develops.

3.4. THE OUTSOURCING APPROACH

What the organization can expect from its internal audit team is outlined in the internal audit strategy. The progressive management has high standards and is aware of what it can obtain from its audit shop. The question of outsourcing arises when the internal team is unable to meet these standards without outside assistance.

The IIA is aware that there are numerous ways in which internal auditing can be provided. Their glossary, which makes reference to external sourcing, defines an external service provider as: An individual or business that is not affiliated with the organization and possesses specialized knowledge, expertise, and experience in a particular field. Actuaries, accountants, appraisers, environmental specialists, fraud investigators, attorneys, engineers, geologists, security specialists, statisticians, information technology specialists, external auditors, and other auditing firms are a few examples of outside service providers. An outside service provider may be hired by the CAE, senior management, or the board. Effective internal auditing departments are ingrained in their organizations, according to research. These departments' work is essential to management's endeavors. A vision statement that is founded on and connected to the overarching organizational vision serves as the foundation for the efficacy of internal auditing, and it is carried out via a strategic plan. A visionary internal auditing department is:

- *Proactive:* It establishes itself as a change agent throughout the organization. It identifies new initiatives to add value to the organization while retaining a clear focus on traditional audit areas such as internal control exposure and potential ethical issues.
- *Innovative:* The innovative internal auditing department searches out the most valuable use of its resources, questions the value of routine audits, and creates opportunities to increase the value of the function. The department invests in technology, people, and the organization and partners with an external provider if it enhances the value of its services.
- *Focused:* Auditing must be responsive to the organization it serves. It must understand and focus on management and audit committee priorities.
- *Motivated:* A motivated auditing staff has a sense of mission, teamwork, and organizational pride. They are open to constructive suggestions and seek input on continuous improvement. They measure user satisfaction and are not resistant to change.
- *Integrated:* Technology should be used to enhance audit productivity and teamwork. Investments should be made in technology that will assist the

organization in continuous monitoring of transactions and identifying potential fraudulent transactions.

A robust department within the company is the source of many of the qualities. External suppliers could score highly on each of these criteria as well. The board, audit committee, and management are responsible for weighing the different aspects and selecting the best course of action for their company. The task has been assigned. Published standards are far removed from the slumbering memory of audit teams of the past who produced endless amounts of pointless reports that were either disregarded or simply accepted. Although this drive has greatly raised the audit profile, it has also raised the bar and put those who have not positioned themselves correctly at risk.

It is recommended that the IA activity employs personnel with qualifications in accounting, auditing, economics, finance, statistics, IT, engineering, taxation, law, environmental affairs, and other related fields, or utilize outside service providers. Not every member must be an expert in every field. It is possible for the board, senior management, or the CAE to hire an outside service provider. Service provider utilized in mergers, IT, valuations, physical conditions, measurement, fraud, actuaries, and the assessment of the internal audit quality assurance program, among other areas. The competence, impartiality, and independence of the outside service provider should all be evaluated by CAE. It is imperative that the CAE evaluates its relationship with the organization and the IA in order to guarantee impartiality. Make sure the work doesn't compromise the external auditor's independence if they are involved. CAE and the service provider ought to go over:

- Objectives and scope of work.
- Matters in engagement communication.
- Access issues.
- Procedures to be employed.
- Ownership of working papers.
- Confidentiality issues.

3.4.1. The Audit Planning Process

Effective planning is essential for a successful audit, and it should involve the client in identifying review areas through relative risk assessment. Due to the large audit universe and the impossibility of auditing everything, long-term planning distributes limited audit resources to it. Auditors need to appear to be carrying out significant tasks.

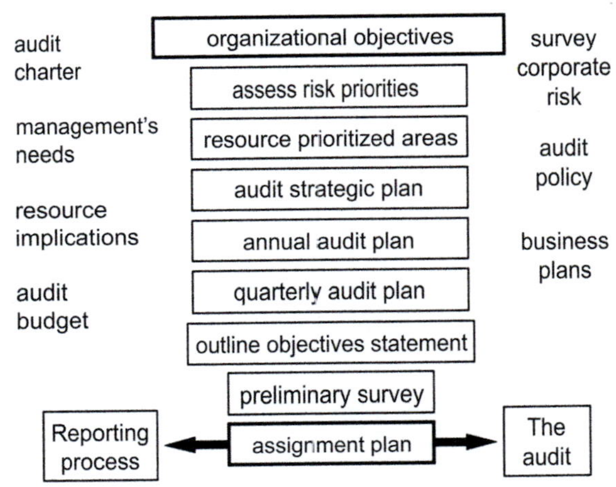

Figure 3.10. *The planning process.*

Source: https://d3i71xaburhd42.cloudfront.net/b332fb5b95d8a06b1b210dcca2334a4701b84a15/220-Figure8.10-1.png.

The worst-case situation is when they appear to be engaged in regular low-level checking in unimportant areas of the company while being unable to carry out delicate high-level investigations on behalf of management. Senior auditors handling significant high-risk matters are typically more important in professional audit services. The audit can function as a component of a well-thought-out system thanks to overall planning. This guarantees the highest priority for all planned work and the most efficient use of audit resources. Figure 3.10 outlines the primary steps involved in the entire planning process.

Some explanations follow:

- *Organizational Objectives:* The organization's goals must serve as the foundation for audit planning. The audit mission must also derive from these goals if they depend on business units receiving corporate services. Before plans can be created, management must make their goals and aspirations clear. Active liaison and communication can help them achieve this feedback.
- *Assess Risk Priorities:* The relative risks of each audit area must be identified, with reference to the corporate risk database.
- *Resource Prioritized Areas:* Suitable resources for these areas must be provided.
- *Audit Strategic Plan:* It is necessary to create a plan to balance the workload with the available resources. This needs to consider all of the opportunities and limitations that are significant both now and in the future. With due consideration for the audit budget, the strategic plan moves us from where we are to where we want to be in a specified amount of time.
- *Annual Audit Plan:* A formal audit plan for the year ahead is expected by most audit committees.
- *Quarterly Audit Plan:* A quarterly plan can be derived from the annual plan. Most organizations experience constant change making the quarter a suitable time-slot for supportive work programs.
- *Outline Objectives Statement:* Audit management can make a one-line statement of expectations from an audit from work done so far in the planning process.
- *Preliminary Survey:* Consideration must be given to important topics for background research in an audit. This can involve anything from a cursory glance through old files and a brief discussion with an operational manager to formal procedures requiring several days' worth of background work and a thorough evaluation of local business risks.
- *Assignment Plan:* We can now draft an assignment plan with formal terms of reference, including budgets, due dates and an audit program.
- *The Audit:* Progress should be monitored with all matters in the terms of reference considered.
- *The Reporting Process:* Planning feeds naturally into reporting so long as we have made proper reference to our plans throughout the course of the audit.

The organization's strategic direction will then naturally inform audit plans, and the underlying process should be adaptable to allow for the reevaluation of scheduled reviews as strategies change. As we take into consideration each facet of audit planning, we should keep in mind the flow of planning components. The field of internal auditing has changed and will continue to change at a rate that many people find unsettling. The CAE faces new challenges as a result of new demands. One area where we must react positively and quickly is audit planning. An established method for organizing audit work entails creating a risk index with the right elements (e.g., materiality, reputational impact, risk associated with state of control, and management requests). As a result, high-scoring audits get priority, even though we might examine everything in a three-year cycle. Throughout the year, we might also carry out thorough transaction testing of important financial systems. A more sophisticated approach is centered on the corporate governance structure (Chambers, 2002).

Here we concentrate audit resources on key areas such as:

- Boardroom arrangements and accountabilities.
- Remunerations committee.
- The role and impact of audit committee.
- The impact of NEDs on the board accountability.
- Factors that encourage financial misreporting.
- Reliability of audit committee and external audit coverage (and independence).
- Control framework in use.
- Reporting on internal controls.
- Risk assessment and risk management arrangements.
- Ethical standards and staff awareness.
- Anti-fraud policies and whistleblowing arrangements.
- Project management (including change programs).
- Control activities and performance management.
- Information systems (security and integrity).
- Communications across and up/down the organization.
- Control assurance reporting and underlying evidence such as CRSA.
- Control environment and ethics and tone at the top.
- Compliance teams and routines. Fraud policies and security.
- Accreditation systems such as ISO 9000, EFQM, IiP.
- HR policies such as staff training, competencies, vetting and learning programs.
- Financial systems and validation routines by financial controller.

The internal auditor aims to "quality assure" the governance framework that the board has established in this manner. It adopts a detached approach and looks at whether the high-level mechanisms are in place and effectively promoting good corporate governance for the relevant year. A risk-based approach, which encourages risk assessment and reviews areas of particular concern, may serve as the foundation of an alternate audit planning procedure.

- Corporate board level risk assessment identifies and classifies key risks (top ten risk policy).
- Risk management assign these risks to responsible managers and ensure they establish a risk management framework (avoid, accept, transfer, insure, contingency plans and/or controls).
- Operational level CRSA programs where risks are identified and associated controls reviewed by

work groups (for action planning).

- Discussion talk to management about their risk assessment and key controls that they are dependent on.
- Risk database prepare a risk database and isolate areas of high risk and controls that are crucial to business success, based on the organization's risk management process in operation.
- The results with the audit committee and allow corporate and operational risk assessment to drive the annual audit plans for assurance and consulting work.

Thus, we concentrate on assisting the board and management in implementing sound risk management procedures before reviewing the areas that continue to raise concerns (i.e. high residual risk) or just go over the essential areas thought to be essential to the success of the business.

The board and senior management have identified high-risk areas through their risk register, and the internal audit plan reflects a combination of these identifications, including assurance-based audits and supporting roles in helping to establish risk management (consulting services). Regarding the scheduling of audit work in relation to risk management and corporate governance, we have several choices. The primary recommendations state that every organization should implement a unique solution that takes into account its environment, organizational culture, and risk tolerance. In response, audit may produce a planning framework that combines elements of the three methods (with differing degrees of emphasis).

Whatever format is adopted the CAE of the future must ensure:

- It fits with the way the organization responds to corporate governance.
- It is mainly driven by the corporate risk register.
- The board/audit committee accepts that this is the best way to apply audit resources.
- It underpins and links into the annual opinion that the CAE provides on the system of internal control.
- It is dynamic, flexible and responds to the changing demands of risk management and accountability.

The IIA.UK and Ireland has issued a position statement on Risk-Based Internal Auditing that argues the following key stages to this advanced approach to audit work.

Risk-based auditing is based around the need to provide independent assurance to the board that:

- The risk management processes which management has put in place within the organization are operating as intended.
- These risk management processes are of sound design.
- The responses which management has made to risks which they wish to treat are both adequate and effective in reducing those risks to a level which is acceptable to the board.
- And a sound framework of controls is in place to sufficiently mitigate those risks which management wishes to treat.

In terms of developing long term audit plans, the risk-based process may be performed along the following lines:

- Corporate objectives.
- Identification of risks to achieving objectives.
- What is the risk appetite of the business?
- Is the risk management processes adequate and effective process for identifying, assessing, managing and reporting on risk?
- For sound processes the organization's view on risk can be used, and where this is not the case, audit will wish to facilitate the identification of risk with management and help refine the overall risk management process.
- Determine risk universe.
- Determine scope and priority of assignments.
- Based on risks select areas for review.
- For each area, review adequacy of risk management process.
- Where risk management is largely okay, determine how management gains assurances, and provide audit assurances. Where this is not the case, facilitate improvements.

3.4.2. Planning the Audit

The high-risk areas that will be the focus of audit coverage over the course of the upcoming year are listed in the annual audit plan. More information is provided by the quarterly audit plan, which outlines the audits that specific auditors will complete over the course of the next three months. An assignment plan will guide and control these resources prior to the start of the full audit and the commitment of resources. We require background knowledge on the intended operation before we can create assignment plans. There will be preparatory work needed; the amount will depend on the audit's size. The fundamentals of the assignment planning and preliminary survey, though the specific audit department's policies will determine the methodology and degree of detail (Figure 3.11). "Internal auditors should develop and record a plan for each engagement, including the scope, objectives, timing, and resource allocation," states IIA Performance Standard 2200, which addresses engagement planning.'

- **Control Objectives**: Control objectives address the risks associated with the work being done and are the good things that business managers want to happen rather than the bad things they want to stop from happening. Some auditors use control objectives to express the intended outcome or goal that will be met by the particular control procedures in order to guarantee that business objectives are met. Once established, it is feasible to consider the risks associated with each of the specified control goals in order to strengthen the aspects of acceptable business practices that pertain to performance and conformance. The disadvantage is that persuading client management of the value of control objectives is frequently challenging.

Note that Implementation Standard 2110.A2 reinforces the scope of internal auditing and provides a framework for control objectives by requiring that the internal audit activity should evaluate risk exposures relating to the organization's governance, operations and information systems regarding the:

- Reliability and integrity of financial and operational information.

- Effectiveness and efficiency of operations.
- Safeguarding of assets.
- Compliance with laws, regulations, and contracts.
- **The Preliminary Survey:** In order to decide on a clear course for the subsequent audit, the preliminary survey aims to gather pertinent data about the operation being examined. The first place to look will be the internal audit files, and any prior audit cover will be taken into account.

  A document titled "outstanding matters" that outlines issues that were not covered by the current audit should be included in every assignment audit file. It is best to speak with the auditor who most recently completed work in the pertinent area because the files and the audit report that follows only provide a portion of the story. It is a good idea to do some background research on the topic of the survey. National research, committee papers, new developments, and upcoming computerized systems may all fall under this category.

  A large portion of this data ought to have been gathered through the corporate risk assessment. To make a good impression, it is always advisable to gather some basic information prior to meeting with management. We can now visit the operational area and have a meeting with the key manager. It is possible to get a summary of the actual risks that the manager in question is facing. By touring the work area, one can get a sense of the audit, and the first impression can be used to point the auditor in the direction of specific issues.

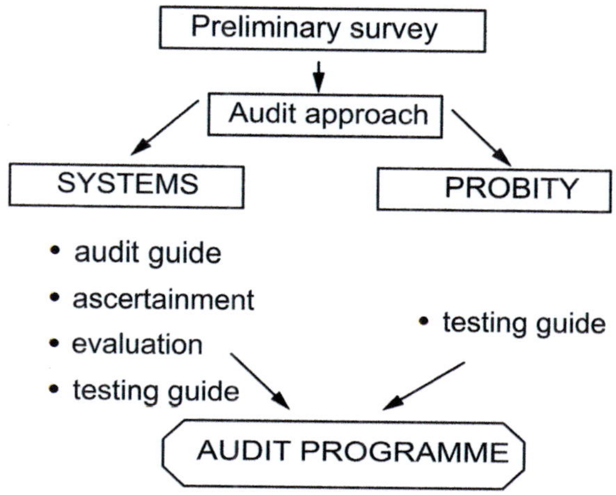

Figure 3.11. *Systems-based approach versus probity.*

Source: https://d3i71xaburhd42.cloudfront.net/b332fb5b95d8a06b1b210dcca2334a4701b84a15/229-Figure9.1-1.png.

Since an audit program is typically connected to a set of predetermined testing procedures, it is important to carefully consider the term audit program. Since the direction of the testing procedures depends on the results of the risk and control evaluation, this does not support the risk-based systems approach. "A document that lists the procedures to be followed during an engagement, designed to achieve the engagement plan" is how the IIA defines the engagement work program. The audit program may consist of the following and be viewed more as an audit guide.

- Outlining the various responsibilities that must be fulfilled. Here, the lead auditor should have a list of important tasks that establish the course of the audit process that will now be followed. In addition to being a helpful planning tool for tracking audit progress, this gives the auditor clear instructions on the tasks that need to be accomplished.

- Outlining the scope of work for a specific operation component. Lists of the different testing procedures can be used for smaller audits that follow a standard procedure. The audit becomes controllable with a defined testing program. It is predicated on the necessary tests, which in the case of basic audits may indicate the quantity of items to be chosen and the method of testing. Control can be strictly enforced by audit management. In a risk-based systems approach, this would not be appropriate because controls are tested after their impact on risks has been evaluated, and testing is not done for its own sake.

This distinction is crucial. Transaction testing is a key component of compliance and probity audits, and the audit program is developed during the preliminary survey phase. This thorough testing program can only be established for risk-based systems auditing once the system has been evaluated and documented. A systems audit's program of work, which may be drafted in its early stages, is essentially an audit guide that outlines the work needed to finish the audit. The program will include deadlines as well as possibly a progress checklist for each audit stage. It serves as a monitoring tool as well as a thorough record of work since it records the date each task is finished and reviewed, which should be noted on the schedule. The assigned auditors may be impacted if the audit techniques are identified. Planning may be necessary for statistical sampling, flowcharting, interviewing, computer-assisted auditing techniques, product inspection, third-party circularization, and other methods as needed. Pre-planning is the time to address resource allocation for these techniques.

To serve as an authorized work plan for the field auditor or auditors, the audit manager must formally approve the audit program. A management tool for managing the audit can be obtained by attaching the program to the related terms of reference and work budget. The audit program provides guidance for the testing phase, but it's important to avoid stifling the auditor's initiative or sense of accountability. While guidance is necessary, there should also be room to consider important questions and form opinions about the current state of controls. The test program for systems audits appears after the majority of the critical evaluation work is finished. It is crucial for compliance audits that the auditor views the program as a tool, not as a goal unto itself. This entails modifying the program to accommodate the audit while maintaining accountability for the final output. It is vital to specify the tasks that must be completed if the audit is being guided by the audit program.

The preliminary survey report: After the work is finished, it is recommended to submit an official preliminary survey report (PSR). Another thing to think about is how crucial it is to establish early access to information and explanations; Implementation Standard 2220 provides assistance in this regard. The scope of the engagement should take into account pertinent systems, records, people, and physical properties, including those that are under the control of third parties, according to A1. The PSR and a brief synopsis of the system to be utilized in creating the assignment plan are sent to the audit manager. The following will be covered in the one or two page PSR:

- An outline of the system under review including systems objectives and boundaries.

- The work undertaken in the preliminary survey.
- An initial opinion on the risk areas based on the key control objectives covering compliance, information systems, safeguarding assets and value for money.
- Recommendations for the proposed assignment in terms of the nature and extent of audit cover now required.
- An appendix with outline systems notes and a draft audit guide/ program for the full audit.

3.5. INTERVIEWING SKILLS

An essential component of audit work is information gathering because the auditor spends a lot of time gathering facts. Asking questions is a good place to start when gathering information, which is why conducting interviews is crucial. Several terms can be used interchangeably with "interviewing," but we define it more broadly as "talking with" in an organized way. The auditor should become proficient in interviewing techniques, and there is a wealth of information available on the subject that will help with this assignment. Interviewing is viewed by us as a procedure, a duty, a predetermined framework, an audit standard, and a test of our comprehension of human nature. The content will address these elements. Effective communication is the foundation of interviews, so it's a good idea to review the fundamentals of communication in order to understand potential problems and how to use figures to improve communication. The message must be sent, and the recipient must determine whether to decode it correctly or incorrectly. All of this is done in opposition to background noise, which is anything that obstructs the delivery and reception of clear messages. The positives are found in the feedback loop, which ensures that the message has been correctly received and understood by feeding back understanding to the sender (Figure 3.12).

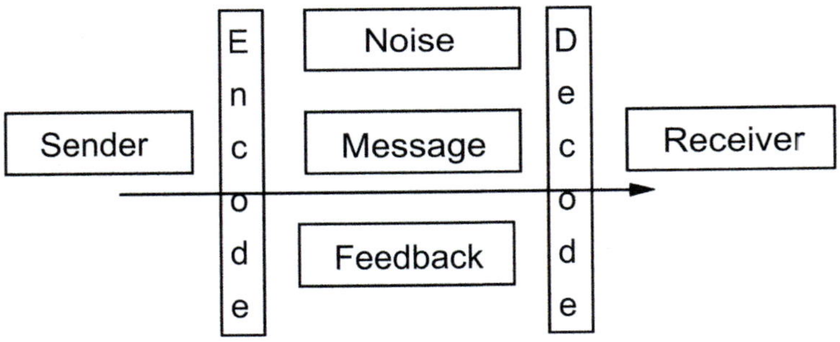

Figure 3.12. *Communications.*

Source: https://d3i71xaburhd42.cloudfront.net/b332fb5b95d8a06b1b210dcca2334a4701b84a15/234-Figure9.2-1.png.

3.5.1. Types of Interviews

A job opportunity is typically on the line in the types of interviews one is likely to have, so being prepared and having a reasonable level of confidence are essential. Formal interviews, phone interviews, panel interviews, sequential interviews, and even walk-in interviews are among the most popular forms of interviews. The candidate must demonstrate his or her abilities in each of these types of interviews and demonstrate why they are the best fit for the position. The most valuable tool in the candidate's toolbox is preparation; regardless of the type of interview, the candidate must be ready to speak intelligently and professionally about the position and their qualifications. Among the various interview formats, a formal interview is arguably the most prevalent. The applicant must meet the employer in person for this type of interview. In a predetermined order, the employer will pose a number of prepared questions, the same questions that they will pose to every applicant. The employer is probably going to make notes about the candidate's responses, and the candidate's responses might be recorded. Numerous inquiries will pertain to fictitious circumstances, prior encounters, and credentials. In an informal interview, the process is essentially the same, but the employer has the freedom to deviate from the pre-planned questions and take the conversation in any direction they see fit.

One of the few interview formats that isn't conducted in person is the phone interview, however this problem can now be resolved with video conferencing. Candidates and employers who live in different parts of the state, nation, or world have a phone interview. In an online interview, questions about relocation and travel may also be asked in addition to the standard questions that applicants would be asked in a face-to-face interview. When multiple people interview a candidate simultaneously, it's called a panel interview. Every individual seated at the table will have a unique set of inquiries to make, and each interviewer will typically concentrate on a particular topic to cover. For example, one interviewer might inquire about background and experience, while another might concentrate more on future objectives. Sequential interviews are closely related to panel interviews. In a sequential interview, multiple interviewers interview the candidate one-on-one rather than conducting the interview at the same time. This frequently entails the candidate having to respond to the same query multiple times for various individuals.

1. **Structured Interviews:** Structured meetings are used for information exchange and acquisition during interviews. Based on a lot of information, we could offer a general example of the format of an audit interview.

- *Greetings:* In order to do this, each person in the interview must be introduced, along with their function and place in the information-gathering process.
- *Goals:* After that, the goals of the interview are clearly stated, and if more information is required, it is given.
- *Queries and Responses:* The interview's main body should then move forward in a way that makes sense and advances the accomplishment of the meeting's initial goals.
- *Conclude:* Rechecking the provided information and any previously agreed-upon issues is the next step.
- *Finalization:* It should be indicated what has to be done next, including scheduling meetings with important staff and other actions. An official expression of gratitude ought to be included in the final interview phase.
- **Behavioral Aspects of Interviewing:** An interview that

seems simple on the surface could go terribly wrong, confusing the auditor and the client. People behave erratically for a variety of reasons, but the most common one is that the auditor does not recognize the behavioral aspects of audit work. When the auditors call, a lot of managers might still be thinking about the aggressive actions of one auditor who left many years ago. Interviewees may be asking themselves the following questions, and the auditor should be mindful of a number of behavioral factors when conducting interviews.

- What do they want from me?
- Are they human?
- Are they assessing me?
- Can I trust them?
- Should I tell them everything?
- What are they writing down?
- What about my problems?
- How can they help me?
- How will their work affect me?
- Who will be blamed if they find any errors?
- Are they going to propose drastic changes?

The possibility that the auditor will alter everyone they come into contact with at work makes them a threat. Change is generally disliked by people, especially when they are unsure of how it will affect them. Any suggested changes may have a negative connotation if they are based on the auditor's findings of levels of unmitigated risk in the manager's area of responsibility. These emotions may influence how the interview goes, so the auditor must take care to carefully explain to the interviewee the purpose of the audit and how it will fit into management's needs. Before engaging in a productive conversation, the auditor may make a clear effort to outline the audit role and methodology during the first few minutes of the interview. It's also critical to specify the actions that will be taken following the interview. The auditor must act in accordance with his or her statements; otherwise, little or no cooperation will be extended. The auditor may be perceived as a senior management spy.

When the management's understanding differs from what the auditor claims they do, it can cause basic conceptual issues. The auditor must constantly combat this in order to debunk misconceptions and establish appropriate working relationships. It is still believed that the auditor is primarily looking at the circumstances at hand rather than the individuals involved, even when the auditor is investigating irregularities. If a problem can be named, this should happen naturally through the process rather than as the result of a witch hunt. Finding a way to balance the assurance and consulting roles is one of the most difficult tasks in the audit role. We sincerely hope that the stereotype of the jackbooted, "find the transgressor" auditor does not extend to our primary responsibility of assurance auditing and prevent us from having productive conversations with staff and management. As long as we act in accordance with our words, candid and open discussions on this subject can anticipate a great deal of client resistance.

2. **Unstructured Interview:** As the name suggests, this is an unstructured interview. The interview has only the structure you provide it. You might be asked a range of open-ended questions during the interview because, in essence, the interviewer is interested in hearing from you. An unstructured interview will sound

less formal and more conversational than a structured one. Inquiries concerning your interests, activities on the weekends, and other lighthearted inquiries meant to reassure you might be made. This casual interviewing approach is preferred by many students, but exercise caution. Employers will occasionally take on this informal tone on purpose to make you feel at ease enough to lower your guard and possibly divulge information that you otherwise would not. In an unstructured interview, be personable without sacrificing your professionalism. While having a light conversation can start the interview off well, make sure the topic always revolves around your qualifications and skills.

3. **Stress Interview:** Interviewers who are hiring for jobs where there is a high level of daily stress in the workplace tend to use this style (i.e., stockbroker, sales, etc.,) In a stress interview, the same questions that are asked in an unstructured or structured interview might be asked. On the other hand, the interviewer's conduct or manner could differ. During a stressful interview, the interviewer might come across as uninterested, obstinate, or uncaring toward you. This kind of interview is intended to gauge how you respond to rejection, indifference, and general stress. It is advised that you concentrate on the question posed during the stress interview rather than the way it is posed in order to succeed. "Strange question" is another distinguishing feature of a stressful interview. To respond to a question like this, divide it into smaller, more manageable parts. For example, some interviewers like to ask, "How many ping pong balls can fit in a 757 jet?" Communicate your decision-making process orally. The interviewer will be more interested in your capacity for problem-solving and logical thought than in whether or not you arrived at the "correct" response. During a stressful interview, the interviewer may occasionally place candidates in awkward situations. For example, candidates might be given a two-hour test and instructed to finish it in thirty minutes.
4. **Behavioral Interview:** One popular technique for conducting job interviews is behavioral interviewing. This strategy is predicated on the idea that past behavior is the most accurate indicator of future conduct. As a result, behavioral interview questions are made to delve into your past experiences to ascertain how you might respond in hypothetical future scenarios. You won't be asked hypothetical questions about how you would respond to a situation if it arose in the future during this kind of interview. Rather, you will be questioned about how you handled a particular circumstance when you previously came across it. Remember that employers aren't concerned with what you should or won't do in the future. They are curious as to what you actually accomplished.

Behavioral interview questions generally start with any one of the following phrases:

- Tell me about a time when you...

- Describe a circumstance when you were faced with a problem related to...
- Tell me how you approached a situation where...
- Share with me an instance in which you demonstrated...

You have to share personal anecdotes in response to questions like these. Your intellectual capacity, leadership, teamwork, personal skills, flexibility and adjustment, drive, communication skills, administrative prowess, and technical aptitude will all be assessed based on these tales. You must first ascertain the abilities and qualities that the employer is looking for in order to get ready for a behavioral interview. Next, consider your previous experiences in education, work, extracurricular activities, and personal relationships to find instances where you amply displayed the skills you have identified. You have to be able to describe these situations clearly and in a way that highlights your advantages during the interview. A comprehensive response should include a description of the following: the situation, the tasks assigned to you, the action you took, and the outcome of that action. This technique of answering behavioral interview questions is known as the STAR Method.

5. **Problem Solving or Case Interview:** Employers assess a candidate's analytical and communication skills with this type of questioning. You will be given a real or simulated problem to think about and solve during a problem-solving or case interview. It's not necessary for you to get the right response. When answering questions of this nature, make sure to think aloud because the interviewer is primarily interested in learning about your mental processes. An answer that shows you can divide an issue into manageable chunks and can think clearly under pressure is considered effective.
6. **Panel Interview:** Before selecting which applicant to hire, employers frequently prefer to get input from a number of staff members. Panel interviews, in which several people interview one candidate at once, are frequently used to achieve this. Make a note of each interviewer's name during a panel interview and address them by name. As you respond, keep your attention on the person who posed the question, but occasionally look the other group members in the eye. Panel interviews can have a variety of styles and tones, but they usually involve questions based on behavior and are more formal in nature.

3.5.2. Types of Questions

While some interviews last only a few minutes or hours, neither of these extremes always corresponds with the auditor receiving all or most of the information that they need. An interview's success is determined by more than just how long it takes.

Although lengthy conversations can be beneficial, they can also lead to ineffective use of time. The deliberate use of various question formats improves interview efficiency. Interviewees are guided by deft use of questioning techniques to address important issues in greater detail while expeditiously addressing specifics.

Types of question include:

- Open questions such as, 'Tell me about your job.'

- Closed questions such as, 'Do you work in the accounts department?'
- Probing questions such as, 'Tell me more about xyz.'
- Confirmatory questions such as, 'Your job description refers to an xyz, is this correct?'
- Clarification along the lines, 'I thought you said that you worked for Mr X?'.

In general one should not use the following types of questions:

- Leading questions such as, 'Surely you check these invoices before approving them?'
- Loaded questions such as, 'You appear to be more qualified than your boss'.
- Trick questions along the lines, 'You say that you have worked here for three and a half years; what date did you start?'

One guideline that needs to be followed is to get feedback continuously during the interview and to have everything verified as much as possible. At the conclusion of the meeting, on more formal occasions, the interviewee should be asked for feedback on the recorded interview. Information from audits is frequently obtained through interviews. Interviews are an intrusion into the interviewee's world, and depending on the rapport built, they may be welcomed or rejected. Skilled auditors efficiently and effectively arrange interviews and obtain information. The audit objectives must be communicated by the auditor in a clear and compelling manner during the two-way interview process. Effective interviewing is hampered by a number of factors, which should be identified and addressed with the help of training sessions and an extensive audit manual.

3.5.3. Ascertaining the System

Risk-based systems auditing is predicated on assessing the entire internal control and risk management system, guaranteeing the accomplishment of operational goals.

Only when the systems under consideration are fully understood—which itself depends on the auditor's capacity to effectively document the system—can this task be completed. There are various other approaches, each with special benefits. (Pickett & Pickett, 2001).

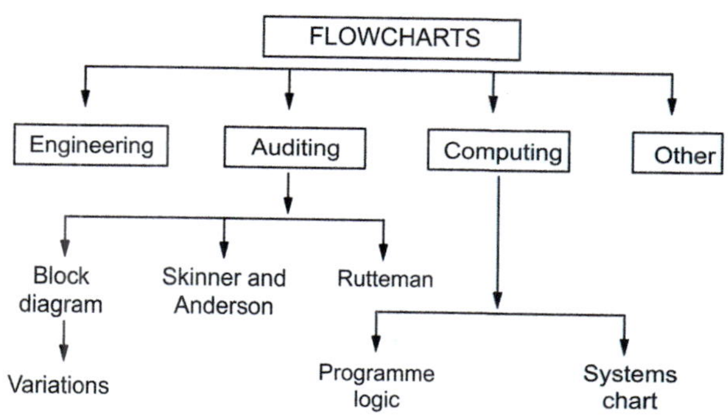

Figure 3.13. *Types of flowcharts.*

Source: https://d3i71xaburhd42.cloudfront.net/b332fb5b95d8a06b1b210dcca2334a4701b84a15/237-Figure9.4-1.png.

The main options that the auditor has for documenting the system are:

- Narrative notes.
- Block diagrams.
- Flowcharts.
- Internal control questionnaire (ICQ).

There are different types of flowcharts which may be shown in Figure 3.13:

Despite clear differences between types of flowchart, there are basic principles per Figure 3.14.

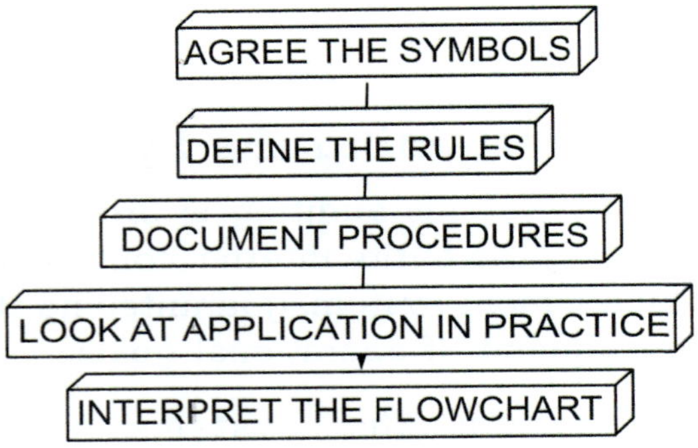

Figure 3.14. *Basic flowcharting rules.*

Source: https://d3i71xaburhd42.cloudfront.net/b332fb5b95d8a06b1b210dcca2334a4701b84a15/237-Figure9.5-1.png.

3.5.4. The Rules of Flowcharting

Flowcharts are detailed representations of documents and information that record most parts of a defined operation. The rules that are applied to audit charts are:

- Provide clear headings and dates so that the system dealt with is clearly identified. Do not make them unnecessarily complicated as this consumes time and may not aid the audit process.
- Look for exception routines and note these so that a complete picture is provided.
- Test the flowchart against the client's understanding of the system.
- Distinguish between operations/processes and controls so that the flowchart can feed directly into the control evaluation procedures.
- Number the events in sequential order as they may be referred to in other audit working papers.
- Keep the narrative brief to avoid making the schedule appear cramped.
- Show destination of all documents by not leaving loose ends.
- Distinguish between information and documentation flow.
- Use a convention of moving through the system top to bottom and from left to right.
- Apply standardized symbols and keys that are fully agreed and detailed in the audit manual.

3.5.5. Evaluation

The evaluation phase of an audit review is arguably the most crucial since it gives auditors the chance to fully utilize their professional creativity. The systems flaws found during the systems evaluation should inform the audit opinion and recommendations. Procedures for audit testing are used to validate the initial assessment regarding the implementation of controls and the impact of control vulnerabilities. The Implementation Standard 2120 of the IIA. According to A4, adequate criteria are required in order to assess controls. Internal auditors should find out how much management has set up sufficient standards to assess whether targets and goals have been met. Internal auditors should use such criteria in their evaluation if they are appropriate. Internal auditors should collaborate with management to create suitable evaluation criteria if they are insufficient. The quality of the remaining audit work will suffer if the evaluation is flawed. The solutions to risk exposures provided by audit recommendations will be inadequate.

1. **Defining the System**: The system under audit is determined by the preliminary survey. The assignment plan's statement on the scope of the audit work will outline the system under review and serve as the basis for evaluation. The model of the system under evaluation must then be examined. There are various ways to conceptualize the system. The first is the prescribed system, which is defined by official documents and procedure notes. Old committee minutes and official reviews that management commissioned may contain information about the original system intentions. This officially agreed format will be followed in the official description of the system. This system may be the one that the organization has officially approved, so the auditor needs to be concerned about it. If it has changed, new approval may need to be requested.

The purported system. This adheres to the guidelines provided by management and system personnel. The system that management intends to implement could be referred to as the planned system.

The emergency/contingency system. Although the system is usually well-defined and implemented, the auditor may want to take into account the existence of an emergency system. This is motivated by the urge to "get things done" in an emergency and could lead to numerous deviations from the established protocol.

The ideal system. By their very nature, published studies on value-for-money and systems control make generalizations about how specific operations can be made better. The desire to create an "ideal system" may be linked to the temptation to lay out ideals for systems control. The auditor's preferred system: The auditor may be persuaded that certain improvements are necessary based on their knowledge of the system's operations and control weaknesses. These could be viewed as the auditor's interpretation of the perfect setup.

Employees' preferred system. Front-line workers and supervisors may have ideas about the kinds of controls that ought to be implemented.

The system that maintains all necessary control features and functions in real-world situations is known as the workable system. It might lie in the middle of the perfect system, management's system, audit's preferences, and staff members' own procedures.

The greatest system. The question of which system is the best emerges. It appears that there are multiple ways to interpret this. The ability of the "best" system to limit risks to management's goals highlights how this criterion ought to be used.

The auditor's understanding of the system should include:

- Understanding the needs of the parties who rely on the system.
- Understanding the adopted success criteria.
- Understanding systems constraints.
- Understanding the overall risk

management arrangements implicit in the system.

2. **Evaluation Techniques**: The system under review is the one that is being used in real life to achieve the operational goals of management. The assessment methodology ought to be grounded in the controls necessary to guarantee that risks to the attainment of goals are minimized without causing significant losses or inefficiencies. Among the methods of evaluation are flowcharts. Along with controls that rely on documentation flows and work organization, these aid in the identification of system bottlenecks, duplication of effort, and duty segregation.

- *Testing of Transactions:* Testing transactions may reveal system flaws that result in error conditions that the tests have detected. When we have the capacity to work with vast quantities of data, we can quickly perform a small number of tests. Since it relies on a haphazard selection and examination of samples rather than a thorough understanding of the operation being reviewed, this cannot be considered a systematic evaluation.
- *Representations with Direction:* It is impossible to dispute the value of information given by those with system knowledge. It would be foolish to disregard management's statement at the beginning of an audit if it indicates that there are unmitigated risks. Middle management, users, employees, and outside parties may file complaints to expedite the review procedure. These remarks would be scrutinized for bias because they required some sort of supporting documentation.

3. **Internal Control Questionnaires (ICQ):** There are numerous standard packages of internal control questionnaires (ICQ), which are frequently used to support the control evaluation process(Figure 3.15). They are comprised of a set of inquiries tailored to a specific function, with the intention that a response of "no" suggests the possibility of a control vulnerability. Is it separate to record income or is it part of the official task of receipting income? A "no" response would imply that official duties are not sufficiently separated. Before testing procedures are implemented, the possible weaknesses are then investigated further and compensatory controls are sought for. ICQs come with a variety of unique benefits and drawbacks.

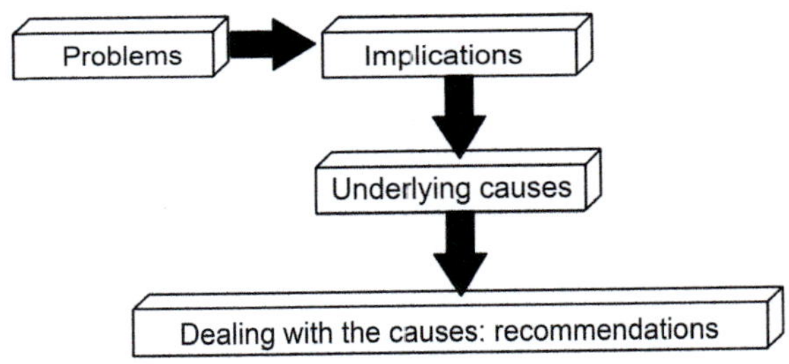

Figure 3.15. *Evaluation.*

Source: https://d3i71xaburhd42.cloudfront.net/b332fb5b95d8a06b1b210dcca2334a4701b84a15/244-Figure9.9-1.png.

a. *Evidence:* A financial database or document's existence can be verified with an internal control questionnaire. For instance, one may inquire about the company's possession of an accounts chart. The auditor can then inquire as to the location of the chart of accounts, if one is present, or plan the audit to proceed without it. The company may not maintain accurate records, in which case the auditor should conduct a more thorough audit, if an employee mentions the existence of the chart of accounts but is unsure of its location.

b. *Employee Controls:* The auditor uses information from internal control questionnaires to ascertain whether staff members verify the work of other staff members. One question on the Arizona Department of Health Services questionnaire concerns an agency's annual vacation policy for its accountants. When an organization's accountants are required to take time off, internal controls are strengthened because other accountants can verify the accuracy of the books while the primary record keepers are away.

4. **Advantages**

- Provides a permanent record of the evaluation stage. As the schedules are completed, they automatically record the response to each key point examined as a ready-made working paper.
- A disciplined, systematic approach to evaluation not depending on the whims and fancies of the assigned auditor.
- Helps audit supervisors as the standard of evaluation is set beforehand through compilation of the ICQ. The expectation that field auditors will ensure full coverage of the defined areas via this process provides a useful management tool for controlling the audit.
- Provides direction to the auditor by setting out clearly the areas that are to be addressed. In this way the auditor can approach an audit armed with the necessary tools, i.e. the ICQ checklists.

There is no need to rethink the control mechanisms that form part of the evaluation process as they are set out in the ICQ. The 'what should be' model is then available to be used to assess the adequacy of existing practices. Some might argue that the ICQ provides indispensable guidance.

- It is simple to use as the questions are directed at control objectives that

should be present in the operation under review.

- The technique can be used by inexperienced auditors who should find it

simple to adapt their work to provide responses to the listed questions.

- It de-personalizes the audit by setting tried, trusted, and objective criteria for the controls in operation. The auditor can defend a charge of being too obsessed with control by referring to the ICQ standards adopted by the internal audit function and not devised in a hit-or-miss fashion.
- ICQs promote a systems-based approach. They emphasize controls as the main source of audit attention, rather than the testing program that may be the main basis for the audit. Controls are deemed by the ICQ to accomplish objectives that support the main thrust of the systems approach.
- Provides good structure and form to the audit by defining beforehand the way systems will be assessed.

Planning is easier as time can be assigned to completing the requirements of the ICQ and the work has a natural start and finish in line with the control standards used.

- It results in comprehensive cover of an area by dealing with all foreseeable points. It is impossible for an auditor to be aware of all control features within an ICQ, particularly the more comprehensive ones. Having the checklist to hand enables one to take on board many factors.

5. **Disadvantages**

- They may result in a stale approach where the auditor tries to look at a set of predetermined, completely predictable factors every year. It might lead to a bureaucratic approach in which the auditor provides little to no real inspiration for the repeated, in-depth inquiries.
- It can become mechanical as the task of completing the never-ending checklist becomes so laborious that the auditor develops a secret desire to leave the profession.
- An auditor whose main concern is finishing schedules without truly understanding why might follow them mindlessly. Giving thorough instructions on audit coverage is one thing, but using form fillers is not acceptable. There might not be enough time to consider the full implications if there are tight deadlines for finishing the schedules.
- Detailed ICQs may stifle initiative. Although more experienced auditors might find this mechanical process frustrating, less experienced auditors might find the detailed guidance helpful. The obsession with finishing the ICQ paperwork may make it difficult to direct resources toward other concerns that have been discussed with client management. To target key risks, a professional auditor needs the freedom to pursue high-level issues all the way to the end.
- Management may feel it is a cumbersome, time-consuming technique. It may look amateurish when the auditor is filling out a checklist that covers everything from crucial issues to unimportant details about unimportant system components. Certain sections of the ICQ will involve asking questions of line management, and finding the necessary answers could be time-consuming. The system auditor may find that certain questions lead to unsuitable responses and that other questions show a lack of comprehension. The majority of these drawbacks result from improper use of the ICQ process, which, in the worst case scenario, leads to the auditor sending management a list of 101 questions.

The ICQ technique can be used in a number of ways to increase efficiency and effectiveness:

- Based on your knowledge of the system being reviewed, adjust the standardized ICQ to the particular situation. Make every inquiry pertinent. The auditor can edit the document on a computer, which makes this task much simpler when automated schedules are used.
- In order to get them to interact with the system, design the questions to

focus on high-risk areas. Questions about pertinent control issues can be directed once the risks have been agreed upon.

3.5.6 Why interview skills are important during audit?

In order to carry out an audit in accordance with the ICAI's auditing standards, the auditor must properly plan the audit, carry it out, gather evidence in accordance with the audit plan, and report the results to management or those charged with governance. There are a number of ways to comprehend an entity in accordance with Auditing Standard SA 315, Identifying and Assessing the Risk of Material Misstatement through Understanding the Entity and Its Environment. It can be accomplished by carrying out analytical procedures, observing and inspecting books, or asking the management, the relevant people, or the person who is probably going to have enough information. Similar to this, when gathering audit evidence in accordance with Auditing Standard SA 500 Audit Evidence, where the primary focus is on gathering adequate and relevant audit evidence, the audit procedure that the auditor is required to carry out—inquiry—provides a crucial audit evidence in conjunction with other audit procedures like observation, recalculation, confirmation, and analytical procedures.

Thus, the interview becomes an essential component of the auditor's risk assessment process. Effective interviewing techniques enable the auditor to obtain a wealth of information that can subsequently be verified through additional audit procedures. Before conducting an interview, it's critical to prepare thoroughly and organize the conversation. To get the information needed and move the audit in the right direction, an efficient interview is crucial. Finding the right person to interview can help you quickly identify the main concerns. It aids in the auditor's evaluation in determining which documents to examine, computer databases to check, and other crucial evidence to gather. Interviews are used to learn more about an entity, comprehend it, and confirm facts. These could be conducted informally or formally through interviews. Notes were taken and/or recordings were made for official interviews. The interviewee may occasionally be asked to sign the notes. The interviewee is advised that if the interview is significant, he or she may need to provide additional evidence for their statements at a later time. To get information about documents and activities, the audit team also holds a lot of informal interviews. Informal interviews may have been handwritten notes, but they were not recorded. These interviews are carried out in order to gather background data, comprehend the organization's characteristics, and gather data necessary for the audit. Interviews can yield information about a person's personal history, their interactions with other members of the organization or entity, and whether or not there have been any employee collusions.

Skills required for conducting effective interview

To be successful, an interview should be thorough. It requires strategic planning, relevant questions and an objective interviewer.

1. Active listener and active observer: In addition to meaning paying closer attention when someone is speaking, the phrase "active listening" also refers to the capacity to decipher nonverbal cues and communication styles. There are

situations when an interviewee's silence says just as much as their words. It is advised to interview one person at a time in order to become a skilled observer.

2. Professional demeanor: Being professional is crucial when doing interviews. Being professional is essential when conducting audit interviews. The auditors have to continue acting as an impartial outsider. This implies that the auditors may attempt to divert your attention from the questions if you succumb to your nervousness and attempt to defuse the situation with humor. Moreover, proposals to conduct the interview over a business dinner may be turned down.
3. Body language and appearance: When it comes to the interview's tone, the auditor must exercise caution. Avoid using hostile body language or an aggressive tone during the interview. The interviewee should not be informed of the private sources used to gather the evidence. If it seems like you're getting too close to the interviewee, that could raise questions about the interview process. Smirking, sarcasm, evasiveness, and stiff body posture are examples of observed behaviors that could indicate dishonesty and damage the auditor's credibility.

Interview & Interrogation

The auditors may turn the interview into an interrogation if they feel they are not getting the whole story from owners and management and significant issues are discovered in the company records. An interrogation puts more pressure on those being questioned to divulge information they might not want to and can come across as accusatory rather than inquisitive. Still, it's always easy to distinguish between an interview and an interrogation. During the audit, interviewers are expected to be ready for a wide range of situations.

Documenting an interview

The process of preparing written transcripts for interviews ought to commence promptly. To ensure further confirmation, the auditor must keep the original notes. In an ideal world, the interview record would include the date, time, place, and participants. Time of key events during the interview can be effectively documented with the use of an interview log. If the interview is thought to be important audit evidence, the details noted should, if at all possible, be verified by the interviewee yourself.

Closing of interview

During the closing of interview, the auditor should try to close the interview with a positive note and leave the door open for additional contact. The facts obtained during the interview should be summarized and the interviewee should be encouraged to say whatever he/ she desires.

3.5.7 Significance of Interview Skills among the Audit Team

The ability to conduct effective interviews is a crucial competency for members of the audit team as it allows them to obtain crucial data, resolve doubts, and comprehend the wider audit environment. Good interviews provide auditors with information about internal controls, management intentions, company culture, and any possible non-compliance or areas of risk that may not be clear from document reviews alone. The information obtained from interviews is frequently crucial in determining the audited entity's process and control gaps, weaknesses, and areas for improvement. These abilities are critical for auditors to establish rapport, promote open communication, and cultivate trust—all of which are necessary for getting frank answers and thorough information. Effective interviewing techniques enable auditors to focus on pertinent questions, listen intently, and delve further into areas where answers might be ambiguous or lacking. In order to get interviewees to go into more detail and provide more nuanced answers, auditors frequently need to pose open-ended questions. Through the use of this technique, important insights that might not be apparent through standard audit procedures or documentation can be found. Knowing when to ask follow-up questions and how to phrase them to avoid putting interviewees on the defensive is another essential skill for conducting effective interviews. Professionals with experience in auditing can handle delicate subjects with grace and tact, keeping the interviewee interested and willing to provide the information needed.

In addition, the ability to conduct effective interviews is essential for comprehending and evaluating the entity's internal control environment. Auditors learn more about how internal controls are created and carried out, whether staff members are aware of and obedient to these controls, and whether there are any unofficial policies that differ from published guidelines by interviewing management and employees. With the aid of this data, auditors can assess the strength, dependability, and risk-mitigation potential of the internal control framework. Auditors can find possible control weaknesses or areas of non-compliance through interviews that may not be found through document review alone. Interviews can highlight discrepancies between documented procedures and actual practices. Proficiency in interviewing also improves the auditor's capacity to identify misbehavior or fraud. Red flags, such as inconsistent statements, hesitation, or signs of discomfort when discussing particular topics, are frequently identified in order to detect fraud. Effective interviewing methods allow auditors to foster an atmosphere of candor and openness, which raises the possibility that anomalies or unusual behavior will come to light. Strong interviewing techniques also allow auditors to detect nonverbal and verbal clues that point to deceit, allowing them to delve deeper into questionable areas and obtain information that could allay or confirm their suspicions.

Asking questions is only one aspect of an interview; another is establishing rapport and trust. Building a strong relationship with interviewees is essential for the audit team because it promotes more honest and open communication. Interviewees are more likely to divulge important information that might otherwise be withheld or omitted when they feel valued and at ease. Strong interpersonal skills enable auditors to establish a non-threatening environment that promotes collaboration and reduces resistance. This is especially crucial when handling delicate topics or when the audit's conclusions could have a big impact on the company. Furthermore, interviewing techniques are important because they aid the audit team in comprehending the ethical climate and organizational culture. Through conversations about issues like employee morale, leadership attitudes, and adherence to ethical standards, auditors can learn more about the organization's overall risk profile and possible problem areas. In order to find the root causes of non-compliance or control weaknesses and to create workable recommendations that are in line with the organization's policies and values, it is imperative to comprehend the cultural context.

An efficient and targeted audit process is also enhanced by well-conducted interviews. Auditors can cut out needless steps and focus their attention on the most important areas by getting concise, direct answers to the most important questions. This focused strategy can improve the audit's overall efficacy, save time and money, and lessen the burden on the audited entity. Additionally, properly conducted interviews can swiftly resolve disagreements and clear up any ambiguities, avoiding miscommunications or arguments that might postpone the audit's conclusion. The preparation of the audit report and the dissemination of findings also require interviewing skills. The context and detail provided by the information acquired during interviews frequently enhance the audit report, making it more thorough and illuminating for stakeholders. Strong interviewing abilities also enable auditors to support their conclusions and recommendations with firsthand testimonies from the organization's staff members and real-world examples, which makes their findings easier to understand and communicate.

CASE STUDY

CASES DESIGNED TO TEACH CRITICAL THINKING AND PROFESSIONAL JUDGMENT IN AUDITING

The three cases, developed in collaboration with KPMG professionals to help audit instructors integrate the KPMG Professional Judgment Framework into the classroom, have been designed to be delivered in a manner that helps students better understand the importance of applying professional skepticism and critical thinking when making judgments and decisions in difficult auditing contexts. To be an effective audit professional in the 21st century, it is important that students learn a structured approach to apply professional skepticism as they critically think about the documentary evidence gathered when they make professional judgments.

Each of the three short cases presented (Hamilton, Pleasant Pasta, and Adams) describes a real-life scenario that was written based on the SEC case document for an actual restatement that has occurred in the recent past. The cases provide a mechanism for educators to illustrate real-life contexts where auditors were not professionally skeptical and did not properly apply critical thinking skills while making important judgments. The identity of each company was concealed by using fictitious names throughout. The primary target audience for these cases is the financial statement auditing class, at either the undergraduate or graduate level.

The cases can be used to help auditing students always remain skeptical about the possibility of fraud. After completing the cases, students should be able to:

- Describe the relevant technical knowledge related to identifying and responding to fraud risks;
- Identify fraud risks in each of the restatement scenarios presented;
- Clarify the issues, objectives and consider the alternatives that may have been available to auditors, given the facts and circumstance in each of the restatement scenarios presented;
- Consider the type of information that could have been gathered and evaluated, given the facts and circumstance in each of the restatement scenarios presented;
- Recognize the importance of reaching an overall conclusion and then carefully documenting the rationale in accordance with professional standards for all judgments made;
- Develop awareness of the most common professional judgment traps and biases (i.e., confirmation, availability, anchoring, and overconfidence) and recognize when to take steps to mitigate these biases.

SUMMARY

- A cornerstone of audit strategy is the corporate assessment of business risk. This establishes an organization's control needs.
- Staff appraisal is a management control that audit would tend to recommend when undertaking an audit where staffing is included in the terms of reference for the work.
- The topic of audit manuals touches upon a number of subsidiary issues including standardization, procedures, controlling creativity and audit approaches, and underpins professional standards for delivering the adopted audit strategy.
- Audit management should delegate work to more junior staff. This can be a powerful way of not only increasing overall efficiency, but also developing auditors.
- The computer has major implications for audit work. Effects range from impact on the audit field to the way audit work is performed to how audit itself uses computers to improve productivity.
- The internal audit strategy tells the organization what it will get from its in-house audit team.
- Planning is fundamental to successful auditing and should involve the client in defining areas for review via the assessment of relative risk.
- Control objectives are the positive things business managers want to happen rather than negative things they want to prevent happening and they address the risks inherent in the work being done.
- Gathering information is a fundamental part of audit work as the auditor spends a great deal of time fact-finding.
- The types of interviews one is likely to go through require preparedness and a fair amount of confidence, as a job opportunity is usually on the line.
- Some interviews go on for hours while others last a few moments and these two extremes do not necessarily coincide with the auditor obtaining full or limited information.
- Risk-based systems auditing relies on evaluating the whole system of risk management and internal control, which ensures operational objectives will be achieved.
- Evaluation may be seen as the most important stage in any audit review since this provides an opportunity for auditors to apply professional creativity to the fullest.

REVIEW QUESTIONS

1. How does a corporation develop and implement an effective risk strategy to mitigate potential threats and capitalize on opportunities?
2. What roles and responsibilities does the internal audit function encompass, and how does it contribute to organizational governance and risk management?
3. What constitutes an audit manual, and how does it guide the procedures and standards for conducting audits within an organization?
4. What are the key steps in the audit planning process, and how do these steps ensure a comprehensive and effective audit?
5. How do audit information systems support the audit process, and what are the key features and functionalities that enhance their effectiveness?

REFERENCES

1. Anderson, U., & Chapman, C. (2002). Implementing the professional practices framework. In *The IIA Handbook Series*. Institute of Internal Auditors (IIA).
2. Australian Stock Exchange. (2003). *Principles of Good Corporate Governance and Best Practice Recommendations.*
3. Basel Committee on Banking Supervision. (2003). *Sound Practice for The Management and Supervision of Operational Risk*. Bank for International Settlements.
4. Chambers, A. (2002). Stakeholders—The court of public opinion. In *Corporate Governance Handbook* (pp. [page numbers]). Tolley's, Reed Elsevier (UK) Ltd.
5. Institute of Internal Auditors—UK and Ireland. (2002). *Corporate Governance and Risk Management*. [Study text].
6. Kubr, M. (2002). *Management Consulting: A Guide to the Profession* (4th ed.). International Labour Organisation.
7. Moon, C. (2002). Internal auditing and business risk: Governance responsibility reporting. *Association of British Insurers Guidelines on Social, Ethical and Environmental (SEE) Issues—Investing in Social Responsibility*, 36–37.
8. Pickett, K. H. S., & Pickett, J. M. (2001). *Internal Control: A Manager's Journey.* John Wiley & Sons, Inc.
9. Weait, M. (2001). The workplace ethic—is it a crime. *Management Today*, January.

CHAPTER

4 Audit Reporting

LEARNING OBJECTIVES

After studying this chapter, you will be able to:

- Explain the significance of audit report;
- Prepare to write an audit report;
- Discuss on subsequent events; and
- Focus on auditor's report on financial statements.

KEY TERMS FROM THIS CHAPTER

Accounting standard
Financial data
Financial ratios
Investors
Creditors
Financial investments
Good governance
Shareholders

INTRODUCTION

An auditor's written opinion about the financial statements of an entity is contained in an audit report. As required by generally accepted auditing standards (GAAS), the report is written in a standard format. Based on the specifics of the audit work the auditor performs, GAAS either mandates or permits certain deviations in the report. The report could be unqualified or qualified. Based on the audit's findings, the unqualified auditors' duty is to express an opinion regarding the financial statements. The statement "we have audited" suggests that the auditor is offering the maximum degree of assurance possible. It is crucial that the person reading the document containing the financial statements understands exactly what the auditors' report covers and, implicitly, what is not. It is the auditors' duty to learn about any events that occurred after the date they signed the auditors' report on the financial statements. However, an auditor might learn of new information about the client after the financial statements and audit report have been released. The auditors may not be further obligated in relation to new information if it relates to a condition that wasn't there when the audit report was issued, or if it refers to the final contingency resolutions or other matters that were disclosed in the financial statements or the auditors' report. However, the new information might be related to facts that were known to the auditors on the date of the audit report, which could have had an impact on the financial statements or the auditors' report.

4.1. SIGNIFICANCE OF AUDIT REPORT

After independent auditors have examined the entity's financial statements and related reports, they issue an audit report that includes their audit's opinion. Financial statements, management accounts, management reports, and other reports similar to compliant reports are among them. These reports are typically released in accordance with the findings of the auditors' expert examination in comparison to the standards or measurement criteria. For instance, auditors check the financial statements of their clients against the accounting standard that was applied in their preparation. These standards may be local GAAP, US GAAP, or IFRS.

The auditors issue the audit report on the financial statements they have just audited after their testing is finished. They will also provide their assessment of the financial statements in this report.

4.1.1. Essentials of Good Audit Report

An auditor's report is a formal opinion, or disclaimer thereof, issued as an assurance service so that the user may base decisions on the audit results by either an independent external auditor or an internal auditor following an internal or external audit. Reports from auditors are regarded as crucial resources for providing users, especially in the business world, with financial data. A lot of third-party users would rather have financial information certified by an impartial external auditor, or they may even demand it. When making decisions about financial investments, creditors and investors consult audit reports from Supreme Audit Institutions (SAI). The value of audit reports comes from bolstering the reliability of financial statements, which in turn increases the trust that investors place in them. Audit reports are used by legislative and anti-corruption agencies in the government to monitor public administrators' actions on behalf of the people. Therefore, auditing reports serve as a citizen's check on the management of public funds, resources, and trust in organizations like local governments, government departments, ministries, and related government bodies that were established to promote good governance.

The essentials of good audit report are as follows:

1. **Simplicity**: A quality audit report should have several key elements, one of which should be simplicity. It ought to be both comprehensible and obvious. It suggests that facts and language that are unclear should not be included in the audit report.
2. **Clarity:** In an audit report, "clarity" denotes cleanliness. This means that information needed to assess and appraise the business's performance should not be withheld from the audit report.
3. **Brevity:** "Brevity" refers to the audit report's succinctness. It is best to avoid repeating data and facts in order to keep the report's length under control.

4. **Firmness:** The report must state unequivocally the extent of the work that needs to be done as well as whether the books of accounts present a "true and fair" picture of the company's situation.
5. **Objectivity:** The report ought to be supported by impartial data. An opinion that is based on data and proof that isn't quantified in monetary terms shouldn't be included in the audit report.
6. **Consistency:** A strong audit report is built on presenting accounting information consistently. A good audit report should consider whether the depreciation charges and stock valuation method have been applied consistently.
7. **Accepted Principles:** The audit report should be based upon the facts and figures that are kept in accordance with generally accepted accounting principles.
8. **Disclosure Principles:** The audit report should be unbiased. It should disclose all the facts and the truth.

4.1.2. Contents of an Audit Report

The basic structure of an audit report as prescribed by the Standards on Auditing is as follows:

a. **Title:** The title should include the phrase "Auditor's Report." This is intended to remind the reader of the credibility an audit adds to the financial statements because of the auditor's independence.

b. **Introductory Paragraph:** The report's first paragraph lists the financial statements that are being audited and indicates that management is in charge of them. It is the auditor's duty to express an opinion regarding those statements in light of the audit's findings. The statement "we have audited" suggests that the auditor is offering the maximum degree of assurance possible. The dates and periods covered by the financial statements that are audited are also specified in the introduction. It is crucial that the person reading the document containing the financial statements understands exactly what the auditor's report covers and, implicitly, what is not. The reader should be informed specifically of what has been audited (the financial statements and the related notes that are, as stated on each page of the financial statements) and what has implicitly not been audited (such as the Chairman's Statements and Report of Directors, financial ratios, and information about stock prices), as an annual report or prospectus typically contains much more information than just financial statements.

c. **Scope Paragraph:** The auditor's reasoning for developing an opinion regarding the financial statements is explained in the scope paragraphs. It is equivalent to certifying that the auditor has adhered to the guidelines set forth by the auditing profession for carrying out an audit to tell the reader that the audit was carried out in line with the Nigerian Standards on Auditing, which are modifications of International Standards on Auditing. The goal of an audit is to collect enough data to allow the auditor to reasonably assure, not to guarantee, that there are no material misstatements in the financial statements. If there is a reasonable possibility that the misstatement would have affected or altered the decision of a reasonable person depending on the financial statements, the misstatement is deemed material. The scope lists the components of an audit. It emphasizes that proof regarding the financial statements' accounting measurements and disclosures was only gathered for testing purposes. The report makes it clear that the main components of an audit are evaluating the client's accounting principles, the estimates included in the financial statements, and the presentation of the financial statements as a whole. Finally, the auditor expressly says that the evidence gathered and assessed during the audit was adequate to bolster the opinion expressed.

d. **Opinion Paragraph:** The auditor's conclusions from the work completed are stated in the opinion paragraph of the report, which is typically the third and last paragraph. The phrase "in our opinion" is meant to convey this element of judgment, rather than a statement of fact or guarantee. The auditor's opinion is a judgment made after analyzing evidence regarding the assertions implicit in the financial statements. In the majority of audits, the auditor concludes that the financial statements "give a true and fair view... in accordance with." In technical terms, the opinion presented here is referred to as an unqualified opinion, i.e., it is an unequivocal opinion that isn't supported by any caveats. A "clean" opinion is a less formal word for an opinion that is not qualified. The standard expectation is that the auditor will be able to provide a positive, unqualified opinion, even though authoritative audit literature describes other types of opinions (qualified opinions, adverse opinions, and disclaimers of opinion). Anything less is typically undesirable and frequently deemed unacceptable by regulatory agencies as well as by the client. The client's financial statements should "give a true and fair view" in accordance with generally accepted accounting principles in order to best serve users of financial statements. As a result, auditors have an obligation to the public and their clients to help clients obtain unqualified opinions by, if at all possible, working to enhance their financial reporting procedures.

e. **Routine Variations in the Standard Report:** The party or parties to whom it is addressed, the statements reported on, the period(s) covered, and the report date are among the standard variations in the wording of the standard report. Unless there are issues or peculiar circumstances that need to be brought to light, an auditor shouldn't make changes to the standard report. This is the case because any deviation from the prescribed vocabulary is typically interpreted as a warning to the reader.

f. **Addressing the Report:** The client company, its board of directors, or its shareholders may all receive copies of the report. The shareholders, not the business or the management, are the auditor's ultimate client. On behalf of a client, an auditor may occasionally be hired to audit the financial statements of a non-client company. If so, the client should receive the report rather than the audited company, its directors, or its shareholders.

g. **Identification of Financial Statements:** It is usually best to identify the financial statements explicitly in the opening paragraph. It is necessary to use the precise name of the business and to list all of the audited statements. These are commonly referred to as the financial statements and include the balance sheet, the statement of cash flows, the statement of income and retained earnings, and accounting policies. Should the report address any additional statements, they ought to be listed as well.

h. **Periods Covered:** Moreover, the timeframes reported on must be mentioned. Reporting on a year's financial statements alongside comparable data from the prior year is standard practice. In their annual report and accounts, companies whose securities are registered with the Securities and Exchange Commission must include a five-year financial summary. The individual financial statements of one or more previous periods that are presented in comparison with those of the current period should be updated in a continuing auditor's report.

i. **Dating the Report:** Due to the time required to close the books, prepare the financial statements, and finish the auditing process, an auditor's report is inevitably released after the end of the period being reported on. "The auditor should date the report on the financial statements no earlier than the date on which the auditor has obtained sufficient appropriate audit evidence on which to base the opinion on the financial statements," according to the International Auditing and Assurance Board (IAAB). Evidence that the entity's full set of financial statements has been prepared and that those in positions of recognized authority have stated that they are taking responsibility for them are examples of sufficient, appropriate audit evidence. ".

4.1.3. Opinion in an Audit Report

There are primarily two kinds of opinions issued by an auditor in his / her audit report:

1. **Unmodified Opinion:** Issued for any audit in which the auditor deems the financial statements to be a true and fair representation of the activities and dealings of the business during the relevant period. "Clean Report" is another term for an audit report that includes an unmodified opinion. Users of an organization's annual reports and financial statements gain trust from an unmodified report. It conveys the idea that the financial statements are fairly free of any misrepresentations and that the outcomes that are shown there are accurate and reasonable.

2. **Modified Opinion:** A modified opinion is published in the audit report whenever the auditor makes specific findings during the audit and determines that the nature of

the findings precludes the issuance of an unmodified opinion. An auditor may conclude to issue a modified opinion for two main reasons: either on the basis of the audit and supporting documentation, determines that there are material misstatements in the financial statements to some extent. Insufficient and inappropriate evidence was obtained to support the conclusion that there are no material misstatements in the financial statements.

There are three kinds of modified opinions which are issued according to the findings and circumstances:

A. *Qualified Opinion:* A Qualified Opinion is given in a situation where:

- The auditor concludes that misstatements are material but the impact is not so high that it would render the whole financial statements unacceptable; or
- The auditor is unable to obtain sufficient or appropriate audit evidence but concludes that there are indications of misstatements in the financial statements (but the degree is not high).
- *Example of a Qualified Opinion paragraph in audit report:* In our opinion, except for the incomplete disclosure of the information referred to in the Basis for Qualified Opinion paragraph, the financial statements give the information required by the Companies Act, 2013, in the manner so required and give a true and fair view in conformity with the accounting principles generally accepted in India:

1. In case of the Balance Sheet, of the state of affairs of the company as at March 31, XXXX;
2. In case of Profit and Loss Account, of the profit/loss for the year ended on that date; and
3. In case of the Cash Flow Statement, of the cash flows for the year ended on that date.

B. *Adverse Opinion:* An Adverse opinion shall be issued by the auditor where he concludes that on the basis of evidence obtained and procedures performed, there are material misstatements in the financial statements and the impact of the same is high.

- *Example of a Qualified Opinion paragraph in audit report:* In our opinion, because of the omission of the information in the Basis for Adverse Opinion paragraph, the financial statements do not give the information required by the Companies Act, 2013, in the manner so required and also, do not give a true and fair view in conformity with the accounting principles generally accepted in India:

1. In case of the Balance Sheet, of the state of affairs of the company as at March 31, XXXX;
2. In case of Profit and Loss Account, of the profit/loss for the year ended on that date; and
3. In case of the Cash Flow Statement, of the cash flows for the year ended on that date.

C. *Disclaimer of Opinion:* When an auditor determines that they are unable to gather adequate and relevant evidence, they must provide a Disclaimer of Opinion. Under such circumstances, the auditor declines to express an opinion on the financial statements since they are unable to do so. The degree and impact of material misstatements are sufficiently high.

- *Example of a Draft Disclaimer of Opinion:* Our assignment involved reviewing the financial reports of ABC Private Limited ("the company"), encompassing the Balance Sheet as of March 31, XXXX, the Profit and Loss Statement, the Equity Statement of Changes, and the Cash Flow Statement for the preceding year, along with the accompanying notes to the financial reports, including a synopsis of key accounting policies. However, we refrain from endorsing the financial reports of the company. The reasons for this are outlined in the Basis for Disclaiming Opinion section of our report, due to the substantial issues that prevent us from obtaining sufficient and reliable audit evidence to support an opinion on these financial reports.

4.1.4. Advantages of Audit Reports

- Provide assurance on Financial Statements. Reports on audits produced by independent, qualified auditors that are operationally independent of the entity's management. The report they released could assist those who use financial statements in determining whether or not the financial information is accurate.
- Prove management integrity on their shareholders. The report may demonstrate whether or not management is being truthful with shareholders because the auditor is independent of management. This has to do with agency theory and principles.
- It is the requirement of law and regulation.

  The majority of nations mandated that entities meeting certain requirements have independent auditors audit their financial statements. These include things like the number of employees, annual turnover, and asset value. An auditor can provide the government with proof that an organization is abiding by the law.
- It is the requirement of shareholders. The majority of corporate shareholders desire an audit of their company's financial statements. Experts have reviewed this report and simplified its language so that most shareholders without a background in finance or auditing could understand it.
- Parent company's requirement. Many parent companies that have subsidiaries operating in the others countries or even in the same country normally required their subsidiaries' financial statements to be audited. This report could help them manage the subsidiary even more effectively.
- Assist stakeholders in comprehending the financial and operational status of the entity. This is most likely the most significant point. Whether or not the entity has a going concern issue must be stated in the auditor report. This covers issues both financial and non-financial that might cause

the entity to file for bankruptcy within the next forceable time frame following the date of the audit report.

4.1.5. Limitation of Audit Reports

- *Scope of Audit Might be Limited by Management:* This is a common conversation regarding auditing issues. According to the audit standard, auditors should be able to access any information that could be useful in obtaining audit evidence or voicing their opinions. In actuality, management might make every effort to stop auditors from obtaining certain private data. These are most likely signs that management lacks integrity or does not fully trust auditors' confidentiality-related ethics. These issues may make it impossible for auditors to offer the highest caliber audit opinion possible.
- *Time too Constraints for Auditors:* In practice, auditor normally face too time constraints which does not provide them enough time to perform their testing as they should be.
- *Auditors' Independence:* Auditors were required by code of ethics to maintain their independence from the audit client. This is to ensure that auditors are impartial in both their work performance and audit opinion issuance.
- *Fraud and Inherent Risks Are Risks That Auditors Might Miss:* According to audit standards, auditors must properly plan their audits and assess risks. This is to guarantee that audit risks are recognized and reduced, and that audit quality is maintained. These measures, however, were unable to completely remove the possibility of a material misstatement in the financial statements. For instance, fraud risks and inherent risks.
- *Auditors Qualification and Competency:* This is the other crucial point. As everyone knows, an individual representing an audit firm must be a CPA in order to operate the firm. However, due to the volume of work and the competition, there may be some issues with the audit report's quality. As you may be aware, there are frequent reports about audit firms receiving fines in multiple cases.

4.1.6. Types of Audit Report

After testing, the auditor found no material misstatements and issued an unqualified audit report on the financial statements. The unqualified opinion of an independent auditor is included in this report. According to the report, the entity's financial statements are prepared, presented honestly and fairly, and adhere to the applicable accounting standards. For all stakeholders who are willing to use the financial statements, this is encouraging news. The opinion paragraph may tell you whether or not the audit report is clean. The unqualified audit report purportedly demonstrated to the shareholders that the financial statements are accurate and fairly presented, devoid of any significant misstatements. Additionally, it implies that the management group has a high standard of integrity with the shareholders. Make sure the auditors issuing the reports are from independent audit firms, though, before disclosing any information about the audit. The majority of shareholders trust the big four audit firms with their information.

- **Qualified Audit Report:** A qualified audit report is a document issued by auditors in response to financial statements on which they discovered material misstatements. However, those substantial falsehoods are not common. For instance, the entity's opening balance included a sizable quantity of inventories that were unverifiable. Regarding the qualified audit report, the auditor issues a qualified audit opinion. However, the auditor will express an unfavorable opinion in their report if they believe that the misstatement is widespread. Only inventories that are mentioned matter in a report like this one. The financial statements contain other accurate and fair information. Because there are material misstatements on the mentioned items or accounts in the financial statements, a qualified audit report has a higher level of seriousness than an unqualified one.
- **Adverse Audit Report:** An adverse audit report is a kind of audit report that is produced in response to material misstatements discovered by auditors in the financial statements. The material misstatements discovered in the qualified audit report are not the same as the misstatements discovered here. They have an impact on other accounts and items in the entire financial statements in addition to being materially misstated for themselves. We refer to these as pervasive. This means that shareholders, investors, and other stakeholders could not trust any of the items and accounts in the entire financial statements. The name of the client, the financial statements that were audited, and the time period covered by the financial statements are all listed by the auditors in this report. The auditor will also list all errors discovered and explain how they have an impact on the users of the financial statements as well as the financial statements themselves. When auditors review financial statements for their own purposes, they typically also disclose all information discovered by Others Maters, which is a warning to financial statement users.
- **Disclaimer Audit Report:** A disclaimer audit report is one that is issued in relation to financial statements when there are issues with the independence of the auditor and those issues make it impossible for the auditor to gather enough audit evidence to bolster their conclusions. This occurs when certain information pertaining to accounts or items in financial statements that auditors are unable to access is thought to be widely and materially misstated. If the limitations are applied solely to the items or accounts that are materially misstated but not frequently, auditors may not issue the disclaimer opinion.

4.2. WRITE AN AUDIT REPORT

The formal opinion of audit findings is contained in an audit report. The audit report is the final product of the audit and can be utilized as a tool for financial reporting, investing, changing operations, enforcing accountability, or making decisions by the recipient individual or organization. Making sure the audit results are communicated in a way that is helpful to the party receiving the audit requires a well-written audit report.

4.2.1. Preparing to Write an Audit Report

1. **Learn About the Various Audit Types:** An audit can take many different forms since it is an official investigation to confirm that correct policies and procedures were followed.

- *Financial Audit:* The most well-known type of auditing is financial auditing, which is the methodical examination of a business's financial reporting to make sure all data is accurate and complies with GAAP.
- *Operational Audit:* An operational audit examines how an organization uses its resources to make sure they are being used as effectively and as efficiently as possible to fulfill the organization's objectives.
- *Compliance Audit:* A program or organization's compliance with laws, policies, regulations, and procedures is assessed through a compliance audit.
- *Investigative audits:* These are usually ordered in cases where it is believed that laws, rules, or regulations have been broken. They may include elements of all the audit types listed above.

2. **Recognize the Fundamental Objectives of Every Audit Report:** Having a general understanding of the main goals of all audit reports is crucial before getting into the details of writing one. You can ensure that your report accomplishes its goals by keeping these points in mind as you get into the specifics of writing one:

- *Illustrating Non-Conformities:* Any audit report's primary objective is to highlight any instances in which the organization fails to meet any required standard, guideline, regulation, or goal. It's critical to specify both the non-conformity and the standard to which it does not adhere. Next, it's critical to provide the evidence that you used to support the non-conformity. Each non-conformity should have sufficient information so that the audit report's recipients can make the necessary corrections.

- *Outlining Positives:* Negatives shouldn't be the only things in an audit report. This is particularly valid for operational audits and compliance reports. This enables the company to concentrate on its strengths and expand upon them into other domains. For instance, you may state, "The audit reveals the current training program has exceeded requirements on-time and on-budget," if you are performing a compliance audit to make sure an organization meets training requirements.
- *Opportunities for Improvement:* Beyond indicating things that are not conforming to requirements (non-conformities), it is important to also indicate high-risk areas, or areas that may be in compliance but are at risk of eventually not complying, or could be improved.

3. **Discover the Various Audit Opinion Types:** It is crucial to recognize that there are four fundamental categories of opinions that can be expressed, particularly when composing a financial audit report. An audit report's tone, structure, and organization are influenced by the opinion you express, and the audit's findings dictate the kind of opinion you should express. The same kinds of opinions can be used in other kinds of audits, such as legal and operational audits.

If an entity's financial statements accurately reflect its financial opinion, then the entity is said to have a clean opinion. When the auditor's work was subject to scope restrictions, a qualified opinion was used. Scope limitations refer to the constraints placed on the audit by the client or other circumstances that prevent the auditor from carrying out all of the audit procedures. If financial information was falsified, an adverse opinion would be applied. Several distinct circumstances can lead to a disclaimer opinion. For instance, there can be issues with the auditee or the auditor's independence.

4. **Consider the Audience for the Report:** An audit report is an official record of an audit project, so it will probably be referred to for re-audits in the future. Who will be reading your report, and what is their level of experience with the language you plan to use? It's important to define every term and acronym you use because common forms of communication could change in the future.

4.2.2. Beginning Your Report

Be familiar with the format of audit reports before starting. Any audit report must adhere to a set of style guidelines, so be sure to familiarize yourself with them before starting to write:

- *Give the Reader a Balanced Perspective by Highlighting Both the Audit's Positive and Negative Findings:* Be specific; stay away from imprecise terminology and repetitive phrasing. For the sake of clarity, use shorter sentences rather than longer ones. In business writing, a word count of no more than 15 to 18 is advised. Additionally, stay away from imprecise intensifiers like clearly, special, key, and reasonable. Avoid using the passive voice. Reading passive voice can be challenging. Saying "No irregularity of operation was found" is preferable. The audit team did not discover any anomalous information. Make use of bullet points to help the reader understand complex material by breaking it up. Make use of terminology that are gender-neutral. Steer clear of audit buzzwords. Buzzwords are vague, overused terms like "tighten controls," "significant risk," and "generally improved."

- *Give a Summary of Your Audit Report:* Read the audit results and create an outline for yourself based on all the sections you will need before you start writing. A typical outline consists of subsections denoted by letters, numbers, or lowercase Roman numerals, and headings denoted by Roman numerals. Choose an organizing method that suits your needs, and then take it from there. For instance, you might think about segmenting the department into several important parts and reporting the results in that manner if you are auditing the procedures for a specific department within an organization.
- *Write Your Introduction:* The introduction overviews information about the audit area, and informs the reader of any background they might need to know before reading the full report.
- *Follow with the Purpose and Scope Methodology:* This section provides information about the audit and should answer the following questions, as well address the methodology used in the audit:

i. Why was the audit conducted?

ii. What was included and not included in the audit?

iii. What was the time period audited?

iv. What were the audit objectives?

- *Continue onto the Statement on Auditing Standards:* This audit is a basic disclaimer people will look for to make sure the audit was conducted correctly. The Statement on Auditing Standards should say the report was conducted according to government standards.
- *Write the Executive Summary: This* is an overview of the audit results. It should present overall conclusions and recommendations related to the Purpose and Scope Methodology. This section must include:

i. A brief description of what was audited, objectives, scopes, and time periods.

ii. Statements of significant action plans.

iii. Overall statements of concerns and conclusions.

iv. Overall audit report rating.

4.2.3. Writing Your Results and Recommendations

Compose a brief introduction for the findings and recommendations section. Results from the audits and suggestions for enhancing the entity being audited are usually included in the audit report's conclusion. A strong report's conclusions and suggestions form its cornerstone. Make a succinct opening statement outlining the information you will be providing before you start writing this section.

- *Understand Condition, Criteria, Cause, and Effect*: The findings of your audit report are reliant on these terms, and understanding and addressing them in each finding is key to a good report.

A description of management objectives and the standards used to assess the program, function, or audited activity is provided in the criteria. The degree to which department management is accomplishing objectives and/or standards is the condition. Objectives may be accomplished entirely, partially, or not at all. A cause is an explanation for why something went well or poorly. The following scenarios could occur: insufficient protocols not being followed, inadequate oversight, or under qualified staff. Effect gives a quantitative description of the outcome of the conditions. When discussing effect, you should address whether there is poor performance, monetary cost, increased risk, or exposure.

- *Make Wise Suggestions:* Making suggestions for improvement for the entity you audited is the last responsibility as an auditor. A lead statement such as "We recommend that the department director: Remember to do the following while writing your recommendations" should list them all together.

i. Be positive. Focus on what is going right at the moment, and how the good aspects of the entity can be applied in ineffective areas.

ii. Be specific. Be very clear as to what specific aspects do not adhere to protocol, and to what concrete steps could be potentially implemented to ensure compliance.

iii. Identify who should act. Does the company need better employee performance or should management be picking up the pace? Make clear who needs to make changes.

iv. Keep recommendations brief. Be succinct - only include details that are necessary to your point.

- *Observe the Correct Format:* Make sure you adhere to the correct format when you are polishing your audit report to send to management.

i. Add a page for the cover: The subject of the audit report and the kind of audit should be covered in three or four lines on the cover page.

ii. The cover page should be followed by a memo: A brief paragraph or two summarizing who and what was audited, who has received or will receive the report, and the distribution schedule should be included in the memo.

iii. The memo is followed by a table of contents that includes an index of the audit's chapters, page numbers, sections, and recommendations.

iv. The report should be written using clear, non-technical language, with appropriate paragraph structure and grammar.

v. Reports are arranged into sections and subsections, each designated with a heading, and chapters, each with a title. Headings ought to be organized from broad to narrow.

4.3. SUBSEQUENT EVENTS

An event that takes place after a reporting period but before the financial statements for that period are released or become available for release is referred to as a subsequent event. Such occurrences might or might not need to be disclosed in an organization's financial statements, depending on the circumstances. A company's normal reporting period is one year. A reporting period, however, need not coincide with the official calendar year, which runs from January 1 to December 31. Companies usually select a year-end that falls during a slow period of activity. Retailers, for instance, typically end their year at the end of January, during the post-holiday season, when inventory is at its lowest. The end of the reporting period and the beginning of the next reporting period are referred to as the cut-off date.

Due to the possibility of incomplete cash cycles, accrual accounting places importance on it. Thus, it's important to know which events will be covered in the current reporting period and which ones will be in the one that follows. Events and transactions are recorded through the deadline. The following events period runs from the cut-off date until the financial statements are authorized to be issued. The type of subsequent event will determine whether or not the financial statements need to be adjusted. Before the cut-off date, transactions and events that alter the measurement of those transactions are recognized.

- *Example:* Before the financial statements are released and after the cut-off date, which is the end of the company's fiscal year, Company A's largest client unexpectedly files for bankruptcy. It is concluded that the major client will only give the company 10% of its outstanding accounts receivable. The event will necessitate a modification to Company A's financial statements.

4.3.1. Types of Subsequent Events

Events that happen after the balance sheet date but before the financial statements and auditor's report are referred to as subsequent events. These events have a significant impact on the financial statements and, as a result, need to be disclosed or adjusted in the statements. Events that follow the date of the balance sheet but take place before the financial statements and auditor's report are released typically fall into one of two categories:

(a) Those that require the adjustments of account balances; and

(b) Those that should not be recorded but should be disclosed in the financial statements.

Developments that offer more proof of the circumstances that prevailed at the balance sheet date and have an impact on the estimates used in the financial statement preparation process are classified as the first kind of subsequent event. A subsequent event that sheds light on circumstances that emerged later and were not present at the balance sheet date is classified as the second kind. The financial statements of the year in which these events occurred should show this, and the statements of the year being reported on shouldn't be adjusted as a result. However, some of these occurrences might be important enough to warrant disclosure; otherwise, the financial statements from the previous year would be deceptive. All transactions as well as other occurrences and situations with a sizable financial impact are included. Acquisitions of businesses and casualty losses are two instances.

Often, the distinction is a subtle one. Declining market conditions after year-end may indicate the existence of a condition that was already present in the inventory at year-end and needs to be adjusted to net realizable value, or it may indicate the existence of a new condition that only needs to be disclosed. In a similar vein, information about a later event that indicates that projected costs are inadequate due to circumstances that arise after the balance sheet date must be revealed. However, if the cause of the deficiency is newly found evidence of circumstances that existed on the date of the balance sheet, then the expense and associated asset or liability accounts on the face of the statements should reflect the evidence.

A third category of subsequent event is one that doesn't need to be disclosed or adjusted in the financial statements and happens after year-end. Events that have no bearing on how financial statements should be interpreted should not be disclosed because doing so could lead to erroneous or unclear conclusions from the notes. It is frequently very difficult to distinguish between events that should and should not be disclosed in the financial statements because every event may have a financial impact. Events that typically shouldn't be included in the financial statements include strikes, changes in customers or management, and new contracts and agreements, though management may be required to disclose information to the public outside of the financial statements. A convenient means of communication in such cases is the Chairman's letter, provided that the events take place prior to the printing of the annual report to shareholders.

As per the section "Subsequent Events," the auditor is supposed to carry out audit procedures that aim to gather adequate audit evidence, confirming that all events that occurred up until the auditor's report date and could necessitate financial statement adjustments or disclosures have been identified. These procedures are additional to those that can be used to particular post-period transactions in order to gather audit evidence regarding account balances as of the end of the period. Examples of such procedures include testing the inventory cut-off and making payments to creditors. However, the auditor is not required to carry out an ongoing review of every issue for which previously used audit procedures have produced satisfactory results. The audit processes would be carried out as close to the date of the auditor's report as is practical in order to find events that might need to be disclosed or adjusted in the financial statements.

Such audit procedures take into account the auditor's risk assessment and ordinarily include the following:

- Reviewing the procedures that management has established to ensure that subsequent events are identified;
- Reading the minutes of the shareholder and governance-related meetings, as well as those of established committees like the audit and relevant executive committees, held following the conclusion of the period, and finding out what was discussed

at meetings for which there are no minutes yet available;

- Reading the entity's latest available interim financial statements and, as considered necessary and appropriate, budgets, cash flow forecasts and other related management reports;
- Inquiring, or extending previous oral or written inquiries, of the entity's legal counsel concerning litigation and claims;
- Reading the minutes of the shareholder and governance-related meetings, as well as those of established committees like the audit and relevant executive committees, held following the conclusion of the period, and finding out what was discussed at meetings for which there are no minutes yet available;
- Whether new commitments, borrowings or guarantees have been entered into;
- Whether sales or acquisition of assets have occurred or are planned;
- Whether the issue of new shares or debentures or an agreement to merge or liquidate has been made or is planned;
- Whether any assets have been appropriated by Government or destroyed, for example, by fire or flood;
- Whether there have been any developments regarding risk areas and contingencies;
- Whether any unusual accounting adjustments have been made or are contemplated;
- Whether any events have occurred or are likely to occur which will bring into question the appropriateness of accounting policies used in the financial statements as would be the case, for example, if such events call into question the validity of the going concern assumption; and
- "When a division, branch, or subsidiary is audited by a different auditor, the auditor will take into account the other auditor's protocols concerning events that occur after the end of the period and the requirement to notify the other auditor of the anticipated date of the auditor's report."

4.3.2. Auditor's Responsibility for Subsequent Events

Whether an event happens after the date of the auditor's report or before determines who is accountable for it. Between the date of the auditor's report and the date the financial statements and auditor's report are released, auditors are under no obligation to obtain any further evidence. However, a lot of auditors think that even though they are not required to look for more proof during that time, they are still obliged to take notice of information that is brought to their attention.

4.3.3. Auditing Procedures in the Subsequent Period

It is the auditor's duty to ascertain whether any pertinent follow-up events have transpired and to talk about the auditing procedures that need to be carried out in the next period. This work is typically divided into two main categories: (a) procedures carried out in order to stay updated on events that will occur in the upcoming period; and (b) completion of auditing procedures carried out for other purposes. As part of the audit of year-end account balances, the latter category includes substantive tests and other auditing procedures that entail examining transactions that occur in the subsequent period. Tests of the client's cash cut-offs, sales and purchase cut-offs, and evaluations of collections and payments following year-end are all part of these procedures. That being said, the auditor is not obligated to conduct any auditing procedures for the period following the report date. The following can be used to summarize the steps involved in staying up to date on events that are happening in the coming period:

- Examine all available records regarding the client's financial situation, including interim financial statements, director, stockholder, and any relevant committee minutes, relevant variance reports, other management reports, and similar materials. An auditor who is familiar with the client will know which areas are volatile or sensitive as well as what information is probably available about them.
- Ask questions concerning things like financing operations, odd entries or adjustments in the accounts, and possible issues found during the audit. An auditor can easily and quickly make those inquiries if they have developed a close working relationship with the client.
- Inquire of client's legal counsel concerning litigation, claims, and assessments; and
- Obtain a letter of representation from client officers describing subsequent events or disclaiming knowledge of any

The auditor may also make other comparisons deemed appropriate under the circumstances as part of the subsequent-period review, including a comparison between the financial statements being reported on and the most recent interim financial statements that are currently available. In a recognized problem area, it may occasionally be necessary to conduct analytical procedures or other substantive tests in the ensuing period. The goal is to determine if a client has fairly assessed the impact of a subsequent event. Tests of the net realizable value of inventories resulting from altered market conditions after year-end are one example of a test that may be necessary to ensure the auditor that a potential subsequent event did not occur.

4.3.4. Responsibilities After Report Date

Evidently, the auditor's duty does not continue after the financial statements are released; responsibility ends there. Finding facts that existed at the time of the auditor's report and later learning of subsequent events that occurred before the financial statements are released differ significantly.

The distinction is as follows:

(a) If the new information refers to:

- A condition that did not exist at the date of the audit report; or
- Final resolutions of contingencies or other matters disclosed in the financial statements or the auditor's report; and
- The auditor having no further obligation.

(b) If the new information:

- Relates to facts existing at the date of the audit report;
- Would have affected the financial statements; or
- Would have affected the auditor's report had the auditor been aware of them

4.4. AUDITOR'S REPORT ON FINANCIAL STATEMENTS

It is crucial to remember that auditor reports on financial statements are not assessments or any other kind of decision-making evaluation that involves assessing entities in order to reach a conclusion. The report solely expresses an opinion regarding the accuracy and lack of material misstatements in the information provided; the user is left to make all other decisions. There are four typical forms of auditor reports, and each one highlights a distinct circumstance that the auditor came across while working. The following are the four reports:

4.4.1. Unqualified Opinion

When an opinion is expressed without substantial reservation regarding any of the topics covered in the Financial Statements, it is considered unqualified. The most common type of report is called an Unqualified Opinion, which is also known as a Clean Opinion because it is often thought of as the equivalent of a doctor giving a patient the all clear.

However, in actuality, the Unqualified Opinion is not a clean opinion because the Auditor can only give a reasonable assurance regarding the Financial Statements, not the company's overall health or the accuracy of company records that are not part of the Financial Statements' foundation. When the financial statements are presented fairly in line with generally accepted accounting principles (GAAP) and are free of material misstatements—that is, when the company's financial condition, position, and operations are fairly represented in the financial statements—an auditor will issue this kind of report. It is the best kind of report that an external auditor can give to an auditee.

An Unqualified Opinion indicates the following:

i. The Financial Statements have been prepared using the Generally Accepted Accounting Principles which have been consistently applied;
ii. The Financial Statements comply with relevant statutory requirements and regulations;
iii. There is adequate disclosure of all material matters relevant to the proper presentation of the financial information subject to statutory requirements, where applicable;

iv. Any changes in the accounting principles or in the method of their application and the effects there of have been properly determined and disclosed in the Financial Statements.

The report has a title and header, a main body, the address and signature of the auditor, and the date of issuance. In order to communicate to the user that the report was impartial in every way, US auditing standards mandate that the title contain the word "independent." The unqualified report's main body typically consists of three main paragraphs, each with a specific purpose and standard wording. However, in an attempt to set themselves apart from other audit firms, some auditors have since changed the structure of the main body (but not the language), even though this change goes against the updated US AICPA auditing standards.

The first paragraph, also known as the introduction, lists the audit work completed and specifies the auditee's and auditor's obligations with regard to the financial statements.

The scope of the audit work, a general description of the work, examples of procedures completed, and any limitations the audit encountered due to the nature of the work are all included in the second paragraph, also known as the scope paragraph.

Additionally, the audit was carried out in compliance with the nation's currently in effect generally accepted auditing standards and laws, according to this paragraph. The auditor's opinion regarding the financial statements and their compliance with generally accepted accounting principles is expressed in the third paragraph, also known as the opinion paragraph.

4.4.2. Qualified Opinion Report

Qualified report is given by the auditor in either of these two cases:

1. When there is a single, non-pervasive misstatement in one or more specific account balances, transaction classes, or disclosures that causes the financial statements to be materially misstated.
2. When the audit evidence for a specific account balance, transaction class, or disclosure that doesn't significantly affect the financial statements is unavailable to the auditor.

With the exception of a paragraph, the report is essentially similar to a Clear Opinion Report. Basis for Qualification comes before the Opinion paragraph and after the Scope paragraph. In addition to its standard wording, the opinion paragraph states that the financial statements present a true and fair picture, with the exception of the subject mentioned in the Basis for Qualification paragraph.

Detailed below:

When the auditor comes across one of the two scenarios that deviate from generally accepted accounting principles but the remaining financial statements are fairly presented, a qualified opinion report is generated. A clean or unqualified opinion is very similar to this type of opinion, but the report says the financial statements are presented fairly except for one particular item that is otherwise misstated. When one of the following two scenarios occurs, an auditor would issue this opinion rather than an unqualified one.

Single deviation from GAAP: When one or more sections of the financial statements don't follow GAAP, this kind of qualification happens (e.g., are misstated), they do not, when considered collectively, impair the fair presentation of the remaining financial statements. One retail company that failed to accurately calculate its building's depreciation expense is an example of this. The auditor qualifies the opinion by outlining the depreciation misstatement in the report and maintains a clean opinion on the remaining financial statements even if this expense is deemed material because the rest of the financial statements do comply with GAAP.

Limitation of scope: This kind of qualification is applied when there are parts of the financial statements that the auditor was unable to audit, but the remaining financial statements passed GAAP audit and were verified. An auditor may not be able to view and inspect a company's inventory of goods, for example. With the exception of the inventory, which could not be audited, the auditor merely declares that the financial statements are fairly presented if they audited the remaining financial statements and are reasonably certain that they comply with GAAP.

The qualified report's language is almost exactly the same as the unqualified opinion; however, after the scope paragraph but before the opinion paragraph, there is an additional paragraph that provides an explanation of the qualification. The opening paragraph remains unchanged from the unqualified opinion, but the scope and opinion paragraphs are slightly altered to reflect the explanatory paragraph's qualification.

The following sentence is added to the first sentence of the scope paragraph so that the user is made aware of the qualification right away. Additionally, this placement notifies the user that the audit was completed without any qualifications for the majority of it: "*Except as discussed in the following paragraph,* we conducted our audit..."

Additionally, a new sentence has been added to the opinion paragraph to remind the user that the auditor's opinion expressly excludes the qualification mentioned. The sentence is changed, depending on the type of qualification, to either state the qualification and the changes that must be made to correct it, or to state the scope limitation and the fact that changes may have been necessary but are not always necessary to correct it. Using the previously mentioned depreciation example, the following phrase is added to the opinion paragraph for a qualification resulting from a deviation from GAAP:

"In our opinion, *except for the effects of the Company's incorrect determination of depreciation expense,* the financial statement referred to in the first paragraph presents fairly, in all material respects, the financial position of..."

For a qualification arising from a scope of limitation, the following phrase is added to the opinion paragraph, using the inventory example mentioned above:

"In our opinion, *except for the effects of such adjustments, if any, as might have been determined to be necessary had we been able to perform proper tests and procedures on the Company's inventory,* the financial statement referred to in the first paragraph presents fairly, in all material respects, the financial position of..."

4.4.3. Adverse Opinion Report

When a company's financial statements contain material misstatements that have a significant impact on the financial statements overall, an adverse opinion report is published about the financial statements. When an auditor finds that an auditee's financial statements are materially misstated and do not, when taken as a whole, comply with GAAP, they issue an adverse opinion. It basically states that the information contained is materially incorrect, unreliable, and inaccurate in order to evaluate the auditee's financial position and operational results. It is regarded as the opposite of an unqualified or clean opinion. If the auditor issued an unfavorable opinion, investors, lending institutions, and governments very seldom accept the auditee's financial statements; instead, they typically ask the auditee to make the necessary corrections and obtain a second audit report.

An unfavorable opinion is typically reserved for situations in which the financial statements materially deviate from GAAP. One instance of this kind of circumstance would be if a business failed to combine a significant subsidiary. The qualified report and the adverse report have similar wording. The scope paragraph is adjusted appropriately, and after the scope paragraph but before the opinion paragraph, an explanation paragraph is added to provide the rationale for the unfavorable opinion. The auditor expressly states in the opinion paragraph of the adverse report that the financial statements are not in compliance with GAAP, which implies that they are unreliable, inaccurate, and do not provide a fair picture of the auditee's position and operations as a whole. This is the most significant change from the qualified report.

"In our opinion, *because of the situations mentioned above* (in the explanatory paragraph), the financial statements referred to in the first paragraph *do not* present fairly, in all material respects, the financial position of..."

4.4.4. Disclaimer of Opinion Report

A Disclaimer of Opinion is issued in either of the following cases:

- When the auditor is not independent or when there is conflict of interest.
- When the limitation on scope is imposed by client, as a result the auditor is unable to obtain sufficient appropriate audit evidence.
- When there are significant uncertainties in the business of client.

When there is a Disclaimer of Opinion, the audit report is substantially altered. The audit report now includes a new paragraph titled "Basis for Disclaimer," which comes before the paragraph about the opinion and after the paragraph about the scope. The phrase "We were engaged to audit the financial statements of XYZ Co." appears in the scope paragraph. Ltd. from We have examined XYZ Co.'s financial statements. Ltd. The phrase "We do not express an opinion on the financial statements of XYZ Co." appears in the Opinion paragraph. Ltd. due to circumstances outlined in the paragraph entitled "Basis for Disclaimer."

When an auditor cannot form an opinion and thus declines to present one on the financial statements, they issue a Disclaimer of Opinion, also known as just a Disclaimer. This kind of report is produced when an auditor attempts to audit an organization but is unable to finish the task for a variety of reasons and does not provide an opinion. Statements on Auditing Standards (SAS) provide certain situations where a disclaimer of opinion may be appropriate:

A lack of independence, or material conflict(s) of interest, exist between the auditor and the auditee (SAS No. 26);

- There are significant scope limitations, whether intentional or not, which hinder the auditor's work in obtaining evidence and performing procedures (SAS No. 58);
- There is a substantial doubt about the auditee's ability to continue as a going concern or, in other words, continue operating (SAS No. 59); and
- There are significant uncertainties within the auditee (SAS No. 79).

Disclaimers are typically issued in the following situations: audits where the auditee willfully withholds evidence or refuses to provide information to the auditor in significant areas of the financial statements; significant legal and litigation issues where the auditee's fate is uncertain (usually government investigations); and going concern issues where the auditee may not be able to continue operating in the near future. If the auditor expressed no opinion, investors, lenders, and governments will usually reject the auditee's financial statements, ask the auditee to address the issues the auditor raised, and request a second audit report. A disclaimer of opinion deviates significantly from the auditor's other reports in that it offers minimal details about the audit process and a paragraph explaining the rationale behind the disclaimer. The letterhead, the auditee's name and address, the auditor's signature and address, and the report's issuance date are still present in the report, but every other paragraph has been significantly altered, and the scope paragraph has been completely removed because the auditor is essentially claiming that an audit could not be carried out. The first sentence in the introduction shifts from We have audited to We were engaged to audit to inform the reader that the auditee requested an audit, but it makes no indication that the audit was finished by the auditor. Furthermore, by leaving out the final sentence of the paragraph, the auditor further declines to take accountability for the incomplete and/or inadequate performance of the audit. The scope paragraph is left out in its entirety because there was essentially no audit done. The auditor is required to provide a brief explanation of the disclaimer's circumstances in an explanatory paragraph, just like with the qualified and adverse opinions. Ultimately, the opinion paragraph completely shifts, saying that the circumstances outlined in the preceding paragraphs prevent an opinion from being formed or from being expressed.

4.4.5. Auditor's Report on Internal Controls of Public Companies

The Public Company Accounting Oversight Board (PCAOB) was created in the wake of the Sarbanes-Oxley Act of 2002 to oversee, control, investigate, and punish public accounting firms and audits of publicly traded companies. Standards for PCAOB Auditing No. 2 now mandates that auditors of public companies provide an opinion on the company's and the auditor's assessment of the company's internal controls over financial reporting, as well as an extra disclosure about the auditee's internal controls in the opinion report. The COSO Opinion is the common term used to describe these new requirements. Either the report on the financial statements is presented after the report on the auditors, or both reports are combined into a single auditor's report, which is updated to include all required disclosures.

4.4.6. Going Concern

As long as it generates or obtains sufficient resources to operate, an entity is said to be a going concern if it intends to continue operating in the near future, which is typically longer than the next 12 months. In the event that the auditee is not a going concern, the entity may not be able to continue operating for the ensuing year. When preparing a report, auditors must take the auditee's ability to continue as a going concern into account. The auditor does not make any changes to their report in the event that the auditee is a going concern. All the same, the auditor must include a going concern disclosure—a paragraph that explains the situation in the audit report either before or after the opinion paragraph—in the audit report if the auditor believes that the auditee is not, or will not, be, a going concern in the near future. We refer to this type of opinion as an unqualified modified opinion.

Unfortunately, because some view this disclosure as a self-fulfilling prophecy, a growing number of auditors are becoming reluctant to include it in their opinions. This is due to the fact that investors, lending organizations, and credit agencies take a dim view of a disclosure regarding a lack of going concern, which lowers the likelihood that the auditee will be able to secure the funding or borrowing it requires to continue operating after the disclosure is made. In such a scenario, the auditor may feel under pressure not to provide a going concern disclosure since the auditee is more likely to cease operating as a going concern and the auditor loses out on possible future audit engagements. A going concern disclosure was absent from the previous auditor's report for almost half (48%) of the public companies that were selected and faced bankruptcy in 2001, according to a study on bankruptcies that year. Furthermore, twelve of the twenty biggest bankruptcies in U.S. history took place between 2001 and 2002, and in their prior auditor's report, none of them disclosed a going concern. Regarding the wording of the auditor's report itself, the disclosure paragraph should explain the situation, the auditor's conclusion that there is a lack of going concern, and the auditee's plan to remedy the situation. The opinion paragraph ought to be followed right away by the disclosure paragraph.

An essential deliverable for any business is the audit report, which summarizes the findings from the entire audit procedure. The audit reports of any business serve as the foundation for the decisions and plans made by users of financial statements, such as investors, lenders, customers, and others. Any financial statement's audit's perceived value is always influenced by the audit report. Since many individuals rely on audit reports and make decisions based on them, the auditor should exercise caution when releasing them. The report should be released by carrying out the duties in an impartial and objective manner. An essential deliverable for any business is the audit report, which summarizes the findings from the entire audit procedure. The audit reports of any business serve as the foundation for the decisions and plans made by users of financial statements, such as investors, lenders, customers, and others. Any financial statement's audit's perceived value is always influenced by the audit report. Since many individuals rely on audit reports and make decisions based on them, the auditor should exercise caution when releasing them. The report should be released by carrying out the duties in an impartial and objective manner.

The basic structure of an audit report as prescribed by the Standards on Auditing is as follows:

Table 4.1. Contents of an Audit Report

Heading	Brief of contents
Title	Title should mention that it is an 'Independent Auditor's Report'.
Addressee	Should mention clearly as to whom the report is being given to. For example Members oMentions that it is the Management's responsibility to Prepare the Financial Statements. f the company, Board of Directors
Management's Responsibility for Financial Statements	
Auditor's Responsibility	Mention that responsibility of the Auditor is to express an unbiased opinion on the financial statements and issue an audit report.
Opinion	Should mention the overall impression obtained from the audit of financial statements. For example Modified Opinion, Unmodified Opinion
Basis of the Opinion	State the basis on which the opinion as reported has been achieved. Facts of the basis should be mentioned.
Other Reporting Responsibility	If any other reporting responsibility exists, the same should be mentioned. For example Report on Legal or Regulatory requirements
Signature of the Auditor	The engagement partner (auditor) shall sign the audit report.
Place of Signature	The city in which audit report is signed.
Date of Audit Report	Date on which the audit report is signed.

Source: https://cleartax.in/s/audit-report

An official opinion or disclaimer issued by an external auditor following an unbiased examination of the financial statements of an organization is known as an audit report. It offers a guarantee on the fairness, accuracy, and compliance of the financial statements with the relevant financial reporting framework to all relevant parties, including shareholders, creditors, and regulators. A few crucial disclosures in the audit report are particularly significant because they include information that is necessary to improve the financial statements' dependability, transparency, and usefulness. With regard to the entity's performance, legal and regulatory compliance, and financial stability, these disclosures assist stakeholders in making well-informed decisions. The opinion of the auditor is among the most significant disclosures in an audit report. In line with the applicable financial reporting framework, such as Generally Accepted Accounting Principles (GAAP) or International Financial Reporting Standards (IFRS), the auditor's conclusion regarding whether the financial statements present a true and fair view is expressly stated in this section. Both modified and unmodified (clean) opinions are acceptable. The absence of material misstatements in the financial statements is indicated by a clean opinion, whereas certain areas of the financial statements' noncompliance with the reporting framework are indicated by a modified opinion, which may be qualified, adverse, or a disclaimer of opinion. This disclosure is essential because it has a direct bearing on the financial statements' credibility and stakeholders' trust in the entity's financial reporting.

An additional crucial revelation is the foundation for the auditor's viewpoint. The rationale for the auditor's opinion is explained in this section, especially if it is updated. This section will describe the type of misstatement, it's possible effect on the financial statements, and the rationale behind the auditor's conclusions if the auditor has issued a qualified or adverse opinion. In the case of a disclaimer of opinion, it will detail the scope restriction or the reason the auditor was unable to gather enough relevant data to create an opinion. This disclosure explains to users the specific areas where the financial statements may be uncertain or deficient, as well as the context of the auditor's opinion. Disclosures regarding material uncertainties pertaining to going concern must also be included in the audit report. A basic accounting principle known as the "going concern assumption" makes the assumption that a business will continue to operate for the foreseeable future. The audit report must clearly state in the event that the auditor finds any circumstances or occurrences that seriously impair the entity's ability to function as a going concern. These uncertainties, the possible effects on the entity's financial stability, and the suitability of management's disclosures about these issues in the financial statements must all be discussed by the auditor. For stakeholders, this kind of disclosure is essential because it indicates possible operational difficulties or financial distress that could affect the entity's long-term viability.

Particularly for listed companies, key audit matters (KAMs) constitute yet another crucial disclosure in the audit report. KAMs are those items in the financial statement audit that, based on the auditor's professional judgment, were most important. They could be high-risk areas, intricate transactions, management decisions or estimates, or any area where the audit encountered significant challenges. For stakeholders, the audit report is more transparent and educational when KAMs are included because they offer more information about the parts of the financial statements that presented the biggest problems or needed the most attention from the auditor. Management's accountability for the financial statements ought to be revealed in the audit report as well. The management of the entity is accountable for the fair preparation and presentation of the financial statements, as well as for the design, implementation, and upkeep of internal controls that guard against or identify fraud and guarantee the accuracy of the financial reporting, as this section makes clear. In addition, it clarifies that management bears the responsibility of determining whether the organization can continue as a going concern and of appropriately disclosing any such uncertainties. To ensure that stakeholders are aware that the auditor's role is to provide an opinion based on their review and not to prepare or guarantee the accuracy of the financial statements, this disclosure is crucial as it clearly outlines the roles and responsibilities between management and the auditor.

A section on the auditor's duties for the financial statement audit is also included in the audit report. This section describes the audit's scope, the auditing standards that were adhered to (such as applicable local standards or the International Standards on Auditing), and the steps taken to gather enough pertinent data to form an opinion. It also covers the duties of the auditor with regard to determining the likelihood of a material misstatement resulting from fraud or error, as well as the suitability of the accounting policies in place and the soundness of the management's major accounting estimates. This disclosure is essential to understanding the scope and character of the auditor's work as well as the degree of assurance the audit offers users of the audit report. Lastly, additional disclosures about the independence and ethics of the auditor are frequently included in the audit report. This disclosure attests to the auditor's independence from the entity in compliance with all applicable ethical standards and attests to the fact that the audit was carried out in accordance with other ethical obligations. This is essential to preserving the audit process's integrity and guaranteeing to stakeholders the objectivity and impartiality of the audit opinion.

The audit report format is the uniform format that the relevant authorities have prescribed for an independent auditor who has been appointed by the company to provide commentary and opinions on the internal accounting and financial health of the company following an examination of the company's various documents. An independent auditor's audit report details the financial situation and internal accounting controls. The organization's stakeholders, investors, shareholders, and board of directors, among others. utilize this report. After examining the organization's financial statements, the auditor is in charge of creating this audit report in a consistent format each year. When putting together the report, the auditor needs to be thorough and objective. Prior to making an investment in any company, investors typically consult the auditor's report. You don't need to conduct your own report analysis because the Audit Report gives you a clear picture of the company's financial situation. The report provides a trustworthy overview of the financial standing of an organization. The first paragraph of an auditor's report provides an overview of the audited financial statements. The audit's nature is briefly described in the scope paragraph. The opinion paragraph contains the auditor's viewpoint.

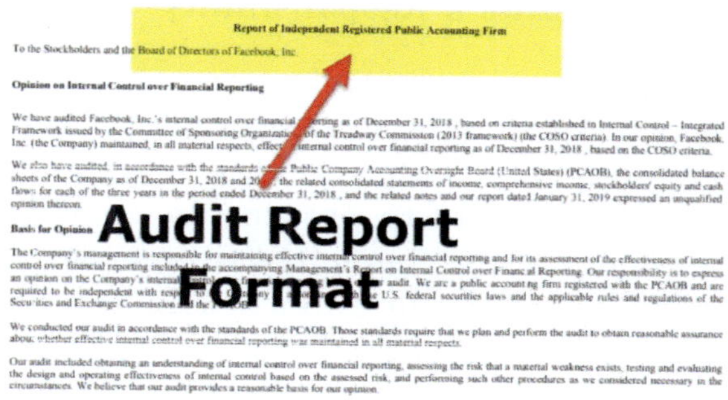

Figure 4.1. A sample format of Audit report.

Source: https://wallstreetmojo-files.s3.ap-south-1.amazonaws.com/2019/05/Audit-Report-Format.jpg

The audit report format is as follows –

#1 - Title

The title should mention - 'Independent Auditor's Report.'

#2 - Addressee

The addressee should mention to whom the report is being presented.

#3 - Introductory Paragraph

A statement that the financial statements described in the report has been audited.

#4 - Management's Responsibility

A summary of the company's cash flows, financial performance, and financial condition should be included in the section of the audit report format titled

"Management's Responsibility for the Integrity of the Financial Statements.". The fact that the organization's management is in charge of the financial statements should be mentioned. To guarantee that the financial records are accurate, it is their duty to design and implement the appropriate financial controls. Keeping accurate accounting records is another duty to avoid fraud.

#5 - Auditor's Responsibility

To obtain assurance regarding the financial statements, it is the auditor's duty to organize and carry out the audit. It is the Auditor's duty to present an objective assessment of the financial statements and to produce an audit report. The report's foundation is the Standards on Auditing. The auditor must follow ethical guidelines in accordance with the Standards.

#6 - Opinion

The Auditor's Opinion is the most important section of an audit report. It makes reference to the impression that was formed following the financial statement audit.

#7 - Basis of the Opinion

It should mention the basis of achieving the opinion as reported and the facts of the premise.

#8 - Other Reporting Responsibility

There are any additional reporting-related obligations. Requirements from regulations might be included. The same must be mentioned by the auditor.

#9 - Signature of the Auditor

The auditor needs to sign the audit report, thereby confirming the report's authenticity.

#10 - Place of Signature

The name of the city in which the signing of the report happened.

#11 - Date of Audit Report

The date on which the audit report is signed/reported;

Sample Audit Report Format Example:

Below mentioned is a sample format of an Auditor's Report:

Independent Auditor's Report to the Members of X Company

Report on the Financial Statements: We have audited the accompanying consolidated balance sheets of X Company (the Firm) as of December 31, 20XX, and the related statements of income, comprehensive income, retained earnings, changes in stockholders' equity, and cash flows for the year then ended, and a synopsis of the accounting policies and other information. We also have audited the Firm's internal control over financial reporting as of December 31, 20XX.

Management's Responsibility for the Financial Statements: The management of the company is in charge of these financial statements. In accordance with generally accepted accounting principles in the United States of America, the Board of Directors of the Firm is in charge of preparing these financial statements, which present a true and fair picture of the company's financial position, financial performance, and cash flows.

Auditor's Responsibility: It is our duty to provide a judgment on these financial statements based on our audit. The audit was carried out in accordance with the widely recognized auditing standards in the US. According to the standards, we must organize and carry out the audit in order to confirm the accuracy of the financial statements and make sure there are no potential frauds or material misstatements. Examining the amounts and disclosures in the financial statements is part of the audit process. Our opinion will have a solid foundation thanks to the audit.

In our opinion, the financial statements referred to above present justly, the financial position of X Company as of December 31, 20XX, conforms to the accounting principles generally accepted in the United States of America. Also, in our opinion, the Firm maintained effective internal control over financial reporting as of December 31, 20XX.

The effectiveness of an internal audit function can be measured among others through follow-up monitoring of management actions following recommendations. An audit finding is the outcome of assessing audit evidence, comparing it to audit criteria, and determining areas for improvement, which is then recommended. An audit report typically includes management actions, along with an owner and a deadline, that are based on recommendations. Audit results are frequently classified as High, Medium, or Low risk. The internal audit function must set up a follow-up procedure as part of the audit cycle to keep an eye on the problems found in the audit engagements and the suggestions made to address these conclusions. The follow-up monitoring procedure generally concentrates on findings with a high and medium risk. For banks, supervisory findings and related actions are crucial. In this particular context, it might be deemed appropriate to incorporate these into the routine follow-up monitoring process of the Internal Audit Function, not only for the recommendations made by the ECB but also for those made by other local supervisors. Last but not least, this paper may also be applicable to other external agents—the most important being the external auditors—who offer advice or best practices regarding internal control issues. In certain banks, the second line of defense handles action monitoring in response to concerns brought up by external agents or supervisors. The Internal Audit function should review implementation as part of the audit engagement to assess the control environment and, additionally, as part of the risk assessment, if it is not carrying out this portion of the follow-up monitoring.

To enable follow-up monitoring, audit findings need to be translated into smart management actions, completed until a specified due date by the respective action owner. The internal auditor needs to review the risk acceptance. The results of the internal audit could be translated either directly into action plans for management that the internal audit function should review, or they could be translated into a consensus document that would be called a "recommendation.". In audit engagements, the actions schedule is a crucial component. Actually, keeping an eye on management's actions reveals a lot about their awareness of risk and risk-taking culture, in addition to other aspects of the issues brought up by the internal audit function. The action owners' formal acceptance of the management actions (or recommendations) with a signature or other equivalent process should be the first step in an adequate monitoring process for the internal audit function's management actions. Next, the action owners' action plan to address any weaknesses found should be reviewed. The approved action plan may, if practical, already be included in the specific audit report. In light of the institution's size and complexity as well as the type and quantity of recommendations provided, the follow-up monitoring procedure ought to be automated to the greatest extent feasible. Establishing an effective monitoring process, accurate reporting, and evidence recording could be facilitated by the implementation of an automated tracking system to which all relevant parties have access. Should senior management accept a finding as risk, the internal audit function will discuss the risk acceptance process and procedure with them. The issue will be brought before the board if they cannot agree.

Management actions reported 'Closed' should be validated by the Internal audit function. A regular monitoring process needs to be established by the internal audit function. Depending on the kind of finding, recommendation, or action (taking importance, impact, etc. into consideration), the intensity of this process could change in accordance with a risk-based approach.). As often as possible, the action plans' implementation status must be updated in accordance with this procedure. The action plan and the conclusion of the findings ought to adhere to a formal procedure. Periodic monitoring or a separate engagement could be used to validate the correct closure of actions. This validation often occurs during the next complete audit engagement, depending on the circumstances and the intricacy of the testing that needs to be done. The internal audit function will appropriately validate this closure by filing evidence if the auditee reports a management action as completed and wishes to close the issue. In certain situations, audit testing for follow-up at a later time is required to guarantee the sustainability of the audit recommendations. The kind of improvement made should be reflected in the audit procedures needed to validate a closed management action. While sufficient testing must be carried out to verify a control's effectiveness, a test-of-one may be suitable for enhancing the control's design. In the event of a highly negative audit rating or significant improvements, independent follow-up audit engagements will be taken into consideration.

The results of follow-up monitoring need to be reported to senior management and the board. The recommendations from the internal audit function that have not been put into practice should be highlighted in this report. The board, the Audit Committee, and senior management must be informed of the results of follow-up monitoring of at least High and Medium risk audit findings through a reporting procedure established by the internal audit function. This report serves to inform the governance bodies on a regular basis of all the major issues that the internal audit function has identified and that have not been sufficiently resolved within the specified time frame. This allows the governance bodies to make decisions about the best course of action. In the event that there is insufficient progress, the reporting format must allow the board, the Audit Committee, and senior management to act appropriately and promptly. Either the internal audit function or the risk function may be responsible for reporting to senior management and the board on the state of the implementation of actions brought forward by supervisors. Follow-up monitoring reports ought to include an overview of the key findings and a synopsis of them. In addition, it ought to provide information at the recommendation level when required and be sufficiently detailed otherwise. There are various methods for completing this reporting, which typically includes both quantitative and qualitative data:

1. **Quantitatively:** Regular progress reporting that provides totaled and comprehensive data, counts and

proportions of open and concluded management actions, details on ageing (the time interval between approving a management action and monitoring it), and information on past-due management actions and recommendations.

2. **Qualitatively:** Overall progress on all closed and pending actions, emphasizing key problems or areas of concern and offering comprehensive details on the actions taken, the state of progress, and any delays that may have occurred.

When evaluating senior management's awareness and risk culture, it is ideal to take their advancement into consideration. Even though the first line of defense is in charge of putting the required controls in place and taking mitigation measures, a poor degree of implementation may point to a weak internal audit function. It might suggest, for instance, that the function lacks organizational independence, that the reporting and escalation protocols are insufficient, that the monitoring procedures are deficient, etc.

ROLE MODEL

CHARLES WALDO HASKINS

Charles Waldo Haskins (January 11, 1852 – January 9, 1903) was an American accountant, and co-founder of the accounting firm Haskins and Sells, a predecessor to Deloitte.

"He was born in 1852 into a leading American family (including uncle Ralph Waldo Emerson)."

Haskins was educated at the Brooklyn Polytechnic Institute, from where he earned a degree in civil engineering, and subsequently completed his studies in Paris. His wife, Henrietta Havemeyer, whom he married in 1885, was from a family even wealthier than his own - the Havemeyer family of New York. Her uncle was three times Mayor of New York, and her grandfather controlled the American Sugar Refining Company ("Domino"). Descended from John Howland, a signer of the Mayflower Compact, Haskins was a New York Member of Sons of Liberty and other local societies along with the local branch of the (Presidents) Adams family (with whom he was also related).

Haskins advocated unified and reliable accounting principles, lecturing widely on history and methods. He was known to describe the public accountant as "the consulting physician of finance and commerce." Haskins stated that the public accountant "understands the anatomy and physiology of business and the rules of health of corporations, partnerships, and individual enterprises. He diagnoses abnormal conditions and suggests approved remedies. His study and interest is the soundness of the world of affairs."

Haskins was heavily involved in codifying qualifications and created the legislation and bodies that defined the first Certified Public Accountant qualifications in the nation for New York State, which were later emulated throughout the US. Haskins served as president of the New York State Society of CPAs and the American Society for CPAs. In 1900, Haskins founded the earliest professional school of business, The School of Commerce, Accounts, and Finance of New York University, and the first university accounting program in America. Haskins was the first dean of the school, a post he held until his death in 1903.[5 An obituary in a leading New York newspaper alluded to his character, accomplishments and circumstances:

"Mr. Haskins occupied a position singular and unique in relation to his fellows in the profession; removed from all the petty jealousies engendered by the battle for a livelihood; possessing means more than ample for the requirements of himself and his personal family, he gave freely in time, money, and influence to every movement designed to place the certified public accountant on a par in the eyes of the world with the professions of law and of medicine."

SUMMARY

- An audit report is a written opinion of an auditor regarding an entity's financial statements. The report is written in a standard format, as mandated by generally accepted auditing standards (GAAS).
- Audit report is the report that contain the audit's opinion which is issued by independence auditors after their examination on the entity's financial statements and related reports.
- The title should include the phrase "Auditor's Report." This is intended to remind the reader of the credibility an audit adds to the financial statements because of the auditor's independence.
- The opening paragraph of the report identifies the financial statements that are audited and states that management is responsible for them. The auditor's responsibility is to give an opinion on those statements based on the result of the audit.
- The opinion paragraph of the auditor's report – usually the third, and final, paragraph – states the auditor's conclusions reached from the work performed.
- The report may be addressed to the client company itself or to its board of directors or shareholders. The auditors have a responsibility to the owners of a business enterprise and therefore the report should be addressed to the members of the company (normally the shareholders), partners or proprietors.
- An audit report with an Unmodified Opinion is also known as a 'Clean Report'. An Unmodified report develops confidence among users of financial statements and annual reports of an enterprise.
- A Disclaimer of Opinion is to be issued by an auditor in cases where the auditor concludes that he / she is not able to obtain sufficient and appropriate evidences.
- Unqualified Audit Report issued by auditor to financial statements when auditor found no material misstatements after their testing. This report contain the unqualified opinion from an independence auditor. The report shown that the entity financial statements are prepared and present true and fair and complying with accounting framework being used.
- Adverse Audit Report is type of audit report that issued to the financial statements when auditors found that there are material misstatements in the financial statements. The misstatements found here are different from the material misstatements found qualified audit report.
- A subsequent event is an event that occurs after a reporting period, but before the financial statements for that period have been issued or are available to be issued. Depending on the situation, such events may or may not require disclosure in an organization's financial statements.

REVIEW QUESTIONS

1. What is audit report?
2. Discuss the contents of an audit report.
3. What is opinion in an audit report?
4. Discuss the types of audit report.
5. How to write an audit report?

REFERENCES

1. Ganesh, M. P., Vijaya, S., & Grace, M. C. (2005). Audit Committee Reports Before and After Sarbanes-Oxley: A Study of Companies Listed on the NYSE. *The CPA Journal, 75*(10), 42–44.
2. Hoffelder, K. (2012). New audit standard encourages more talking. *CFO Magazine*.
3. Messier, W., & Emby, C. (2005). *Auditing & Assurance Services: A Systematic Approach*. McGraw-Hill Ryerson Limited.
4. Public Company Accounting Oversight Board (PCAOB). (2013). *Auditing Standard No. 16: Communications with Audit Committees*.

CHAPTER

5

Internal Audit

LEARNING OBJECTIVES

After studying this chapter, you will be able to:

- Define the fundamentals of internal auditing;
- Discuss on numerous types of internal auditing; and
- Access the approaches of internal audit.

KEY TERMS FROM THIS CHAPTER

Accounting system

Bank reconciliation

Physical inventory

Auditor

Internal control

Risk management

INTRODUCTION

Internal auditing is the phenomenon that occurs when a department or organization is assigned the responsibility of impartially and independently reviewing both the processes and the system. Internal auditing is carried out directly within an organization while keeping company standards in mind. There are those who mistake it for statutory audits, which are not the same as internal audits. The process of organizing, leading, and carrying out internal audits—which are thorough, impartial assessments of a company's policies, practices, procedures, and accounting controls—is known as internal audit management. Assuring that a company is successfully managing its risks and operations, as well as assessing the suitability and efficacy of its risk management, control, and governance procedures, are the main objectives of internal auditing. Internal auditing is an objective process that adds value and enhances an organization's operations. By employing a methodical approach, it assists organizations in achieving their goals. It also examines how well governance and risk management are working. The internal audit function needs to be in constant adjustment to the shifting demands of the business environment and the organization itself. It also needs to be in line with the organization's strategic goals and the risks it faces. The Internally Generated Report, or IGR for short, was its previous name.

5.1. FUNDAMENTALS OF INTERNAL AUDITING

Internal auditing is a free-standing, impartial assurance and consulting practice that aims to enhance an organization's performance. By bringing a methodical, disciplined approach to assess and enhance the efficacy of risk management, control, and governance processes, it aids an organization in achieving its goals. Internal auditing provides insight and recommendations based on analyses and assessments of data and business processes, which act as a catalyst for improving an organization's governance, risk management, and management controls. Internal auditing adds value to governing bodies and senior management by being an unbiased, independent source of advice, all while upholding integrity and accountability.

Internal auditing is defined as "the independent appraisal activity within an organization for the review of the accounting, financial, and other operation as a basis for protective and constructive service to the management" by the Institute of Internal Auditors. It's a control mechanism that works by gauging and assessing how well other control mechanisms are working. Although its primary focus is on accounting and finance, it can also appropriately handle operational issues. "

Here are various definitions of Internal Auditing prevailing, which can be stated as follows:

1. Internal Audit is a management tool, performed by employees of the organization to ensure correctness in accounting data and to detect fraud by way of periodical review of organizational system and procedures.
2. Internal auditing is the ongoing, methodical process by which staff members or outside organizations designated specifically for this purpose investigate, report on, and analyze an organization's records and operations. Essentially, it is management auditing, and the extent of the audit varies based on the type and scale of the business.
3. It is a control system concerned with examination and appraisal of other control mechanisms.
4. Internal Audit is an extension of and as such is complimentary to statutory audit.

To put it briefly, internal auditing is the evaluation of a company's performance and control methods. An internal audit is an assessment carried out by an internal auditor chosen by the company's management with the goal of identifying the weak points within the organizations. It involves looking at and assessing different organizational activities as well as providing support to the management team so they can carry out their duties effectively and efficiently. When they do not jeopardize their independence, internal auditors serve as experts in various teams, particularly development teams, and as partners with other organizational components. To fulfill the following requirements, the internal auditor audits the accounts and other pertinent records every day, every week, or every period.

- To find out whether the business has adhered to all laws, rules, policies, procedures, and ideals, an internal audit may be carried out.
- To determine whether the current internal control system is appropriate for the size of the company and sufficient in terms of effectiveness.
- To make sure that all of the organization's assets are adequately protected; if not, he informs management of the issue and offers recommendations.
- To identify the organization's weak points and offer suggestions for improving them.
- To determine whether the organization is operating smoothly, effectively, economically, and efficiently.

5.1.1. Necessity of Internal Audit to Management

By providing assurance services for its internal customers regarding governance, control, and risk management procedures, internal auditing helps the organization's management carry out its guiding and monitoring responsibilities in an effective and efficient manner. By providing objective, independent information, improvement recommendations, and training supervisors and staff in the use and comprehension of monitoring procedures and self-evaluation of business and other organizational activities, internal auditing adds value and helps the organization achieve its objectives. Internal auditing establishes and carries out its own goals while incorporating the organization's values, which also serve as a guide for the auditors' work. For the following reasons, internal auditing has grown in importance as a management tool:

- An expert service to examine the standards of operational efficiency in business is internal auditing.
- In terms of overall management control, internal auditing is capable of independently evaluating a variety of issues and making improvement recommendations.
- Independent evaluation and review by Internal Audit can guarantee the accuracy and timeliness of MIS and management reporting, which is the foundation for decisive actions by upper management.
- An organization's internal audit system ensures the effectiveness of its internal control systems, including its accounting control systems.
- Internal Audit performs evaluation and review from an impartial perspective to guarantee the sufficiency, dependability, and accuracy of financial and operational data.
- Internal auditing has the ability to overcome personality traits, power ego, and potential conflicts of interest within the company.
- It guarantees adherence to accounting policies and procedures.
- An internal auditor can be a great help to management when it comes to bringing in new clients, promoting new goods, and starting new initiatives for business growth or diversification.

5.1.2. Objectivity of the Internal Auditor

Every internal auditor should have a goal-oriented mindset and be sufficiently independent to exercise discretion, voice opinions, and make recommendations in an unbiased manner.

- Despite being employed by the company, the internal auditor should not have any conflicts of interest stemming from business or personal connections, financial stakes, or any other type of interest in a company or activity that is being audited.
- The internal auditor must be free from unjustified influences that would limit or alter the scope or manner in which he performs his duties, or that would override or materially impair his judgment regarding the contents of the internal audit report.
- When auditing an activity over which he has authority or responsibility, the internal auditor should not permit his objectivity to be compromised.
- When major modifications to the internal control system are being considered, as well as when new systems are being implemented, it is advisable to consult an internal auditor who can offer advice on the appropriate control standards.
- This need not compromise the auditor's objectivity when they subsequently review those systems. In general, an internal auditor shouldn't perform non-audit tasks; however, in the rare event that he does, he should make sure management is aware that he is not acting in that capacity.

An internal audit's primary goal is to provide unbiased information to higher management, governmental agencies, etc. These objective data cover a wide range of topics, such as environmental control, organizational risk, and much more. Each person who attends the internal audit is referred to as an internal auditor, and they are all sent by their respective organizations.

a. **Appropriate Control:** One of the primary goals of an internal audit is to maintain appropriate control over the organization. The management requires appropriate assurance that the firm's efficiency and the veracity of its financial records are maintained. The Internal Audit assists in determining both. Ideal

b. **Accounting System:** An internal audit thoroughly examines the organization's accounting system. Vouchers, transaction authority, and mathematical accuracy are all areas where internal auditing is useful. Every entry is checked to lower the possibility of errors or frauds.

c. **Review of Business:** An internal audit is responsible for examining a company's financial and operational aspects. The Internal Audit procedure examines the business's errors, strengths, and weaknesses. Asset protection is achieved through the internal audit process, which verifies and values an asset. Internal Audit specifically audits the authorization in the event of any unusual transactions, such as the purchase, sale, or revaluation of assets.

d. **Keep an Eye Out for Errors:** At the conclusion of a fiscal year, financial records are reviewed for errors. Internal auditing, however, allows errors to be found and fixed right away. Fraud detection is one of internal audit's other primary goals. In actuality, internal audit benefits the company because it makes employees less likely to engage in fraudulent activity. There won't be any time to commit fraud and the Internal Audit procedure will operate smoothly, which will reduce the amount of fraud that occurs within an organization.

5.1.3. Scope of Internal Auditing

The potential for internal auditing now encompasses broader ideas of community governance, such as power and risk, acknowledging that organizations are essentially structured to manage risk and promote beneficial governance. The biggest difference is that internal auditors are thought to shift from being faultfinders to advisors. The Auditee is the customer that internal auditors should look out for. Similar to working with a client, the internal auditor (Wood, 2012) should clearly communicate with the auditee, involve management in the process of developing the audit, take into account organizational risks that could potentially cause audit anxiety, collaborate with managers to identify appropriate solutions, have a discussion of the findings prior to formally reporting, and solicit feedback from the auditee for the improvement of audit practice. Some companies that conduct extensive internal audits are currently using internal audit as a training ground for aspiring managers because it offers an overview of the entire company. With a body of knowledge, professional credentials, code of ethics, independent career advancement, and a quality control system, internal auditing has emerged as a distinct profession. A significant portion of the advancements in internal auditing have happened in the private industry. But the public sector has also begun to recognize the significance of this role. There have been multiple waves of thought in the public sector. The development of the decolonized nations and the reconstruction of the economies destroyed by the Second World War quickly took precedence. Planning, import substitution, and a fixed exchange rate excited everyone. When the theory began to exhibit limitations, it functioned well for a few years. Global nationalizations have become widespread due to the challenges posed by socialism and concerns surrounding the Cold War. The Government began to swell in size. The public sector grew significantly in size. The realization that the public sector needs to operate in an environment of economy, efficiency, and effectiveness resulted from this. Value-for-money and performance measurement requirements gained traction. These worries about the efficacy and efficiency of the public sector remained persistent and were largely unaddressed until a global wave of privatization swept the globe, even though there was some dissatisfaction with the frameworks for value for money auditing and performance measurement that governments had put in place. Demands for appropriate regulation of the recently formed privatized enterprises arose as a result of the privatization. This was accompanied by a plethora of concerns from a far wider and more powerful range of stakeholders regarding good governance, transparency, and accountability of the public sector.

"The examination and evaluation of the adequacy and effectiveness of the organization's system of internal control and the quality of actual performance" is how the Institute of Internal Auditors defines the scope of internal auditing. Thus, the assessment of internal control and the caliber of actual performance are the two main focuses of internal auditing. One of the management's control tools is internal auditing, which works to support the entire organization by assessing the effectiveness and sufficiency of risk management, governance procedures, quality of operations, and internal control. The organization receives information, advice, recommendations, evaluations, and analyses from the internal audit. The goal is to determine whether the internal control system works effectively enough for management to be reasonably confident that the goals and objectives will be met, that operations are efficient, that reporting is trustworthy, that assets are protected, and that laws and regulations are followed. This is done by also considering the information provided by external auditors. The five operational areas that make up internal audit, as defined by The Institute of Internal Auditors, are as follows.

1. **Reliability and Integrity of Financial and Operating Information:** Internal Auditors should review the reliability and integrity of financial and operating information and the means used to identify, measure, classify and report such information.
2. **Economical and Efficient Use of Resources:** Internal Auditor should ensure the economic and efficient use of resources available.
3. **Compliance with Laws, Policies, Plans, Procedures, and Regulations:** Internal Auditor should review the systems established to ensure compliance with those policies, plans and procedures, law and regulations which could have a significant impact on operations and should determine whether the organization is in compliance thereof.
4. **Accomplishment of Established Goals for Operations:** Internal Auditor should review operations, programs to ascertain whether results are consistent with established objectives and goals and whether the operations or programs are being carried out as planned.
5. **Safeguarding of Assets:** Internal Auditor should verify the existence of assets and should review means of safeguarding assets. The business transactions of an organization may be broadly divided into phases.

5.1.4. Internal Auditing Process

Internal auditors usually carry out a wide range of duties to accomplish this goal, such as reviewing financial statements, expense reports, inventory, financial data, budgeting and accounting procedures, and developing risk assessments for every department. In order to identify potentially harmful errors or falsehoods and identify ways to increase productivity, thorough notes are taken, employee interviews are carried out, work schedules are monitored, physical assets are confirmed, and financial statements are carefully examined. Following the completion of the investigation by an internal auditor, the results are submitted in a formal report. The audit report outlines the procedures followed, the findings, and, if required, recommendations for potential enhancements. It is typically given to the company's senior executives. When recommendations for changes are made, it is typical for an internal auditor (Christ, Marc & David, 2019) to be asked to conduct a follow-up audit in order to assess the effectiveness of the suggested changes' implementation. Effectively run publicly traded companies also conduct internal audits to make sure the business is adhering to all applicable federal, state, and SEC regulations. On the other hand, businesses also need to make sure that their accounting procedures adhere to the generally accepted accounting principles (GAAP).

5.1.5. Principles of Internal Auditing

The basic principles of establishing internal audit in a business concern are:

1. **Independence:** The internal audit department should have an independent status in the organization. The internal auditor must have sufficiently high status in the organization. He may be required to report directly to the board of directors.
2. **Objectives:** The objectives of the internal audit function should be made very clear and unambiguous. The objective should be properly communicated so that internal audit is not viewed as "over the shoulder check" by other departments.
3. **Clarity in Scope:** The scope of internal audit department must be specified in a comprehensive manner. The department must at all times, have authority to investigate from the financial angle, every phase of organizational activity under any circumstance.
4. **Definition of Duties:** The internal audit department's duty is to review operations as part of the internal control system. It should not be involved in performance of executive actions.
5. **Internal Audit Department:** The size and qualification of staff of the internal audit department should be commensurate with the size of the business. The cost of internal audit department should not exceed the benefits expected to be derived from it.
6. **Reporting:** The program of internal audit should be time-bound. There should be provisions for periodic reporting on various operational and other aspects.
7. **Follow-up and Review:** There should be sufficient scope for the follow-up action on the various points raised in internal audit report. Top management should take active part in ensuring compliance with action points raised in the report.
8. **Relationship with Statutory Auditor:** The copy of the internal audit report should be made available to the statutory auditor, who can deal with the same in the manner as he deems fit.

5.1.6. Evaluate an Internal Audit Project

An internal audit is a thorough examination of a business's finances and operating practices. This review may cover an organization's entire division or just one. Auditors will carefully examine the project and compile reviews based on their observations. An internal audit takes a lot of time and money to complete. However, the advantages of a speedy, precise audit will greatly exceed that expense. The process must be evaluated and the reviewers must be examined in order to determine how cost-effective your company's internal auditing procedure is.Check that the auditing agents are kept apart from the other employees. For internal auditors to remain impartial and perform a true audit, they must be kept totally apart from the rest of the workforce. Examine how effective the internal auditing procedure is. Examine both the process's speed and the accuracy of the finished product. Provide suggestions on how to improve speed and accuracy in order to guarantee future audits that are more productive. Examine the audit's entire scope. Whether it is an audit of a single department or the entire organization, an internal audit starts with a defined objective. See how closely the auditors adhered to protocol in order to accomplish the goal by reading over the audit team's notes. Examine each auditing team member's performance individually. Examine each set of notes to determine whether each auditor adhered strictly to the assignment given to him. Examine how well the managing auditor has managed the process and managed her employees. Express your gratitude to her and the auditing team for a job well done, along with suggestions for improvement.

5.1.7. Audit Procedures and Techniques for an Internal Audit

You can assess how well your company's internal control system is working with a semi-annual or annual internal audit. An internal audit looks for evidence of fraud, waste, or abuse at your company as well as weaknesses in internal control, as opposed to an external audit's focus on evaluating whether financial statements follow generally accepted accounting principles. Using internal auditing methods and procedures is crucial to implementing risk management successfully.

1. **Audit Procedures and Goals:** By examining risk-management strategies and operational procedures for flaws and shortcomings, an internal audit assists you in evaluating and enhancing internal business controls at your organization. Assessing current processes and procedures is usually the first step in an audit procedure. Auditors then assess whether audit results adhere to internal policies and procedures as well as federal and state laws and regulations by analyzing and comparing the results against internal control objectives. Finally, auditors put together an audit report that they give to the company owner.
2. **Techniques for Indirect Assessment and Observation:** The goal of assessment is to ensure that your internal auditors are knowledgeable about internal control protocols and have the ability to ascertain whether staff members are adhering to internal control guidelines. By employing an indirect assessment technique to begin the internal audit process, auditors aim to minimize any disruption to the regular workflow. Examining current documentation, such as departmental control policies, manuals, and flowcharts, is one of these. Making audit trails that follow particular procedures from beginning to end is another popular method of assessment. Internal auditors use methods from the second phase, such as one-on-one interviews and process observations, when audit trails or document reviews are unable to adequately address auditor inquiries.
3. **Analysis Methods for Testing Data:** Audits aren't just for identifying systemic shortcomings or unethical behavior. They also assist in locating mistakes or misstatements in the financial

statements of your business. If an internal auditor believes there is a risk to an internal control process, they can use analysis techniques to target specific data or test data at random. Transaction matching, a physical inventory count, audit trail computations, and recalculating previously reconciled financial statements, such as a monthly bank reconciliation, are examples of substantive procedures.

4. **Audit Reporting Procedures:** Your Company's internal auditing process comes to an end with the completion of a final internal audit report. Reporting can include an interim report in the form of a memo or preliminary report, but it always includes a formal report. An interim report often contains results that are important or sensitive that the auditor feels the business owner should know about right away. A final report is more formal and contains recommendations for modifications or enhancements to internal controls and control procedures, as well as an overview of the methods and approaches employed to complete the audit and a description of the audit findings.

5.1.8. Benefits of an Internal Auditor (IA)

Even though it's not required by law, a lot of businesses decide to hire internal auditors. Thorough internal audits are thought to be essential for promptly resolving problems, upholding a positive reputation, and avoiding financial waste. Internal auditors' (IAs') reports can support a business's growth and optimal operation. Because of this, a lot of executives consider them to be an essential expense. Even though it's not required by law, a lot of businesses decide to hire internal auditors. Thorough internal audits are thought to be essential for promptly resolving problems, upholding a positive reputation, and avoiding financial waste. Internal auditors' (IAs') reports can support a business's growth and optimal operation. Additionally, internal auditors prepare the business for success during the yearly external audit. An internal auditor's primary responsibility is to assist in identifying and resolving problems before an external auditor has the opportunity to do so. Because of this, a lot of executives consider them to be an essential expense.

5.1.9. Difference Between Independence, External, and Internal Auditor

Audits are carried out to confirm that a business's procedures and documentation adhere to rules or guidelines. Financial audits are conducted to safeguard the interests of shareholders and the general public, and they are among the most strictly regulated and frequently discussed audit types. Additional audit types evaluate software development procedures, management system procedures, safety and environmental procedures, and a variety of scenarios unique to a given industry. The need for auditor independence is a universal requirement of audit process, regardless of the subject matter being audited. An appeal for objectivity can be found in the idea of auditor independence. An audit's performer shouldn't be connected to the party being audited. There is no chance of bias influencing the audit findings because there is no relationship. Absolute objectivity is hard to achieve in corporate settings because relationships are made when a business hires an internal auditor or enters into an agreement to pay for external or internal audit services. To further encourage auditor objectivity in these circumstances, industry standards, professional ethics policies, and governmental regulations are put in place.

1. **Internal Audit Independence:** Direct hires or contract workers of the business under audit are internal auditors. According to Accounting Tools, their general objectivity may be questioned because they have to satisfy management in order to be paid. The goal of rules to reduce bias is to get rid of conflicts of interest. There is a conflict of interest when an auditor audits something they personally support, which may lead one to doubt the audit's conclusions. Successful internal auditors are unable to conduct audits of the tasks, procedures, departments, or teams that they currently oversee or were previously in charge of.
2. **External Audit Independence:** External auditors are employed by companies that the auditing company has contracted with. These auditors are subject to the same stringent regulations as internal auditors. The regulations forbid external auditors from having any kind of affiliation, including financial ones, with the company they are auditing, unlike internal auditors. The integrity of the audit results may be compromised if the auditor has a conflict of interest stemming from prior employment with the company being audited or from discussions regarding potential employment opportunities with the company.
3. **Consultant Auditors:** Internal auditors are not able to operate in a completely independent manner from the company they are auditing due to their very nature. These auditors are permitted to provide consultative services, which gives managers ideas to enhance how things are done. They also have a tendency to know precisely where to look for mistakes or issues. Offering the company being audited any services other than auditing is strictly forbidden for external auditors; doing so would create a relationship and create a conflict of interest.
4. **Qualifications for Internal and External Auditors:** Internal and external auditors may even attend the same training sessions and are typically trained to look for similar items. Nonetheless, certification procedures will vary. The hiring company will decide what credentials and certifications an internal auditor needs. A regulatory board sets requirements for the credentials and qualifications of an external auditor.

5.2. INTERNAL AUDITING TYPES

The management of an organization established internal audit as a self-governing assessment function to review the internal control system as a service to the organization. Internal audits assess a company's internal controls, including its corporate governance and accounting procedures. They also look into, assess, and report on the adequacy of internal control as it relates to the proper, economical, and successful use of resources. These audits support accurate and timely financial reporting and data collection, as well as compliance with laws and regulations. Businesses employ internal auditors to perform tasks on behalf of their management teams. By finding issues and fixing mistakes before they are found in an external audit, these audits also give management the resources they need to achieve operational efficiency. Given that managers are now legally liable for the accuracy of their company's financial statements under the Sarbanes-Oxley Act of 2002, internal audits are essential to a business' operations and corporate governance. In addition, SOX mandated that an organization's external audit include a documentation and review of its internal controls. Internal audits not only guarantee that a business abides by rules and regulations but also offer some risk management and protection against possible fraud, waste, or abuse. The outcomes of internal audits offer management recommendations for enhancing existing procedures that aren't operating as planned. These procedures may include supply-chain management and information technology systems. Internal audits can occur every day, every week, every month, or every year. Audits may occur more frequently in some departments than in others. For quality control, a manufacturing process might undergo daily audits, but the human resources department might only undergo annual audits.

5.2.1. System Based Audit

It alludes to a thorough analysis of the internal control framework with the aim of determining how well the controls are operating. Its purpose is to evaluate the completeness and correctness of financial statements, the economy, efficiency, and efficacy of operations, as well as the legitimacy and regularity of the underlying transactions. Following a systems-based audit, several transactions, account balances, etc., should be substantively tested to ascertain whether the auditee's financial statements are complete and accurate, the underlying transactions are lawful and regular, and/or the effectiveness, efficiency, and economy requirements have been met. An audit strategy that pertains to a client's internal controls is known as a system-based audit strategy. Using this audit methodology, auditors carry out the audit using the internal control systems of the client. The auditors must prove that the client's internal control systems are adequate and suitable in order for that to be feasible. In contrast to the substantive procedures audit approach, this method approaches audits in a different way. The internal control systems of a client are the main focus of the system-based audit approach to auditing. Auditors may believe that the client's financial reporting system will be less risky if they can rely on those systems. That does not, however, mean that the system-based audit approach will not necessitate work in addition to internal control system testing.

- **Work:** When using a system-based audit approach, auditors first examine the internal control systems of their clients. The basic control systems and operational procedures of the client must be understood by the auditors. Above all, they need to evaluate the financial reporting-related internal controls. The effectiveness of these internal controls in stopping, identifying, and fixing misstatements must be evaluated by auditors. The test of controls is the main process auditor's use in system-based audits. Auditors evaluate two facets of the client's internal controls using this process. The first concerns whether controls are in place where they ought to be. The effectiveness of those controls in producing the desired results is the second question. Auditors may apply the system-based approach if they determine that the client's internal control systems are effective. Nevertheless, auditors are unable to carry out a system-based audit if those systems are insufficient or inefficient. However, that does not mean that the work that auditors do using this method is over. Auditors must still test other areas even though system-based audits concentrate on internal controls. However, in comparison to other audit techniques, the testing threshold might be more lax. The preliminary results of the evaluation of the internal controls assist auditors in determining the extent of substantive testing that is required. The number of substantive tests conducted will decrease with the level of confidence auditors can place in the client's internal control systems.
- **How the Information System Audit is Different from Financial Audit?** While information system audit is primarily concerned with data security, the efficacy of IT infrastructure, and the design of the system's internal control, financial audit aims to determine whether the financial statements present a true and fair view of the business financial position and are free of any material errors. The System Audit Procedure comprises the subsequent six steps.

i. *Step 1: System Review:* Through observation of installation procedures, staff interviews, and review of installation documentation, the auditor attempts to gain an understanding of the organization's information system in this first step. The auditor looks for any weaknesses in the management control at this point.

ii. *Step 2: Measuring Information System Vulnerability:* In this step, each computer and application is looked at separately to determine which is the most vulnerable. The auditor reviews the quality protocols at this point.

iii. *Step 3: Identification of Potential Threats:* All potential external and internal system threats are identified in this step, including those posed by programmers, system security staff, regular users, software vendors, data entry operators, and others.

iv. *Step 4: Verifying Internal Controls:* In this step, the system auditor assesses how well the internal controls of the information system are performing and verifies that each control is operating correctly. Additionally, the auditor looks for any gaps in internal control systems.

v. *Step 5: Final Evaluations:* The auditor conducts a number of tests to assess each of the information system's component parts in this last and final step of the system audit. These tests consist of verifying data with external sources, comparing computerized and manual data, and ensuring data flow and authorization.

- **Advantages and Disadvantages**: Auditors can benefit from the system-based audit approach in a number of ways. With this method, auditors can work with less work. As a result, it can assist auditors in saving time and concentrating on more important tasks. This method may also highlight issues with the client's accounting reporting setups. The system-based audit approach is not without its limitations, though. Not concentrating on the risks is among the most important of these. The risk-based audit approach is more appropriate for audit engagements that auditors deem risky.

5.2.2. Performance Audit or Operational Audit

An independent evaluation of an organization's operations to ascertain whether particular programs or functions are carrying out as intended to meet predetermined objectives is known as a performance audit. Since most government organizations receive federal funding, performance audits are usually connected to government agencies at all levels. It evaluates the degree to which the program, activity, or body has been managed effectively, efficiently, or economically. It should be evident from the audit objectives—which must be looked at—that a specific performance audit will not necessarily attempt to draw conclusions regarding all three of the aforementioned factors. However, the effectiveness of the audited entity must be taken into general consideration when conducting audits of economy or efficiency. It might be preferable for the entity to do the right thing poorly than the wrong thing well. A performance audit in the public sector looks at a program's efficacy and efficiency with the intention of making changes. The term "program" can refer to government entities, activities, organizations, programs, and functions, as per the Generally Accepted Government Auditing Standards (GAGAS). The U.S. has established guidelines for the audit standards. The Government Accountability Office (GAO)'s main goal is to offer unbiased data that can be utilized to cut expenses and make other improvements. An audit's specific goals may differ. These could include a program's efficacy, economy, and efficiency as well as adherence to legal requirements. The breadth of an audit's purview allows it to identify fraud and inefficient procedures that undermine a program's declared goals. The GAO lays out three categories of standards for the performance audit: general, field, and reporting.

a. **General Standards:** These standards address topics like professional judgment, quality control (QC), and the auditor's and the audit process's competency. The general standards aim to guarantee the auditor's competence, independence, and compliance with internal quality controls.

b. **Field Standards:** Planning, obtaining information for assessment, and creating high-quality documentation are all covered by field standards. This topic aims to delineate the goals, their rationale, and the approach that will be taken to achieve them.

c. **Reporting Standards:** Reporting standards deal with the information contained in the report and how the results are presented. These address the audit report's format and specify who should receive the report and how.

- **Purpose:** Performance and operational audits are types of engagements that offer assurance by comparing specified criteria, like defined business practices, requirements, or measurements, with adequate and appropriate evidence. In order to help management and those in charge of governance and oversight make better decisions, lower costs, enhance program performance and operations, and promote public accountability, performance audits offer objective analysis. The goals of a performance audit can be very different and can include compliance, internal control, program efficacy, economy, and efficiency evaluations, as well as prospective analysis. In these categories, some examples of audit objectives are as follows.

Evaluating whether the audited entity is adhering to sound procurement practices; Assessing whether incurred or proposed costs are in compliance with applicable laws, regulations, contracts or grant agreements; Evaluate whether the program's purpose, the manner in which it is to be conducted, the services delivered, the outcomes, or the population it serves are in compliance with laws, regulations, contract provisions, grant agreements, and other requirements. Estimating the extent to which legislative, regulatory, or organizational goals and objectives are being achieved.

- **Benefits of Performance Audits:** After a performance audit is finished, the management of the particular program or organization receives the results. Their intention is to apply the results to enhance procedures in a way that will enable them to meet their objectives. To determine whether management has adopted any of the audit findings and whether there has been any improvement as a result, a follow-up performance audit is usually conducted. An essential function of performance audits is to promote government accountability. Governmental organizations are held to objective standards for carrying out the duties that they are legally required and authorized to carry out through performance audits. Overseeing the appropriate, lawful, and economical operation of public services and programs, higher-level appointed staff members and elected officials examine the audit findings. The results' release enables the general public to determine whether particular programs are worthy of their tax dollars and to use that knowledge to cast informed ballots.

5.2.3. Financial or Accounting Audit

It assesses how accurate accounting is as well as associated processes and behaviors. It evaluates whether the transactions supporting the financial statements are lawful and regular, as well as the completeness and accuracy of the financial statements of the activity, program, or body under audit. Nonetheless, internal auditors are primarily responsible for assessing the internal control system, per the definition of internal auditing. Thus, the controls that guarantee the accuracy of accounting data and financial reporting are of greater importance to internal auditors than accounting itself. The process of examining a company's financial records to make sure there hasn't been any fraud, misrepresentation, or financial mismanagement is known as financial auditing. It is also required to submit audited reports to specific authorities and organizations. An audit is the examination and confirmation of the financial statements and documentation of a business by an auditor. The company's records and statements are checked by the auditor to make sure they accurately and fairly depict the business's financial condition and transactions. The accounts are also examined to determine whether they conform to recognized accounting standards and whether any errors or unethical practices were made in the computation and preparation of the financial statements.

An audit verifies the efficacy of the company's internal controls in addition to the financial records and statements. An audit looks at the accounting procedures and suggests ways to make them more efficient. It offers a professional assessment on the possibility of process improvement. Typically, management or the board of directors chooses auditors. They are chosen to be individuals who have no affiliation with the company or its accounting procedure. This guarantees impartial and objective evaluations of the company's financial statements, controls, and accounting system. You can feel secure knowing that the financial statements that are provided to the company's owners, shareholders, and investors are accurate. An audit also verifies that the financial accounting procedures being used comply with company policies and recognized accounting standards. This prevents the financial statements from being manipulated by employing incorrect accounting procedures and calculation techniques. An extensive, in-depth analysis of a business's financial statements and accounts is called a financial audit. The audit is carried out by an unbiased third-party auditor, who bases his audit opinion on the most recent financial statements. This data aids in directing controls and decision-making.

There are many reasons a company conducts financial audits

- To ensure the accuracy of the books and financial statements
- For regulatory compliance with state or federal financial laws
- To demonstrate accurate financial statements for lenders or investors
- To improve the company's internal controls and accounting processes

A financial audit looks at all historical data regarding operations: financial statements, books of accounts, invoice processing, and more. A skilled auditor or certified public accountant (CPA) uses these sources to ensure a company's statements about its financial position are reliable.

- **Reviewed During a Financial Audit:** A financial audit considers every aspect of your financial process and documentation. During a typical audit, expect your auditor to review several pieces of financial information to render an independent opinion.
- **Account Balances and Transactions:** Documentation of the account balances and transaction history for each account covering the duration of the review period
- **Historical Documents:** Documents about the company's founding, such as articles of incorporation and bylaws
- **IRS Documentation:** IRS communications and documents, such as exemption letters and returns
- **Internal Documents:** Policies and procedures documentation, such as financial reporting processes, personnel handbooks, accounting procedures, and security documents
- **Commitments:** Financial commitments, such as loans, lease agreements, employee benefits, and other liabilities the company must pay
- **Financial Statements:** Previous cash flow statements, balance sheets, and income statements that provide context for the other financial reporting activities within the organization
- **Benefits of a Financial Audit:** A financial audit provides various internal and external benefits to companies, financial planning professionals, investors, and lenders.
- **Error Detection:** An audit compares known financial data (such as trial balances, previous year totals, and other sources of verified data) to find discrepancies and problems in order to determine the financial accuracy of the books. Unusual data or trends may be revealed by the error detection process.
- **Fraud Deterrent:** Your auditor may look over internal controls like dual control and the segregation of duties while conducting the audit. They might check for adjustments to accounting estimates or erroneous payment requests. A forensic audit looks into the potential for fraud and looks for patterns and data that may indicate wrongdoing.
- **Cost Reduction:** Audits take an in-depth look at the organization's financial performance. They help identify areas for improvement, streamlining, and cost-cutting.
- **Resource Allocation:** A financial audit helps leaders decide how to spend available capital. It may reveal areas of over- or under-spending that help align allocation with organizational goals.
- **External Reporting:** Reassurances regarding the company's sound financial management practices are necessary for investors and lending institutions. A financial audit's reporting aids businesses in showcasing their financial procedures and capacity for repayment.
- **Preparing for a Financial Audit:** An audit requires planning and

preparation, but with enough time and thought ahead of time, the process can go smoothly and provide useful information. To cut down on friction during the research and reporting process, start your audit planning with these three fundamental steps. Find the relevant financial data and gather all the documentation needed for the audit's review period. Incorporate trial balance information, the book of accounts, the general ledger, financial statements, IRS paperwork, and accounting supporting documentation. Gather internal documentation: Assemble internal documents, such as department manuals, handbooks, accounting standards of practice (SOPs), and bylaws, or process guidelines. Communicate with internal and external stakeholders: To foster openness and collaboration in the audit process, talk about pertinent data and dates with the finance team, accounting team members, external auditors, and others. Issues and discrepancies should be discussed in advance in order to be addressed and settled quickly.

5.2.4. Compliance Audit

It assesses the degree to which the organization complies with pertinent laws, rules, policies, plans, procedures, and contracts. Since the auditor measures the performance of the organization using laws, policies, and regulations as a yardstick, compliance is typically included in all audits. As a result, there is no separate section on compliance audit in these guidelines; instead, the topic is covered in all audit instructions that follow. An extensive examination of an organization's adherence to legal requirements is called a compliance audit. Over the course of a compliance audit, audit reports assess the rigor and completeness of security policies, user access controls, risk management procedures, and compliance preparations. Depending on an organization's status as a public or private business, the kinds of data it manages, and whether it transfers or retains sensitive financial data, different aspects of the audit are scrutinized.

- Examples of Compliance Audits
- A Sarbanes-Oxley Act compliance audit would have to prove that any electronic communication is backed up and secured with a reasonable disaster recovery infrastructure.
- Healthcare providers that store or transmit e-health records, including personal health information, are subject to HIPAA, or Health Insurance Portability and Accountability Act, laws and regulations.
- Financial services companies that transmit credit card data are subject to Payment Card Industry Data Security Standard requirements.

In each case, organizations must demonstrate compliance by producing an audit trail, often generated with data from event log management software as well as internal and external audits.

- **Internal Compliance Audits vs. External Compliance Audits:** Employees of a company perform internal compliance audits to assess overall risks to security and compliance and to ascertain whether the organization is adhering to internal policies. Throughout the fiscal year, internal audits take place, and management teams utilize the reports they receive to pinpoint areas in need of development. Internal audits compare the goals of the organization to output and strategic risks. Formal audits carried out by impartial outside parties are known as external compliance audits. They adhere to a particular format that is specified by the compliance regulation that is being evaluated. Reports from external audits assess whether a company is adhering to corporate, state, or federal laws, policies, and guidelines. Regulators use an auditor's report to determine potential fines for noncompliance, and the C-suite uses it to demonstrate regulatory compliance. Internal audits can be used by an external compliance auditor to assess compliance and regulatory risk management initiatives more thoroughly.

- **Overview of an External Compliance Audit:** Meetings between company representatives and compliance auditors to discuss compliance checklists, policies, and the audit's parameters precede external compliance audits. The auditor reviews staff performance, examines internal controls, evaluates documentation, and verifies departmental compliance. Members of the C-suite and IT administrators are typically subjected to a series of targeted questions by compliance auditors. These may include what users were added and when, who has left the company, whether user IDs have been revoked, and which IT administrators have access to vital systems. By tracking and documenting authentication and controls in their IT systems, IT administrators can use event log managers and powerful change management software to get ready for compliance audits. The expanding market for governance, risk, and compliance software can assist CIOs in demonstrating to auditors that a company complies with regulations in a timely manner and in avoiding expensive fines or penalties. After that, auditors produce a final audit report after reviewing all business compliance procedures. Compliance auditors furnish business executives with information regarding the organization's degree of compliance adherence, any infractions, and recommendations for enhancement. Eventually, they release the audit report to the public.
- **Importance of Compliance Auditing:** An organization can find areas for improvement and identify flaws in its regulatory compliance procedures with the aid of compliance auditing, whether internal or external. In certain situations, the advice given by a compliance audit can lower risk and lessen the possibility of legal issues or federal fines for noncompliance. Similar to the laws that govern them, compliance programs are always changing as new regulations are introduced and old ones are revised. An outline of internal business processes that can be modified or enhanced when rules and specifications change is provided by compliance auditing.

5.3. TACTICS OF INTERNAL AUDIT

According to the Institute of Internal Auditors, an internal audit assists a business in making sure it has the right controls, governance, and risk management procedures in place. It is by definition an independent task carried out by an individual or group that is qualified to offer unbiased results and suggest remedial actions. A strong internal auditing program can reduce expenses for your business by rapidly identifying and fixing flaws. Internal auditors are responsible for a broader range of tasks and are subject to different reporting requirements than external auditors, who are primarily focused on financial risk.

- **Evaluate Internal Controls:** Companies implement controls as a way to manage risk and make it more likely that everyone is working toward the same goals and objectives. Internal auditors assess controls related to financial compliance, data and information security, and operational efficiency. These controls can be detective in nature, looking for errors or irregularities after the fact, or preventive in nature, intended to stop errors from being introduced. Auditors examine objectively how these controls support the objectives of the organization.
- **Monitor Regulatory Compliance:** Internal audits play a crucial role in corporate governance by assessing how well the organization's policies, procedures, and standards meet its goals and satisfy its stakeholders in a morally and legally compliant way. It usually assumes an advisory capacity, alerting the leadership team to matters pertaining to control. According to the Marquette University Risk Unit, the audit also evaluates adherence to local, state, and federal laws and regulations. Within organizations or sectors that have experienced previous governance problems, internal audits may adopt a more formal oversight role. For instance, if a company has been involved in legal issues due to financial irregularities, this is probably a breach of corporate ethics and calls for an official response from internal audit.
- **Mitigate Risk Factors:** Every business faces risks, and internal auditors concentrate on problems that might keep the organization from achieving its goals. An organization's risk tolerance, risk detection and mitigation strategies, and effective risk communication and monitoring are all examined by internal audit. Providing reassurance that risks have been appropriately defined and assessed is one of its primary purposes. For example, an internal auditor may find that new risks—like the potential disruptive impact of a new technology—aren't being adequately taken into account. The owner or leadership group would be informed of this shortcoming by the auditor.

- **Document Findings:** An internal auditor's primary responsibility in a company is to report findings to the chief risk officer or the chief financial officer. The business owner or management will ultimately decide what to do after reading these reports, even though they might offer suggestions for fixing issues. The goal of internal audits is to find problem areas, fairly report them to management, and provide ownership with the data it needs to decide how best to address shortcomings moving forward.

5.3.1. Internal Audit Compliance

An internal audit department is a division of a corporation that makes sure that internal policies, guidelines, and procedures are sufficient and adhere to industry regulations, standards set by human resources, and recommendations from top management. Significant operational risks are another goal of internal auditors, who also report them to senior managers and see to it that corrective measures are put in place.

- **Purpose:** An internal auditor examines internal controls and procedures within a company to make sure they are sufficient, efficient, and compliant with legal requirements. (Controls are measures implemented by managers of a company to prevent losses resulting from theft, mistakes, or technological malfunctions. Problems with internal control are appropriately resolved by an efficient control. A sufficient control specifies the guidelines that workers must adhere to in order to complete tasks and make choices. Adherence to corporate policies and regulatory requirements are the two levels of compliance that internal auditors concentrate on (Wood, 2009).
- **Function:** An internal auditor is a specialist in finance and accounting with a four-year degree from an accredited business college. A master's or doctorate in auditing or finance is frequently held by an auditor, particularly a senior specialist in the field. A professional certification, such as the Certified Public Accountant (CPA) or Certified Internal Auditor (CIA) designations, is acquired by certain auditors. A compliance-focused audit specialist needs to be proficient in risk management and have strong written, verbal, and graphic communication skills.
- **Types:** Financial, technological, regulatory, and operational audits are the four categories of audits. Generally speaking, an audit is a procedure that verifies compliance by assessing if practices are operating as intended and complying with rules or regulations. An operational audit concentrates on the controls in an organization's day-to-day operations, including human resources programs and payroll processing. A financial audit examines the internal workings of accounting records. A technology audit verifies that software and information systems are operating as intended. A regulatory audit, also referred to as a compliance audit, verifies that staff members follow the law.
- **Expert Insight:** A consultant or a professor from a university may be

hired by an internal audit manager to assess review procedures and offer suggestions for improvement. This usually happens when a section or an area that is being reviewed calls for specialized knowledge or abilities. For instance, to assist in performing compliance tests on the fund's market and credit risk calculation procedures, the audit manager of a mutual fund might engage a scholar with expertise in quantitative finance.

- **Misconceptions:** An internal auditor's position does not call for a professional certification, in contrast to that of an external auditor (e.g., CPA). Internal audit reports are not made available to investors or regulators; instead, they are not made public. Although generally accepted auditing standards (GAAS) must be applied to evaluate processes or controls and an internal auditor must be independent from the area under review, professional rules do not require this specialist to follow the same ethical standards (e.g., preventing conflicts of interest) in the role of an outside auditor.

5.3.2. The Importance of the Internal Audit Function in a Company

If you believe your small business could be making more money and using less resources, an internal audit can help you identify areas where you can cut costs and save time by looking at employees' daily tasks and highlighting areas that could use improvement. Audits also reveal areas of waste in the company, as well as instances of dishonest spending or improper employee transactions. Invest regularly in internal audits as a means of achieving long-term success; the benefits will be realized eventually.

- **Detecting Fraud and Theft:** Employee theft costs small businesses millions of dollars annually. Employee fraud can take many different forms, such as cash theft, check tampering, skimming customer payments, using company credit cards improperly, and improper payroll transactions. You might think that your company doesn't have enough employees to conduct audits or develop internal audit policies to address these issues. Nevertheless, you can still set up a program to keep an eye on employees' work and behavior even with a small team. Declaring that financial transactions will be internally audited could actually deter employees from abusing company resources.
- **Monitoring Internal Controls:** Fraud detection is not the only task involved in a formal internal audit. Regularly reviewing policies and procedures guarantees that your company reduces its vulnerability to fraud and other losses. One such area of loss prevention is the review of credit lines that are extended to customers. Internal audits check for compliance with any credit extension policies you may have developed. Creating a credit policy with the goal of lowering bad debt is useless if it is not implemented.
- **Improving Operational Practices:** Operational audits look at a company's procedures rather than its financials. Is your company running as efficiently as possible?

Inefficient operations raise costs without boosting revenue. An operational audit could identify these inefficiencies or highlight time spent on pointless documentation. Is your company adhering to the relevant regulations? Being aware of your noncompliance with a rule before the government does can help your company stay out of trouble and prevent fines and other legal actions. A quickly growing business must keep an eye on compliance with human resource laws as new hires come on board. Internal audit is essential in examining these operations.

- **Planning Your Internal Audit:** Though it's unlikely that your small business can afford to hire an internal audit department, you can set up a system for monitoring your business and employees with careful planning. You can still get the data you need from this less formal system to enhance your financial and operational controls. Two persons must collaborate in order to complete such an internal audit. By doing this, personality conflicts are avoided and the auditor is kept from just reviewing his own work. It also gives the team members a chance to talk about the outcomes and write an unbiased report for ownership.

5.3.3. Internal Audit and Business Risk

According to conventional definitions, internal auditors are internal accountants who regularly and continuously review financial records and internal controls. The likelihood that a business will suffer losses from operations disruptions brought on by internal issues or external circumstances is known as business risk. The traditional role of internal audit is evolving: there is a push to integrate it as partners with business risk management. Internal audit is seen by supporters as a useful tool for verifying risk managers' assessments in programs designed to reduce business risks.

- In the past, internal auditors have been responsible for ensuring that financial records are accurate, assessing the effectiveness of internal controls, and protecting the company from the one and only risk of fraud. The Risk and Insurance Management Society, Inc. has drawn attention to the growing function that internal auditors play in the realm of business risk. (RIMS) and the Institute of Internal Auditors (IIA) in a collaborative report on articulating internal audit and risk management's mutual roles and responsibilities. According to the report, Cisco Systems, Hospital Corporation of America, TD Ameritrade, and Whirlpool Corporation are among the major corporations that have created their own framework for internal audit participation in risk management.
- One of the main responsibilities of risk managers is to identify business risk. Prioritizing a risk involves determining its likelihood and expected consequences after it has been identified, examined, and evaluated. Risk assessments often weigh the potential cost of mitigating a risk against the potential cost of doing little or nothing to prevent it. For instance, yearly insurance costs could be higher than the equipment's

estimated replacement cost in the event that it is stolen. In these situations, accepting a loss would end up saving money in the long run. Internal auditors can test risk managers' assumptions about costs and business risks, and this can yield valuable insights.

- It is management's ultimate responsibility to manage business risks. Internal auditors are being asked more and more to assist in making sure that internal controls are in place and that significant business risks are being addressed as risks are recognized and managed.
- Ernst and Young list the top ten requirements for internal audit when assessing risks associated with sustainability and climate change. New business risks arise from investments in alternative energy and conservation. The majority of concerns are about financial strains, legislative changes, compliance, effects on business operations, and reputational consequences for the company. A crucial role is usually played by internal auditors in determining the extent of these risks.

5.3.4. Checklist for an Internal Audit of a Company

A company's adherence to both internal and external standards is evaluated through an internal audit. A small business owner can verify that their company is following its policies and procedures on a regular basis by using an internal audit checklist. Potential noncompliance issues are highlighted by internal audit results, allowing the company to take corrective action without consulting regulators. An audit committee or department is not necessary for an organization to perform an internal audit.

A list of the business functions that require an audit is the first checklist item that any organization should have. For the purpose of making sure that its business plans are sound and strategic, every organization should audit its management function. To make sure staff members are adhering to uniform protocols intended to optimize performance, a business should audit its operations. Lastly, in order to prevent fraud, a company audits its financial procedures. To make sure that compliance lasts over time, management conducts the audit procedure again on a regular basis. The organization and strategy plan of the business are confirmed by the management audit. The auditor looks over the company's aims and objectives to make sure that the organizational structure backs up its objectives. In a similar vein, the objectives of every worker should be linked to the company's overarching objectives. The auditor also examines the organizational charts of the business to make sure that managers answer to the owner and employees report to them for performance.

An operational audit evaluates how well the company's primary function is performing. The operational audit checklist consists of items such as an evaluation of the company's timely delivery of goods and services, if the company has sufficient contracts with its vendors, how the company onboards new hires and verifies the effectiveness of that training, how the company maintains relationships with its customers, and so on. The auditor also evaluates how well the company's sales representatives perform and how frequently they update their expertise of the industry, rivals, and relevant technologies for the company's operations. The regulatory requirements, including corporate governance and tax filings, are the main focus of the financial audit. The auditor confirms that the business has obtained the licenses and permissions required to carry out its operations. The auditor reviews the company's financial records to make sure that business and personal records are kept separate and that the accounting system is accurate and supported by source documents. A financial audit additionally validates that the business pays taxes and insurance as required by law, provides the promised fringe benefits, and accurately computes each employee's pay.

5.3.5. Internal Audit vs. Consulting Role

The financial watchdogs of a company are its internal auditors. Their job is to independently assess operating procedures and conduct an objective analysis of a company's financial records without interference from management. Internal auditors who work as consultants concentrate on a particular division rather than the entire business. The responsibilities of an independent auditor and a consultant may become conflicted as a result.

- **The Internal Audit:** An internal audit involves the audit committee, the department being audited, and the internal auditors. The department's internal business operations are the main topic of discussion. The internal auditors examine departmental workflow, examine manuals, and select documents at random. Auditors search for indications of fraud and poor asset management. They also evaluate risk control measures. The audit committee receives the internal auditors' findings directly. After reading the report, the audit committee meets with the department manager to go over the audit findings.
- **Auditor as Consultant:** In contrast to an internal audit, a consultation involves just the department manager and the internal auditor. The internal auditor (Pett, Kristall, & Mack, 2017) serves as a consultant and has no managerial or decision-making authority. The auditor will look over the department's protocols and watch the workers at work. The internal auditor will serve as a consultant, offering suggestions for enhancements and advice. The internal auditor collaborates with managers to put the changes into effect and help with staff training.
- **Auditor vs. Consultant:** Using staff internal auditors as consultants entails a number of risks. As consultants, the auditors don't seem to be working for the company as a whole, but rather for a particular manager or department. It may seem as though the auditor has lost their independence and objectivity. When the former auditor who is now a consultant is required to audit, or supervise an audit of, her own prior work, a conflict of interest may develop. Furthermore, the number of internal auditors employed by a corporation is limited. The number of auditors available to carry out internal audits across the entire organization is decreased when they serve as consultants for their own business.
- **Auditor and Consultant:** The function of the internal auditor is changing as a result of business owners and executives. One of the main concerns of management is controlling and managing risk.

Management wants internal auditors to assist in creating and implementing risk controls, not just provide an audit report. Internal auditors still have difficulty striking a balance between their growing consulting role and their historical independence and objectivity.

5.3.6. Weaknesses in an Internal Audit Control System

An effective internal audit control system resembles a healthy diet and fitness regimen. It consists of all the policies and procedures you have in place to safeguard the assets of your company, just like the steps you take to protect your health. The property, furniture, equipment, and money itself are all considered assets. Intangible assets include things like brand awareness and reputation for your company.

- **Internal Audit Control Systems Types**: Internal audit systems come in two primary varieties: detective and preventive. The purpose of preventive systems is to avert issues. They are the component of exercise, a balanced diet, and vitamins. Detective systems, like the diagnostic tests your doctor performs when you're sick, are made to find issues that have already happened. Both are present in the best internal auditing systems. To control losses, proactive preventive measures are essential. However, in the event that an issue occurs, your system also needs to have a detective component. The detective element consists of a set of rules for handling issues. Since detection shows that the preventive controls are operating as intended, it should be continued.
- **Strengths of Internal Control:** A good internal control system does the following:
  - Controls risk.
  - Operates effectively and efficiently.
  - Protects tangible and intangible resources from waste and theft.
  - Prevents fraud.
  - Proactively identifies potential issues and reactively deals with them quickly when they occur.
  - Generates prompt and accurate reporting.
  - Measures progress toward your goals.
  - Complies with all laws and regulations that apply to your business.

The Enron and Lehman Brothers scandals are two well-known instances of internal control issues. Both large corporations went bankrupt, but not before their losses caused countless losses that affected countless lives. More recently, an estimated $21.7 million was lost by Kenya Airlines as a result of inaccurate billing and undercharging for excess baggage.

- **Weaknesses of Internal Control:** Although creating a robust internal control system from the beginning is the best course of action, internal audit control system flaws are typically fairly simple to resolve. However, you must first identify them. Strong physical security, such as locks, alarms, cameras, and restricted access to your company's assets, is a sign of internal control deficiencies. If any of these components are absent from your internal control system, you have them. Job responsibilities and roles for employees are clearly stated. Divided up the work of employees, especially when it came to handling money. You run a significant risk of improper handling of the money if one person is in charge of handling everything, from receiving it to depositing it in the bank. The consent of management or owners regarding who is responsible for what on a regular basis and when a specific task needs supervisory approval.

Asset security includes things like who can operate which equipment, who has the business's keys, and who can access cash and inventory. Frequent evaluations of business performance are necessary to ensure that goals are being met, that earnings are within target, and that budgets are balanced. Regular reconciliations involve comparing various data sets to make it simple to spot inconsistencies and issues. Inventory is regularly compared to sales to make sure that no stock is lost to theft or waste. A disaster recovery strategy to guarantee asset protection and data backup. If a natural disaster strikes or damage occurs to your place of business, you should be able to quickly recover or resume operations. Although there are a lot of items on this list, the time invested in creating a robust internal audit control system is money well spent. By identifying and promptly resolving losses when they occur, as well as preventing losses as much as possible, it can save you a significant amount of money over time.

5.3.7. Top-Down Approach for Audit of Internal Controls

When conducting an audit of internal controls, the top-down approach is meant to enable the auditor to choose which controls to test and identify risks in a methodical manner. The auditor starts the top-down approach by getting a general understanding of the organization and the sector in which it works. Examining the company's financial statements and gaining general business knowledge are two ways to achieve this. The auditor then examines the entity-level controls of the business to make sure that adequate policies and processes are put in place to identify misstatements—whether the result of fraud or error—as soon as possible, preventing material misstatements from having an impact on the financial statements. Entity-level controls over the period-end financial reporting process and those pertaining to the control environment are the two most significant categories. Controls over the control environment should evaluate the extent to which management upholds moral principles and integrity, as well as whether the audit committee or the board of directors has taken on accountability for the completeness and accuracy of the financial statements and internal controls. The methods used to enter data into the general ledger, the extent to which IT is used in the financial reporting process, the kinds of adjusting and consolidation entries, and the participation of management, the board of directors, and the audit committee in the period-ending financial reporting process should all be evaluated as controls over the process.

Controls over management override, the organization's risk assessment procedure, centralized processing controls, operations monitoring controls, and other control monitoring controls are additional entity-level controls that need to be considered. It's critical to realize that entity-level controls differ in terms of their scope and accuracy. While some entity-level controls are specifically made to keep an eye on the efficacy of the other controls, others only indirectly impact the possibility of finding or preventing material misstatements. The auditor needs to run fewer tests on controls the more exact the control. The auditor then notes any noteworthy accounts, disclosures, and pertinent claims associated with them. In essence, risky financial statement assertions are relevant assertions. Financial statement assertions demonstrate that a transaction has really happened, is finished, accurately valued, has given the company ownership, and has been appropriately reported on the financial statements. Therefore, any of these financial statement assertions that are particularly prone to being misrepresented and could result in the financial statements being materially misstated would be considered relevant. Larger accounts, those that are more likely to contain misstatements, those that are highly complex, those that have a higher volume of transactions during the period, those that have realized losses during the period, those that involve a high likelihood of related party transactions within the account, and those that have seen a significant change in the accounting methods from the previous year are all examples of significant accounts and disclosures that demand greater attention. Going through the financial statements and brainstorming all the ways that each account and disclosure could have been misstated will help the auditor identify as many risky areas as possible. Both the internal control audit and the financial statement audit will use the same risk factors, key accounts and disclosures, and pertinent assertions. An auditor conducting a multi-entity audit should utilize the consolidated financial statements to pinpoint important accounts and disclosures.

The auditor must next determine the most likely sources of misstatement. The auditor needs to accomplish a number of goals in order to do this. One of these goals is for the auditor to demonstrate any weaknesses in an organization's internal controls that might lead to material misstatements in the financial statements and the steps management has taken to mitigate those risks. Conducting walkthroughs is the most effective method for the auditor to accomplish these goals.

When an auditor conducts a walkthrough, they trace a transaction from its beginning to the financial records, ensuring that all control procedures were carried out correctly. It is crucial that the auditor performs these kinds of operations independently and keeps meticulous records of the people and information technology utilized in each processing step. The top-down approach's last stage is deciding which controls to test.

In order to assess whether or not a specific risk has been adequately addressed, the auditor should test each control that is most crucial. Testing both controls might not be required if they address the same risk. Furthermore, if a single control adequately manages both risks, it might not be necessary to address them individually. When all of these internal controls are tested, the auditor will have a conclusion regarding how well internal controls over financial reporting work.

In summary, an auditor can identify specific risk areas in a company's internal controls over financial reporting by using the top-down approach, which is a systematic method of risk assessment. The auditor can then choose the most appropriate tests to ensure that these risks are adequately addressed. Under the top-down approach, auditors must first gain an understanding of the company and its sector, then proceed to the entity-level controls of the company, major accounts and disclosures, and their pertinent assertions. After that, they must confirm that they have a comprehensive understanding of all the risks, and lastly choose which controls need to be tested to ensure that all risks have been addressed.

5.4 BASIS OF CHECK LISTS

An organization's internal control system is evaluated through internal auditing. It examines a number of topics, such as organizational goals, legal and regulatory compliance, and financial reporting procedures. You can find opportunities for improvement and previously unidentified risks or issues with the aid of an efficient internal audit process. Internal auditing can also help you strengthen data governance, improve operational efficiency, raise staff morale, and improve the accuracy and dependability of financial statements. One tool that helps auditors through the audit process is an internal audit checklist. Many industries, such as manufacturing, services, and more, frequently evaluate whether their current performance and procedures satisfy specific standards. The checklist should be tailored to the particular requirements of the business and may include things like financial report reviews, staff interviews, and assessments of the infrastructure for information technology. An internal audit checklist can help you ensure that every aspect of the company is examined. The list ought to address a variety of topics, including risk management, quality control, and compliance with relevant laws and regulations. To ensure that nothing is overlooked, every item needs to be thoroughly examined.

Let's look at these seven key factors that go into a quality audit:

1. Provide reasoning for your audit

Providing an explanation for the audit's necessity is crucial because it can give employees the impression that their work is being watched over and examined. You should specify the scope and audit criteria in detail. This will guarantee that everyone cooperates throughout and assist staff in understanding the significance of the procedure. Although there are many reasons why you might need to perform internal or external audits, the following are some of the most typical ones.

- identifying areas for improvement
- meeting compliance requirements
- increasing financial accuracy
- monitoring the accuracy of internal processes

Whatever the reason, it's important to make it clear so everyone is on the same page.

2. Establish the goal for internal auditors

After outlining the rationale behind your audit, it's time to establish a target. This should be the main goal that all participants in the process can work toward. For instance, internal auditors will concentrate on finding areas where processes and procedures can be improved if your objective is to raise financial accuracy. Financial statements, records, reports, and other documents where anomalies might occur should be examined by internal auditors. Similar to this, your internal audit manager will focus especially on business practices, policies, and procedures that may be in violation of the law or regulations if that is the main objective. It's critical to make sure everyone involved in the goal-setting process is aware of what needs to be accomplished and how they can contribute. Also, your objective needs to be reachable and reasonable.

3. Determine the type of audit

After establishing the goal for your internal audit, you'll need to decide on the type of audit that best fits your needs. To determine your internal audit plan, consider your goal and the areas you need to examine.

Internal audits can be divided into three categories:

- **Financial audits.** You can use these to examine and verify financial statements and identify areas where changes or improvements could be made.
- *Operational audits.* An auditor can evaluate the efficiency and effectiveness of operational processes and procedures, such as quality control, workflow, staffing levels and administration.
- *Compliance audits.* Compliance with applicable laws and regulations is essential to any organization. These audits examine policies, procedures and practices to meet all applicable laws and international standards.

4. Request the necessary documents

Requesting the documents you'll need for the process is crucial because audits will need a lot of documentation. This includes reports, financial statements, and other documents and records that are relevant to your audit evidence. Because it automates the collection and tracking of documents, software created to support quality internal audits can frequently make this process simpler. It is also expected that all requested documents are current. Get the most recent financial statements, for instance, if you're performing a financial audit. Results that are not up to date may be misleading. It can be helpful to identify areas for improvement and to provide additional context if you have an audit trail, such as audit reports from prior years. For these reports' data to be helpful, they must, however, adhere to current internal auditing standards.

5. Identify performance indicators

Performance metrics assess how successfully a company is accomplishing its goals. Both qualitative and quantitative indicators can be used, and they should be customized to the particular objectives of your audit. Performance indicators might include cash flow, profitability, return on investment (ROI), and net income, for instance, if you're performing a financial audit. Qualitative metrics such as employee engagement scores or customer satisfaction surveys are also applicable.

6. Start the documentation review

An internal audit cannot be successful without a thorough examination of every document.

Auditors ought to carefully go over each document, making notes as they go, and looking for any anomalies or inconsistencies. Create a system to help you keep track of your findings. Included in this should be your observations and recommendations, as well as the notes you took during the document review process. When looking through documents, you should be meticulous. The accuracy of your results can be severely impacted by even small mistakes.

7. Create an action plan to address areas of improvement

What really adds value to your internal audit is an action plan. Internal audit reports will be used to pinpoint any areas in need of improvement and create a strategy to deal with them.

Your action plan ought to outline the precise procedures, deadlines, and materials required to produce the intended outcomes. Setting goals along the route makes it easier to monitor development over time.

5.4.1 Why is an Internal Audit Checklist Important?

For multiple reasons, an internal audit checklist is necessary. It guarantees that every audit is carried out methodically and consistently and offers a framework that can be used as a guide throughout.

Consistency across Audits

Every audit that uses an internal audit checklist adheres to the same standards. This consistency makes it simple to compare various audits or organizational sections, which facilitates the identification of trends, patterns, and areas in need of improvement.

Comprehensive Coverage

Using an internal audit checklist guarantees that no part of the company is missed when conducting the audit. Finding possible risks and weaknesses across the entire organization depends on this thorough coverage.

Facilitates Communication

An organized checklist is a useful tool for stakeholder and auditor communication. It promotes openness and trust by making the audit's procedures, expectations, and scope clear.

Efficiency in the Audit Process

An audit checklist saves time and effort during the planning and execution of audits, increasing efficiency. It gives auditors a precise road map, removing uncertainty and encouraging timely audit completion. The foundation of any successful audit procedure is an internal audit checklist. The secret is to tailor it to the particular needs and specifications of your company. Keep in mind that your audit will be more successful if your checklist is more thorough.

5.4.2 Components of Check List

The item on an internal audit checklist ought to describe every step of the audit procedure, from preparation to conclusion. You can complete the audit process step-by-step and without missing anything if you compile all of the necessary components into a handy list. It guarantees accuracy and consistency while also streamlining the audit process. Having said that, the following items should be included in an internal audit checklist according to the various audit stages.

1. **Initial Audit Planning**

- Identify the scope and objectives of the audit, including the specific areas and processes to be examined and the goals to be achieved.
- Establish a comprehensive audit timeline, outlining key milestones and deadlines to ensure timely completion of the audit.

- Gather detailed information about the area to be audited, including relevant documents, records, and data sources, to support a thorough and effective examination.
- Develop a preliminary audit program that outlines the audit procedures, techniques, and methodologies to be employed, ensuring a structured and systematic approach to the audit process.

2. Involve Risk and Process Subject Matter Experts

- To ensure a comprehensive audit, it is essential to involve subject matter experts in risk management and process controls.
- Before conducting the audit, it is crucial to discuss the potential risks associated with the specific area to be audited.
- By leveraging expert insights, you can refine the audit program and ensure that all relevant risks are addressed effectively.

3. Frameworks for Internal Audit Process

- It is important for organizations to adopt suitable internal audit frameworks such as COSO (Committee of Sponsoring Organizations of the Treadway Commission) and COBIT (Control Objectives for Information and Related Technologies) to ensure effective governance and risk management.
- When implementing an internal audit framework, aligning it with the company's objectives and regulatory requirements is crucial. This ensures the framework supports the organization's strategic goals and addresses compliance obligations.
- Additionally, organizations should customize the chosen framework to cater to their unique needs. This involves adapting the framework to the organization's size, industry, and specific risk profile, enabling a more tailored and effective internal audit process.

4. Frameworks for Internal Audit Processes

- Embrace and modify audit methodologies, tools, and templates to enhance efficiency and effectiveness.
- Guarantee compliance with the standards established by professional organizations such as the IIA or AICPA.
- Integrate industry-leading practices to continuously improve audit processes and outcomes.

5. Initial Document Request List

- Identify the documents required for the audit, such as financial statements, invoices, contracts, and relevant policies.
- Request the necessary documents from the auditee well in advance, ensuring a sufficient timeline for preparation.
- Thoroughly review the obtained documents to understand the area to be audited, analyze the information, and identify potential risks or areas of concern.

6. Preparing for a Planning Meeting with Business Stakeholders

- Prepare a comprehensive agenda outlining the topics to be discussed and the desired outcomes of the meeting.

- Identify and invite key stakeholders with a direct interest or involvement in the matters to be addressed during the meeting.
- Prior to the meeting, proactively share the initial audit plan with the stakeholders to gather their insights and ensure alignment.

7. Preparing the Audit Program

Summary and Purpose of the Audit Program

- Establish the purpose of the audit, which is to assess the effectiveness and compliance of the organization's internal controls and processes.
- Summarize the audit processes to be followed, including conducting interviews, reviewing documentation, performing tests, and analyzing data to gather evidence and evaluate the organization's adherence to policies and procedures.

Process Objectives and Owners

- Clearly define and document the objectives of each business process to ensure clarity and alignment with organizational goals.
- Identify and assign owners to each process who will be responsible for its execution, monitoring, and continuous improvement. This ensures accountability and effective management of the processes.

Process Risks

- Identify and list all potential risks associated with each process, considering internal and external factors.
- Evaluate the potential impact and likelihood of each risk by analyzing historical data, industry standards, and expert opinions.

Controls Mitigating Process Risks

- Identify and document control measures that have been implemented to mitigate the identified risks.
- Conduct regular evaluations to assess the effectiveness of these controls in managing and reducing the identified risks.

Control Attributes

- Define the specific attributes and characteristics of each control measure, outlining their purpose and intended effects.
- Clearly articulate the procedures and methods for testing each control measure, ensuring accuracy and reliability in assessing their effectiveness.

Testing Procedures and Methods for Controls to be Tested During the Audit

- Establish clear and comprehensive procedures for testing each control to ensure effectiveness and accuracy.
- Carefully select testing methods that align perfectly with the audit objectives, taking into account the specific requirements and desired outcomes.

8. Audit Program and Planning Review

- Thoroughly review the audit program to ensure its completeness and identify potential areas for improvement.
- Carefully align the audit plan with the defined audit objectives and the overarching goals of the company.
- Once all necessary adjustments have been made, finalize the audit

plan and promptly share it with all relevant stakeholders for their awareness and input.

5.4.3 Process of Checklist

An organization's corporate governance procedures and internal controls are carefully assessed by internal audits. It highlights risks related to privacy and information security and determines whether there are sufficient rules, regulations, and processes in place to prevent unlawful activity.

Internal audits are essential for organizations because they provide insight into the efficacy of controls, validate advancements, and guarantee ongoing improvement. Ignoring the need for an internal audit in favor of an external one would result in increased audit time and expenses, non-compliance risks, and lost opportunities for improvement.

Helps ensure strategic alignment

Internal audits assist in ensuring that controls and policies are implemented according to plan and are free from flaws.

They draw attention to both flourishing and failing areas, providing an unbiased perspective on the trajectory of an organization. This makes it easier to comprehend areas for improvement and impending difficulties.

Proactively identifies potential risks

Internal audits assist in ensuring that implemented policies and controls are as intended and are devoid of any vulnerabilities. By highlighting both successful and failing areas, they provide an unbiased perspective on the trajectory of an organization. This aids in comprehending future obstacles and growth prospects.

Uncovers compliance gaps

Examining any deviations from compliance requirements is a requirement of internal audits. This increases the organization's preparedness for certification procedures and speeds up the start of any necessary corrective action. Additionally, it saves external auditors time by reducing the amount of time they must spend requesting remediation.

Litmus test for internal control effectiveness

Internal audits assist in determining whether internal controls are being implemented as intended and are successful in thwarting possible threats. It helps foster trust among stakeholders and clients by reassuring the company that its security force is well-trained.

Ensures Continuous refinement

Ensuring security and compliance are continuous pursuits. Internal audits support the organization's continuous improvement and vigilance. Internal audit feedback that is well-integrated can assist the organization in effectively responding to and adapting to the changing threat landscape.

5.4.4 Risk Description

Identifying and recording possible risks that might have an impact on the accomplishment of organizational goals is necessary when creating a risk description for an internal audit checklist. A precise, concise, and pertinent risk description for the area under audit is required. Here's a guide on how to structure a risk description in an internal audit checklist:

1. **Risk Title**

   Example: Data Privacy Breach

2. **Risk Description**

   What is the risk?

   Example: The risk of unauthorized access to sensitive customer data due to insufficient access controls.

   Why does this risk exist?

   Example: Lack of robust password policies and multi-factor authentication.

   Potential Impact

   Example: Legal penalties, loss of customer trust, and financial losses.

   Risk Category

   Example: Compliance, Operational, Financial, Strategic.

3. **Risk Factors**

   Internal Factors

   Example: Outdated IT infrastructure, inadequate staff training.

   External Factors

   Example: Changes in regulatory requirements, cyber threats.

4. **Existing Controls**

   Example: Regular security audits, encryption of sensitive data, staff training programs.

   Effectiveness of Controls

   Example: Controls are partially effective, with gaps in monitoring and response protocols.

5. **Risk Likelihood**

   Example: Medium (Based on past incidents and current control effectiveness).

6. **Risk Impact**

   Example: High (Considering potential legal consequences and reputational damage).

7. **Audit Procedure**

   Example: Review access control policies, conduct interviews with IT security personnel, and assess compliance with data protection regulations.

8. **Residual Risk**

   Example: After implementing existing controls, the risk remains Medium due to the persistent threat of external attacks.

9. **Recommendations**

   Example: Implement multi-factor authentication, update security protocols, and increase the frequency of security audits.

10. **Risk Owner**

    Example: Chief Information Security Officer (CISO)

11. **Date of Last Review**

    Example: September 1, 2024

12. **Audit Conclusion**

    Example: The risk of a data privacy breach is significant, and further actions are required to mitigate this risk effectively.

13. **Follow-Up Actions**

    Example: Schedule a follow-up audit in 6 months to review the implementation of recommended controls.

14. **Documentation & Evidence**

    Example: Attach relevant documents such as security policies, audit trails, and compliance reports.

15. **Sign-Off**

    Example: Signed by the auditor and risk owner on completion.

This checklist should be customized based on the specific risks relevant to the area being audited.

By providing detailed risk descriptions and associated information, internal audit teams can more effectively assess and mitigate risks within the organization.

5.4.5 Controls

An instrument that helps auditors navigate the audit process is the internal audit checklist, which lists particular risk areas to look at, controls to assess, and protocols to adhere to. Within this checklist, effective risk control necessitates a multifaceted approach comprising goal-setting, risk assessment, design of suitable controls, ongoing effectiveness monitoring, and strategy adjustment in response to discoveries and shifts in the risk environment. The first step in risk management is to precisely outline the goals and parameters of the audit. Understanding the organization's objectives in terms of strategy, operations, finances, and compliance will help the audit team determine which areas are most important and where possible risks could have the biggest effects. Establishing specific goals makes it easier to concentrate the audit's attention on the most pertinent risk areas and guarantees that the checklist addresses all significant facets of the company's operations and internal controls. The checklist should, for instance, include checks on authorization processes, physical security measures, and asset management policies if the goal is to protect assets. Conducting a risk assessment is the next step after objectives have been set. This entails determining the likelihood and potential impact of each risk, then ranking them. A thorough inventory of potential risks, divided into categories like operational, financial, compliance, and strategic risks, should be included in the internal audit checklist. Every risk is assessed by the audit team in order to ascertain its importance and relevance to the goals of the company. High-risk areas are given more attention and scrutiny during the audit process thanks to this assessment, which enables the organization to concentrate its resources on the most important risks.

Following risk identification and assessment, the company needs to create and put into place the necessary risk controls. These controls may be of the preventive, investigative, or remedial types. Preventive controls, such as stringent financial authorization protocols, extensive access controls, and background checks on hiring staff, are intended to avert risks from materializing. Detective controls, like reconciliations, audits, or monitoring activities, are designed to find risks that have already happened. Corrective controls, such as incident response plans or contingency strategies, are aimed at reducing the impact of risks once they have manifested. Every risk area should have a detailed description of the controls in place, along with an assessment of their efficacy and design, on the internal audit checklist. Using the internal audit checklist to control risk requires regularly testing the efficacy of controls. In order to ascertain whether the controls are functioning as intended and are adequate to reduce the risks that have been identified, the audit team should conduct thorough testing. This may entail doing sample checks, staff interviews, process observations, and documentation reviews. For example, if data security controls are on the checklist, the audit team could examine user access logs, look for unauthorized access, or test the organization's reaction to a cyberattack simulation to see if access controls are working as intended. An organization can take remedial action by identifying any gaps, weaknesses, or failures in the controls through effective testing.

An efficient risk management framework requires ongoing monitoring of risks and controls in addition to testing. Procedures for routinely examining and updating the risk assessment and control measures should be included in the internal audit checklist. This may entail regular monitoring, audits on a periodic basis, or the tracking of important risk indicators with automated tools. The organization can quickly identify changes in the risk environment and take appropriate action thanks to continuous monitoring. For instance, the organization should evaluate the impact of newly introduced regulatory requirements on current controls and update the checklist to reflect any necessary modifications. Additionally, the checklist ought to stress how crucial internal reporting and communication are to the organization. All levels of management and stakeholders must promptly and accurately share information in order for risk control to be effective. The audit team should make sure that management is promptly informed of any significant findings, such as control flaws or new risks. This guarantees that risks are recognized, given appropriate priority, and handled appropriately. Steps for recording findings, making action plans, and monitoring the application of recommendations should all be included in the checklist.

Training and awareness are two more essential components of risk control listed in the internal audit checklist. Workers need to be aware of the value of risk management and how they fit into the overall maintenance of efficient controls. Procedures for assessing the suitability of training courses and staff awareness campaigns ought to be on the checklist. The audit team may, for example, examine the frequency and subject matter of training sessions on cybersecurity, fraud prevention, and regulatory compliance. Making sure staff members are knowledgeable and trained contributes to the development of a risk-aware culture within the company, which lowers the possibility of mistakes, non-compliance, or fraudulent activity. Finally, the internal audit checklist needs to be flexible and dynamic. Risks are dynamic; they evolve over time as a result of both internal and external variables, including changes in the economy, technology, regulations, and organizational size. As a result, the checklist needs to be updated and reviewed frequently to account for modifications to the risk environment. This involves adding new risks, changing the controls that are already in place, or modifying audit procedures in light of previous conclusions or new trends. A dynamic checklist makes sure the company manages risks in an adaptable and proactive manner.

CASE STUDY

WORLDCOM ACCOUNTING AND AUDITING SCANDAL

Founded initially as a small company named Long Distance Discount Services in 1983, it merged with Advantage Companies Inc to eventually become WorldCom Inc, naming its CEO as Bernard Ebbers.WorldCom achieved its position as a significant player in the telecommunications industry through the successful completion of 65 acquisitions spending almost $60 billion between 1991 and 1997, whilst also accumulating $41 billion in debt. During the Internet boom WorldCom's stock rose from pennies per share to over $60 a share as 'Wall Street investment banks, analysts and brokers began to discover WorldCom's value and made "strong buy recommendations" to investors.' During the 1990's WorldCom evolved into the 'second-largest long distance phone company in the US' mainly due to its aggressive acquisition strategy.

A cycle became apparent in the marketplace where an acquisition was seen as a positive move by the analysts leading to higher stock prices of WorldCom. Consequently this allowed WorldCom to gain greater financing and backing for further acquisitions repeating the cycle. One of the most significant and largest acquisitions was that of MCI Communications Inc in 1998, becoming the largest merger in US history at that time. British Telecommunications were also in the running for the takeover of MCI Communications making a $19 billion bid, when Bernard Ebbers the CEO of WorldCom decided to place a counter bid 1.8 times higher than that of what BT had placed, at $35 billion. Evidently this takeover was agreed and the merger between the two brought MCI WorldCom into second position behind that of AT&T in the telecommunications market.

However, from 1999 to early 2002, CEO of the company, Bernard Ebbers along with other senior management used fraudulent and improper accounting methods to mislead investors and other directors. Their fraudulent accounting method had mainly two approaches: 'The reduction of reported line costs' and the 'exaggeration of reported revenue'. These practices were to ignore the generally accepted accounting principles (GAAP) in addition to not informing the users of the financial statements of the changes to the previously used accounting practices. This was done to reduce their E/R ratio, the main key performance indicator used to measure the performance of telecommunications companies. It is the relationship between their main expenses; line costs (the rental of telephone lines) to its revenues and the lower figures consequently produced more recommendations by analysts increasing stock prices.

The eventual failure of WorldCom was caused by the disruption of the cycle, as discussed before, when the planned acquisition of Sprint Corporation in 1999-2000 was stopped by pressures from the US Department of Justice and the European Union over concerns of it creating a monopoly. As a result WorldCom lost its main growth strategy and left Bernard Ebbers few options to enhance the business further. Either they had to consolidate all the previous acquisitions into one efficient business, which they had failed to do so far, as they had only concentrated on the takeovers or to find other creative ways to sustain and increase the share price.

The CEO chose the latter and in July 2002 WorldCom filed for Chapter 11 bankruptcy after disclosures were made about the improper accounting methods used to inflate revenue's and reduce expenses. By the end of 2003, it was estimated that the company's total assets had been inflated by around $11 billion.

The Fraud

The members of senior management were engaged in a continuing series of improper accounting manipulations to try and achieve market expectations on growth, making the financial reports more appealing. This was achieved through basic fraudulent methods, including changes to financial estimates, early revenue recognition, erroneously capitalization of the long term assets, as well as alteration of the reserves in order to improve the earnings picture.

WorldCom's managers modified their assumptions on accounts receivables, by adjusting the amount of uncollectible bills owed to the company and as a result increased the total amount of accounts receivable. Managerial assumptions played two important roles here; firstly they determine the amount of funds reserved to cover bad debts, as the lower the perceived need of non-collectable bills, the smaller the reserve required. This resulted in manipulation of the reserves, reducing them when needed to increase earnings. Secondly, when selling receivables to third parties the assumptions are used to identify the quantity available for sale, which WorldCom utilized. This manipulation was easily achieved as many of the WorldCom's customers were small, start-up telecommunication businesses with little data and history of repayment likelihood, leaving a large degree of judgement from management to set these figures.

Line cost accruals were exploited in a similar way to that of the bad debt reserves, due to the judgement needed in deciding upon figures. Line cost accruals estimates are extremely difficult to make with precision, being best practice to adjust them frequently. This, of course, provides further opportunities for falsification. With the importance of line costs to the company's bottom line and with Ebbers promise to reduce expenses; the accruals were adjusted on a regular basis to improve the company's overall margins, maintaining the high growth rate now expected by the market. WorldCom's finance chief, Sullivan later admitted to the court that he falsified financial statements of the company and in particular ordered the General Accounting department to reduce Wireless' Division's expenses by US$150 million.

In fact, during the second quarter of 2000, the total accounts receivables at WorldCom Inc rose 12.6% to US$926 million, but the allowance only increased by US$443 million, or 3.5%, leading to higher earnings of $69 million.

The large acquisition of MCI gave WorldCom another opportunity to fiddle its books as it could now apply its dubious methods to all the new assets and expenses of MCI.

Therefore they started reducing the book value of some MCI assets whilst also increasing the value of goodwill by the same balancing amount. This gave greater flexibility for achieving their targets as smaller amounts of expenses were taken against earnings by spreading the charges over decades rather than the year it was incurred. 'The net result was WorldCom's ability to cut annual expenses, acknowledge all MCI revenues and boost profits from the acquisition.'

Next, there was the existence of a 'Corporate Unallocated Revenue Account', which included entries of corporate level adjustments. This was to assist Ebbers in adjusting the performance of WorldCom by profit smoothing, such that the predicted 15% year on year growth could be achieved. The access to the "Corporate Unallocated Schedule", which was an attachment to the Monthly Revenue Schedule, was only available to the senior management. This schedule included the journal entries to the revenue account that erroneously increased the revenue of the company.

According to US GAAP Code 605, the account of such sort is fictitious, as it does not satisfy the criteria, and thus could not be treated as a legal form of revenue. The management, knowing this fact, restricted the number of people who had access to the monthly revenue, so that the fraud in revenue recognition would not be discovered. In addition to that, WorldCom tended to recognise the revenue, which was yet to be received from long term contracts, even before the actual service was provided. This, of course, was another violation of the US GAAP.

Furthermore, in a bid to reduce line costs, WorldCom capitalised the excess capacity expenses that were not generating revenue. The reason given was that these lines are costs which should have been incurred after the related benefits were generated. Although this arrangement does not oppose the classification of asset in FASB Concept Statement No 6, 'Assets are probable future economic benefits obtained or controlled by a particular entity as a result of past transactions or events,' there was no proper business or accounting rationale for these procedures. The latter include journal entries of $798 million and $560 million, made to capitalize 'line costs' during 2001.

Indeed, according to FRS 16, costs that are related to day-to-day servicing, or wear and tear repairs of Property Plant and Equipment (PPE) would be expensed, unless the PPE is enhanced as a result of the expenditure. Consequently, we can see that WorldCom has wrongly classified its expenses as an asset account despite the PPE not being enhanced at any state. This would lead to the reduction of expenses, increment in total assets, and ultimate increase in profits as well as a stronger balance sheet. Lastly, other reserves were also manipulated to manage earnings. The reserves, which were often set aside by WorldCom to cover foreseeable costs and losses, were inflated to create 'hefty slush funds' that could be used to increase profits.

Auditing Issues

Actions of the company's management yielded an environment where fraud activities were easily accomplished. For this reason, the internal audit function, designed to supervise and hold employees accountable, was suppressed by a few senior members in an attempt to limit their exposure to the sensitive information. This was achieved by senior management keeping the internal audit department understaffed, generally under qualified and busy with other projects as well as retaining information from them. They also hampered efforts from internal auditors to find information once they became wary of the accounting processes used. The effort to delve into the financials was brought by Cynthia Cooper the Vice President of internal audit who did eventually help uncover the truth by gathering information after-hours to avoid suspicion and supervision by her repressive bosses. Cynthia questioned external auditors Arthur Anderson over some of the methods and they refused to respond initially eventually stating that they had approved the methods and that she should leave it at that. The internal controls meant to help supervise were controlled by the directors so proved useless as information could be changed, stopped or edited.

Arthur Andersen's involvement being the Auditors of WorldCom would have been to find the irregularities in the company's accounts. The level of complexity of the fraud found in WorldCom were more of judgement as opposed to those complex issues raised through Enron (who Arthur Anderson also audited), yet they were still missed. However following their failure at Enron, WorldCom switched to KPMG as their auditing firm. The resulting implication for Arthur Andersen is that it lost Public trust and was implicated in the frauds of both Enron and WorldCom due to not fulfilling their duties.

Corporate Governance and Accountability Issues

WorldCom's failure was down to a multitude of underlying issues and shortcomings. Firstly, one might have to blame the system of the market for their method of assessing the value of a company solely on its share value. This created situations where a company could behave in an unsolicited manner. The pressure of achieving targets led to the company creatively constructing some of its financials to meet expectations laid down by the market, which might have been over-optimistic.

The aggressive acquisition strategy used by Ebbers was brought through from his previous ventures where he found himself adept at raising money, mainly due to his likeable personality. The appointment of a CEO that had little knowledge and no background in the phone technology market led to Ebbers doing what he knew; raising funds and this was used on these acquisitions. However in his quests he failed to consolidate these companies into one efficient business leaving only one route to improve stock values; more acquisitions. The failure to consolidate the firms was also assisted by his remuneration package being to myopic only focussing on quick profits as opposed to measurement over a period of years focussing on sustainable growth. Subsequently this focussed his attention on increasing share prices now as he received large amounts of his remuneration in shares, and an increase in share price increased his wealth, in the short run anyway.

Infectious greed was apparent among the investors and market, expecting and demanding maintained high returns. Ebbers owning many shares in WorldCom may have also been overtaken by this, however as a CEO he must also promote and act in the best interests of the company and this is where he failed his fiduciary duty to all shareholders and stakeholders. This meant the continuance of the fast growth acquisition strategy which was detrimental to the company's long-term success.

The culture of WorldCom was another problem that was among the underlying causes of its downfall, being apparent in all aspects of the company, but mostly passed down the ranks from top management starting with Ebbers. A downfall of the firm was the absence of accountability from some of the top management. Ebbers tried to argue in his defence that he was a hands-off director who wasn't involved in the detailed aspects of the firm and hence not involved in the fraud, however he had the authority and forced others to comply. There was no direct accountability on him to align his and the firm's objectives of providing true and fair accounts, as there were little repercussions for his actions. He was able to gamble with other people's money whilst either increasing his value of shares and remuneration when successful or having a severance payment if the company starts failing.

This culture also enticed dubious business transactions with the appointment of Salomon Smith Barney being among many. Smith Barney became and remained WorldCom's investment banker only after allocating the executives large amounts of shares in a planned IPO's, which could be construed as a bribe.

The audit committee and the rest of the board not only failed to oppose Ebbers and his CFO, Scott Sullivan, but even financed Ebbers and others with large loans. Consequently, Ebbers was allowed to continue with other pursuits setting up and running other companies utilizing loans from WorldCom. The latter, of course, has created several conflicts of interest and independence issues, as well as allowing the attention of the CEO to divert from his core responsibilities.

Effects of Fraud

- **Effects on WorldCom**

The bankruptcy case of WorldCom was considered to be unprecedented in terms of its scale until the breakdown of Lehman Brothers in 2008. While the debtors of WorldCom were protected from some losses, WorldCom's shareholders received nothing.

Within days, the stock of not so long ago major player in the telecommunication industry fell well under $1. By the same token, 17,000 WorldCom employees lost their jobs together with insurance and pensions, which have collapsed along with the share price.

Three years after the fraud was revealed, Bernard Ebbers, who had already left the company's CEO position, was found guilty and sentenced to 25 years of prison for the charges of fraud, conspiracy and filing false documents. On April 2004 WorldCom emerged from Chapter 11 under the name of MCI with Michael Capellas as new CEO and CFO Robert Blakely. Supported by 200 employees of the company's external auditor

KPMG and an additional 600 people workforce from Deloitte & Touch they then had the task of settling the company's remaining debt of $35 billion. Eventually, in February 2005, MCI ceased to exist as an independent company when it was bought by Verizon Communications for $8.4 billion.

WorldCom's fraudulent activities gradually took its toll on the entire U.S. telecommunications industry. Equipment manufacturers such as Lucent Technologies, Nortell Networks, and Corning which have initially been benefitting from WorldCom's fictitious profitability and projections ultimately suffered with depressed stock prices and were forced to lay off work forces, too. WorldCom's then larger rival, the telecommunication company AT&T (American Telephone & Telegraph) had been laying off tens of thousands in the late 90's as it was trying to match WorldCom's phantom profits which eventually led to its acquisition by Baby Bell SBC Communications in December 2005.

- **Legislative Consequences**

The WorldCom scandal could potentially have discredited US GAAP standard setting provoking the assumption that the fraud could only have occurred due to deficient accounting principles. However, there is a broad consensus that the WorldCom disaster was rather a failure of corporate governance. Following the downfall of Enron, the Securities and Exchange Commission had not yet enacted any new laws. However, after the senior management of WorldCom was charged with fraud, the Congress was pushed to answer the critics through legislative actions. Thus, a new US federal law, the Sarbanes-Oxley Act (SOX) emerged in 2002. It now applies to any company registered with the SEC and contains eleven sections that specify duties concerning the issues of corporate governance, compliance and disclosure.

In answer to the fact that at Worldcom, members of the senior management have been involved in the fraud, CEOs and CFOs can now be directly and individually be held responsible for the accuracy of financial statements. Moreover, it is no longer allowed to give credit to their directors or officers as WorldCom did to Ebbers. Concerning the relationship to the auditing company it includes guidelines stipulating that audit firms cannot provide any additional services that may compromise their independence and auditors can not in any way be involved in management decisions. Moreover, a new auditor rotation system that requires audit partners to change every five years and audit firms every seven years respectively has been imposed.

The most notorious section of the SOX is section 404 which requires the implementation and periodic evaluation of an internal auditing system and it has became the main contributor to the increased compliance costs. Since its introduction, companies have spent millions of dollars to comply with the new law which has increased accountability but, as critics say, also suppresses innovation. It can also be seen to be unfair and a overburden to the smaller listed companies as the similar priced compliance costs take a greater share off their revenues, leading a lot many institutions delisting and some even listing elsewhere, such as the UK where a lighter hand on governance has been implemented.

In Europe, the reactions to the Worldcom accounting scandal of the U.S. included the implementation of the mandatory 'Annual Corporate Governance Statement'. The Company Act 2006 has replaced the Memorandum and Articles of Association with a single document followed by the attempt to shorten the time limit on information delivery for small companies from ten to seven months after the financial year end. Alteration of the statement of duties of directors also took place together with the Operating & Financial Review being introduced for large firms. All of these changes were to try and bring shareholders and other stakeholders closer to their investments to supervise them more closely.

ACTIVITY

Evaluate student participation in group discussions, the depth of their analysis of internal controls, and the quality of their recommendations for improvement. Assess their understanding of the role of internal auditing in organizational effectiveness and risk management.

SUMMARY

- Internal Audit is a phenomenon for when an organization or department is tasked with providing their independent reviews of the system in an unbiased way along with the processes. Internal Audit is performed within a company in a direct manner with keeping the company standards in mind. Some people confuse it with statutory audits, from which Internal Audits are quite different
- Internal Auditing is an independent, objective assurance and consulting activity designed to add value and improve an organization's operations. It helps an organization accomplish its objectives by bringing a systematic, disciplined approach to evaluate and improve the effectiveness of risk management, control, and governance processes.
- The internal auditing supports effective and efficient discharging of the guiding and monitoring duties of the organization's management by producing assurance services for its internal customers relating to governance, control and risk management processes.
- The main purpose or objective of an Internal Audit comes as the provider of objective information to the upper management, government bodies, etc. Such objective information includes that of the control over the environment, risks for the organization, and much more. Each of the individuals who come for the Internal Audit are known as Internal Auditors, who are themselves sent by their organization.
- The possibility of internal auditing currently embraces wider concepts of community governance: risk and power – recognizing that organize exists within an organization basically to manage risk and advance valuable governance. The most significant vary is that the internal auditors are estimated to modify their mindset: from faultfinders to advisers.
- Once an internal auditor has completed the examination, the findings are presented in a formal report. The audit report describes how the audit was done, what it discovered and, if necessary, suggestions for what improvements could be made. It is usually presented to senior executives at the company. If changes are recommended, it's common for an internal auditor to be asked to complete a follow-up audit to determine how well the advised changes have been executed.
- An internal audit is an in-depth review of the finances and procedures of a company. This review can encompass one department of a company, or the entire business. Auditors will methodically delve into the project and write reviews from observational notes. An internal audit is a time-consuming process that can be quite costly.
- Audits are performed to verify that a company's processes and records are in compliance with standards or regulations. Among the most commonly discussed types of audits and the most stringently governed are financial audits, which are performed to protect public and shareholder interests.

- A performance audit is an independent assessment of an entity's operations to determine if specific programs or functions are working as intended to achieve stated goals. Performance audits are typically associated with government agencies at all levels as most government bodies receive federal funding.

REVIEW QUESTIONS

1. Why is internal audit essential for effective management oversight and decision-making within an organization?
2. What are the key areas and functions covered under the scope of internal auditing, and how do they contribute to organizational governance and risk management?
3. What criteria and metrics should be used to evaluate the success and effectiveness of an internal audit project?
4. What are the most effective audit procedures and techniques employed in internal auditing, and how do they ensure comprehensive and reliable audit outcomes?
5. In what ways do information system audits differ from financial audits in terms of objectives, scope, methodologies, and outcomes?

REFERENCES

1. Alles, M. G. (2015). Drivers of the use and facilitators and obstacles of the evolution of big data by the audit profession. *Accounting Horizons, 29*(2), 439–449. https://doi.org/10.2308/acch-51035.
2. Christ, M. H., Eulerich, M., & Wood, D. A. (2019). *Internal Auditors' Response to Disruptive Innovation*. Internal Audit Foundation. ISBN 978-1-63454-062-9.
3. Parker, S., & Johnson, L. A. (2017). The development of internal auditing as a profession in the U.S. during the twentieth century. *Accounting Historians Journal, 44*(2), 47–67.
4. Pett, J., Kristall, M., & Mack, D. (2017). Opportunity from disruption. *Internal Auditor, 74*(3), 57–60.
5. Wood, D. A. (2009). Internal audit quality and earnings management. *The Accounting Review, 84*(4), 1255–1280. https://doi.org/10.2308/accr.2009.84.4.1255.
6. Wood, D. A. (2012). Corporate managers' reliance on internal auditor recommendations. *AUDITING: A Journal of Practice & Theory, 31*(2), 151–166. https://doi.org/10.2308/ajpt-10234.

CHAPTER

6

Audit Procedures of Government Organizations, Local Bodies & NGOs

LEARNING OBJECTIVES

After studying this chapter, you will be able to:

- Understand the objectives and principles of government auditing;
- Describe the unique characteristics of local government audits; and
- Discuss the methodologies and techniques used in conducting miscellaneous audits.

KEY TERMS FROM THIS CHAPTER

Accountability
Authorizations
Financial repercussions
Government agency
Transparency
Acquisitions
Bankruptcy
Forensic accounting
Stakeholders

INTRODUCTION

A special audit is a narrowly focused audit that solely examines a particular aspect of the operations of an organization. An audit of this kind could be started by a government agency, but it could also be approved internally or by any other organization. When there is a suspicion that rules or regulations have not been followed in an organization's financial management, special audits are required. Audits relating to, for example, duties, authorizations, responsibilities, and internal control guidelines can be conducted in addition to looking into violations. Special audits are frequently associated with bankruptcy or corporate reorganization. In these situations, the audits are conducted in accordance with the bankruptcy advisory board's recommendations. Special auditing refers to a focused examination and evaluation of specific aspects of a company or organization's financial activities, internal controls, and compliance with laws and regulations. Unlike general audits, which cover the entirety of financial statements and operations, special audits target particular areas of concern or interest. These audits can be initiated for various reasons, such as suspected fraud, discrepancies in financial records, regulatory requirements, mergers and acquisitions, or stakeholder requests. The scope of a special audit is narrower and more defined, allowing auditors to delve deeply into the specific issues identified. This concentrated approach facilitates a thorough analysis of the targeted area, enabling the detection of irregularities, inefficiencies, and areas of non-compliance. The process of a special audit begins with a clear definition of objectives and scope, set forth by the initiating party, such as the board of directors, regulatory bodies, or external stakeholders. Auditors then gather relevant information through interviews, document reviews, and data analysis. The focus might be on particular transactions, departments, or processes, depending on the underlying concerns. For example, in cases of suspected fraud, auditors might scrutinize cash flows, procurement processes, and expense reports. They use various audit techniques, including forensic accounting methods, to trace transactions and verify their legitimacy. Additionally, auditors assess the effectiveness of internal controls and risk management practices related to the area under review. A critical aspect of special auditing is its flexibility and adaptability. Unlike regular audits, which follow a standardized approach, special audits are tailored to the unique circumstances of each case. This customization allows auditors to address the specific needs and concerns of the stakeholders, providing them with detailed insights and actionable recommendations. The findings from a special audit are typically presented in a comprehensive report, outlining identified issues, their implications, and suggested corrective actions. This report serves as a valuable tool for management to make informed decisions and implement necessary changes.

Furthermore, special audits play a significant role in enhancing transparency and accountability within an organization. By addressing specific concerns, these audits help restore stakeholder confidence and ensure that the organization operates with integrity and compliance. They also contribute to improving internal controls and operational efficiency, reducing the risk of future discrepancies and financial mismanagement. In regulated industries, special audits can help organizations demonstrate their commitment to regulatory compliance, thereby avoiding potential legal and financial repercussions.

6.1. GOVERNMENT AUDIT

Even in developing nations, government auditing has a fairly long history dating back to the days of organized government. Government audits' concept, content, and scope have evolved to reflect the nations' political, social, and economic developments. Additionally, it has addressed the demands of the administration. Its goal is to guarantee that the executive is held accountable for public revenue and expenditures. All government spending is primarily controlled by the Parliament and, in the case of States, the State legislatures through demands for funding. The fundamental tenet of this control is that no expense may be made unless approved by the State Legislatures or the Parliament, and funds for each such expense must come from either the State or the Consolidated Fund of India. Following the incurrence of expenses and account closure, the Public Accounts Committee reviews the prepared Appropriation Accounts. Therefore, legislative or parliamentary control is used both before and after money is actually spent.

There has been a massive surge in government activity, which has resulted in higher capital, revenue, and expenditure as well as higher receipts and borrowings to cover the increased spending. Government has entered the business sector, but this is not the same as government enforcing regulations and maintaining law and order. The nature and scope of audits had to change due to the evolution of government and the complexity of its operations, which included regulatory duties in a global setting. From accounting and regularity checks to an assessment of the outcomes of government operations, auditing has changed over time. Government auditing was initially mostly focused on expenses, just like auditing elsewhere. Auditing of tax and non-tax receipts was gradually undertaken. As public enterprises expand quickly, another important area of specialization, i.e. commercial audit was established. In addition, a sizable number of government-funded noncommercial autonomous organizations working in a variety of development, academic, scientific, and social research domains are mandated to undergo audits from the perspective of public accountability. In addition to adopting the fundamentals of auditing as understood and applied in the field to meet the needs of governmental transactions, government auditing has introduced fresh ideas, methods, and processes to the audit field. The U.S. N. The handbook on government auditing and developing countries provides a thorough definition of government auditing, which is as follows:

Government auditing is the systematic, objective, professional, and independent examination of a public entity's financial, administrative, and other operations carried out after they have been carried out in order to evaluate and verify them. The report that is produced after the audit includes conclusions and recommendations for future actions from the responsible officials as well as an explanation of the audit findings and, in the case of financial statement examination, a statement of the appropriate professional opinion regarding the fairness of the presentation.

Public accounting of government funds is facilitated by government audits. Together with accountability for the officials in charge of implementing them, it also offers public accounting for the operational, management, program, and policy aspects of public administration. In addition to highlighting the shortcomings of the lower hierarchy, audit observations based on factual data collection also assist supervisory level officers in implementing corrective actions. Government audits are not designed or equipped to act as investigative bodies, following every anomaly or misdemeanor to its inevitable conclusion. The primary goal of auditing is to help the administration while also making sure that the administration is held accountable to the legislature. However, an inherent part of the auditing function is to criticize administrative actions when appropriate. Since the criticism is offered in a constructive manner, this must be understood and accepted in the appropriate spirit.

6.1.1. Expenditure Audit

One of the main elements of government audit is the audit of government spending. The fundamental guidelines for auditing expenditures are to make sure that funds are available and that the limits on expenditures are set by a responsible authority.

These standards are:

a. That the expenses incurred comply with the applicable provisions of the statutory enactment and the Financial Rules and Regulations established by the appropriate regulatory body. The term "audit against rules and orders" refers to this type of audit.

b. That the expenditure has been authorized by competent authority with either special or general sanction. This type of audit is known as the sanctions audit.

c. The availability of funds that have been approved by the appropriate authority and from which expenses may be made. This type of audit is known as an audit against funding provision.

d. That the expense is incurred responsibly, taking into account broad and general financial propriety principles. Proprietary audit is another term for this type of audit.

e. That the numerous plans, initiatives, and projects that have required significant financial outlays are being managed profitably and producing the anticipated results. The term "performance audit" refers to this type of audit.

Each of the above audits is discussed in detail in the following paragraphs:

1. **Audit Against Rules and Orders:** The purpose of an audit against rules and orders is to verify that the expenditure complies with all applicable provisions of the Constitution as well as the laws and rules enacted under it. Additionally, it aims to ensure that the spending is compliant with the financial guidelines, policies, and directives provided by an appropriate authority.
2. **Sanctions Audit:** The auditor must make sure that every expense is subject to a general or special sanction from the appropriate authority. The goal of the sanctions audit is to confirm that the expenditure is appropriately covered by a sanction and to confirm that the sanctioning authority is qualified for the task at hand based on the authority granted to it by the Constitution's provisions, the law, any rules or orders made thereunder, or the guidelines for the delegation of financial powers established by a qualified authority.

3. **Audit Against Provision of Funds:** An audit against provision of funds attempts to determine whether the expenses incurred were for the intended use of the grant and appropriation, and whether the total amount of those expenses did not surpass the appropriation.

4. **Propriety Audit:** In "propriety audit," auditors look for instances of unjustified, preventable, or infructuous spending even when the money was spent in accordance with the laws and regulations in place. Over time, it became apparent that regularity audits by themselves were insufficient to adequately safeguard the public interest in the executive authorities' financial decisions. Even though a transaction satisfies every requirement of the regularity audit in terms of the different legal formalities pertaining to rules and regulations, it may still be extremely inefficient. A school building may be built, but utilized five years after it is finished, a case of avoidable expenditure, or a building intended for the installation of a telephone exchange may be built but not used for the same purpose, resulting in infructuous expenditure. Hence, audit should make an effort to ensure a respectably high level of public financial morality by examining the soundness, consistency, and economy of transactions. Due to these factors, the audit authorities have evolved the audit against propriety and are now combining it with their regularity audit function. It is challenging to create clear guidelines that will govern the audit process in opposition to propriety. The acceptance of such an audit objective rests on its ability to appeal to the auditors' and those whose financial transactions are being audited for propriety's common sense and straightforward reasoning. Nonetheless, the Audit Code establishes a few broad guidelines that have long been accepted as benchmarks for financial propriety.

Audit against propriety seeks to ensure that expenditure conforms to these principles which have been stated as follows:

A. The expenditure should not be prima facie more than the occasion demands. Every public officer is expected to exercise the same vigilance in respect of expenditure incurred from public moneys as a person of ordinary prudence would exercise in respect of expenditure of his own money.

B. No authority should exercise its powers of sanctioning expenditure to pass an order which will be directly or indirectly to its own advantage.

C. Public moneys should not be utilized for the benefit of a particular person or section of the community unless:

(i). The amount of expenditure involved is insignificant; or

(ii). A claim for the amount could be enforced in a Court of law; or

(iii). The expenditure is in pursuance of a recognized policy or custom; and

(iv). The amount of allowances, such as travelling allowances, granted to meet expenditure of a particular type should be so regulated that the allowances are not, on the whole, sources of profit to the recipients.

One could argue that enforcing economy in public spending is the duty of the executive departments. The purpose of an audit is to alert the appropriate authorities to instances of improper, avoidable, and infructuous spending as well as wastefulness in public administration.

5. **Performance Audit:** The audit's purview has expanded to include performance audits, full scope audits, efficiency, economy, and effectiveness audits. Efficiency audits examine whether different plans and projects are carried out, their operations are managed economically, and whether they are producing the anticipated results, i.e. the relationship between the resources used to produce goods and services and the output of those resources; and an analysis intended to determine the degree of economical and efficient operation. An economy audit examines whether the government has used its financial, human, and physical resources wisely as well as whether the agencies in charge of approving and allocating funds have kept an eye on economy. An evaluation of a program's, scheme's, or project's performance in relation to the overall targeted objectives and the effectiveness of the means used to achieve the objectives is called an effectiveness audit. Anywhere it is applied, efficiency-cum-performance auditing is an unbiased analysis of the financial and operational performance of a program, authority, organization, or function with the goal of finding areas where more economy and effectiveness can be achieved. The process for carrying out a performance audit includes selecting the subject, doing a preliminary investigation, organizing and carrying out the audit, and reporting.

6.1.2. Audit of Receipts

Although it is not as common nor as historical as the audit of expenditures, the audit of receipts has become established in certain nations. An audit like this allows for verification;

i. Whether the designated authorities have accurately assessed, realized, and credited to the government account all revenues or other debts owed to the government;

ii. Whether the relevant department or agency has created sufficient rules and processes to ensure an efficient check on case allocation, collection, and assessment;

iii. Whether or not such rules and processes are really followed;

iv. Whether sufficient safeguards are in place to guarantee the timely identification and examination of anomalies, duplicate reimbursements, counterfeit or fraudulent refund vouchers, or other income loss resulting from dishonesty, deliberate failure to levy or collect taxes, or carelessness in issuing refunds; and

v. Systems and procedures are reviewed to ensure that internal processes are sufficient to ensure accurate and timely accounting of demands, refunds, and pursuit of dues all the way to final settlement. Suggestions for improvement are also made.

The fundamental tenet of an audit of receipts is that, while individual cases of assessment, demand, collection, refund, etc., are important, it is more important to focus on the general than the particular are significant in the context of test checking. To evaluate the efficacy of the assessment process, a review of the court rulings made by tax authorities is conducted.

6.1.3. Audit of Stores and Stocks

In accordance with the tasks assigned, an audit of the stores' and stocks' accounts has been developed as a component of the expenditure audit. An audit is carried out to determine whether the regulations controlling the acquisition, receipt, and issuance, custody, sale, and inventory control of stores are well-crafted and appropriately implemented. The intention is also to notify the government of any inadequacies in the amount of stores maintained or flaws in the control system.

The audit of store purchases is carried out in the same way as the audit of expenditures: it verifies that the purchases are legitimate, cost-effective, and compliant with the purchase rules established by the relevant authorities. The auditor must confirm that the receiving and inspecting units have provided the quality and quantity certificates, and that the prices paid are fair and consistent with those specified in the contract for the supply of stores. The audit particularly brings cases of unprofitable store purchases and losses caused by subpar or faulty store quality. Accounts of receipts, issues, and balances are examined for accuracy, correctness, and reasonableness of stock balances, paying special attention to the established standards for stock holding level of consumption. The report makes special mention of any excess or idle stock, and regular stock verification is carried out to confirm its existence.

6.1.4. Audit of Commercial Accounts

Public enterprises are required to maintain commercial accounts and are generally classified under three categories:

i. Departmental enterprises engaged in commercial and trading operations, which are subject to the same laws, financial and other regulations as other government departments and agencies;
ii. Statutory bodies, corporations, created by specific statutes mostly financed by government in the form of loans, grants, etc.; and
iii. Government companies set up under the Companies Act.

6.1.5. The Role of External Auditors in Corporate Governance

One important and ever-changing facet of business is corporate governance. The interactions between different stakeholders in deciding the course and performance of corporations are known as corporate governance. The board of directors, management, and shareholders make up the majority of participants. The process of overseeing and managing a company's directors is known as corporate governance. Assuring management's accountability to shareholders and other stakeholders is one of the two pillars of corporate governance, the other being supervision and monitoring of management performance. Up until now, the two most crucial fundamental components of sound corporate governance have likely been "full disclosure" and the presence of independent auditors and directors, each of whom has a different method for verifying that the information supplied by the company is accurate and fairly stated. Companies are expected to fully comply with regulatory requirements and professional pronouncements that outline the contents of full disclosure. Because the external director and external auditor are independent, the directors and auditors will need to put in a lot of distance in order to reassure shareholders that their tasks have been completed.

1. **Role of External Auditors in Corporate Governance:** A crucial part of the corporate governance structure is played by external auditors. They carry out one of the most significant corporate governance audits that support the oversight of management's operations. Financial statement audits improve the accuracy of disclosures, boosting public trust in the openness of the business. In terms of corporate governance, external auditors' job is to ensure that the management and board of directors are behaving responsibly with regard to the investment interests of the shareholders. Maintaining objectivity allows the external auditors to make sure that the company's internal controls are robust and efficient, which benefits the shareholders. Additionally, external auditors can support the Board of Directors' ability to oversee the financial reporting process more effectively by collaborating with the audit committee and communicating with internal auditors.

Nonetheless, since the audit function is limited in its ability to combat fraud, it is necessary to recognize the "audit expectations gap." During an audit, it is not reasonable to expect the external auditor to discover every fraud and mistake. The external auditor must declare in the annual report that the financial statements present a true and fair view, in accordance with the Cadbury Report. It is crucial to understand that the external auditor's role does not include preparing the financial statements, assuring the accuracy of the data in the financial statements, or ensuring the company will continue as a going concern. The Cadbury Report made clear that the question was not whether an audit was necessary, but rather how the external auditors could guarantee that the audit was carried out efficiently and impartially.

Nonetheless, since the audit function is limited in its ability to combat fraud, it is necessary to recognize the "audit expectations gap." During an audit, it is not reasonable to expect the external auditor to discover every fraud and mistake. The external auditor must declare in the annual report that the financial statements present a true and fair view, in accordance with the Cadbury Report. It is crucial to understand that the external auditor's role does not include preparing the financial statements, assuring the accuracy of the data in the financial statements, or ensuring the company will continue as a going concern. The Cadbury Report made clear that the question was not whether an audit was necessary, but rather how the external auditors could guarantee that the audit was carried out efficiently and impartially.

2. **Auditor Independence:** It is expected of external auditors to report on the company impartially and independently of the organization. In actuality, auditors need to be independent in order to carry out their duties properly. To give the investing public the confidence to base their decisions on the financial statements, they must carry out their duties in the

most impartial and trustworthy way possible. The Cadbury Report states that the close bond between auditors and company managers as well as the auditors' desire to build positive relationships with their clients may have an impact on auditor independence. Providing non-audit services is one of the many risks to auditor independence because such services can be very profitable. Contracts for non-audit services can only be acquired by auditors who have a positive working relationship with management. The Cadbury Report emphasized that in order for external auditors to collaborate with company management rather than against it, a balance must be struck, and in doing so, they must serve shareholders. This is a challenging route. The simplest approach to guarantee that this equilibrium is reached is to create audit committees and efficient accounting guidelines.

The Cadbury Report advised every business to form audit committees. The interests of shareholders are represented by audit committees. In addition to overseeing the financial reporting process to promote sound corporate governance, they are also thought to be qualified to guarantee that the management whose financial statements are being audited and the external auditor have a suitable working relationship. The 2003 Smith Report made clear that the audit committee must take the initiative to bring up concerns with directors rather than ignoring them. The report also emphasized that independent non-executive directors should make up the majority of the audit committee. Comprehensive details about the functions and duties of the audit committee should be included in the company's annual reports.

3. **Lessons from Financial Scandals: Collapse of Enron:** The Texas-based energy trading company Enron is the first scandal to rock the auditing industry (Balsam, Krishnan, & Yang, 2003). The trust in auditors and the accuracy of financial reporting have both been severely damaged as a result. There were doubts about the external auditors' independence and the quality of the audit. Enron's accounting and auditing practices in this instance were dishonest. Enron's auditor, Arthur Andersen, participated in the company's dishonest accounting and auditing. One of the main causes of the company's demise is the audit function's failure. Enron established four special purpose entities (SPEs) called "The Raptors." SPEs are created so that a business can collaborate with other interested parties to form a joint venture in order to carry out a particular transaction. The other parties to this transaction won't be exposed to the risks that are typically connected to the business's operations. U. Under certain circumstances, companies may be able to record the gains and losses of SPEs without disclosing their assets and liabilities thanks to generally accepted accounting principles (GAPP). Enron was able to avoid consolidating certain SPEs and thus adding more than $1 billion in debt to its balance sheet. The issue is that these entities were included in the core financial statements despite their losses rapidly reaching billion-dollar levels. Subsequently, it emerged that Enron suffered significant losses. After a precipitous decline in the company's stock price, Enron

filed for bankruptcy in December 2001.

There are numerous instances of Enron's dishonest accounting throughout the company. For instance, the business declared profits from a joint venture with Blockbuster Video that was never fulfilled. Enron restated its financial statements in 2002, a move that actually resulted in a $600 million decrease in reported profits. Actually, for the financial statements from 1997 to 2000, the process led to a $628 million increase in debt and a $591 million decline in cumulative profit. The earlier exclusion of three off-balance sheet entities was the primary cause of the disparity in the profit figures. Due to this profit inflation, the business was able to increase its earnings per share (EPS). The company was discovered to have established multiple off-balance sheet entities in order to remove significant amounts of debt from its accounts in addition to manipulating the accounting figures to inflate the earnings. These kinds of special purpose organizations can be used to conceal liabilities from the balance sheet of a business, giving the impression that the financial statements are much better than they actually are. This indicates that a sizable portion of liabilities that were primarily attributable to another legal entity were exempt from disclosure requirements on Enron's financial statements. The conflicts of interest between the external auditor and management are the reason behind all these problems and the question of "why did Enron's auditor allow this type of activity?"

Since Arthur Andersen has a conflict of interest due to the large consulting fees it received from Enron, they have been accused of using lax standards in their audits. In 2000, Andersen received $27 million for consulting services in addition to $25 million for auditing Enron's books. Arthur Anderson was paid US$55 million in 2001 for services other than auditing. Despite reporting on the company's financial statements, Arthur Andersen did not alert the shareholders to any fraud. This is as a result of management's involvement in the fraud. Even though the company was losing money, Kenneth Lay, who served as CEO from February 1986 to February 2001, received US$ 152 million in compensation. In the event that Andersen reports, they most likely won't be appointed in the ensuing years or work on non-audit projects. In particular, companies develop close relationships with their external auditors over time. Once more, it may have an impact on the auditing function and independent judgment. In this instance, Arthur Anderson's employees frequently switch positions within Enron. The function of corporate governance is impacted by these conflicts of interest. Members of Enron's internal audit committee have also developed serious conflicts of interest, which has prevented the committee from carrying out its duties of overseeing external auditing and internal control. As an illustration, Lord Wakeham, a member of the audit committee, had a consulting agreement with Enron concurrently. This demonstrates that, if they had been independent, those in positions of responsibility ought to have been able to spot fraudulent activity. Several members of Enron's board of directors have demonstrated a willingness to engage in fraudulent activities. It's also because conflicts of interest undermined the non-executive directors.

6.2. AUDIT OF LOCAL BODIES

In an urban setting, a municipality is a unit of local self-government. The administration of a locality—a village, town, city, or any other area smaller than a state—by a body representing the local populace, with a fair amount of autonomy, the ability to raise at least some money through local taxes, and the expenditure of that money on services that are considered local and, therefore, distinct from state and central services—is commonly understood to be what is meant by the term "local self-government." The following categories broadly group the expenses that corporations and municipalities incur: (a) general administration and revenue collection; (b) public health; (c) public safety; (d) education; (e) public works; and (f) other items like interest payments, etc. The main sources of funding for local governments are property taxes and octroi; additional municipal taxes include show taxes, profession taxes, taxes on non-mechanized vehicles, taxes on advertisements, taxes on boats and animals, tolls, and others. The state government may also award various kinds of grants to local entities.

a. **General Purpose Grants**: These are primarily intended to substantially bridge the gap between the needs and resources of the local bodies.
b. **Specific Purpose Grants**: These grants which are tied to the provision of certain services or performance of certain tasks.
c. **Statutory and Compensatory Grants**: These grants, under various enactments, are given to local bodies as compensation on account of loss of any revenue on taking over a tax by state government from local government.

6.2.1. Financial Administration

It would be imminent on the part of the auditor to understand financial administration of local bodies before embarking upon the audit. Some of the aspects are as under:

1. **Budgetary Procedure:** This is designed to support the dual goals of controlling spending and maintaining financial accountability. The primary goal is to make sure that funds are raised and used by the executive departments in compliance with laws and regulations and within the parameters of approval and sanction granted by the legislature or council, which is typically the body that sets tax rates and spending caps. State-by-state variations exist in municipal budget formats and heads of accounts. The corporation and municipalities differ from one another. The fact that revenue and capital items are not strictly segregated in municipal budgets is a noteworthy characteristic; the majority of capital transactions are typically covered by a "head" called extraordinary items. However, a number of

special funds exist, such as roads or, occasionally, distinct budgets for particular municipal tasks (e.g., education) or business endeavors (e.g., transportation, energy, sanitation, and water supply etc.).

2. **Expenditure Control:** The existence of a distinct division between the legislative and executive branches of government is a prerequisite for the financial control mechanisms implemented at both state and federal levels. It is challenging for the municipal council's executive to serve as both its inquisitorial body and its legislative body because of the council's integration of legislative and executive powers. Furthermore, the presence of an independent finance officer answerable to the municipal council or its executive committee is incompatible with the division of executive powers and functions within municipal government. This means that the only method left for regulating municipal spending is the state government's external audit system.

3. **Accounting System:** The format of municipal budgets and accounting has come under fire for being neither clear nor easy to understand, at times offering an abundance of information and other times insufficient data. A suitable management information system is not supported by either of these circumstances.

6.2.2. Local Bodies

The external control of municipal expenditure is exercised by the state governments through the appointment of auditors to examine municipal accounts.

The important objectives of audit are:

(a) Reporting on the fairness of the content and presentation of financial statements;

(b) Reporting upon the strengths and weaknesses of systems of financial control;

(c) Reporting on the adherence to legal and/or administrative requirements;

(d) Reporting upon whether value is being fully received on money spent; and

(e) Detection and prevention of error, fraud and misuse of resources.

Another tool for financial control used by local governments is auditing. The privilege of ultra vires is attached to this provision. An audit may "surcharge" a local government action if it goes beyond its legal authority. This practice dates back to the colonial era, and it is becoming less and less common even in England. This could potentially be attributed to the growing proficiency of local government officials. The learned author also believes that all municipal institutions should have an internal auditing system in place in addition to the external audit. Internal audit should be conducted by employees of the institutions themselves. It ought to be carried out continuously in accordance with a clearly defined program. As a component of an entire internal financial control system, the work of the internal audit should be reliable to the external auditor. In situations where municipalities are small or have inadequate staffing, there may not be an internal audit. In such cases, the external auditor must conduct in-depth investigation. As previously mentioned under government audit, "value for money" audits are receiving more and more attention. This type of audit focuses on determining whether urban institutions are carrying out their duties in an efficient, economical, and effective manner—sometimes referred to as "the three Es."

6.2.3. Audit of Non-Governmental Organizations (NGO's)

NGOs are non-profit organizations that seek financial support from members, donors, or contributors in addition to volunteering their time, effort, and skills to further their social goals, which include educating the public, offering healthcare, helping the underprivileged financially, managing emergencies and disasters, and providing education. Thus, charitable organizations, voluntary health and welfare agencies, research foundations, hospitals, senior living facilities, and religious organizations would all fall under this definition of an NGO. Grants and donations, a fund-raising initiative, member fees for technical assistance or services rendered, subscriptions, gifts, the sale of produce or publications, and other sources are the primary sources of funding.

Donations and grants that are the result of a promoter's contribution are classified as capital receipts and are represented as liabilities on the non-profit organization's balance sheet. These could take the shape of a revolving fund contribution or a corpus contribution. Contributions to an NGO's capital or corpus are referred to as corpus contributions. Generally speaking, donors must indicate whether their gift or donation will be included in the NGO's overall corpus. Usually, these contributions are made in relation to the total amount of money that an NGO needs. Contributions and grants made to a revolving fund have the purpose of rotating the amount by providing short-term loans for projects to other NGOs or beneficiaries, recovering the loan to provide another short-term loan, and so on. However, depending on the limitations set forth by the organization making the contribution (for the revolving fund) or by the guidelines established by the relevant NGO in this regard, any interest received from the beneficiary on such short-term loans from the fund could either be added back to the fund or credited to the Income and Expenditure Account.

Donations and grants received for the purpose of acquiring particular fixed assets are those whose main requirement is that the non-profit organization receiving them build, buy, or acquire the assets in question. NGOs frequently receive in-kind donations. These contributions consist of possessions like real estate, structures, cars, office supplies, etc. and items associated with projects or programs, like food, books, clothing, bedding, building supplies, and raw materials for training, e.g., reeds, wool, fabric, etc. An NGO can use funds for a variety of purposes, such as program or project expenses, maintenance costs, establishment costs, office and administrative costs, charitable giving, and donations.

The auditor may focus on the following while organizing the audit:

i. Familiarity with the work, areas of operation, mission, and vision of the non-governmental organization.

ii. Keeping abreast of pertinent statutes, particularly in light of recent changes, circulars, and court rulings. Act of 1976 on Foreign Contributions (Regulation), Act of 1860 on Societies Registration, Act of 1961 on Income Tax, etc. as well as the statute-related Rules.

iii. Examining the organization's legal structure as well as its bylaws, articles of association, and rules and regulations.

iv. Examining the organizational chart of the NGO, followed by the financial and administrative manuals, the project and program guidelines, the requirements and formats of the funding agencies, and any applicable budgetary policies.

v. Reviewing the minutes of the Board, Governing Body, Management, and Committees in order to determine how decisions affect the financial records.

vi. Examine and confirm the applicability of the NGO's internal controls, procedures, internal checks, and accounting system.

vii. Setting of materiality levels for audit purposes.

viii. The nature and timing of reports or other communications.

ix. The involvement of experts and their reports.

x. Review the previous year's Audit Report.

The audit program should include in a sequential order all assets, liabilities, income and expenditure ensuring that no material item is omitted.

i. *Corpus Fund:* The donations and grants received for the corpus should be validated specifically based on the letters provided by the donor(s). With the Investment Register and the actual investments in hand, the interest income should be verified.

ii. *Reserves:* Attest transfers from projects or programs accompanied by letters from donors and NGO board resolutions. Verify the transfer of the asset's gross value from the capital reserve to the general reserve as well as any adjustments made throughout the year.

iii. *Ear-Marked Funds:* Review the guidelines set forth by the donor institutions, the NGO's board resolution, and the policies and procedures governing the ear-marked fund schemes.

iv. *Project/Agency Balances:* Attribute payments and expenses in accordance with donor agreements for every balance.

v. *Loans:* Loan agreements vouch for the loans, and receipts and counterfoils are issued.

vi. *Fixed Assets:* Attest to all asset purchases, sales, and disposals, including depreciation and related authorizations. Verify the donor's letters and grant agreements as well. Verify the title of any immovable property, etc.

vii. *Investments:* Verify that the investments are physically in the name of the NGO by checking the Investment Register. Check that any additional investments or disinvestments have the approval of the relevant authorities and that the principal and interest amounts are recorded in the bank accounts.

viii. *Cash in Hand:* At the end of the year, physically confirm the cash in hand and impress balances to see if they match the books of accounts.

ix. *Bank Balance:* Verify the information for past due and unadjusted amounts by consulting the bank reconciliation statements.

x. Stock in Hand: Confirm the quantity and valuation of the stock in hand and get a certificate from management.

xi. *Program and Project Expenses:* Confirm the conditions for carrying out the program or project with the donor(s) supporting it. Consequently, for programs/projects involving contracts, make sure income tax is withheld, deposited, and returned on time. Additionally, confirm the terms of the contract.

xii. *Establishment Expenses:* Ensure that all employee state insurance, life insurance premiums, provident funds, and administrative costs are withheld, contributed, and deposited in accordance with the deadlines. Verify additional office and administrative costs like travel, stationery, and postage.

6.3. MISCELLANEOUS AUDITS

A wide range of audits that are not directly connected to financial statements or regulatory compliance are referred to as "miscellaneous audits." These audits, which aim to evaluate different processes, systems, and practices to ensure efficiency, effectiveness, and adherence to established standards or best practices, can cover a wide range of topics and areas within an organization.

6.3.1. Audit of a Sole Trader

There is no legal requirement for a sole proprietor to have an audit of their accounts. But a lot of these people have their financial statements audited because of legal obligations, like stock brokers or bank directives for loan approval, etc. As a result, he is able to decide on the parameters of the audit as well as how it will be conducted. For instance, he can specify that the auditor will also prepare the final statements of account or that only a portion of the audit will be conducted. He can also specify that only a portion of the accounts will be examined. Additionally, he has the authority to determine if the audit will be conducted annually or continuously. Based on these factors, it is preferable that the written contract appointing the auditor in this situation specify the exact nature of the work the auditor is expected to perform. This lessens the chance of miscommunication. In the event that the auditor's appointment is not documented, the auditor ought to correspond with his client, outlining the extent of his responsibilities. In order to get the client's approval, he should mention any restrictions that may have been placed on his work while doing so.

6.3.2. Audit of a Firm

Typically, the partners in a firm choose to appoint the auditor based on their own judgment or to fulfill a requirement outlined in the partnership agreement. The partners also decide on his compensation. It is crucial that the appointment letter explicitly outline the kind and extent of the audit that will be done as well as any restrictions that may apply to his work. An audit of a partnership firm is not required by the Partnership Act. However, for the purpose of verifying the adjustments made to the partners' accounts regarding profits and losses, interest and compensation, capital contributions, and so forth. The provisions of the Act pertaining to this matter, particularly those regarding the powers and audit of partners and their entitlement to profit and capital under various conditions, must be understood by the auditor. In particular, the auditor may make sure that the Institute's accounting standards are followed. If a statute requires the company to have its accounts audited, the auditor must qualify the report if there is any non-compliance with accounting standards. Alternatively, it wouldn't need to be qualified; just the disclosure of non-compliance with the accounting standards would be adequate. Additionally, he should review the partnership agreement and take note of the clauses pertaining to the following issues before beginning the audit.

1. The moniker and manner in which the enterprise will function.
2. Any predetermined length of time for the partnership, if any.
3. The capital contribution that each partner will make; this could be a fixed amount or could change annually.
4. The duration, at the conclusion of which the partnership's accounts will be closed on a regular basis; the ratios in which profits will be distributed to partners or losses will need to be borne by them; and whether any partner will be exempt from bearing losses.
5. The rules pertaining to the upkeep of books of account and the factors that need to be considered in order to calculate the profits of the company that the partners can split, e.g., the establishment of reserves, the depreciation allowance, etc., additionally, the window of time during which accounts can be reopened to address a clear mistake.
6. The partnership's ability to borrow money (when not implied, as in the case of non-trading firms).
7. The interest rate that will be applied to partners' capital contributions and loans, as well as the interest rate that will be assessed on their current accounts and drawings.
8. Whether any salaries are due to the partners, or if withdrawals against profits are allowed, how much of them?
9. The responsibilities of the partners with regard to the management of the company's business, including the partners who will serve as managing partners;
10. Who will manage the company's bank account? The ways in which the partnership's excess funds will be invested?
11. The rights and powers of partners, as well as their implied authority to guarantee the company's credit or hold it accountable, will be subject to limitations and restrictions.

In the absence of a partnership agreement, the provisions of the Act which concern the auditor are the following:

i. Each partner is required to contribute an equal amount of capital.
ii. The partners share equally in profits and losses.
iii. The partners are not entitled to any interest on capital.
iv. Where a partner is entitled to interest on the capital subscribed by him, such interest will be payable only out of profits.
v. A partner is entitled to interest at 6 per cent per annum on his advances and loans over and above the capital.
vi. Every partner can take part in the management of the business. A partner is, however, not entitled to receive any remuneration for taking part in the conduct of the business.
vii. Every partner has the right to inspect and to take a copy of any of the books of the firm.
viii. A partner is entitled to be indemnified for all payments made and liabilities incurred by him in the ordinary course of business or in the preservation of the firm's property.

ix. The property of the firm must be held and used by the partners exclusively for the purpose of business.

x. If a partner derives any profit for himself from any transaction of the firm or from the use of the property or business connections of the firm or the firm name, he must account for that profit and pay it to the firm; also the profit from any competing business carried on by a partner without other partners' consent must also be accounted for and paid to the firm.

xi. In the absence of any usage or custom of trade to the contrary, the implied authority of partner does not empower him to:

- Submit a dispute relating to the business of the firm to arbitration;
- Open a bank account on behalf of the firm in his own name;
- Compromise or relinquish any claim or portion of a claim by the firm;
- Withdraw a suit or proceeding filed on behalf of the firm;
- Admit any liability in a suit or proceeding against the firm;
- Acquire immovable property on behalf of the firm;
- Transfer immovable property belonging to the firm; or
- Enter into partnership on behalf of the firm.

xii. The firm is liable to third parties:

- If a partner, acting within the scope of his, receives money and misapplies it, or
- If the firm in the ordinary course of the business receives money, which is misapplied by a partner.

xiii. No person can be introduced as a partner without the consent of the other partners.

xiv. Any differences arising as to ordinary matters connected with the business are to be decided by the majority of the partners, but no change can be made in the nature of the business without the consent of all the partners.

xv. If, on the death or retirement of a partner, no final settlement has been effected and the business is carried on by the surviving or continuing partners, the outgoing partner or his estate has the option of claiming:

- Such share of profits as may be attributable to his share of the assets; or
- Interest at 6 per cent per annum on his share of partnership assets.

xvi. On dissolution of the partnership, every partner has the right to have the goodwill of the business sold for the common benefit of all the partners.

xvii. On a dissolution of the firm, the losses, including deficiencies of capital must be made good: (a) first out of profits; (b) next out of capital; and (c) lastly, by the partners individually in the proportion in which they share profits.

xviii. On the dissolution of the firm, assets are to be applied in the following order: (a) in paying the firm's liabilities to third parties; (b) in repaying partner's advances and loans; (c) in repaying partner's capital; and (d) the residue if any, is to be divided amongst the partners in the proportion in which they share profits.

- *Advantages*: On broad considerations, the advantages of audit of accounts of a partnership could be stated as follows:

i. The likelihood of a disagreement developing between the partners is reduced because audited accounts offer a practical and trustworthy way for them to settle accounts. In light of this, it is customary for the partners to provide and accept this as binding upon them, unless a glaring error is discovered within a predetermined amount of time after the accounts have been signed.

ii. When a partner retires or passes away, audited financial statements that have been approved by the other partners provide trustworthy documentation for determining what is owed to the retiring partner or to the partner's representative regarding their respective portions of capital, earnings, and goodwill.

iii. An audited partnership's accounts are typically recognized by the Income Tax Department as the foundation for determining the partners' assessable income and for resolving their Wealth Tax liability.

iv. When making loan decisions, banks and potential buyers of the company rely on audited statement of accounts as proof of the company's financial stability and profitability.

v. When negotiating someone's admission as a partner, audited statements of account can be useful, particularly if they are available for several prior years.

vi. An audit serves as a strong defense against a working partner or partners taking unfair advantage of the company, particularly when those partners are not directly involved in the day-to-day operations of the business.

Matters which should be specially considered in the audit of accounts of a partnership:

i. Attesting to the fact that the duly authorized partner's letter of appointment explicitly outlines the type and extent of the audit that the partners have in mind, including any restrictions that may apply to the auditor's ability to perform.

ii. Examining any minute books that may be kept to document policy decisions made by partners, particularly those that deal with capital and extraordinary expense approval, loan financing, asset purchases, unusual contracts, and other non-routine matters.

iii. confirming that the partnership agreement, or any later extensions or modifications thereto, authorizes the business the partnership is engaged in.

iv. Determining whether the books of account seem reasonable and appropriate given the nature of the partnership's business.

v. Confirming in general that no partner's interests have been adversely impacted by anything the partnership has done that it was not permitted to do by the partnership deed or by any breach of a clause in the partnership agreements.

vi. Verifying that the accounts have accounted for the partnership's share of the company's tax liability before calculating the profit divided among the partners.

vii. Confirming that the partners have split the earnings and losses according to the agreed-upon profit-sharing ratio.

From the aforementioned procedures, it can be seen that the audit of a partnership, like the audit of any other commercial endeavor, ends with the verification of the profit and loss account and the balance sheet to make sure these accurately reflect the firm's current state of affairs. An important aspect of this type of audit is looking over the partnership agreement with the goal of allowing the auditor to report to the partners if any partner's interest has been negatively impacted due to the firm engaging in activities for which it was not authorized or in violation of any partnership agreement provisions.

- *Reports on Accounts of Sole Traders and Partnerships:* In the case of partnerships and sole proprietors, there is no required format for the auditor's report. Frequently, the sole proprietors' and companies' auditors only have two things to say about the audited accounts: "Audited and found correct" or "Examined and found correct." Since it does not indicate the scope of the account examination that has been done, this type of reporting is not advised. The purpose of the Guidance Note on Members' Duties regarding Engagements involving Financial Statement Compilations is to offer guidance on the professional responsibilities of Institute of Chartered Accountants members when they undertake engagements involving the compilation of financial statements or other financial information, as well as the format and content of the report that is issued in connection with such a compilation. This is done to prevent users of the statements from misinterpreting the association of the member's name with the financial statements as having been audited by him. For the member, the goal of a compilation engagement is to gather, categorize, and summarize financial information using accounting expertise rather than auditing expertise. This typically means distilling complex data into a form that is manageable and comprehensible without the need to verify the claims that support that information. The processes in place are not intended to allow the member to voice any opinions regarding the financial data. However, because the service was provided with due care and professional competence, users of the compiled financial information benefit in some way from the member's involvement.

In most cases, a compilation engagement entails the preparation of financial statements, which may or may not be a full set of financial statements.

Additional financial information may also be gathered, categorized, and summarized. Engagements to offer restricted support to a customer in the creation of financial statements (e.g., choosing a suitable accounting policy) do not belong in the category of financial information compilation.

6.3.3. Audit of Small Companies

The auditors' roles and responsibilities with regard to each small business client are the same as those in larger audits, and a successful completion of the work necessitates the deft application and adaptation of auditing principles to the particular situation. The arrangement and scope of the work should be precisely defined and documented, especially since the relationship with the directors is usually less formal. Thus, the following paragraphs list several issues that small businesses face as well as procedural details that are crucial in this regard:

1. **Letter of Engagement**: It is recommended that the auditor provide their client (Beattie, Fearnley, & Hines, 2015) with a detailed scope of responsibilities regarding the audit as well as any further work that needs to be done, and that they receive an acknowledgement of this information.

   Upon engagement, the auditors ought to elucidate to the directors the management's duties regarding the compilation of the accounts and the implementation of an internal control framework that is suitable for the enterprise's requirements. The letter should also outline the auditors' ability to rely on a reliable system. This should then be verified in writing, possibly in the letter of engagement.

2. **Internal Control**: At an early stage in the audit, the auditors should take care to bring to the directors' attention their findings on the system of internal control.

Problems in small companies arise in the application of auditing principles and procedures. Due to inadequate staff they are unable to apply these principles in totality. These problems mainly arise from:

a. Substantial domination of the accounting and financial functions by one person; and

b. Limitations in the effectiveness from the audit point of view of the system of internal control rendered inevitable by the small number of employees.

In most small businesses, one or both of the aforementioned points can be found in considerable amounts. From an audit perspective, the primary distinction between the small and large companies will be how much the internal control system and staff organization ensure that each employee's work is verified independently or complements the work of others. Internal checks and balances, while useful in small businesses for their intended purpose of monitoring management behavior, would fall short when used as a check on management itself. These restrictions on internal control's efficacy from an audit perspective may lessen its value to the point where the auditors will have to think about expanding their audit procedures. This will necessitate them testing more transactions and stepping up the processes for confirming assets and liabilities, such as stocktaking verification and direct communication confirmation of debtor balances. When a small number of employees leads to deficiencies in internal control, the internal control letter should acknowledge this and offer recommendations for strengthening the system. These would usually take the form of recommendations for improving the director's oversight and control in such situations.

Despite the extension of comprehensive audit procedures, it will become necessary in small business audits to rely more heavily on management representations, which are frequently not corroborated by external evidence or by the opening of records kept by other company employees. In these situations, the auditors may not be able to rely on their examination of the company's records, the evidence at their disposal, and their awareness of all the circumstances affecting the business in order to determine whether or not the representations made by management are consistent with and supported by the evidence. They have to decide if the available evidence taken as a whole is sufficient and consistent enough in their opinion to support these representations to their satisfaction. The auditors may rely on the records as a foundation for the creation of accounts that present a true and fair picture if, under the circumstances, they believe the records are sufficient and have been appropriately maintained. If they are unable to accomplish this, though, they will need to make sure that the reservation they need to make is stated in the report.

3. **Letter of Representations**: A letter of representation on the company's letterhead addressed to the auditors should be obtained following a discussion with the directors at the end of the audit and prior to signing the auditor's report. These letters serve to document management's position on important issues pertaining to the account, such as ownership and the methodology for determining the total amount of assets, liabilities, and contingent liabilities. They also serve as a reminder to management of their obligations. But these letters don't absolve the auditors of their duties in any way.

6.3.4. Audit of Charitable Institutions

In the case of the audit of a charitable institution, attention should be paid to the following matters:

1. **General**

a. Examining the charter that established the nonprofit organization. It may register as a trust or as a company limited by guarantee under the Societies Registration Act, 1860. The provisions of any state legislation affecting the charitable institution's accounts and audit should be considered if it is a public trust.

b. Checking to see if the institution is being run as the legislation that established it intended.

c. Analyzing the internal control system, particularly with reference to the accounting of collected amounts.

d. Carefully examining the income and making sure that the funds have been consistently and promptly deposited into the bank.

2. **Subscriptions and Donations**

i. Ascertaining, if any, the changes made in amount of annual or life membership subscription during the year.

ii. Whether official receipts are issued;

iii. Verifying that sufficient controls are placed on unused receipt books;

iv. Acquiring all receipt books for the review period;

v. Verifying that the cash book and counterfoils match in a test; any cancelled receipts will be carefully examined;

vi. Acquiring the printed list of donations and subscriptions and comparing it to the total collections indicated in the accounts;

vii. Reviewing the internal check system regarding funds received from box collections, flag days, etc. and comparing the amount representatives receive to the correspondence and official receipts; paying close attention to the controls placed in place over collections and the measures implemented to guarantee that every collection has been accounted for; and

viii. Confirming the total amount of donations and subscriptions received with any numbers disclosed in reports, etc. published by the nonprofit.

3. **Legacies**: Verifying the amounts received by reference to correspondence with any figures and other available information.

4. **Grants**

i. Vouching the amount received with the relevant correspondence, receipts and minute books.

ii. Obtaining a certificate from a responsible official showing the amount of grants received.

5. **Investments Income**

a. Attesting to the sums obtained along with the interest and dividend counterfoils.

b. Verifying the interest calculations on securities with fixed interest rates.

c. Verifying that, in the event that any investment is sold, the correct dividend has been received division or bought cum. division.

d. Examining the dividend amounts obtained in relation to the investment schedule and conducting additional research on any investments held for which no dividend has been paid.

6. **Rents**

a. Examining the rent roll and inspecting tenancy agreements, noting in each case:

- The amounts of the rents, and
- The due dates.

b. Vouching the rents on to the rent roll from the counterfoils of receipt books and checking the totals of the cash book.

7. **Special Function, etc.**

Attesting to the total income and expenses for any unique events, e.g., plays, concerts, and so forth held in support of the charitable organization with any required cash statements and vouchers. Specifically, confirming that, after accounting for returns, the proceeds from every ticket sold have been tracked down.

8. **Income Tax Refunds**: Since charitable institutions are exempt from paying income tax, it should be evident that a refund of the income tax has been received when it has been subtracted from investment income. To do this, one must: (a) verify the income tax refund using correspondence from the income tax department; and (b) verify the claim repayment computation.

9. **Expenditure:**

a. Attesting to the payment of grants and confirming that no trustee, director, or managing committee member has profited directly or indirectly from them, and that the grants have only been given for charitable purposes or purposes falling within the scope of the objectives for which the charitable institution was established.

b. Confirming the schedules of securities held and inventories of both movable and immovable properties through examination of the securities, title deeds, and test-based physical verification of the movable properties.

c. Checking bank and cash balances.

d. Verifying that any money donated with a specific intention has been used for that intention.

6.3.5. Audit of Educational Institutions

The special steps involved in their audit are the following:

1. Look over the Trust Deed, or the Regulations in the case of a college or school, and make a note of all the clauses pertaining to accounts. Refer to the Act of the Legislature and the Regulation framed thereunder in the case of a university.
2. Go over the minutes of the Governing Body or Managing Committee meetings, taking note of any resolutions that impact accounts and making sure they have been properly followed. Pay particular attention to the decisions made regarding the management of bank accounts and the approval of expenses.
3. Verify that the system of internal checks in place ensures that demands made against students are appropriately raised by comparing the names entered in the Students Fee Register for each month or term with the corresponding Class Registers, which display the names of students on rolls and the test amount of fees charged.
4. Verify fees received by following the collections in the Fee Register and comparing counterfoils of granted receipts with entries in the Cash Book to ensure that the income from this source has been properly recorded.
5. To determine whether fees paid in advance have been carried forward and whether irrecoverable arrears have been written off with the approval of the relevant authority, add up the various columns of the Fees Register for each month or term.
6. Unless the Managing Committee has decided otherwise, compare admission fees with admission slips that have been signed by the institution's head and ensure that the money has been credited to a capital fund.
7. Verify that the person granting the free studentship and concessions is authorized to do so, keeping in mind the rules that the Managing Committee has prepared.
8. Verify that penalties for absenteeism, late payments, etc. have been properly authorized and either collected or remitted.
9. Verify that the hostel fees were paid before the students' accounts were closed and their caution money deposits were reimbursed.
10. Check the rent rolls, etc., to confirm the rental income from landed property.
11. Attest to income from investments and endowments, as well as interest and dividends; check the securities with regard to assets held.
12. Use the grant memo to confirm any grants from the government or local authorities. Find out why any expenses have been rejected for grant purposes if they have.
13. Report any past due balances for fees, rent for the dorm, etc. Managing Committee in order.

14. Verify that, unless they are non-refundable, caution money and other deposits made by students upon admission have been recorded as liabilities on the balance sheet and have not been transferred to revenue.
15. Ensure that any income over prizes has been accumulated and invested with the corpus, and that the investments representing endowment funds for prizes are kept apart.
16. Confirm that the staff's Provident Fund funds have been invested in the right securities.
17. Acknowledge donations, if any, using the list that is included in the yearly report. If a donation was intended for any particular purpose.
18. Attest to all capital expenditures in the customary manner and confirm them with the Committee's approval, which is recorded in the minute book.
19. Vouch for all establishment expenses in the customary way and inquire about any excessively high expenditure under any heading. If an annual budget was created, make sure that the Managing Committee properly approved any excess under any heading over the allocated sum. If not, mention it in your report to the Committee.
20. Verify that the Committee has approved and minuted the staff salary increase.
21. Verify that all bills are properly authorized and approved before being paid, and that the system for ordering inspections upon receipt and issuance of provisions, food, clothing, and other equipment is effective.
22. Check the inventories of all equipment, supplies, clothing, furniture, and stationery, among other items. Values applied to different items should be tested, and these should be verified using the Stock Register or comparable inventories from the prior year.
23. Verify the return of taxes withheld from investment income (interest on securities, etc.) since the institutions are typically exempt from paying income taxes, has been claimed and recovered.
24. Lastly, check the yearly financial statements and make sure that distinct financial statements for the staff provident fund, games fund, hostel, and poor boys fund, among other things, have been prepared (Hegazy, Sabagh, & Hamdy, 2015).

6.3.6. Audit of Hotels

Any hotel audit involves a number of issues, some specific to the business, like controlling cash assumes larger proportions. In a hotel, almost every sales location accepts both cash and credit. The total sales reported and the total bills issued by the sales point—which could be a bill roll or a set of bills with numerical controls—should be reconciled by the auditor. To make sure that all bills are included in the total, this numerical control needs to be verified. Next, the cash portion of the sales has to be verified against the cash books and the credit sales in total as well as in detail against the bills of the guests.

The special problems in a hotel audit can be summarized as follows:

1. **Internal Controls**: One of the biggest issues in any hotel is pilfering, so it is crucial to have internal

control. It is the management's duty to implement measures that will reduce leakage as much as possible. Their ability to prepare regular, maybe weekly, trading accounts for every sales point and closely examine the resulting profit percentages—investigating any deviations from the expected form—provides as proof of their success. These regular trading accounts for the period under review should be obtained by the auditor, who should then review them and get justification for any apparent deviations. An auditor faces a very serious issue if a hotel's internal control is inadequate or even fails. The auditor has to rely heavily on the gross margin reported by the accounts because many of his clients' records are ephemeral. As a result, he will have to expand the scope of his audit tests and think about qualifying his audit report if a material margin discrepancy remains unexplained.

2. **Room Sales:** The night auditor or the receptionist in large hotels typically posts the charge for room sales to the guest bills. The guest register is usually the source of these entries, so audit tests should be performed to make sure that the right number of guests are being charged for the right amount of time. To make sure they have been duly authorized, any discrepancy between the charge rates on the guests' bills and the regular room rate should be looked into. A daily report detailing the rooms that were occupied the night before and the number of beds kept in each room is typically prepared by the housekeeper in many hotels. The auditor should make sure that there are enough reports available so that he can test them with the guest register and with each guest's bill individually, as this report is not usually kept on file forever.

3. **Stocks:** Every hotel has easily transportable and marketable inventory, especially when it comes to food and drink. In order to maintain control over each unique store area and sales point, it is crucial that all movements and transfers of such stocks are accurately documented. Tests should be conducted by the auditor to guarantee that all of this documentation is processed accurately. Large amounts of stock should be stored in locked areas, with the department manager holding the key. Only dependable staff should be given access to the key, and unauthorized individuals shouldn't be allowed in the store areas unless they are closely supervised. It is especially important to monitor any movement of goods into or out of the stores, as it is not uncommon for an empty crate to be mistakenly removed in place of a full one. Many hotels value their stocks continuously throughout the year using specialized, qualified valuers. The balance sheet stock figure at year's end is then almost always based on this kind of valuation. Even though these valuers are not affiliated with the audit client, it is crucial that the auditor confirms to himself that the sums included for these stocks are appropriate. The auditor should think about participating in the actual stock take and performing specific pricing and calculation tests in order to reassure himself of this. Given that

the data will have been compiled separately from the hotel, the scope of these tests may be restricted.

4. **Fixed Assets:** Each hotel is likely to have a different set of fixed asset accounting policies. On the other hand, a lot of hotels use stock accounting to account for some quasi-fixed assets like silver and cutlery. This may cause confusion between individual stock items and comparable assets that are recorded using a fixed assets approach more commonly. In these situations, it's critical that stock items have extremely specific definitions, and the auditor should conduct tests to make sure the definitions have been strictly adhered to.

5. **Casual Labor:** In the hotel industry, casual labor is used extensively. Often, the documentation kept on these wage disbursements is insufficient. By advising management on appropriate controls, the auditor should make sure that deception occurs on this account.

6. **Other points**

a. Bills are typically made on behalf of travel agents or booking agencies for ledgers that are received through them. The auditor should ensure that funds are retrieved from booking or travel agencies in accordance with the permitted credit terms.

b. The commission that booking agents or travel agents receive, if any, should be verified by consulting the relevant agreement.

c. The auditor must make sure that accurate records are kept for renting out halls and other spaces to special guests, and that these records are recovered using the tariff.

d. Using K as a reference, the auditor should confirm a few restaurant bills. O. T. (Kitchen Order Tickets) or a foundational document. This would allow the auditor to confirm that revenue cycle controls are in place.

e. The auditor should confirm that expenses for remodeling and redecorating the hotel are capitalized while expenses for significant additions and alterations to the building are treated as deferred revenue expenditures.

f. The auditor is responsible for making sure that the accounts accurately reflect the occupancy-in-progress at the balance sheet date. (vii) The auditor should ensure that all food and occupation taxes collected from tenants have been turned over to the appropriate authorities.

CASE STUDY

CASE STUDY ON CORPORATE GOVERNANCE: ENRON SCAM

Enron is an energy-based company in Houston, Texas that deals with the energy trade on international and domestic based. Enron Corp. Is one of the world's largest energy, commodities and Services Company was created out of merger of two major gas pipe line in 1985.

Enron was created by merge between Houston Natural Gas and Internorth. Houston's gas's CEO Kenneth lay headed the merger of the two companies. After that Kenneth lay become the CEO of Enron. Earlier Enron was solely involved with the distribution and transmission of electricity and gas of United States.

In merger, Enron incurred a large amount of debt, and which resulted deregulation, after this Enron was no longer had the rights of its pipelines. The company had to find a way to generate profits and cash flow. Kenneth lay hired Jeffrey Skilling to work for Enron as an accountant. Skilling suggested the practice of buying gas from a network of suppliers and selling it to it consumers at the fixed price with a contract.

Enron was interested in the expansion, building, and operation of the pipelines, power plants, and other infrastructure. After just a year of operation Enron merged with a company called spectrum seven, a company whose chairman and CEO is the former president of United States, George W. Bush After just a year of operation. In 1999, Enron tried to expand their company by creating the Azurix Corporation, a water utility company. Overall, the Azurix Corporation proved unsuccessful financially. The Azurix Corporation, due to their failure to make an entrance into the market, went under.

Enron allegedly became successful, trading over eight hundred different products worldwide. Enron was named "America's Most Innovative Company" by Fortune magazine from 1996 to 2001. Enron was on Fortune's "100 Best Companies to work for In America" in 2000. The company's future appeared to be bright and promising continued success.

Enron faced many accusations of building links to political power. The company's connection to George W. Bush, and Houston's local politics has received much attention in recent past. In 1986, Enron was involved with Bush's company in joint drilling for oil. There are reports that Kenneth Lay and George W. Bush even shared friendship. Kenneth lay has employed politicians who have worked under George W. Bush also signed off on a law that deregulated Texas's electrical markets, which coincidentally resulted in large profits for Enron. The company also had political links that reached outside of the United States. Enron created a massive and highly expensive power plant in India, even though many Indian citizens and the World Bank strenuously objected. Allegedly protesters in India were beaten up and arrested. The United States ambassador to India, who opposed the plant eventually, joined the board of Enron oil and gas

The screws came loose in August 2001, when Jeffrey Skilling, the CEO resigned from office for unknown reasons. By October 2001, Enron experienced its first quarter where they did not report a profit. On November 8th, 2001 Enron told the SEC it was restating its earnings since 1997, reducing income by $.

Enron Scandal

In Enron's original natural gas business, the accounting had been fairly straightforward in each time period, the company listed actual costs of supplying the gas and actual revenues received from selling it. However, when skilling joined the company, he demanded that the trading business adopt mark- to -market accounting, citing that it would reflect "true economic value". Enron became the first non-financial company to use the method to account for its complex long- term contracts.

Mark-to-market accounting requires that once a long-term contract was signed, income be estimated as the present value of net future cash flows. Often, the viability of these contracts and their related costs were difficult to judge. Due to large discrepancies of attempting to match profits and cash, investors were typically given false or misleading reports. While using the method, income from projects could be recorded, which increased financial earnings. However, in future years, the profits could not be included, so new and additional income had to be included from more projects to develop additional growth to appease investors. However, Enron later expanded its use to other areas in company to help it meet Wall Street projections.

Here are some detailed frauds in the Enron's financial statement:

1. Enron's auditor applied reckless standards in their audit, which was showing conflict between interests.
2. Enron financial statement showed the booking costs of cancelled projects as assets, with the rationale that to no official letter had stated that the project was cancelled.

This method was known as "the snowball", and although it was initially dictated that stay under $90 million, it was later extended to $200 million where all found "strange transactions". Like "erratic cash flow" and huge debt.

Enron was estimated to have about $23billion in liabilities, both debt outstanding and guaranteed loans. Citigroup and JP Morgan Chase in particular appeared to have significant amounts to lose with Enron's fall. Additionally, many of Enron's major assets were pledged to lenders in order to secured loans, throwing into doubt what if anything unsecured creditors and eventually stockholders might receive in bankruptcy proceedings.

Impact

The collapse of Enron, the largest bankruptcy in U.S history, which led to thousands of employees losing their jobs and their life saving plans tied to the company's stock, which was calculated as 401(k). Reputation of Andersen, Enron's auditing firm, is damaged after company official admitted that thousands of Enron documents were destroyed.

Those events lead to flurry of probes, including a criminal investigation by the U.S justice department of Enron. The SEC and the Labor department – as well as six congressional committees-is also investigating the company's collapse. Enron officials have donated millions of dollars to Republicans and Democrats alike.

At the heart of Enron's troubles were numerous outside partnerships, set up to keep debt off its books, which were reviewed by Andersen. In addition, it was revealed that Enron has paid no income taxes in four of the last five years, using almost 900 subsidiaries in tax-haven countries and other techniques.

A major issue brought to light by the scandal is Andersen dual role as Enron's auditor and consultant, which critic's claim is a serious conflict of interest. Andersen has been accused of overlooking the huge sums of money kept off Enron's books because Enron represented a potential $100 million -a- year in fees to the auditor. Enron fired Andersen as the feuding corporations both came under growing scrutiny for their roles in the collapse of the world's largest energy trading company.

ACTIVITY

To engage students in understanding the purpose, scope, and procedures involved in conducting a special audit. Evaluate student participation in group discussions, the depth of their analysis of the special audit scenario, and the quality of their proposed audit strategies. Assess their understanding of the specialized nature of special audits and their ability to apply auditing principles in unique contexts.

SUMMARY

- A special audit is a tightly-defined audit that only looks at a specific area of an organization's activities.
- Special audits are needed when it is suspected that laws or regulations have been violated in the financial management of an organization.
- Government audit is as old as organized governments and has fairly long pedigree even in developing countries. The concept, content and scope of government audit have developed in tune with the political, social and economic development of the countries.
- The basic standards set for audit of expenditure are to ensure that there is provision funds authorized by competent authority fixing the limits within which expenditure can be incurred.
- Audit against rules and orders aims to ensure that the expenditure conforms to the relevant provisions of the Constitution and of the laws and rules made thereunder.
- The auditor has to ensure that each item of expenditure is covered by a sanction, either general or special, of the competent authority.
- The scope of audit has been extended to cover efficiency, economy and effectiveness audit or performance audit, or full scope audit.
- Effectiveness audit is an appraisal of the performance of programs, schemes, projects with reference to the overall targeted objectives as well as efficiency of the means adopted for the attainment of the objectives.
- Audit of the accounts of stores and stocks has been developed as a part of expenditure audit with reference to the duties and responsibilities entrusted.
- The system of financial control obtaining in the state and central government level is conditioned by the fact that there is a clear demarcation between the legislature and executive.
- Donations and grants received in the nature of promoter's contribution are in the nature of capital receipts and shown as liabilities in the balance sheet of NGO.
- Miscellaneous audits refer to a broad category of audits that are not specifically related to financial statements or compliance with specific regulations.
- The auditor to a firm is usually appointed by the partners either on the basis of a decision taken by them or to comply with a condition in the partnership agreement.
- The duties and responsibilities of the auditors in respect of the individual small company client are the same as in larger audits and the satisfactory accomplishment of the work requires the skillful adaptation and application of the principles of auditing to the individual case.

REVIEW QUESTIONS

1. What do you understand by the term 'government auditing'?
2. Mention the points to be considered in the audit of a leasing company involved in the leasing of capital goods.
3. Mention the important matters requiring the attention of the auditor in the audit of a charitable institution.
4. In respect of government audit, explain:
- Propriety Audit
- Audit of Stores and Stocks
5. Discuss the problems which are encountered while shifting from manual-based accounting records to computer-based accounting records.
6. You have been appointed auditor for the first time of a small partnership firm carrying on business for last several years. What special information you would obtain before commencing the audit?
7. What would be your duties and responsibilities towards its audit problems and how would you overcome them?

REFERENCES

1. Balsam, S., Krishnan, J., & Yang, J. (2003). Auditor industry specialization and earnings quality. *Auditing: A Journal of Practice & Theory, 22*(2), 71–97. https://doi.org/10.2308/aud.2003.22.2.71.
2. Beattie, V., Fearnley, S., & Hines, T. (2015). Auditor–Client interactions in the changed UK regulatory environment: A revised grounded theory model. *International Journal of Auditing, 19*(1), 15–36. https://doi.org/10.1111/ijau.12043.
3. Carcello, J., & Nagy, A. (2004). Client size, auditor specialization, and fraudulent financial reporting. *Managerial Auditing Journal, 19*(5), 651–668. https://doi.org/10.1108/02686900410534082.
4. Casterella, J. R., Francis, J. R., Lewis, B. L., & Walker, P. L. (2004). Auditor industry specialization, client bargaining power, and audit pricing. *Auditing: A Journal of Practice & Theory, 23*(1), 123–140. https://doi.org/10.2308/aud.2004.23.1.123.
5. Cenker, W. J., & Nagy, A. L. (2008). Auditor resignations and auditor industry specialization. *Accounting Horizons, 22*(3), 279–295. https://doi.org/10.2308/acch.2008.22.3.279.
6. Dunn, K., & Mayhew, B. (2004). Audit firm industry specialization and client disclosure quality. *Review of Accounting Studies, 9*(1), 35–58. https://doi.org/10.1023/B:RAST.0000010911.28983.62.
7. Ettredge, M., Heintz, J., Li, C., & Scholz, S. (2007). Auditor realignments accompanying implementation of SOX 404 reporting requirements. *Working Paper*, University of Kansas.

8. Fan, J. P., & Wong, T. J. (2005). Do external auditors perform a corporate governance role in emerging markets? Evidence from East Asia. *Journal of Accounting Research, 43*(1), 35–72. https://doi.org/10.1111/j.1475-679X.2005.00167.x.

9. Francis, J., Stokes, D., & Anderson, D. (2006). Is earnings quality higher when auditors are city-specific industry leaders? *Working Paper*, University of Missouri.

10. Gerakos, J., & Syverson, C. (2015). Competition in the audit market: Policy implications. *Journal of Accounting Research, 53*(4), 725–775. https://doi.org/10.1111/1475-679X.12087.

11. Hegazy, M., Hegazy, I., & Kamar ElDawla, N. (2015). Audit quality control measures: A practical investigation. Paper accepted for presentation and publication in the 38th Annual Congress of the European Accounting Association proceedings, Glasgow, April 28–30.

12. Hegazy, M., Sabagh, A., & Hamdy, R. (2015). The effect of audit firm specialization on earnings management and quality of audit work. *Journal of Accounting and Finance, 15*(4), 143–164.

13. Hribar, P., Kravet, T., & Wilson, R. (2009). A new measure of accounting quality. *Working Paper*, University of Iowa and University of Texas at Dallas.

14. Huang, Y., & Scholz, S. (2012). Evidence on the association between financial restatements and auditor resignations. *Accounting Horizons, 26*(3), 439–464. https://doi.org/10.2308/acch-50268.

15. Kothari, S. P., Leone, A. J., & Wasley, C. J. (2005). Performance-matched discretionary accrual measures. *Journal of Accounting & Economics, 39*(1), 163–197. https://doi.org/10.1016/j.jacceco.2004.11.002.

16. Landsman, W. R., Nelson, K. K., & Rountree, B. R. (2009). Auditor switches in the pre- and post-Enron eras: Risk or realignment? *The Accounting Review, 84*(2), 531–558. https://doi.org/10.2308/accr.2009.84.2.531.

17. Lawrence, A., Minutti-Meza, M., & Zhang, P. (2010). Can Big 4 versus non-Big 4 differences in audit quality proxies be attributed to client characteristics? *The Accounting Review*. Advance online publication. https://doi.org/10.2308/accr.2010.85.1.1.

18. Lazer, R., Livnat, J., & Tan, C. (2004). Restatements and accruals after auditor changes. *Working Paper*, New York University.

19. Lee, H., Mande, V., & Ortman, R. (2004). The effect of audit committee and board of directors' independence on auditor resignation. *Auditing: A Journal of Practice & Theory, 23*(September), 131–146. https://doi.org/10.2308/aud.2004.23.2.131.

CHAPTER

7

Depreciation

LEARNING OBJECTIVES

After studying this chapter, you will be able to:

- Define the concern of depreciation;
- Prepare to measuring depreciation; and
- Examine the depreciation within organization.

KEY TERMS FROM THIS CHAPTER

Computer equipment
Income statement
Journal entry
Purchase brands
Tax systems
Computer system
Income tax systems
Physical deterioration
Purchase decision

INTRODUCTION

Depreciation is the gradual reduction in value that many assets go through. For instance, during the course of several years of ownership, cars typically lose value. Age, market conditions, and wear and tear are a few examples of factors that may contribute to this decline. Certain assets, like real estate, appreciate in value over time. Depreciation can be quite shocking in certain circumstances. When a car owner tries to sell their vehicle later, it can be frustrating because new cars, for example, are notorious for losing value practically as soon as they leave the lot. Computer equipment depreciates even faster than other items because, like appliances, it becomes technically obsolete very quickly. When buying a new asset, people should definitely take this value decline into account, especially if they anticipate needing to sell the asset at a later time. Investigating the rate of loss for different new purchase brands, models, and makes can occasionally be very illuminating and provide information that may affect a final purchase decision. It is imperative to consider potential market fluctuations that may affect the appreciation or depreciation of an asset. For instance, in a down economy, a suburban house may lose value, but a car with low fuel consumption may gain value.

Since depreciation is an expense of doing business, many tax systems have particular rules governing it. In these instances, the word is used as an accounting term, and its usual meaning is somewhat altered. For instance, when a business purchases a computer system, it can deduct the entire cost of the system at once or over time in installments as the system's value decreases and revenue is still being generated. An accountant uses accumulated depreciation to write off an even amount of money each year by dividing the item's cost by the number of years remaining in its expected life. The write-off amount in accelerated depreciation is higher in the initial years and lower in the subsequent years. When writing off assets, depreciation has a number of important benefits. For instance, a large purchase's cost can be spread out over a number of tax years, offering a tax benefit over time rather than all at once. When it comes to filing taxes, tax accountants usually give their clients advice on the best course of action.

7.1. CONCERN OF DEPRECIATION

For tax and accounting purposes, the process by which a business accounts for the depreciating value of its assets is referred to as depreciation. Asset value is decreased by depreciation on a residual basis. Additionally, it lowers the current year's profits. Depreciation is a measure of a fixed asset's declining value. The life of an asset determines whether its value decreases. The way that assets are used determines how long they last. The process of distributing a tangible asset's purchase price over the course of its useful life is known as depreciation in accounting and finance. Depreciation is the systematic reduction of a fixed asset's recorded cost until the asset's value is zero or insignificant, as stated in accounting terminology. Structures, furnishings, office supplies, machinery, etc. are examples of fixed assets. The only exception is land, which cannot be depreciated because its value increases over time.

A fixed asset's cost can be partially offset by the revenue it generates thanks to depreciation. The matching principle requires this since revenues and related costs are recorded during the accounting period in which the asset is utilized. This aids in obtaining a comprehensive image of the revenue generation process.

An accounting technique called depreciation is used to distribute an asset's cost over the course of its useful life. Depreciation shows how much of an asset's value has been spent over a specific amount of time. Businesses can use one of several approaches to depreciate assets for accounting and tax reasons. Equipment and machinery are expensive assets. Companies can use depreciation to spread out the cost of an asset rather than realizing the entire cost in the first year and match depreciation expenses to related revenues in the same reporting period. This enables the business to deduct an asset's value over time—specifically, its useful life. Businesses regularly deduct depreciation from their costs in order to transfer the cost of their assets from their balance sheets to their income statements. When a business purchases an asset, it records the transaction as a credit to lower cash (or increase accounts payable), which is also recorded on the balance sheet, and as a debit to increase an asset account. The income statement, which lists revenues and expenses, is unaffected by either journal entry.

At the end of an accounting period, an accountant books depreciation for all capitalized assets that are not yet fully depreciated. The journal entry consists of a:

- Debit to depreciation expense, which flows through to the income statement
- Credit to accumulated depreciation, which is reported on the balance sheet

The term "depreciation" refers to two different interpretations of the same idea: (1) an actual decline in an asset's fair value, such as the yearly value reduction of factory equipment due to use and wear, and (2) the accounting statement's allocation of the asset's original cost to the periods during which it is utilized (depreciation with the matching principle). Hence, depreciation is the process of writing down the cost of a tangible asset (like equipment) over its useful life and the reduction in asset value. Long-term assets are depreciated by businesses for tax and accounting reasons. A business's or entity's balance sheet is impacted by an asset's decline in value, and its income statement is impacted by the accounting method used to depreciate the asset, which in turn affects net income. Usually, the cost is divided among the anticipated use periods of the asset as depreciation expense.

7.1.1. Causes of Depreciation

Depreciation is the ratable decrease in a fixed asset's carrying value. The goal of depreciation is to fairly represent the actual consumption of the underlying asset, resulting in a carrying amount that, by the time the asset's useful life is up, is substantially less than its salvage value. However, why is depreciation even necessary?

The causes of depreciation are:

- **Physical Deterioration or Wear and Tear:** The assets' quality and performance start to deteriorate as they are used. The careless use of the assets also contributes to physical deterioration. Wear and tear from erosion, dust, decay, and other factors also occurs when the asset is being used. One of the main factors contributing to physical deterioration and wear and tear in assets is their exposure to natural forces such as wind, rain, and sun. The asset cannot be returned to its original state or quality, no matter how cautiously or carefully the user handles it.
- **Obsolescence:** To become obsolete or out of date is to undergo obsolescence. We are a part of the technological age. New technologies appear quickly after they are developed. Antiquated products become obsolete due to advancements in technology. We can observe how the release of the iPhone 7 has affected the iPhone 6 model. The iPhone 7 has made the iPhone 6 outdated. Even well-maintained old machinery can become outdated as new technologies are developed.
- **Inadequacy:** The inability to use the same asset as a result of the firm's growth and size changes is referred to as inadequacy. If sales rise to 10,000 units, the 2,000-unit mobile phone manufacturer will need to invest in new and upgraded equipment.
- **Accidents:** Errors happen to everyone. Additionally, human error results in accidents. Accidents are inevitable, regardless of the company's level of safety measures and quality control.

The factors listed above all point to the cause of the decline in the value of assets that are currently being used. These value losses could occur all at once or gradually over the course of the asset's economic life. The company makes annual provisions for depreciation in order to record this value decline. There are several ways to figure out how much. Let's examine a few of the well-known ones. Equipment damage or destruction is a variation on the depreciation concept. In the event that this occurs, the equipment needs to be valued and potentially written off to reflect its decreased useful life. Asset impairment is a further variation in which an asset's carrying cost exceeds its market value. If impairment happens, the difference is attributed to expenses, thereby lowering the asset's carrying value. An asset's impairment or damage can be regarded as a cause of depreciation because they both affect the amount of depreciation that still needs to be recognized.

7.1.2. Tax Depreciation

The majority of income tax systems permit a tax deduction for the recovery of business asset costs or income generated. Both individuals and businesses are permitted to take these deductions. When assets are used up immediately, the cost can be written off as an expense right away or included in the cost of goods sold. Generally speaking, the cost of assets that are not being used right now must be postponed and eventually recouped, for example through depreciation. Certain systems allow the cost to be fully deducted, or at least partially, in the year that the assets are purchased. Some systems permit the use of a depreciation method or percentage to spread out the cost of depreciation over a certain life. Regulations differ significantly between nations and may also change within a nation depending on the kind of asset or taxpayer. The same depreciation lives and methods that are specified in many systems for financial reporting must also be used for tax purposes. Different rules apply to real property (buildings, etc.,) under most tax systems. as well as private property (apparel, etc.).

- *Reduce Taxable Income:* Claiming tax depreciation lowers your taxable income. This can significantly reduce your tax bill, effectively putting more money back in your pocket each year.
- *Improve Cash Flow:* By reducing your tax liability, you effectively increase your annual cash flow. This can be particularly beneficial for property investors who rely on rental income.
- *Maximize Investment Return:* Depreciation is a non-cash deduction – it doesn't come out of your pocket on an annual basis. Claiming it ensures you're maximizing the return on your investment property.

Property Value Appreciation: Even as your property appreciates in market value, you can still claim depreciation on the building and its fixtures and fittings, enhancing the investment's profitability.

1. **Capital Allowances**: An annual deduction of a predetermined percentage of the cost of depreciable assets is a common system. This is commonly known as a capital allowance, which is the term used in the United Kingdom. Both individuals and companies are able to deduct expenses for assets that were put into service during or prior to the assessment year. Capital Cost Allowances in Canada are set percentages of assets that belong to a certain class or kind of asset. The type of asset determines the fixed percentage rates. The capital allowance deduction is calculated by multiplying the fixed percentage by the tax basis of assets placed in service. These percentages are specified by the nation's tax legislation or regulations. The total set of assets, sets or pools by year (vintage pools), or pools by asset classes may be used as the basis for capital allowance computations. There are just three methods for

depreciation (Goldschmidt, Yaaqov, & Amiram, 1991).

2. **Tax Lives and Methods**: Certain systems define lives according to property classes that are established by the taxing authority. Several classes are defined by the Canada Revenue Agency according to the kind of property and its intended use. The Internal Revenue Service publishes a detailed guide that details the asset lives and applicable conventions under the United States depreciation system. Additionally, the table includes specified lives for a few frequently used assets (e.g., automobiles, computers, and office furniture) that take precedence over the business use lives. U. S. Tax depreciation is calculated using either the straight-line method or the double-declining balance method, depending on the taxpayer's preference. Percentages to be applied to an asset's basis for each year it is in service are specified in IRS tables. An asset's first deduction for depreciation occurs when it is put into service.

3. **Additional Depreciation:** For a portion of the cost of depreciable assets purchased in the current tax year, many systems permit an additional deduction. A £50,000 first-year capital allowance is offered under the UK system. There are two of these deductions available in the US. Up to $500,000 in depreciable tangible personal property costs can be written off in 2013. The deduction is completely eliminated for companies that purchase more than $2,000,000 worth of real estate in a given year. Furthermore, the majority of other depreciable tangible personal property entitles to an additional first-year deduction of 50% of its cost. Similar first year or accelerated allowances are provided by certain other systems.

4. **Real Property:** Longer depreciable lives are mandated by many tax systems for land improvements and buildings. The kind of use can affect these lives. Depreciation on real estate may be claimed using either the straight-line method or a small fixed percentage of the cost in many of these systems, including the US. For bare land, there is typically no depreciation tax deduction permitted. In the US, the straight-line method is used to depreciate residential rental buildings over a 27.5-year or 40-year life, other buildings over a 39- or 40-year life, and land improvements over a 15- or 20-year life.

5. **Averaging Conventions:** Calculating depreciation on each asset a business owns necessitates extensive record-keeping, particularly if assets are added to or partially disposed of after acquisition. Nevertheless, a lot of tax regimes allow all comparable assets purchased in the same year to be merged into a single pool. After that, a single computation of depreciation is made for each asset in the pool. There must be assumptions made in these computations regarding the acquisition date. A taxpayer in the US is able to utilize a mid-month convention for real property and a half-year convention for personal property. All property of a specific type is deemed to have

been acquired at the halfway point of the acquisition period under such a convention. In the acquisition period (and also in the final depreciation period if the life of the assets is a whole number of years), one-half of a full period's depreciation is allowed. According to US regulations, if the last quarter comprises more than 40% of the year's acquisitions, a mid-quarter convention must be held for each property.

7.1.3. Fixed Assets Accounting

Many pieces of equipment are likely to be broken, thrown away, or stolen without any entry being made in the accounting records for their disposal if internal controls over plant and equipment are not carefully designed. Then, the asset accounts will be inflated, and it is likely that depreciation schemes for those equipment units that are missing will go on. As a result, incorrect depreciation charges and the omission of losses on plant asset retirement will cause net income to be misstated. The use of controlling accounts and subsidiary ledgers for plant and equipment is a crucial control mechanism that prevents the failure to record the retirement of assets. Every major category of plant assets, including land, buildings, office equipment, and deal very equipment, usually has a serpent assets account and associated depreciation accounts in the general ledger. For instance, the general ledger will include the office equipment account along with the associated accounts for depreciation expense and accumulated deportation. The office equipment account in the general ledger includes entries for a range of products, including desks, dictaphones, filing cabinets, and typewriters. The cost of each item, its estimated useful life, book value, insured value, and other data that may be required by management as a basis for decisions on such matters as replacement, insurance, and taxation cannot be adequately maintained in this one general account.

For office equipment and all other general ledger accounts that represent numerous distinct units of plant property, a subsidiary ledger should be created. In a manual accounting system, the subsidiary ledger might be a card life, with a separate card for each piece of property, like a desk or typewriter. The asset's name, identification number, cost, useful life, depreciation, cumulative depreciation, insurance coverage, maintenance, and gain or loss upon disposal are all listed on each card. Every purchase of office supplies is recorded on a card in the subsidiary ledger as well as in the controlling account. Similar to this, each time a piece of office equipment is disposed of, it is recorded in the subsidiary ledger as well as the controlling account. A plant and equipment ledger also provides the benefit of easily accessible data for the recurring computation of depreciation and for entries documenting the disposal of specific property. Additionally, there is a stronger foundation available to support the date on tax returns, secure appropriate insurance coverage, and bolster claims for losses incurred on insured property. It is standard procedure in well-managed businesses to control plant and equipment expenditures by creating a budget that accounts for all planned acquisitions at least a year in advance. A thorough inventory of the assets currently owned, including their cost, age, and remaining useful life, is a prerequisite for creating such a budget.

- **Plant and Equipment:** Contrarily, current assets are more or less in a state of flux, experiencing little adjustments on a regular basis. Transactions that alter the amount of investment in a business's plant and equipment tend to be rare and involve relatively large amounts of money. Even so, internal accounting control procedures used by a business usually cover all transactions, whether they have to do with current assets or plant and equipment. The two groups' auditing processes are different. The balance on hand is of concern to the auditor when auditing current assets at the date of the balance sheet. With regard to plant and equipment, the auditor is concerned with all changes that took place during the audit period, regardless of the type of audit that is being performed. ALL of any substantial amount that either increase or decrease the value of such assets must be examined. Changes that occurred during the year are not substantiated in detail, with the exception of audits designed as complete audits.

- **Land:** Land that is utilized for business operations should be recorded differently from land that is purchased for speculation or investment. The accounting processes for the two categories of land are very different. While land acquired as an investment is classified with other investment assets and applicable expenses are sometimes capitalized, they are treated as non-operating or financial expenses. Land held for business use is shown on the balance sheet as part of plant and equipment, and expenses associated with it are operating expenses. The building that may be situated on land that is purchased for use in running a business should always be recorded separately from the land itself. The main reason for this is that, unlike land, where depreciation is typically not taken into account when calculating operating costs for businesses, buildings are subject to depreciation and must be treated as operating costs. When an auditor discovers that a building and some land are listed in the same real estate account, he ought to suggest that the buildings and land be kept apart, each with a distinct value. This will make it easier to calculate a building's depreciation separate from its land.

As land is essentially a company's most permanent asset, the auditor should make sure that the land account is charged with (1) the original cost, (2) the costs associated with the purchase, including the cost of tracing the title, recording the deed, paying commissions, and any other costs that equate to an increase in the purchase price, and (3) the costs associated with subsequent improvements that raise the land's value, like grading, draining, building approaches, sewer assessments, and treat improvements. Frequently enough. Improvement assessments are deducted from current operating costs. However, the land account should be billed for these expenses, when a piece of land is sold. The cost price should be credited to the land account, and any profit or loss on the difference between the cost and the selling price should be recorded separately. The original cost of the land plus the cost of any improvements made to it will always be represented as the balance of the land account under this procedure.

- **Vehicles:** Every organization that has vehicles must have a vehicle politics. This will write down the policy on a range of cases such as:
  - Insurance

- Depreciation
- Repair and Maintenance
- Purchasing, disposal and replacement
- Private usage of it by staff
- What needs to be done when an accident happen?
- Driver training and qualifications
- Carrying the passengers

In the budget procedure, replacement and repair costs have to be reasonable. Every vehicle needs to have a journey log in order to assess the cost of operation per kilometer and keep a close eye on private use. Purchasing fuel with cash carries a certain amount of risk; it may be safer to open an account with a reliable fuel supplier and make monthly checks instead.

- **Buildings:** When acquiring buildings through the purchase of real estate, the buildings and land should be valued separately, with cost serving as the basis for the valuation. Value should be calculated using cost plus additions and improvements minus depreciation when preparing annual reports. The buildings are typically listed at cost, with depreciation subtracted, for balance sheet purposes. The buildings' book values are added to the disparity. The question of whether the accounts for land, buildings, and other types of plant and equipment should be marked up from cost to a higher current value ascertained by an appraisal occasionally comes up. Working papers that separate the various buildings should be prepared by the auditor as part of the building account audit. The book values at the start of the audit period and the cost of any additions or deductions made during the period should be displayed in these working papers. These beginning and ending balances ought to match the account on the books as well as the amount of the building and ending balance on the balance sheet as both dates.

7.1.4. Advantages and Disadvantages of Depreciation

In economics and finance, the term "depreciation" is commonly used to describe the gradual loss of value. Every asset, including currency, stocks, real estate, and automobiles, is subject to depreciation. Numerous factors, including deterioration, obsolescence, and economic factors like the asset's demand, can cause depreciation. There are benefits and drawbacks to depreciation.

- **Durable Goods Depreciation**: Products that don't quickly deteriorate or wear out are considered durable. Automobiles, furniture, and electronics are a few examples of durable goods. Because of normal wear and tear and the emergence of better alternatives, most durable goods eventually lose value. For consumers who purchase brand-new goods, the depreciation of durable goods is a drawback because the value of new goods tends to depreciate more quickly. However, depreciation of goods benefits consumers who buy used goods; often, slightly used durable goods that are still functional can be found for a small portion of their original cost.
- **Real Estate Depreciation:** Real estate depreciation usually benefits

those looking to buy real estate and hurts those who already own it. For example, a person who is currently renting an apartment can purchase a home for less money if home prices decline, but the seller of the home will receive less money for the sale. Because local governments can impose higher taxes on homes with higher values, real estate depreciation may also be detrimental to their ability to collect real estate taxes.

- **Stock Depreciation:** The depreciation of a specific stock benefits those who do not own it and may want to buy it, but it hurts those who do own it and is comparable to real estate depreciation. Among stock traders, "buy low, sell high" is a common maxim. Stock depreciation lowers the stock's trading price, enabling investors to buy more shares for less money. To put it another way, depreciation enables investors to purchase low.
- **Currency Depreciation:** Devaluation, also known as currency depreciation, is the process of a currency's value declining in relation to other global currencies. Depreciation of currency typically works to the benefit of exporters and disadvantages importers. Foreign goods will become more expensive if the value of the dollar declines. As a result, customers in the U.S. to place a lower demand on imports. Conversely, less valuable dollars make it less expensive for foreign nations to purchase American-made goods.

7.1.5. Provision for Depreciation

Depreciation is a cost that is allocated as an expense and has the effect of decreasing a fixed asset's value while it is being used by a business. It is a non-cash expense that must be yearly charged to the profit and loss account, which reduces profit margin and raises free cash flow. Fixed assets have a lengthy lifespan. They are not purchased primarily for resale, but rather to help with business operations. Because of the profit they contribute to base on how long they are useful, they are in fact revenue-generating assets (Liapis, Konstantinos, & Dimitrios, 2015). Fixtures, buildings, vehicles, and machinery are examples of depreciable items. The following are some causes of asset depreciation:

1. **Obsolescence:** Assets are replaced because new and more efficient technology has been developed.
2. **Depletion or Exhaustion:** The values of assets such as mines, quarries and oil wells diminish due to the extraction of raw materials from them.
3. **Passage of Time:** Assets which have limited period of life in terms of years. The term amortization instead of depreciation is often used to refer this.
4. **Physical Deterioration:** Assets become worn out after used. It becomes less cost-effective to perform and spend more to maintain and repair.

The two most common methods used to calculate depreciation expense are:

1. **Straight Line or Fixed Installment Method:** An equal amount of depreciation over the estimated useful life of an asset is allocated for each year.
2. **Reducing Balance or Diminishing Balance Method:** Depreciation is calculated as a fixed percentage

based on the book value of an asset at the beginning of the accounting year but not the cost of the asset.

- **Provision for Depreciation in Financial Statements:** Accumulated depreciation is recorded in the depreciation provision. Due to the asset contra account, there is a credit balance that is displayed on the balance sheet as a deduction from the associated fixed asset. Over time, both the book value of the fixed asset and the balance of the depreciation provision increase. Depreciation account provision is a business liability. The current value of fixed assets will be reflected in the company's balance sheet through the depreciation account provision. The accumulated depreciation will be transferred from the credit side of the provision for depreciation account upon the sale of the asset. Next, we'll contrast it with the asset's sale price. Profit will be realized from the sale of the asset if the sale price exceeds the asset's current book value after depreciation has been adjusted.
- Reasons for Including Provision for Depreciation in Financial Statements

1. **To Match the Earning Revenue:** The primary motivation is to equalize the revenue earned. The matching idea is directly tied to depreciation. A concept known as the "matching concept" aligns related revenues and expenses. According to the matching concept, revenues cannot exist without expenses because expenses in a given accounting period represent the cost of the assets used to generate revenue. Without expenses, revenues cannot be generated. Consequently, the net profit or loss for that period will be determined by matching the expenses with the revenues earned during that same period. As an illustration, take ABC Woodworks Company, a woodworking company that buys its own specialized equipment. When ABC Woodworks Company invests in a new custom piece of equipment, it is built to last for many years. This indicates, in accounting terms, that the machine is used throughout multiple reporting periods, not just the one in which it was bought.
2. **Technological Obsolescence:** In addition, the reason for depreciating assets is the obsolescence of technology. Generally speaking, technological obsolescence happens when a new product is developed to replace the previous model. The company will need to purchase a new machine in order to continue producing goods after a current one has reached the end of its useful life. For instance, the market value of revenue will be extremely low if the technology is out of date. At that point, the company will deduct (i.e. completely depreciated), the technology and the requirement to purchase new, cutting-edge technology emerge.
3. **Wear and Tear:** Wear and tear is the third cause of depreciation. Wear and tear is the term used to describe how an asset has physically deteriorated as a result of use. The assets would have more wear and tear the more we used them. An asset's physical deterioration can occur for a variety of reasons, such as erosion, accidents, friction, etc. Not only is general wear and tear a cause of depreciation, but it also is.

7.1.6. Capital Budgeting and Depreciation

One key idea in capital budgeting is depreciation. This is because it should ideally not affect the cash flows as it is a non-cash expense.

It is added back during cash flow calculations for this reason. We still have the depreciation in cash because it never really left our bank account in the form of expenses. Therefore, on the surface, it might seem that depreciation had no impact at all. Initially, it was subtracted from the net income as shown in the income statement. The effect was then neutralized when we calculated cash flows by adding the same amount back.

- **Depreciation and Taxation:** Depreciation is a non-cash expense, it is true. Depreciation, however, is tax deductible. Therefore, the amount of taxes we pay is influenced by the amount of depreciation we pay. Recall that in order to determine profit before taxes, we deduct the amortization and depreciation amount from EBIDTA when calculating net income. This is the amount subject to taxation, from which we calculate the profit after taxes. Consequently, a larger depreciation amount will result in a lower taxable profit and, ultimately, a smaller tax payment. Therefore, depreciation reduces the amount of taxes paid, which indirectly affects cash flow. As a result, a high depreciation may even improve cash flows!
- **Depreciation Tax Shield:** The exact amount of taxes that were reduced because of depreciation can be calculated. This is known as the depreciation tax shield. Let's understand this with the help of an example:

	With Depreciation	Without Depreciation
EBIDTA	$2000	$2000
Depreciation	$500	$0
PBT	$1500	$2000
Tax @ 40%	$600	$800
PAT	$900	$1200

Now, as we can see that when we consider depreciation the tax paid is lower by $200 i.e., we pay $600 in taxes as opposed to $800. Therefore, $200 is the tax shield. However, we need not go through the entire calculation to come up with the amount of the tax shield.

- **Shortcut to Determine the Amount of the Tax Shield:** It is possible to simplify the calculation. We can calculate that we have saved $040 in taxes for every $1 in depreciation. Therefore, all we have to do to calculate the tax shield is multiply the total depreciation amount by the ongoing tax rate. For instance, let's consider $500 * 0.40. This comes out to exactly $200, which is what we got from the laborious computation up above. We must realize that the amount of the tax shield will change depending on the rate of depreciation. Therefore, when comparing accelerated depreciation techniques to straight line techniques, the former will offer a larger upfront tax shield. Additionally, the time value of money principle is applicable because we will be discounting the values of these tax shields. This is the reason why the accelerated depreciation method will be used instead of the straight-line method.

7.2. MEASURING DEPRECIATION

The process of assigning expenses to the proper time frame is called depreciation. Accountants are required to report financial statements in accordance with generally accepted accounting principles (GAAP); however, they are free to choose from a variety of acceptable approaches. Depreciation is regarded by economists as capital consumption. They measure depreciation in two different ways: either by valuing the equipment's depreciation in relation to its opportunity cost or to its replacement cost, which will yield earnings that are comparable.

The most profitable alternative use of equipment that is lost by using it for its current purpose is known as opportunity cost. Measuring the opportunity cost is the issue. Joel Dean suggests that one way to calculate opportunity cost is to calculate the value decline over the course of a year. When capital equipment, such as in a thermal power project, has no other use, this method cannot be used. Under these circumstances, replacement cost serves as a suitable depreciation measure. The cost of the new asset and the remaining value of the old asset are used in this method to calculate the asset's depreciation.

However, depreciation is only documented when an asset is replaced. Public utility companies such as railway and electricity companies use this method. Depreciation is an allocation of under-expenditure over time, according to accountants. These depreciation charges and allocations are based on implausible presumptions, like constant prices and a predetermined rate of obsolescence. Depreciation is charged in a variety of ways, all of which are crucial. Although there are other ways to calculate depreciation, the Straight-Line Method and the Written down Value Method continue to be the most widely used approaches.

- Straight Line Method
- Written Down Value Method
- Annuity Method
- Insurance Policy Method
- Machine Hour Rate Method
- Depletion Method
- Revaluation Method
- Depreciation Fund Method

Consider how each of these can be used, depending on the situation.

7.2.1. Straight-Line Depreciation Method

The straight-line depreciation method is the most straightforward and widely used technique for figuring out depreciation expense on the income statement. The straight-line depreciation method is the simplest to understand, despite its intimidating appearance. Since most businesses don't require the most complex methodologies, the calculation is simple and works for most of them.

- **How to Calculate the Straight-Line Depreciation Method**: The purchase price or acquisition cost of an asset must be subtracted from the salvage value at the time of retirement, sale, or other disposal in order to compute the straight-line depreciation method. The asset's useful life—a term used in accounting jargon—is then calculated by dividing this amount by the total number of product years that the company can reasonably expect it to benefit from.

In other words, writing it out like a math problem:

Straight Line Depreciation = (Purchase Price of Asset – Approximate Salvage Value) ÷ Estimated Useful Life of Asset

- **An Example of a Straight-Line Depreciation Calculation:** You choose to spend $5,000 on a new computer server for your small business. You project that the parts will have $200 in salvage value at the end of its useful life, which you can sell to partially recover your costs. Computers can only be used for a maximum of five years under current accounting regulations. Since your company has always upgraded its hardware every three years, you think that this is a more accurate estimate of the computer's useful life because you will probably be getting rid of it then.

Using this information, you can calculate the straight-line depreciation cost as follows:

- **Step I:** ($5,000 purchase price - $200 approximate salvage value) ÷ 3 years estimated useful life
- **Step 2:** $4,800 ÷ 3
- **Answer:** $1,600 annual straight-line depreciation expense
- **Understanding How Depreciation Charges Fit with the Income Statement, Balance Sheet, and Cash Flow Statement:** In the example we just calculated, here is what would actually happen, assuming you bought the computer for cash.

1. $5,000 would be moved from the cash and cash equivalents line of the balance sheet to the property, plant, and equipment line of the balance sheet.
2. At the same time, the cash flow statement would show a $5,000 outflow for capital expenditures.
3. For three years, $1,600 would be charged to the income statement annually. Accordingly, you would actually show profits reduced by $1,600 in year one, $1,600 in year two, and $1,600 in year three, even though you parted with $5,000 in year one and $0 in each subsequent year.
4. Each of those $1,600 charges would be offset by accumulated depreciation, a contra-account under property, plant, and equipment on

the balance sheet that essentially lowers the asset's carrying value. For instance, following the first year, the balance sheet would reflect a $5,000 computer, which would be deducted from the $1,600 accumulated depreciation contra-account, leaving a $3,400 net carrying value.

- 5. After three years, the asset would be retired by management, the carrying value would be $200 on the balance sheet, and the straight-line depreciation method would have finished. There would be no carrying value under the balance sheet's fixed asset line, the sale price would eventually return to cash and cash equivalents, and any gain or loss over or below the estimated salvage value would be recorded.
- **The Use of the Straight Line Depreciation Method, Or Any Other Depreciation Method, Can Result In Tax Timing Differences in the Reported Financial Statements**: One peculiarity of applying the straight-line depreciation method to the reported income statement is that management may choose to apply more accelerated depreciation methods on tax returns than on the reported financial statements prepared in accordance with GAAP regulations, provided that Congress passes laws permitting such methods. Management will probably take advantage of this since it can raise intrinsic value when it happens. In particular, taking the tax deduction upfront by accelerating depreciation on the tax return can result in more money saved this year, even though the reported earnings figures more accurately reflect economic reality due to the smoothed nature of the straight-line depreciation method. That's money that could be used for expansion in the future or increased owner dividends. (You are aware that a dollar today is typically worth more than a dollar tomorrow due to the time value of money. Nevertheless, this gives rise to an issue. There is a discrepancy between the accounting and tax records. Luckily, as the so-called tax timing differences work themselves out over the asset's useful life, they will eventually equalize. Special adjustments must be made to the reported financial information contained in the 10-K filing and annual report in the interim. The details of these changes don't matter to you at this time. In short, the difference between the income statement and cash flow statement will be adjusted for by creating a unique deferred tax asset on the balance sheet. That deferred tax asset will gradually decrease until the straight-line depreciation schedule's end, when the reported income to the IRS and GAAP align.
- **The Straight-Line Depreciation Calculation Should Make it Clear How Much Leeway Management has in Managing Reported Earnings in any Given Period:** You may have noticed by now that management appears to have a great deal of leeway in deciding how high or low reported earnings are for any given period. You're correct. Depreciation rules influence that, particularly for companies with a high asset count. However, for the majority of significant asset classes, there

are widely recognized depreciation estimates that offer some limitation. These can be found in documents referred to as Asset Life tables. For instance, The Clorox Company, one of the biggest producers of cleaning supplies in the world, claims that its computations employ the following depreciation schedule:

- Land improvements are depreciated over 10 to 30 years
- Buildings are depreciated over 10 to 40 years
- Machinery and equipment are depreciated over 3 to 15 years
- Computer equipment is depreciated over 3 years
- Capitalized software cost is depreciated between 3 to 7 years
- Furniture and fixtures are depreciated between 5 to 10 years
- Transportation equipment is depreciated over 5 to 10 years

7.2.2. Written Down Value Method

The value of an asset after depreciation or amortization is known as written-down value. It is computed by deducting cumulative amortization or depreciation from the asset's initial value, and from an accounting standpoint, it represents the asset's current value. A fixed percentage of the original cost is deducted in the first year of depreciation using the written down value or reducing balance method of depreciation. Nevertheless, in the ensuing years, depreciation is computed using the same fixed percentage based on written down values that progressively decrease over the asset's anticipated working life rather than the asset's original cost. Although the rate of depreciation is a set percentage, the annual amount allotted in this instance gradually drops. While this may all sound a little complicated, allow me to dispel any confusion with the example that follows (Natarajan, Harikrishnan, & Ajitha 2016).

- **Example:** A machine was purchased for $1,00,000, the estimated useful life of which is 8 years. The estimated salvage value of the machine at the end of its useful life is $20,000. It was decided to charge depreciation at 10% every year on the written down value of the machine. The results under the written down value method after charging depreciation for 8 years will be as shown in the table below:

*WDV = Written Down Value

Year	Cost/WDV	Depreciation @ 10% on WDV	Net Book Value (at the end of the year)
1	1,00,000	10,000	90,000
2	90,000	9,000	81,000
3	81,000	8,100	72,900
4	72,900	7,290	65,610
5	65,610	6,561	59,049
6	59,049	5,905	53,144
7	53,144	5,314	47,830
8	47,830	4,783	43,047

In the straight-line method depreciation example we looked at the conclusion of the eighth year, only $20,000. This represents the salvage value, and it was all that was left to be written off. But in this case, where the written-down value method of depreciation is being used, the asset's net book value at the end of the eighth year is $43,047.

There is still $(43047 – 20,000) = 23047 that needs to be written off. Therefore, under the written down value method, a higher percentage rate is required to reduce the asset to its disposable value in a given amount of time.

This is due to the fact that, unlike with the straight-line method of depreciation, the fixed rate of depreciation is applied to the asset's written down value or diminishing balance rather than the asset's original cost. The written down value method or the diminishing balance method will never bring an asset's net book value down to zero for the same reason. In a scenario where the estimated life of the Asset and the residual value of the asset can be reasonably estimated, the rate of depreciation may be calculated by the following formula:

Rate of Depreciation under WDV Method

$$\text{Rate of Depreciation} = 1 - \sqrt[n]{\frac{\text{Salvage Value}}{\text{Cost}}}$$

where n = estimated life of the asset in years.

- **Assumptions of the Written Down Value/ Reducing Balance Method of Depreciation**: The written down value or the diminishing balance method of depreciation is based on the following assumptions:
- The service potential of an asset gradually reduces with the passage of time.
- As an asset becomes old the cost of repairs and maintenance related to that asset gradually increases.

When an asset's working life cannot be reasonably estimated and it will need more repairs in the future, the written down value method of depreciation can be used. For instance, buildings, machinery, and plants, etc. Let's talk about a few benefits of the written-down value depreciation method.

- **Advantages of the Written Down Value Method of Depreciation**

1. This method is simple to understand and easy to operate. A separate calculation need not be made in respect of every addition to the main asset.
2. The amount of annual depreciation reduces with the reducing balance of the asset.
3. When the machine is new and has low repair costs, there is more depreciation than in previous years. As a result of increased use and asset wear and tear in later years, the amount of depreciation decreases and the amount of repairs rises. As a result, the overall cost of depreciation and repairs stays relatively constant over time. This aids in removing significant fluctuations in yearly earnings or losses.
4. Since the majority of depreciation is charged in earlier years, this method addresses the issue of assets becoming obsolete. This feature makes it simple and practical to replace the assets before their estimated useful lives are up.
5. This method is recognized by tax authorities and other legal bodies.

In spite of having so many advantages this method is not free from demerits. Below we will see some of the demerits of the written down value method of depreciation.

- **Disadvantages of the Written Down Value Method of Depreciation**

1. Under this method the book value of an asset cannot be reduced to zero.
2. The rate of depreciation has to be very high if the written down value is to be brought down to its estimated scrap value.
3. This method is not suitable for an asset having a very short life. The calculation of the rate of the depreciation becomes very difficult and creates problems in this case.

It is appropriate to use the written down value or reducing balance method of depreciation for expensive and worn-out assets like machinery, trucks, and other heavy-duty vehicles, where there is a residual value and where the question of repairs is crucial.

7.2.3. Annuity Method

The cost of the asset is treated as an investment under the annuity method of depreciation, and interest at a fixed rate is computed on it. The owner would have received interest if he had made an external investment of the same amount as the asset's cost. Therefore, in addition to the asset's usage costs, the proprietor loses the interest mentioned above when they purchase the asset. Depreciation is therefore computed to account for both of the aforementioned losses. The annual depreciation amount is calculated using the annuity table. The annuity method is especially useful for assets with high costs and long, fixed lives, such as e.g., Leasehold real estate, including buildings and land. The objective of the annuity method of depreciation is to maintain a steady rate of return on an asset.

To employ the annuity method, follow these steps:

1. Estimate the future cash flows that will be associated with an asset.
2. Calculate the internal rate of return on those cash flows.
3. Multiply the internal rate of return by the initial book value of the asset.
4. Subtract the result from the cash flow for the current period.
5. The residual value is the depreciation to charge to expense in the current period.

There is no general accepted accounting principle that supports the annuity method. This method of depreciation is also known as the compound interest method.

For assets with a high initial cost and a long lifespan, like real estate and buildings secured by leases, the annuity method of depreciation is helpful. Using this method has certain drawbacks, such as the possibility of frequent recalculations depending on the asset and its potential difficulty of comprehension. Additionally, as depreciation decreases annually, it may eventually become burdensome for profit and loss accounting.

7.2.4. Insurance Policy Method

Using this method, an insurance company receives the annual depreciation as premiums and issues an insurance policy equal to the asset's cost.

When an asset reaches the end of its life, the insurance company pays the amount specified in the policy, and a new asset is bought. The Insurance Policy Method involves purchasing an endowment policy from an insurance provider for a sum of money that is adequate to replace an asset. The main distinction between it and the sinking fund method is that we use insurance police rather than investments. The insurance policy's term will match the asset's lifespan. Using this approach, an insurance policy is obtained for the replacement cost of the asset.

The policy's amount is designed to cover the cost of replacing the asset once it wears out. Each year, a premium payment in the amount of depreciation is made. The money is received at maturity after continuing to accrue at a specific rate of interest.

The money received in this way is used to replace the old asset with a new one. Using this approach, the asset is secured in addition to receiving money for replacement. The asset is protected against loss at the time the policy is taken out. The method works with expensive assets that are squandered. At its initial cost, the asset account is still in place.

- Merits (Insurance Policy Method):
- It provides adequate funds for replacement of assets.
- Better security is provided to the investors by assumption of risk by Insurance Companies.
- The Insurance Company will pay a stipulated amount with which replacement of asset can be made.
- **Demerits:**
- This method is more expensive since Insurance Company keeps its own margin.
- When policy is surrendered for one reason or other, there is greater loss.
- The method is unsuitable, where additions are made to assets during the period.

7.2.5. Machine Hour Rate Method

The Machine Hour Rate Method of Depreciation is applicable to assets, such as plants and machines, whose lives can be measured in hours. As a result, we must maintain track of the total number of machine working hours used in a given fiscal year. This total serves as the machine's depreciation for that fiscal year. To compute depreciation, we must first determine the machine hour rate. This figure is then multiplied by the total number of hours the machine is used in a given fiscal year. The machine hour rate can be used to quickly calculate the value of various overheads. We can compute the value of depreciation using the machine hour rate method because it is one of the primary overheads of the business. We determine the total life of any fixed asset based on its working hour's life, in accordance with the machine hour rate method of depreciation. Next, we divide the actual fixed asset cost by the fixed asset life expressed in hours. We will calculate the depreciation rate per hour by dividing. The machines will be the primary target of this approach. As a result, we have substituted the word machine for fixed asset in the formula below. By adjusting the machine cost, scrap value, and estimated life in hours, you can use the following formula to find the hourly depreciation rate for any other fixed asset.

$$\text{Hourly Depreciation Rate} = \frac{\text{Original Cost of Machine - Scrap Value}}{\text{Estimated Life of the Machine in Hours}}$$

Now, we have to see, how many hours our fixed asset worked. By multiplying working hours of fixed assets in year with depreciation rate per hour, we will calculate the amount of annual depreciation.

Annual Depreciation

={Working of Machine in a Year} X Hourly Depreciation Rate
(Calculate in hours)

- **For Example:** A machine was acquired on 1st April 2004 at a cost of $ 45000, the cost of installation was $ 5000. It is expected that its total life will be 1,00,000 hours. During 2004, it worked for 8,000 and during 2005 for 12000 hours. Write up the machinery account for 2004 and 2005.

Hourly Depreciation Rate = Cost of machine + cost of installation / estimated life

HDR= 45000+5000/1,00,000 = $0.50 per hour

Dr.	Machinery Account				Cr.
Date	Particular	Amount	Date	Particular	Amount
1st April. 2004	Bank Account (Buying the machine) Bank Account (Installation cost)	45000 5000	31st Dec. 2004	Depreciation Account {8000 hours X $ 0.50 per hour} Balance C/d	4000 46000
		50000			50000
1st Jan. 2005	Balance B/D	46000	31st Dec. 2005	Depreciation Account {12000 hrs X $ 0.50 per hour}	6000
			31st Dec. 2005	Balance C/d	40000
		46000			46000
1st Jan. 2006	Balance B/D	40000			

- **Advantages:** Machine hour rate method of absorption of factory overheads has certain advantages.

  It helps to compare the relative efficiencies and cost of operating different machines.
- It brings to light the existence and extent of idle time of machines.
- It enables the management to decide how far the use of machine work is preferable to manual work.
- It is most scientific, practical and accurate method of recovery of manufacturing overheads.
- Cost reports prepared with the help of such rate are dependable and can help the management in decision-making.
- It provides useful data for estimating cost of production, setting standards and for fixing selling prices for quotations.
- It provides ready method for measuring the cost of idle machines if separate rates for fixed and variable overhead rates are calculated. When hourly rate is fixed on the basis of anticipated running hours of the machine, there is under-absorption

of fixed overhead expenses if actual running hours are less than the estimated.

- **Disadvantages:** Machine hour rate method of absorption of factory overheads has certain disadvantages.
- It involves additional work in assessing the working hours of machines and thus it is a costly method.
- It does not take into account expenses that are not proportional to the working hours of machines.
- It gives inaccurate results if manual labor is equally important.
- It is difficult to estimate the machine hours especially when production program is not available in advance.
- Blanket rate cannot be used and it makes the method more costly.

7.2.6. Depletion Method

Essentially, the depletion method accounts for natural resources instead of depreciation. Depreciation is typically allowed on the depletion unit basis for wasting assets, such as mines and quarries, which must be replaced. This means that an annual amount is allocated to represent the capital outlay that has expired based on output comparisons with the estimated total contents of the mine, etc. Consequently, five cents will be deducted for each tonne of stone raised if a $5,000 stone quarry with a 100,000-ton stone capacity is purchased. In order to extract natural resources such as coal, oil, wood, metal, salt, and others, entities in the extraction and mining industry have fixed assets such as mines, quarries, and wells. In contrast to the property, plant, and equipment utilized during the duration, these assets are depleted through extraction. The depletion method is used to calculate depreciation for such assets. Depletion is the division of the cost of a natural resource over a given time period according to the rate of resource consumption.

In order to determine periodic charge, we need following pieces of information:

1. Cost of natural resource also called depletion base
2. Determination of depletion rate for which we need following two items:
1. Expected total reserve available for extraction that expressed in particular unit of measurement e.g., tonnage, cubic feet etc.
2. Quantity of resource extracted in the period

Cost of natural resource is determined like other fixed assets of the entity. General principle is that all such costs that are specifically incurred to bring the assets into its intended use are included as cost of the asset. In case of natural resource cost includes:

1. **Purchase Cost of the Asset:** this is the price paid to acquire the land or property where extraction will be done.
2. **Exploration and Drilling Costs:** This covers the price of the labor spent locating the natural resource's position and examining possible extraction points. These expenses are incurred long before the extraction process really begins. The entity may choose to use the "total approach," in which case all incurred costs are treated as asset costs, or it may choose to add only those costs that were incurred upon successfully "hitting" the resource. In the latter case, unsuccessful attempts will be treated as losses.

3. **Extraction and Development Cost:** this includes all such efforts, assets both tangible or intangible that were necessary to extract the resource and includes machinery, temporary sight constructions, licenses, legal fee etc.
4. **Restoration and Rehabilitation Costs:** once the extraction work is concluded, entities are often duty bound to restore the location back to its natural state instead of leaving the spill and destruction behind. This cost is also added as cost of natural resource or in other words depletion base.

Depreciable value, also known as "depletable" value, is calculated by subtracting any residual value from the depletion base after the cost of the natural resource has been established. Depletion rate and unit of production method depreciation are similar. The entire amount of resource in a given unit is estimated by a surveyor or expert, and at the conclusion of each period, the units extracted are divided by the total units available. The depletion rate is simply 0.02, or 2% (100/5000), if the total estimated coal in the mine is 5,000 tonnes and 100 tonnes have been extracted thus far. The depletion rate can also be expressed in dollars rather than percentages. Depreciable value is then divided by the total amount of resource. For instance, if the total estimated amount of coal is 500,000 and the quarry has a depreciable value of $50,000, the depletion rate would be 10 cents per ton extracted. To compute depreciation using the depletion method, the entire formula is:

Depletion for the current period= Units consumed this periodTotal units of natural resourcex cost-residual value

- **Example–Depletion Method of Depreciation:** Methane gas is extracted by Uchali Corporation. Probability indicates that the methane reserves in the Soon Skesar valley are of superior quality. The cost of the plot of land has already been determined to be $1 million. A local company is hired to conduct the survey and identify the drilling point at a cost of $250,000. The preparation of the site will cost $100,000, and after extraction is finished, the entity is obligated to return the area to its natural state. Twenty years from now, the plantation is expected to cost 200,000. (Ignore the effect of time value). The resource is thought to contain 10 million cubic feet of gas, with no value for salvage. Uchali extracted 200,000 mcf of gas during the current period.

Considering the same example as above. Suppose, the next year latest survey report tells that recoverable gas is lesser than before estimate. It is found to be only 8 million. In second year, entity extracted 500,000 mcf of gas.

If estimates change, then their adjustment is made prospectively by adjusting the depletion rate and not retrospectively just like methods of depreciation in which change of estimate is dealt prospectively. The net book value for second year is 1,519,000 (1,550,000 – 31,000). With 8 million now in total and 500,000 mcf of gas extracted in second year, the depletion charge will be calculated as following:

Depletion for 2nd year = 500,0008,000,000×1,519,000

Depletion for 2nd year = $94,938

- **Advantages and Disadvantages of Depletion Method**: Some advantages and disadvantages of depletion method of depreciation are given below:

- *Advantages:*

1. It provides a method to charge amortization/depreciation for the companies dealing in natural resources, as these assets are different in nature and consumption from other fixed assets like car, building etc.
2. The method itself is easy to understand.

Disadvantages:

1. The method is simply used for a periodic reduction in the cost of the asset and it is unlikely that the carrying amount of the asset shows the real market value of the asset.
2. The method is highly subjective especially the number of units to be extracted is difficult to estimate.

7.2.7. Revaluation Method

The assets are revalued annually under the depreciation method of revaluation. The technique is typically used to calculate depreciation on a variety of low-cost fixed assets, such as small tools, livestock, patents, copy rights, and other assets whose values fluctuate frequently and whose lifespan is highly unpredictable. As a result, usable items are periodically inventoried and valued at cost, regardless of prevailing prices. The periodic depreciation expenses are thus given by the excess of the opening over the closing inventory. A company using the revaluation model can choose to carry a fixed asset at its revised value. The amount carried on the books following the revaluation is equal to the asset's fair value less cumulative depreciation and impairment losses. This method requires one to keep revaluing fixed assets often enough to guarantee that the carrying amount never deviates significantly from the fair value over the course of any given period. Only under international financial reporting standards (IFRS) is this option available. Certain fixed assets may have highly variable fair values, requiring revaluations as often as once a year. Revaluations that occur once every three to five years are deemed acceptable by IFRS in the majority of other cases. There are two approaches to handling depreciation that has accrued since the last revaluation when a fixed asset is revalued.

The choices are:

- Force the carrying amount of the asset to equal its newly-revalued amount by proportionally restating the amount of the accumulated depreciation; or
- Eliminate the accumulated depreciation against the gross carrying amount of the newly-revalued asset. This method is the simpler of the two alternatives.

To ascertain a fixed asset's fair value, use a market-based appraisal conducted by a certified valuation specialist. Use a different approach to determine an estimated fair value if a fixed asset is so specialized that a market-based fair value cannot be determined. Utilizing discounted future cash flows or estimating an asset's replacement cost are two examples of such techniques. Recognize the increase in other comprehensive income and place it in equity in an account named "revaluation surplus" if the decision is made to use the revaluation model and the revaluation raises the carrying amount of a fixed asset. However, recognize the revaluation gain in profit or loss to the extent of the prior loss (thereby erasing the loss) if the increase reverses a revaluation decrease for the same asset that had previously been recognized in profit or loss. Recognize the decrease in profit or loss if a revaluation lowers the carrying value of a fixed asset. Recognize the decline in other comprehensive income to balance any credit balance in the revaluation surplus for that asset, though, if there is one. The reduction in other comprehensive income offsets the amount of any equity that has already been recorded as a revaluation surplus. Any related revaluation surplus should be transferred to retained earnings in the event that a fixed asset is derecognized. The difference between the depreciation based on the asset's original cost and the depreciation based on its revalued carrying amount is the amount of this surplus that is transferred to retained earnings.

- **Advantages and Disadvantages of Revaluation Method of Depreciation**: The major advantages and disadvantages of revaluation method of depreciation are given below:
- *Advantages:*

1. The method is very simple and straightforward to understand.
2. This method could be applied to a variety of assets upon which assessment of inflow of financial benefits individually could not be estimated easily.
3. Where a business has many small assets, this method could be applied to all the assets collectively assuming all the smaller assets as one big asset.

- *Disadvantages:*

1. It may be the case that the asset could not be revalued every year or the cost of asset may not decline. In such a case no depreciation could be charged on the asset.
2. The sum of depreciation that is charged to the assets does not show a steady pattern.
3. The implementation of this method could become costly as revaluation exercise requires assistance from experts and so sometimes result in costs exceeding its benefits.
4. The revaluation is a judgmental area and the amount of depreciation to be charged depends upon it. So, if the revaluation is not carried accordingly the amount of depreciation charged could be miscalculated.

7.2.8. Depreciation Fund Method

This method allows for the replacement of an asset when it becomes useless in addition to accounting for depreciation. Using this method, an annual fixed amount is credited to the Depreciation Fund Account rather than the Asset Account and debited to the Depreciation Account or Profit and Loss Account. Every year, the asset is recorded in the books at its original cost. The money is invested in gilt-edged securities and is credited to the Depreciation Fund. Similar securities are also used to invest the interest on this kind of investment. It is easy to convert the securities into cash. An annual purchase of investments is made. Investments are liquidated when an asset loses value, allowing for the acquisition of new assets without negatively impacting the financial situation. This approach is specifically used when it's desirable to replace an asset when its useful life is coming to an end in addition to simply writing it off. Depreciation is set aside in a way that, when combined with compound interest, will cover the cost of a new asset less any scrap value that may need to be replaced.

- **Definition and Explanation:** The annual depreciation amount is placed into a fund under the sinking fund or depreciation fund methods. Every year, the same amount is invested in government papers or other gilt-edged securities outside the company, equal to the annual depreciation. The fund receives the income from investments, which is promptly reinvested. This procedure is followed for the duration of the asset's life, and at its conclusion, an amount equal to the asset's purchase price is accumulated in the fund. After that, the entire investment is sold, and the money raised from the sale is used to buy a new asset. This method's unique feature is that the money needed to purchase the new asset can be obtained through sinking funds or depreciation. Consequently, the business's working capital is safeguarded. The sinking fund approach is particularly useful for expensive machinery used in large-scale industries.
- **Entries:** The entries to be made will be as follows:

At the end of the first year:

1. Debit profit and loss account and credit depreciation fund account with amount of annual depreciation.
2. Debit depreciation fund investment account and credit bank account with an equal amount.

At the end of each subsequent year:

1. Debit bank account and credit depreciation fund account with amount of interest earned on investment.
2. Debit profit and loss account and credit depreciation fund account with amount of annual depreciation.
3. Debit depreciation fund investment account and credit bank account with amount of annual depreciation plus interest received.

In the last year:

1. Debit bank account and credit depreciation fund account with amount of interest earned on investment.
2. Debit profit and loss account and credit depreciation fund account with amount of annual installment.
3. Debit bank account and credit depreciation fund investment account with proceeds of sale of investment. Any profit or loss on sale of investment should be transferred to depreciation fund account.
4. Debit the account of new asset and credit the bank account with cost of replacement.
5. Debit depreciation fund account and credit the account of old asset which has now become useless.

Note: In the last year this amount should not be invested in the purchase of investments.

The asset for which this depreciation fund is being created will appear at its original cost, but the balance sheet prepared during the period of building up the depreciation fund will show the depreciation fund account on the liabilities side and the depreciation and depreciation fund investment account on the asset side. An extract of the sinking fund table, from which the annual depreciation amount to be provided for the depreciation will be determined, is provided below.

- **Sinking Fund Table**: Periodic deposit which will amount $1

$$\frac{i}{(1+i)^{n-1}}$$

Period	3%	4%	5%	6%
1	1.000000	1.000000	1.000000	1.000000
2	.492611	.490196	.487805	.485437
3	.323530	.320348	.317209	.314110
4	.239027	.235490	.232012	.228591
5	.188355	.184627	.180975	.117396
6	.154597	.150762	.147017	.143363
7	.130506	.126610	.122820	.119135
8	.112456	.108528	.104772	.101036
9	.098434	.094493	.090690	.087022
10	.087231	.083291	.079505	.075868
15	.053767	.049941	.046342	.042963
20	.037216	.033582	.030243	.027185
25	.027428	.024012	.020952	.018277
30	.021019	.017830	.015051	.012649
35	.016539	.013577	.011072	.008974
40	.013262	.010523	.008278	.006442
45	.010785	.008262	.006262	.004701
50	.008866	.006550	.004777	.003444

7.3. DEPRECIATION WITHIN ORGANIZATION

Instead of having a significant expense in the first year and no expenses in subsequent years, depreciation enables you to spread the cost of capital assets, or business assets that last longer than a year, over a number of years. Depreciation generally distributes costs over an item's useful life, but in certain circumstances, you can use accelerated depreciation to claim costs sooner and save money for your company.

- **Tax Savings:** You can deduct those expenses from your taxes at a faster rate if you can write off your capital assets. This reduces your tax liability as soon as possible. Let's take the case where you purchase a new delivery truck for $40,000. You get a $4,000 annual deduction if you have to depreciate it equally over a ten-year period, and the full benefit is not realized for ten years. You can recover the entire cost in five years if you can depreciate it in that time. This means you can deduct $8,000 annually.
- **Debt Reduction:** Early tax payment reduction can save a company money, especially when starting a new business and needing to take out loans to finance operations. For instance, if the accelerated depreciation on a new car lowers your annual taxes by $2,000, that's $2,000 less that you will need to borrow during the first few years of the business and pay interest on. These tax advantages can be very important to a developing company, particularly if your enterprise needs large capital expenditures.
- **Separate Tax Accounting:** Theoretically, since a larger portion of the cost is written off as an expense in the initial years after the purchase, claiming a larger portion of your depreciation expenses on your taxes would result in lower profits on paper early on. That isn't always the case, though, as businesses are able to maintain separate sets of books—one for general accounting purposes and another for tax purposes—with the second set employing a different depreciation schedule. The depreciation method you use for accounting purposes must take into account the use and increasing obsolescence of certain capital investments, as required by Generally Accepted Accounting Principles. For instance, let's say that an exceptional accelerated depreciation deduction under the tax code enables you to write off the full cost of a $20,000 oven purchase. You may have to spread those costs more precisely over the oven's useful life in accordance with GAAP accounting standards by using a different technique, such as double declining-balance depreciation or straight-line depreciation.
- **Warning:** Using rapid depreciation when budgeting for future costs causes your depreciation deductions to run out sooner, which increases the amount of taxable

income your company will have in later years after the depreciation allowances are exhausted. In the event that you are a startup and do not anticipate significant profits for a few years, the depreciation deductions may be worth more in five years than they are now. For instance, let's say that after a few years of being in the 15% tax bracket, your business takes off in year five, putting you in the 35% bracket. If you took advantage of rapid depreciation, you might have already depleted all of your deductions, which could have saved you 35 cents for every dollar in subsequent years instead of 15 cents.

7.3.1. Depreciation of Revalued Assets

An asset with a lifespan longer than a year cannot have its whole cost written off by a business at once. Instead, it must take yearly depreciation expenses and spread out the deductions over the asset's useful life. You can use the straight-line or declining balance methods to depreciate the cost less salvage value. U. S. and there are differences in global guidelines for revaluing assets.

- **Cost Method:** Long-lived assets cannot have their value increased using the cost method. The U.S. and the International Accounting Standards Board both approve of this approach. S. commonly accepted accounting guidelines. A long-lived asset may not have its book value increased by the cost method, even if its fair value has increased. On the other hand, impairment-related reductions in fair value allow you to record losses. You credit the asset and debit the loss to an income account. Determine the future depreciation amount by recalculating it using the reduced carrying value. If you modify a partially depreciated property's estimated lifetime or salvage value, you should update your depreciation schedule accordingly and report any income effects for the current year in your financial reporting.
- **Revaluation Method:** The revaluation method, which enables a business to periodically recognize the fair value of long-lived assets and modify the carrying value upward or downward, is also approved by the International Accounting Standards Board. When the price at which an asset would be sold freely fluctuates, fair value also does. If the asset is valued higher, the gain is credited to "other comprehensive income" and deducted from "revaluation surplus," which is a component of owners' equity's "accumulated other comprehensive income" section. Moving ahead, the revaluation surplus is depreciated using the same process as the asset's depreciation. Never retroactively alter the amount of depreciation that has already occurred.
- **Improvements:** When a property is improved, it is treated as a distinct depreciable asset. Any addition or partial replacement that increases the usefulness or lifespan of an asset qualifies as an eligible improvement. Any regular maintenance and repair expenses you incur to keep a fixed asset in operation are deducted from your

income. But you have to treat an improvement as a new asset and depreciate it separately if you replace or repair a long-lasting asset in a way that raises its value, makes it more useful, or extends its service life.

- **Disposition:** A partially depreciated property must be reclassified to an asset account like "non-current assets held for sale" and depreciation must stop if you choose to sell or otherwise dispose of the property. Any gain or loss from a sale is reported on the income statement in relation to the asset's impaired and depreciated value. In order to determine how much depreciation to claim in the disposition year if you depreciated the property in accordance with the modified accelerated cost recovery system and sold it before the recovery period ended, you must follow the applicable timing conventions.

7.3.2. Deduct a Charitable Contribution of Depreciated Assets

You might be able to deduct charitable contributions from your income if you donate business assets to a good cause. However, the deduction becomes a little trickier when the assets have depreciated over time. Determining the tax basis, figuring out the amount of ordinary income for each asset, and making reasonable valuation estimates are all necessary steps in the depreciated asset deduction process.

- **Fair Market Value:** First, estimate the fair market value, or FMV, of the depreciated assets to find out how much you can deduct. The full value of an asset is typically the most that can be deducted from your taxes as charitable contributions. The Internal Revenue Service points out that formulas, like a set percentage of an asset's acquisition cost, are not used to calculate FMV. It is more accurate to use the price you can get at the time of donation from a willing buyer. When estimating fair market value (FMV), factors to take into account are the state of each asset, prices found for recent and comparable sales, the cost to your company of replacing the asset, and, if relevant, expert opinions.
- **Depreciation and Adjusted Basis:** The adjusted tax basis of each depreciated business asset must be ascertained before donating it. An asset's adjusted basis is the total of all acquisition costs, which include the asset's purchase price, sales taxes, freight, and installation costs, less the total of all depreciation deductions made. Your charitable contribution deduction is equal to the fair market value (FMV) of the asset if its adjusted basis is greater than its FMV on the donation date. However, there is an extra step involved in determining how much you can deduct when FMV exceeds adjusted basis. This is figuring out how much of the difference between FMV and adjusted basis is considered ordinary income.
- **Ordinary Income Gain:** Every depreciable asset used in a business is regarded as "ordinary income property." The tax regulations may require the recognition of ordinary income rather than a long-term capital gain when ordinary income

property is sold at a gain—that is, when the sales price, or FMV, exceeds the adjusted basis—up to the total of all depreciation taken or the difference between FMV and adjusted basis, whichever is less. Even though you donate the assets, you still need to figure out how much ordinary income you would have received if you had sold the asset at fair market value. This is so because the amount of your charitable deduction is limited by the tax laws to the FMV of the asset less the amount of ordinary income that would arise from this fictitious sale.

- **How to Deduct:** Determining the amount of your charitable deduction typically requires more work than figuring out how to claim it. Charitable deductions are taken as an itemized deduction on Schedule A if you report business income on your personal return (i.e., you are a sole proprietor, partner, shareholder of a S corporation, or member of a limited liability company that does not elect to be taxed as a C corporation). Form 1120, the corporate income tax return, is where C corporations and other entities that choose to be taxed jointly report all charitable contribution deductions.

7.3.3. Calculate Beginning Year Accumulated Depreciation

The accounting and tax principle of depreciation recognizes the useful life of a physical, long-term asset—that is, an asset with a lifespan longer than a year—and takes wear and tear into consideration. A business can move a certain amount of an asset's cost from the balance sheet to the income statement through depreciation. On the income statement, depreciation expense is shown, and on the balance sheet, the cumulative effect of this expense is shown as accumulated depreciation.

- **Depreciation:** Using tables it provides, the Internal Revenue Service determines the useful life of the assets your business owns. Companies are only required by the IRS to expense assets with useful lives of less than a year or with shorter holding periods. When these short-term assets, like inventory, are purchased, their entire cost is shown on the income statement. The income statement does not show purchases of any other assets, such as machinery, furniture, and property (but not land). Rather, the asset's value is shown on the balance sheet, and depreciation expense shows the item's cost over time on the income statement.
- **Accumulated Depreciation:** The total amount of depreciation your business has to pay for all the years since the asset was bought or put into use is known as accumulated depreciation. As accumulated depreciation is deducted from the asset's initial cost and appears as a negative balance immediately beneath the asset, it is considered a contra account to a long-term asset. Accrued depreciation typically shows up on your company's balance sheet under property, plant, and equipment.
- **Beginning Year Accumulated Depreciation:** Depreciation expense is typically recorded by small businesses either quarterly or annually on their income statements.

As a result, the income statement at the end of the year will reflect the entire year's depreciation expense. Your company's year-end balance sheet won't reflect any depreciation for the current year if your company follows an annual depreciation schedule. Only the total depreciation up to the end of the prior year will be displayed. Your year-end balance sheet will display three quarters' worth of current year depreciation in addition to past accumulated depreciation if your business follows a quarterly depreciation schedule.

- **Beginning Year Continued:** The balance sheet of your business receives the profits or losses and depreciation from the year-end period, while the income statement is reset to zero at the beginning of the year. Add the depreciation expense from the income statement to the accumulated depreciation from the previous period to get the beginning year accumulated depreciation.
- **Example:** Every year, your company computes depreciation. By year's end, your balance sheet indicates $250,000 in total depreciation on PP and E. $50,000 in depreciation expense is shown on your income statement for the year. Your balance sheet's accumulated depreciation rises to $300,000 at the start of the year, comprising $250,000 and the $50,000.

7.3.4. The Advantages of Amortization & Depreciation

Accounting and tax payment techniques such as amortization and depreciation allow business owners to gradually spread the costs of large purchases and financing projects. Small businesses benefit from amortization and depreciation because they produce a more consistent accounting of costs and revenues, which facilitates budgeting and increases tax payments. Both amortization and depreciation, though they pertain to different kinds of assets, are tax deductible as business expenses.

- **Accrual Accounting:** Accrual accounting allows a business owner to record expenses and income closer to the actual time they occur because it makes use of concepts like amortization and depreciation. When a business buys a large asset, like buildings or machinery, it uses these over many years to help produce earnings, profits, and sales. These assets eventually reach the end of their "useful life" and must be replaced. As per the legal website Nolo, accrual accounting provides business owners with an enhanced view of their long-term profitability; however, it may also complicate the process of monitoring cash flow.
- **Useful Life:** Generally accepted accounting principles include amortization and depreciation. The Internal Revenue Service has regulations on how businesses must amortize and depreciate expenses in order to claim business tax deductions. The IRS releases tables showing the useful lives of the most often deducted assets for a variety of assets.
- **Straight-Line Depreciation:** Two categories of depreciation exist. Straight-line depreciation is the simplest and most popular method of calculating depreciation because

it allows you to gradually lower an asset's value over the course of its useful life. Using this method, you could claim $5,000 annually as a business expense for a $50,000 machine that has a ten-year useful life.

- **Accelerated Depreciation:** Accelerated depreciation is an additional technique. In this case, business owners deduct more in the early years following the asset purchase and less in the later years of the asset's useful life. The business will receive the tax break early but will have fewer deductions later if it takes larger deductions up front. This might prove to be a poor idea for a developing company, particularly if the owner eventually moves into a higher tax bracket and has to pay more taxes on a higher amount of reported income.
- **Amortization:** Intangible assets, such as software, non-compete clauses, patents, brand names, licensing agreements, copyrights, and R&D expenses, are subject to amortization. An asset's acquisition costs, including labor and other expenses, can be capitalized and amortized. Amortization allows companies to spread out asset costs over time and obtain a more consistent accounting of revenue and expenses than depreciation does.

7.3.5. The Straight-Line Depreciation Method in Capital Projects

Capital projects, by definition, call for an initial outlay of funds, typically for fixed assets like real estate, machinery, or automobiles. The expense of those capital expenditures shows up on the income statement over time as depreciation rather than as expenses right away. The straight-line method, which is the most straightforward and popular approach, provides you with a yearly depreciation expense that is constant.

- **Method:** Under straight-line depreciation, the annual depreciation expense is reported in the same amount. (The name comes from the fact that if you were to graph the expense over time, it would look like a straight, horizontal line. Let's say you are creating a budget plan for a capital project that calls for an equipment purchase of $15,000. You anticipate that the equipment will last ten years and that you will be able to sell it for two thousand dollars at that point. The $13,000 total that needs to be depreciated is made up of the $15,000 purchase price less the $2,000 you anticipate recovering over time. Given that the equipment is expected to last ten years, you will record a $1,300 annual depreciation expense.
- **Profit and Taxes:** Depreciation is merely an accounting technique for distributing the equipment's cost over the course of its useful life. This has an impact on your capital project's net income, or the profit the project reports on paper. The profit from the project goes toward your total business profit, which influences your tax liability. (Other business forms transfer their profits to their owners, who are responsible for paying taxes on them.) Corporations pay taxes on their profits. Taxes on business

profit will be paid in either case. Year over year, the impact on profit stays the same under the straight-line method. In the event that you were in the 25% marginal tax bracket and you took out $1,300 in depreciation expenses annually, you would save $325 in taxes annually.

- **Cash Flow:** Owners of businesses are aware that profit is essentially just a number on paper. It's a term from accounting. It is not the same as cash flow, which is the description of actual money entering or leaving your company. The fact that you will require $15,000 for equipment at the start of the project does not change based on the depreciation method your company employs. Despite not having an immediate impact on profit, that represents a negative cash flow. However, depreciation is an expense that is not paid for with cash. Even though you're declaring $1,300 in annual equipment expenses, which lowers your profit, you're not really spending $1,300 in cash. That money has already been spent. The only way depreciation affects cash flow, in actuality, is through tax savings—you'll save $325 in taxes annually.
- **Accelerated Depreciation:** While the most popular depreciation method is straight-line, there are other options as well. Some techniques record higher costs in the early years and lower ones in the later years, which speeds up depreciation. As a result, profit is decreased more significantly in the initial years, and the majority of the tax savings are also shifted to those years. Tax savings are cash that can be taken out by the business owner or reinvested in the company. The sooner you can start realizing the savings, the better, as cash now will have more buying power (and more potential for investment) than the same amount of money years from now.

7.3.6. Depreciation Method Gives the Highest Net Income

By lowering your taxable net income, depreciation claims help you pay less in taxes. While it's generally preferable to pay less in taxes, there are situations in which you may want to make sure your net income doesn't look excessively low. Using this information, you can plan how to deduct the cost of assets your company purchases in order to reduce the effect on your profit margin.

- **Depreciation Options:** Together with the Section 179 deduction, the Internal Revenue Service provides two different forms of depreciation. Certain capital asset purchases can be written off as expenses in the year of purchase thanks to the section 179 deduction, which spares you from having to depreciate the asset. Although you have the option to use the alternate depreciation system, the general depreciation system is used to depreciate most assets. Generally speaking, you can write off assets over a shorter time period using the general depreciation system. Under the general depreciation system, you can also choose to accelerate depreciation; under the alternative depreciation system, you can only use the straight-line method.

- **Current Year Net Income:** Extend your depreciation as much as you can if you want to increase your net income this year. As an illustration, you could depreciate assets rather than write them off under Section 179. With the five-year recovery life of data processing equipment under the general depreciation system, depreciating $20,000 worth of computer purchases will cut the $20,000 hit to your net income to just $4,000. Although you have the option, once you depreciate purchases using the alternative depreciation system, you will be forced to continue using that method for the asset's whole life.
- **Future Net Income:** Maximize your future net income by taking as much depreciation as possible now. Every depreciable asset you purchase will eventually be written down to zero value, regardless of the schedule you select. For instance, your company's net profit will be severely impacted if you claim the Section 179 deduction on a $20,000 computer purchase this year, but you won't be required to claim any additional depreciation over the following four years. The additional benefit of this is that you will save more money on taxes up front.
- **Income or EBITDA:** While increasing your net income may be beneficial, some companies are more concerned with EBITDA, or earnings before interest, taxes, depreciation, and amortization. They believe that EBITDA more closely reflects a company's actual cash flow because net income can include components that don't really reflect how well a business is doing right now. There is a compelling argument to focus on the depreciation method that best serves your overall objectives rather than worrying too much about your net income, since your business's sales and actual costs will remain the same regardless of how you choose to depreciate the assets you purchase.

7.3.7. Adjust Accumulated Depreciation

When an asset's value decreases over its service life and production activity, it is recognized in accounting as depreciated. There are several ways to calculate depreciation expense, including the straight-line and declining balance methods. An asset's accumulated depreciation is the total, cumulative depreciation on the asset since it was placed in service, whereas depreciation expense refers to the depreciation incurred on the asset in the current year.

- **Accumulated Depreciation:** One type of contra-asset account is accumulated depreciation. The asset's net book value, or the asset's current carrying value on the balance sheet of the company, is the result of offsetting the asset's cost against the cost of the related fixed asset. Accumulated depreciation has a normal credit balance because it is a contra-asset account. This essentially indicates that while decreases to the account are debited, increases to accumulated depreciation are credited.
- **Asset Capitalization:** In order to illustrate the adjustment of accumulated depreciation as a result of depreciation expense, let

us suppose that a company spends $8,000 on machinery on January 1st. Three years are predicted to be the asset's useful life. When the asset is purchased, management anticipates that it will be sold for $800 when its useful life is up. The asset will be capitalized as follows on the company's books on January 1st: Debit Cash 8,000 Credit Machinery 8,000.

- **Annual Depreciation:** The asset's yearly depreciation, calculated using the straight-line method of depreciation, will be $2,400. This is calculated by dividing the asset's total cost of $8,000 by its three-year residual value of $800. As stated in Section 1, the asset's net book value at the end of the first year is determined by the asset's cost of $8,000 less accumulated depreciation of $2,400, or $5,600. The asset's annual depreciation is recorded to the company's general ledger at year-end with the following entry: Debit Depreciation Expense 2,400 Credit Accumulated Depreciation 2,400. The asset will have $4,800 in total depreciation at the end of the second year. The asset's carrying value will be $800 and its accumulated depreciation will total $7,200 at the end of the asset's third year of use.
- **Sale of the Asset:** On December 30, after the asset's third year, the business sells it for $1,200, a little more than management had projected. The machinery sale will be documented as follows: 8,000 Credit Machinery 8,000 Gain on Sale 400 Debit Cash 1,200 Debit Accumulated Depreciation 7,200 This journal entry eliminates the asset and accumulated depreciation from the books. At this point, the increase in cash as well as the gain from the asset's sale (the asset's $1,200 sales price less its $800 carrying value) are also recorded.

7.3.8. Calculate the Accumulated Depreciation Under the Units of a Production Method

When a company purchases a long-term asset, it accounts for wear and tear on the income statement by recording a portion of the asset's cost as a depreciation expense each period. The amount of depreciation recorded each period under the units-of-production depreciation method is determined by how much the asset was used by the business. The total amount of depreciation expense charged thus far is known as accumulated depreciation. You must be able to compute the depreciation expense for each period in order to determine the accumulated depreciation for an asset in your small business.

- **Depreciable Cost:** Depreciable cost is the total value of an asset that can be written off during its useful life. It is equivalent to the asset's initial purchase price less its salvage value, or its estimated worth at the end of its useful life. Let's take an example where your small business spends $25,000 on a company car that it plans to sell for $10,000 after five years. $15,000 is its depreciable cost, or $25,000 less the $10,000 salvage value.
- **Depreciation Expense per Unit:** The depreciable cost divided by the total number of units of output the asset is expected to produce

over its life by the business is the depreciation expense per unit. The kind of asset determines which output unit you should use. For example, you could use machine-hours for a piece of equipment, printed pages for a copy machine, or miles driven for a car. Assume, using the earlier example, that you plan to drive the car 100,000 miles during its lifetime. $15,000 divided by 100,000 equals $0.15, which is the depreciation expense per mile.

- **Figuring Accumulated Depreciation:** The amount of depreciation expense in an accounting period is calculated by multiplying the number of units produced by the asset during the period by the unit depreciation expense. The total of all the depreciation taken in earlier periods plus the depreciation expense for the current period is known as accumulated depreciation. Assume, using the preceding example, that you drove 15,000 miles in the second year and 20,000 miles in the first. Depreciation costs for the first year come to $3,000, or $0.15 times $20,000. The depreciation for the second year is $2,250. At the conclusion of the second year, the total depreciation is $5,250, which is equal to $3,000 plus $2,250.
- **Accumulated Depreciation on the Balance Sheet:** On the balance sheet, a business records accumulated depreciation that is less than the asset's original cost and records the asset's book value either next to or below the accumulated depreciation. The original cost less cumulative depreciation is book value. The asset's book value decreases with each period as accumulated depreciation increases. The asset's book value and salvage value are equal at the end of its useful life, after it has undergone complete depreciation. In the preceding example, the car's book value will be $10,000 and its accumulated depreciation will be $15,000 after five years.

7.4 THE SIGNIFICANCE OF AUDITING IN DEPRECIATION

In order to ensure that a company's financial performance and health are accurately represented, auditing depreciation is an essential part of financial statement audits. The methodical distribution of tangible fixed asset costs over their useful lives, or depreciation, has a direct effect on the balance sheet and income statement. It impacts total assets through accumulated depreciation as well as net income through depreciation expense. Giving stakeholders a true and fair picture of a company's financial position, an accurate audit of depreciation helps ensure that these financial statements are fairly presented in compliance with pertinent accounting standards like GAAP or IFRS. Key financial metrics like profitability, return on assets, and debt covenants can be distorted by inaccurate or manipulative depreciation, which could mislead creditors, investors, and regulatory agencies. Depreciation audits are therefore crucial to preserving the accuracy of financial reporting. Depreciation auditing is important because it affects how financial decisions are made. Reliable cost allocation is ensured by accurate depreciation calculations, which benefits management by enabling them to make well-informed decisions about capital investments, asset management, and budgeting. A company's taxable income is impacted by depreciation, and mistakes in tax filings may result in penalties or legal issues with the government. Auditors confirm that a client's depreciation policies are reasonable, consistent, and in line with the business's economic realities. This entails assessing the residual values, useful lives, and depreciation methods (such as straight-line or declining balance) of assets to see if they appropriately represent the consumption of the financial benefits derived from those assets.

Identifying possible hazards of a material misstatement pertaining to depreciation is a critical responsibility of auditors. In deciding which useful lives or depreciation techniques will maximize profitability or satisfy earnings targets, they evaluate the possibility of management bias. Auditor signals of aggressive accounting practices or earnings management can be identified by assessing adjustments to depreciation methods or assumptions. Monitoring major asset additions, subtractions, and impairments is another aspect of auditing that makes sure all of the changes are appropriately recorded. For example, auditors check that assets that are written off or impaired appropriately and that capital expenditures are properly recorded. Understating expenses and overstating assets could otherwise inflate earnings and mislead stakeholders. This process reduces that risk. Maintaining compliance with legal and regulatory requirements is another important function of the depreciation audit. In terms of how fixed assets and depreciation are handled, businesses have to abide by national and international accounting standards, tax laws, and corporate governance guidelines. As a result, there is a lower chance of financial penalties, legal issues, or reputational harm. Auditors assist clients in meeting these obligations. They also confirm the accuracy, completeness, and level of transparency of the disclosures made in the financial statements, including the methods and rates of depreciation, changes in estimates, and accumulated depreciation, so that interested parties can comprehend the company's performance and financial status.

Additionally, auditing depreciation promotes uniformity and comparability in financial reporting among peers in the same industry and across periods. A company's comparability to its competitors allows investors and analysts to assess its performance, and consistency in the application of depreciation policies allows stakeholders to compare financial performance over time. Auditors confirm that if a company modifies its depreciation policy or estimates, the justifications are legitimate and appropriately stated in the financial statements. This degree of examination strengthens the financial statements' credibility and increases confidence among creditors, investors, and other stakeholders. Auditing depreciation also aids in the detection and prevention of fraud. Sometimes management will purposefully manipulate depreciation in order to get the desired financial outcomes. For example, a business may reduce depreciation expense to boost profits by changing the asset's useful life or residual value. By recalculating depreciation expense for a sample of assets, comparing actual depreciation rates to industry standards, and analyzing trends in depreciation expense in relation to changes in the asset base, auditors can detect manipulations of this kind.

Audit Procedure

- Obtain an understanding of entity's process of charging depreciation and amortization.
- Acquire access to the entity's fixed asset register. There's always a chance that a business will either charge capital expenditures directly to income and expense statements to lower its profit or capitalize revenue-related expenses to increase it. In order to limit this risk, auditors should physically verify the fixed assets, or those with a significant value, as there is always a chance that fictitious assets have been capitalized in the books. They can also choose to check the asset's nature from the fixed asset register. Ensure that the appropriate approval is obtained from the designated person for each addition or deletion by obtaining a list of all such changes.
- Select the sample of assets from the Fixed Assets Register, on materiality considerations and verify the rates of depreciation and depreciation calculations.
- Obtain the list of all the components identified by the management.
- Ensure Intangible assets like patents, goodwill, copy rights have been properly amortized over the period.
- Ensure depreciation is charged on the assets from the date when it is ready to use and not from the date of actual usage.

- Ensure depreciation on revalued amount has been properly accounted from revaluation reserve.
- Calculate depreciation in accordance with the Income Tax Act of 1961. Verify that additions match those made in accordance with the Companies Act and the opening WDV to the Tax audit schedule for the assessment year that precedes the year that is being audited.
- Analyze records for arithmetic accuracy, conduct independent computations, and gather audit evidence regarding the overall reasonableness of amortization and depreciation expenses. Calculate the annual depreciation expense, for example.
- Ensure that the depreciation and amortization has been charged as per the useful lives of PPE and intangible assets.
- Ensure that residual values have been properly verified as that impacts the computation of depreciation.
- Ensure that the depreciation and amortization has been computed prospectively whenever there is any change in useful lives of PPE and intangible assets.

Need for Depreciation

- To ascertain the true profit of the year, it is desirable to charge depreciation.
- To ascertain true value of assets, depreciation should be charged and without correct value of assets, true financial position of the company cannot be ascertained.
- Instead of withdrawal of overstated profit, it is desirable to make provisions to buy new asset and replace the old asset. Accumulated value of depreciation provides additional working capital.
- Depreciation help us to ascertain uniform profit in each accounting year.
- Depreciation is also useful to gain advantage o tax benefits.

7.4.1 Auditor's Duty Regarding Depreciation

The Auditor cannot be held responsible for estimating the working life of an asset; it is the job of an expert value.

- A company can adopt different methods for different type of assets provided that the methods are adopted consistently over the years.
- If a business decides to adopt new depreciation techniques, depreciation must be recalculated using the new techniques starting on the asset's first day of use. If there is a loss, the difference between the amount of depreciation charged under the old rate and the amount computed under the new rate should be credited to the general reserve; if there is a profit, the difference should be debited to the profit and loss account.
- As per the Companies Act's Schedule II, depreciation is assessed pro rata up to the date of sale or disposal of any asset that is sold or disposed of during the same year. Analogously, in the event of a fixed asset addition, depreciation will be billed pro rata.

- Account must disclose method of depreciation.
- Depreciation must be according to provisions of Companies Act and Income Tax Act.
- If depreciation is charged more than prescribed rate, Auditor should examine whether it is based on some professional and technical advice.
- Depreciation should be charged on revalued amount, if there is revaluation of assets.

7.4.2 Depreciation and Amortization Journal Entries of a Client

In order to conduct an audit of a client's depreciation and amortization journal entries, you should first assess whether the client's depreciation and amortization policies adhere to the relevant financial reporting framework (e.g. IFRS or GAAP). Examine the customer's fixed asset register to make sure all listed assets are appropriately valued and classified. Additionally, make sure the depreciation schedule, residual values, and useful lives follow the company's guidelines and accepted practices in the sector. Examine whether these policies are being applied consistently over various time periods. To make sure the client's calculations are accurate, recalculate the amortization and depreciation costs for a sample of assets. Examine the general ledger entries in comparison to the supporting records, including the fixed asset register and computations, to ensure that all pertinent assets are appropriately recorded. Check that disposals or impairments are appropriately recorded and timely reported, as well as that new assets are capitalized appropriately. Analyze any notable variations in amortization and depreciation costs from previous periods in order to spot any odd patterns or disparities that need more research. Determine whether these changes are the result of significant asset additions or disposals, changes in the depreciation schedule, or adjustments to the useful lives. Make sure that all depreciation and amortization-related modifications or reclassifications are appropriately recorded and approved. Assess whether depreciation and amortization costs are reasonable in relation to the asset base and business operations by using analytical techniques like ratio analysis. Lastly, confirm that all depreciation and amortization disclosures—such as methods, useful lives, and accumulated depreciation—are accurately disclosed in the financial statements and adhere to the applicable accounting standards. This thorough method aids in guaranteeing that amortization and depreciation entries are precise, comprehensive, and compliant with relevant accounting standards.

Step 1: Understand the client's policies and methods

Understanding the client's policies and procedures for asset amortization and depreciation is the first step. Examine their estimates, accounting policies, and amortization and depreciation disclosures. Additionally, you ought to find out about any modifications to the procedures and policies, as well as the rationale behind them. You ought to contrast the client's procedures and policies with the relevant industry norms and accounting standards.

Step 2: Test the existence and valuation of the assets

The assets that are subject to amortization and depreciation must be identified and valued. This is the next step. You should ask the client for the asset register or schedule so you can confirm the specifics of the assets, including the description, cost, acquisition date, useful life, residual value, method of depreciation or amortization, and cumulative depreciation or amortization. To confirm their existence, you should also examine the tangible assets or get attestations from other sources. To evaluate if the asset valuation is reasonable, you should carry out analytical tasks like comparing the amortization or depreciation expense with the previous year, the budget, or the industry average.

Step 3: Test the accuracy and completeness of the journal entries

Testing the completeness and accuracy of the journal entries for amortization and depreciation is the third step. To confirm that the amounts, dates, accounts, and descriptions in a sample of journal entries are accurate, you should follow the entries back to the original documents, which could be contracts, agreements, or invoices. It is advisable to verify the precision of the depreciation and amortization computations through mathematics and confirm that they align with the client's guidelines and procedures. To make sure the journal entries are recorded in the appropriate accounting period, you should also run a cut-off test.

Step 4: Test the presentation and disclosure of the journal entries

Testing the disclosure and presentation of the depreciation and amortization journal entries is the fourth step. To make sure that the assets and accumulated depreciation and amortization are appropriately presented and measured on the balance sheet, as well as that the depreciation and amortization expenses are appropriately classified and reported on the income statement, you should go over the financial statements and the notes. Additionally, you must make sure that the client provides all pertinent information regarding their policies and procedures, estimates and presumptions, and modifications to their depreciation and amortization policies and procedures.

Step 5: Evaluate the audit evidence and identify any issues

The assessment of the audit evidence and the identification of any problems or inaccuracies with the journal entries for depreciation and amortization constitute the fifth step. You should take into account whether the audit evidence is appropriate and sufficient, as well as whether it confirms or refutes the client's claims. Additionally, you must find and notify the client and the audit team of any substantial or material misstatements, deviations, or inconsistencies in the journal entries. In the audit working papers, you should also record your audit procedures, results, and conclusions.

Step 6: Form an audit opinion and issue an audit report

The final step is to form an audit opinion and issue an audit report on the depreciation and amortization journal entries. It is important to take into account how any problems or mistakes may affect the overall reliability and fairness of the financial statements. Any changes or corrections that the client suggests or makes should also be taken into account in terms of their materiality and importance. The next step is to give your assessment of whether the journal entries for depreciation and amortization comply with applicable accounting standards and do not contain any material misstatements. In your audit report, you should also mention any restrictions, qualifications, or suggestions.

7.4.3 Regulatory Requirements for Depreciation

The balance sheet and income statement are impacted by depreciation, which is the methodical distribution of tangible asset costs over their useful lives. The International Financial Reporting Standards (IFRS) worldwide and the Generally Accepted Accounting Principles (GAAP) in the US offer a framework for how businesses should compute and report depreciation. The aforementioned standards mandate that organizations utilize uniform depreciation techniques, ascertain rational useful lives, and take into account any remaining value during the distribution procedure. By ensuring compliance with regulatory requirements, auditing reduces the possibility of financial misstatements that could deceive creditors, investors, and other stakeholders. Because there is a chance of significant misstatements or financial result manipulation, depreciation audits are necessary. According to regulatory standards like GAAP and IFRS, businesses must apply the proper depreciation techniques—such as units of production, declining balance, or straight-line—based on the asset's nature and anticipated use. The role of auditors is crucial in ensuring that the depreciation method selected accurately represents the true pattern of economic benefits derived from the asset. Auditors also evaluate if the residual values and useful life estimates match the asset's state, usage, and industry norms. Key metrics like net income, asset values, and tax obligations can all be greatly impacted by inaccurate estimates or improper methods used in financial statements. Auditors assist in making sure these suppositions adhere to legal requirements and are logical, consistent, and thoroughly documented.

Auditing depreciation is crucial to ensuring compliance with tax laws and avoiding penalties because it has substantial tax implications as well. Financial reporting standards may not align with the particular regulations that apply to a given jurisdiction when it comes to depreciation calculations for tax purposes. For example, in order to promote investment in specific asset classes, tax authorities may mandate that businesses use specific depreciation methods or offer options for accelerated depreciation. Auditors review the company's depreciation schedules to make sure the correct amounts are reported for tax purposes and that they adhere to these tax regulations. This audit procedure lowers the possibility of financial penalties, helps avoid future conflicts with tax authorities, and guarantees that the company's tax filings are accurate and defendable. Adequate disclosure of depreciation-related information in the financial statements is another regulatory requirement. Companies are required to disclose the depreciation methods, useful lives or depreciation rates applied, gross carrying amount of depreciable assets, and cumulative depreciation under standards like GAAP and IFRS. Any modifications to estimates, such as those pertaining to residual value or useful life, or adjustments to the depreciation technique, must be disclosed together with the reasoning behind the modification. To make sure these disclosures fairly depict the company's financial situation, auditors check them for accuracy, completeness, and transparency. This examination aids in the assessment of the company's performance and asset management procedures by investors and other stakeholders, as well as in understanding the underlying assumptions of the financial statements.

Assessing the comparability and consistency of depreciation practices over time and between entities is another critical task for auditors. Companies must adhere to regulatory standards and consistently apply depreciation methods in order to prevent manipulating asset values or earnings. Any modifications to the depreciation policies must have sufficient justification and disclosure.

Auditors make sure that these adjustments are founded on actual changes in circumstances or in accordance with changing industry standards, rather than being made arbitrary in order to achieve targeted financial results. For stakeholders who depend on financial statements to make educated decisions—investors, creditors, and analysts—this consistency and comparability are essential. Depreciation auditing also aids in the identification and prevention of asset management fraud.

To boost profits or reach budgetary goals, management may manipulate depreciation by changing residual values, useful lives, or depreciation procedures. Strong internal controls are necessary under regulatory frameworks to thwart such manipulations, and auditors evaluate the efficacy of these controls as part of their audit processes. Auditors can spot anomalies or warning signs of possible fraud by carrying out substantive tests and analytical procedures, such as recalculating depreciation for particular assets, comparing depreciation rates to industry standards, and examining trends in depreciation expense. This guarantees that the company's financial statements accurately reflect its actual financial performance and position and contributes to the integrity of the financial reporting process.

7.4.4 Compliances under the Deprecation

Making sure that a business's depreciation policies comply with all applicable tax laws and accounting standards, such as International Financial Reporting Standards (IFRS) or Generally Accepted Accounting Principles (GAAP), is the task of an auditing compliance under depreciation. According to the regulations governing depreciation compliance, businesses must choose a suitable depreciation method, calculate the useful life and residual value of assets with accuracy, and apply these calculations consistently throughout reporting periods. It is the auditor's responsibility to confirm that these conditions are satisfied and that the financial statements accurately depict the state and performance of the company's finances. The main guideline for depreciation compliance is that the depreciation method should match the manner in which the business uses the asset's economic benefits. The units of production method, the declining balance method, and the straight-line method are examples of widely recognized techniques. The process of distributing an asset's cost over its useful life varies depending on the method used. The simplest and most popular approach, the straight-line method, distributes the depreciation expense equally over the asset's useful life. A faster consumption of the asset's economic benefits is reflected in the higher depreciation costs charged in the early years of the asset's life by the declining balance method, an accelerated depreciation technique. By basing the expense on the quantity of units produced or the number of hours used, the units of production method links depreciation expense to the asset's actual usage. Auditors look for alignment between the selected method and the asset's use within the organization in order to audit compliance. For instance, an accelerated depreciation method might be more appropriate if it is anticipated that an asset's benefits will diminish quickly. Auditors also confirm that the estimates of residual value and useful life are reasonable and supported by reliable data, such as engineering reports, industry standards, or past performance. Regular reviews of these estimates are necessary to account for any changes in the market or technological developments that may have an impact on the asset's lifespan or value.

The formula for calculating depreciation under the straight-line method is:

$$\text{Depreciation Expense} = \frac{\text{Cost of Asset} - \text{Residual Value}}{\text{Useful Life}}$$

This formula ensures that an equal amount of depreciation expense is allocated to each accounting period over the asset's useful life. For the declining balance method, the formula is:

$$\text{Depreciation Expense} = \text{Net Book Value} \times \text{Depreciation Rate}$$

where the depreciation rate is often a multiple (e.g., 150% or 200%) of the straight-line rate, and the expense decreases as the asset's book value reduces. For the units of production method, the formula is:

$$\text{Depreciation Expense} = \frac{\text{Cost of Asset} - \text{Residual Value}}{\text{Total Expected production}} \times \text{Actual Producation}$$

These formulas are used by auditors to recalculate depreciation costs for specific assets and confirm that the amounts reported are accurate. Ensuring appropriate disclosures in the financial statements is another aspect of auditing compliance under depreciation. To ensure transparency for stakeholders, the depreciation method of choice, useful life estimates, residual values, and any modifications to these policies must be sufficiently disclosed. Through this disclosure, stakeholders can comprehend how the company's asset management and financial performance are impacted by depreciation. Auditors ensure that the company's depreciation practices are transparent, equitable, and compliant with regulations by conducting thorough testing, recalculations, and disclosure verification.

ACTIVITY

CALCULATING DEPRECIATION USING DIFFERENT METHODS

- **Objective:** To demonstrate and compare various depreciation methods (straight-line and reducing balance) for different types of assets.

Distribute asset details (cost, useful life, salvage value) for several hypothetical assets to each student or group. Ensure each asset has enough information to calculate depreciation using both methods.

- **Assessment:** Evaluate students based on the accuracy of their depreciation calculations, their ability to apply different methods, and their understanding of how depreciation methods impact financial statements.
- **Extension:** For advanced students, introduce more complex scenarios such as partial-year depreciation, changes in useful life estimates, or tax implications of depreciation methods.

SUMMARY

- Depreciation is a decline in value experienced by many assets over time. For example, cars tend to depreciate over the course of several years of ownership. Factors like wear and tear, the conditions of the market, and age can all have an impact on this decline. Some assets grow more valuable or appreciate over time, such as real estate. In some cases, depreciation can be quite staggering.
- Depreciation is a term used for tax and accounting purposes that describes the method a company uses to account for the declining value of its assets. Depreciation reduces the value of assets on a residual basis. It also reduces the profits of the current year. Depreciation indicates reduction in value of any fixed assets. Reduction in value of assets depends on the life of assets. Life of assets depends upon the usage of assets.
- Depreciation is a ratable reduction in the carrying amount of a fixed asset. Depreciation is intended to roughly reflect the actual consumption of the underlying asset, so that the carrying amount of the asset has been greatly reduced to its salvage value by the time its useful life is over.
- Most income tax systems allow a tax deduction for recovery of the cost of assets used in a business or for the production of income. Such deductions are allowed for individuals and companies. Where the assets are consumed currently, the cost may be deducted currently as an expense or treated as part of cost of goods sold.
- Depreciation calculations require a lot of record-keeping if done for each asset a business owns, especially if assets are added to after they are acquired, or partially disposed of. However, many tax systems permit all assets of a similar type acquired in the same year to be combined in a pool. Depreciation is then computed for all assets in the pool as a single calculation. These calculations must make assumptions about the date of acquisition.
- Depreciation allows you to spread the cost of capital assets -- business assets that last more than one year -- over several years rather than having a large expense in the first year and no expenses after that.
- A company cannot deduct the entire cost of a long-lived asset -- one with a lifetime more than one year long -- all at once. Rather, it must space out the deductions over the useful lifetime of the asset by taking annual depreciation expenses. You can depreciate the cost minus salvage value using the straight-line or declining balance methods. U.S. and international standards for how to revalue assets differ.
- Donating business assets to charity may allow you to take a charitable contribution deduction. When the assets have been depreciated over the years, however, the deduction is a bit more complicated. Deducting depreciated assets requires reasonable valuation estimates, determination of tax basis and calculating the amount of ordinary income for each asset.

REVIEW QUESTIONS

1. Why is understanding the causes of depreciation crucial for financial reporting?
2. What role does tax legislation play in determining depreciation rates?
3. How does the provision for depreciation impact financial statements?
4. Why might businesses choose the straight-line method over other depreciation methods?
5. What types of assets typically use the depletion method for depreciation?
6. What challenges or considerations arise when depreciating revalued assets?

REFERENCES

1. Goldschmidt, Y., & Gafni, A. (1991). A managerial approach to costing fixed assets in health care organizations: The role of depreciation and interest. *Health Care Management Review, 16*(4), 55–65. https://doi.org/10.1097/00004010-199101640-00008.
2. Lentini, V., & Gimenez, G. (2019). Depreciation of human capital: A sectoral analysis in OECD countries. *International Journal of Manpower, 40*(7), 1254–1272. https://doi.org/10.1108/ijm-07-2018-0207.
3. Liapis, K. J., & Kantianis, D. D. (2015). Depreciation methods and life-cycle costing (LCC) methodology. *Procedia Economics and Finance, 19*, 314–324. https://doi.org/10.1016/s2212-5671(15)00032-5.
4. Natarajan, H., & Ajitha, P. (2016). Truthful bidding for cloud resources based on competitive cloud auction, costing, and depreciation. *International Journal of Computer Science and Engineering, 3*(3), 9–12. https://doi.org/10.14445/23488387/ijcse-v3i3p102.
5. Satriani, D., Saifudin, A., & Sunarya, P. A. (2020). *Perbandingan penggunaan* straight line method dan double declining balance method pada aset PT. Delimas Lestari Jaya. *CICES, 6*(1), 1–10. https://doi.org/10.33050/cices.v6i1.870.

CHAPTER

8 Professionalism

LEARNING OBJECTIVES

After studying this chapter, you will be able to:

- Explain the concept of a new professionalism: changes and continuities;
- Define the internal auditing standards and due professional care;
- Discuss the quality concept of internal audit activity;
- Explain the internal review and external review of auditing; and
- Discuss about marketing the audit role.

KEY TERMS FROM THIS CHAPTER

Audit committee assurance
Empowerment
New public service management (NPSM)
Organizational controls
Corporate governance
Managerial interference
Occupational value
Quality control

INTRODUCTION

The most crucial quality to have when conducting an audit is professionalism. Although no facility is flawless, it is your responsibility as a skilled auditor and correctional administrator to assist the facility in becoming compliant rather than placing them in an unfavorable position. The ethical climate and internal control system of the company have been regularly observed and reported on by these practitioners, who have also methodically evaluated risks and offered suggestions for enhancing risk-mitigating procedures. In addition, they have given management and the audit committee assurance, direction, and clear communication about following rules and regulations, risks to the organization's operations and reputation, and actions to improve corporate governance. The legislation has been far more menacing and the task of compliance has been more difficult for organizations that had not maintained these procedures. Facilities look up to auditors because they are the association's representatives and because of their knowledge and skill. Facilities who encounter an unprofessional auditor may become permanently jaded about the advantages of accreditation and may decide to discontinue the process altogether, or they may decide to treat auditors as role models. Some staff members may find the audit process extremely unpleasant if an unprofessional auditor is present, as they are already under a lot of pressure from their superiors to perform well on the audit. Regardless of the actual condition and standards of the facility, unqualified auditors can affect how well facilities perform in the accreditation process.

8.1. A NEW PROFESSIONALISM: CHANGES AND CONTINUITIES

A government initiative to support commercialized and institutionalized forms of professionalism has resulted in changes to professionalism. Brint has talked about an epochal transition from the language of trusteeship to the language of expertise within this framework. The majority of professional occupations and expert groups are being profoundly impacted by organizational principles, strategies, and methods, which are changing their identities, structures, and practices. It's arguable whether a "new" kind of professionalism is developing because there are aspects of continuity and aspects of change. To determine whether or not professionalism will endure as an occupational value, it is crucial to ascertain precisely what has changed and what the same remains. Undoubtedly, aspects of change include things like bureaucracy, output and performance metrics, standardization of work practices, and hierarchy—all of which are more indicative of organizational than of professional forms of occupational control.

Repurposing professionals as managers and using normative techniques became a key component of the strategy when service sector professionals demonstrated persistent resistance to change and difficulty in managing. The discourses of professionalism, quality, customer service, and care are intertwined with the enterprise discourse. The ideological tenets of autonomy, discretion, innovation, and empowerment also tempt professionals. Furthermore, the need for explicit auditing and accounting of professional competences is actually increased by attempts to quantify and demonstrate professionalism. As a result, management requests for goal-setting, performance reviews, and quality control and audits are reinterpreted as efforts to advance professionalism. It is imperative to acknowledge, nonetheless, that performance and output metrics also embody a "discourse of competition," or as Broadbent put it, "individualization." The risk is that rivalry jeopardizes both collaborative efforts and collegial support, while social cohesiveness and institutional action are compromised. Therefore, while the pursuit of professionalism and accountability is driven by individualism and fierce competition, it also serves as a bureaucratic tool for regaining and controlling a professionally staffed, market-oriented business.

Furthermore, certain traits, especially the professionalism that emerged under the banner of new public service management (NPSM), appear to indicate the existence of a new and unique kind of professionalism. These variations include the focus on community controls and governance, the balancing of numerous competing agencies and interests, and the repurposing of professionals as managers. Thus, normative values and self-regulated motivation are increasingly used in public sector professions to achieve control. Professional services firms combine the language of quality and customer care with the concepts of empowerment, autonomy, innovation, and discretion to create a discourse of enterprise. Furthermore, this is a discourse about individualization and competition, where a person's success or failure as an organization is correlated with their own performance. All of these elements combine to form potent worker/employee control mechanisms that leverage professional values in the workplace to advance effective organizational management. In a lot of ways, regulatory, centralizing governments are redefining professionalism and accountability as quantifiable in an effort to show the value of public service budgets. However, it's important to recognize some of the ways that occupational professionalism still functions before we can fully accept the decline and potential demise of occupational forms of professionalism. According to Adler, there is potential for mutual support between the market, hierarchy, and community rather than for them to be mutually exclusive. Increased market pressures frequently result in an increase in community-based practices that align with occupational forms of professionalism, such as cooperative working and multidisciplinary teams.

Table 8.1. *Changes and Continuities in Professionalism as Occupational Value*

Changes	Continuities
Governance	Authority
Management	Legitimacy
External forms of regulation	Prestige, status, power, dominance
Audit and measurement	Competence, knowledge
Targets and performance indicators	Identity and work culture
Work standardization, financial control	Discretion to deal with complex issues, respect, trust
Competition, individualism, stratification	Collegial relations and jurisdictional Competitions
Organizational control of the work priorities.	Gender differences in careers and strategies
Possible range of solutions/procedures defined by the organization	Procedures and solutions discussed and agreed within specialist teams

Source: https://journals.openedition.org/spp/docannexe/image/4955/img-1.jpg.

Both structural and relationship aspects and characteristics are included in these changes and continuities; crucially, however, the changes are primarily structural, while the continuities typically center on relations. Furthermore, these alterations and continuity have been recognized and demonstrated at the macro (i.e., social) as well as mezo (i.e., institutional/organizational) levels of examination, but noteworthy micro (i.e., variations in local organizational contexts and various work locations. So what are the implications for practitioners and their clients? What are the opportunities and challenges of evolving aspects of professionalism as an occupational value? Is occupational professionalism worth preserving as a unique alternative and contrasting way of controlling work and workers (compared with organizations and markets) and with value for both practitioners and their clients?

- **Consequence and Challenges:** Researchers interested in various occupational groups in Europe and North America are documenting the effects of and challenges to professionalism as an occupational value, and research ties with organizational sociologists are growing. Additionally, there are some preliminary signs that policymakers may be moving away from managerialism or significantly redefining some aspects of New Public Service Management (NPSM) with regard to specific service work. Any correlation between the organizational changes and challenges to occupational professionalism and a decline in professional values is still theoretical as there is no concrete evidence to support it. Furthermore, a number of complicating factors make it challenging to establish a causal relationship. The demystification of some aspects of professional knowledge and expertise; instances of practitioner malpractice and "unprofessional" behavior; media exaggeration and oversimplification; political interference; significant fee and salary increases in specific professional sectors; and divisions between commercial (corporate clients) and social service (state-funded) practitioners are some of the complicating context factors (some general, some nation-specific). These factors are further compounded by the growing trade union activism on behalf of professionals, all of which carry a perception of self rather than public interest. Furthermore, it is true that strong professionals have frequently resisted organizational controls and managerial interference. Many public service organizations (e.g., hospitals and universities) are intricate professional bureaucracies that are distinguished by the participation of several professional associations. These groups frequently have high status, which gives them both power and authority, and a history of having some degree of autonomy over their working methods. Furthermore, it is difficult to standardize and quantify the "outputs" of these organizations—and the professionals who work there. Services of this kind would seem to be inappropriate for both market and organizational controls when it comes to defining and standardizing the nature of the work process and when it comes to defining the work's outputs and what success looks like.

Hence, one of the many complicating factors is the potential growth of organizational forms of professionalism and the decline in occupational professionalism. Nonetheless, it can be said that employee control strategies used by organizations have impacted the work of practitioners within professional associations. Targets have been imposed in the fields of education, medicine, and even law enforcement, and these actions have had "unintended" effects on how work is prioritized and organized. Specifically, target achievement has become more important than other, less quantifiable duties and responsibilities. Form filling, more regulations, and bureaucracy take time that could be better spent serving clients. Standardizing work processes, maybe with the help of software, is a good way to keep an eye on underachievers, but it can also work against professionals who are inspiring, creative, and inventive. Professionalism is changing as a result of an emphasis on enterprise and economic contracting, as well as internal and external markets. Professionalism in accounting, audit management, and tendering demands practitioners to formalize their qualifications for assessments and contracts. "Service products to be marketed, price-tagged, individually evaluated, and compensated are defined as professional work; in that sense, it is commodified." Organizations that provide professional services are evolving into enterprises in terms of identity, hierarchy, and logic. Instead of adhering to the professional institution's ethical codes, the organization defines and places restrictions on potential solutions for client problems and difficulties. The identification of organizations' role as institutional entrepreneurs encompasses their ability to lobby the state to modify professional regulations to their advantage.

Professional work relationships must adapt as a result of the commodification of professional service labor. The traditional employer/professional trust relationship changes when practitioners join an organization and become employees, requiring oversight, evaluation, and auditing. By the creation of quasi-markets, customer satisfaction surveys and evaluations, quality measures, and payment by results, relationships between professionals and clients are also being transformed into customer relations. Key indicators for transforming welfare services into a market are the development, dissemination, and publication of quality and target measurements. The service itself is becoming more and more standardized, consumer interests are shaping it, and it is modeled after similar offerings from other producers. Professionals are becoming more connected to their workplace than to professional associations and institutions due to the growing emphasis on marketing and selling expert solutions. Customers replace clients, and the work organization now defines, relates to, and evaluates professional work competencies in the main (Adler, Kwon, & Hecksher, 2008).

- **Opportunities:** Using the previously identified list of changes and continuities, it would seem important to try to retain some form of occupational control over both work processes and relationships. The challenges to professionalism as an occupational value seem numerous, but are there any opportunities associated with these changes which might improve the conduct and the practice of professional service work and be advantageous for both practitioners and their clients? Are there some advantages in the combination of professional and organizational logics, of hybrid organizations and organizationally located professional projects, for controlling work and workers? It is possible to argue that identity, work culture, specialist teamwork, discussions among specialists, and the formation and maintenance of knowledge and expertise all improve the conduct of professional work and its practice while being advantageous to practitioners and their clients. However, all aspects would require evaluation and assessment through research. Certain items that organizations seem to find important actually seem less relevant and even detrimental to their ability to exercise professional control over their work. These consist of performance indicators, targets, and auditing measurement. These characteristics have been demonstrated on multiple occasions to skew work priorities, protocols, and processes, having "unintended" negative effects on clients and practitioners. Credentials, governance, and external regulations are some other aspects of organizational change that may have some positive effects (like transparency and control over more extreme professional powers) but may also have negative effects (like more bureaucracy, form-filling, and paperwork). All of these require time that, according to the profession, would be better spent on client interaction and service work as those terms are defined by the profession rather than the workplace. These factors would appear to have costs and benefits, so it would be necessary to continuously assess whether they were appropriate for professional work.

From the combination of the logics of professionalism and organization, there are other opportunities that might prove more advantageous. Using Human Resource Management (HRM) from the company into professional hiring practices, processes, and procedures is one of them. Work contracts, job descriptions, formal interview and selection processes, employment rights and benefits, appeals procedures, sick leave and coverage, maternity, childcare, and other absences are just a few examples of the many tools that have helped professionals in organizations. These tools have largely replaced less formalized ways to network socially and through informal recommendations. In fact, HR practices have improved equality of opportunity and diversity while also playing a major role in the 20-year spectacular growth in professional employment. The transparency of what were frequently obscure, even "mysterious," arrangements regarding promotion, career advancement, departmental relationships, and links within the organization has also increased as a result of the standardization and formalization of procedures for hiring, retaining, and career development. The majority believed that less codified procedures were unfair and inequitable because they only benefited a small number of privileged practitioners. Consequently, greater transparency may lead to a shift away from the sponsorship of the wealthy few and toward career decisions based on individual circumstances. In general, though, the integration of HRM policies and procedures from the organization into professional employment practices has been a chance and beneficial for practitioners and their work. Career disparities, including those based on gender and ethnicity, are evidently still present, as is a certain dependence on networking and unofficial advice and recommendations.

The growing understanding that managerialism and organizational management are not only complex but also multifaceted and multilayered appears to account for additional opportunities. As a micro-level strategy, there is some evidence, primarily from health professionals like nursing and midwifery but also now from medical doctors and teachers, of individual practitioners acquiring qualifications in management with the clear intention of furthering their careers. Management is used to control, and sometimes limit, the work of practitioners in organizations. However, management is also used by practitioners and by professional associations themselves as a strategy both in the career development of particular practitioners and in order to improve the status and respect of a professional occupation and its standing. This can also be seen as a collective mobility strategy in the case of health professionals, like nurses and midwives, as middle and senior hospital management is increasingly seen as a career opportunity for those with the necessary management training, experience, and drive. It's also worthwhile to take note of Langer's work regarding social work in Germany as a mezo level tactic. In order to elevate social work as a professional occupation in the field of social services work, management training is being incorporated into master's level programs for social workers in Germany. In response to the European Union's efforts to harmonize higher education across the continent, Germany has seen a significant increase in Master's programs, allowing social workers—in this example—to apply for leadership roles in social services departments and nonprofit organizations. Thus, these developments can be understood as strategies at the micro and mezzo levels in relation to social work. Organizations can also serve as venues for professional dominance and control, as well as objects of it. Abbott first discussed jurisdictional conflicts and negotiations, but these days they take place inside companies as opposed to the larger context of labor markets and educational institutions. Occupations within organizations try to organize and manage tasks and task divisions according to their own professional interests. The medical field can continue to maintain its dominance through cultural authority and legitimacy, but other professions must use competition—especially with regard to competences—to gain control over organizational decision-making. Armstrong talks about the struggle among management experts (accounting, engineering, and personnel) to occupy important roles and decision-making positions in big businesses. In this sense, organizations serve as venues for both professional and inter-professional competitions.

8.1.1. Characteristics of Professionalism

There's much more to being a professional in your field than just dressing in a coat and tie or holding a prestigious title and college degree. Being professional also means acting professionally when conducting business. There are several crucial traits that true professionals have that are applicable to almost any kind of business.

- **Appearance:** A professional looks well-groomed. Make sure you adhere to the dress code established by your company, if not exceed it, and take extra care in how you present yourself to potential or current clients.
- **Demeanor:** You should project confidence without coming across as cocky. Whether you're speaking with coworkers, superiors, or customers, always be courteous and articulate. It's important to maintain composure even in stressful situations.
- **Reliability:** It will be expected of you as a professional to find a way to complete the task. Reliability is also demonstrated by answering inquiries from others and keeping your word when you make commitments.
- **Competence:** Professionals distinguish themselves from the rest of the pack by striving to become experts in their field. This can entail taking classes, going to seminars, and earning any relevant professional designations in order to further your education.
- **Ethics:** Professionals that work with patients, attorneys, and public accountants are required to follow a strict code of ethics. You should always act ethically, even if your industry or company doesn't have a formal code.
- **Maintaining Your Poise:** A professional has to remain

composed in the face of difficulty. You shouldn't act in the same way toward a coworker or client, for instance, if they treat you aggressively.

- **Phone Etiquette:** Another crucial element of professional conduct is phone manners. This entails answering calls using your entire name, business name, and title. Make sure you listen carefully to the other person and avoid taking over the conversation.
- **Written Correspondence:** During written correspondence, keep your letters brief and to the point. Your tone should be polite and formal without being "stuffy." This also applies to email correspondence.
- **Organizational Skills:** A professional can quickly and easily find what is needed. Your work area should be neat and organized, and your briefcase should contain only what is needed for your appointment or presentation.
- **Accountability:** At all times, professionals are responsible for their actions. Admit your mistakes and, if you can, work to correct them. Avoid trying to assign responsibility to a coworker. If the error was made by your company, own up to it and try to fix it.

8.1.2. Importance of Professionalism in Business

Whether a company is small or large, maintaining a professional image at work is essential to its long-term success. In order to guarantee that the aims and objectives of the business are fulfilled, employee interactions and relationships with customers are crucial. Employee performance is enhanced when there is a professional attitude and demeanor at work, which inspires pride in the job done. Professional managers encourage their staff to conduct themselves in a way that promotes the success of the entire company, setting a suitable example (Bourgeault, & Benoit, 2009).

- **Establish Boundaries:** Boundaries between acceptable and inappropriate office behavior are established in a professional manner. Although most managers are in favor of a lively and pleasurable work atmosphere, boundaries need to be established to prevent miscommunication and confrontations. Employees that behave professionally avoid going too far in their talks and other interactions with clients, superiors, and other employees.
- **Encourage Improvement:** Success is more likely in a workplace where staff members act and dress professionally. Professional dress codes promote career development and personal growth in the workplace, according to Dress for Success, a nonprofit organization that assists businesswomen in obtaining appropriate work attire. Professional appearance and behavior make employees feel good about themselves and motivate them to deliver better work for their clients.
- **Maintain Accountability:** Businesses that deal directly with customers have an obligation to give them the best service and to show them in the best possible light. When giving clients written information, professionalism matters. Expertly crafted business

plans, company reports, and other written communications support companies in maintaining service quality accountability. The Small Business Administration states that it matters how the paperwork is submitted.

- **Promote Respect:** In the business world, professionalism fosters respect for clients, supervisors, and coworkers. By acting professionally, one can avoid being disrespectful by avoiding gossip and improper, personal conversations. Employee respect for the customer and the business partnership is demonstrated by maintaining a professional demeanor when dealing with unruly clients.
- **Minimize Conflict:** In a formal business setting, conflicts are less likely to occur. Conflicts that cannot be effectively resolved are rare among coworkers who behave professionally and respect one another's boundaries. Professionalism in the workplace has additional advantages in varied settings where clients and businesspeople have a range of viewpoints and opinions. Businesspeople can avoid upsetting people from diverse backgrounds or cultures by acting professionally.

8.1.3. Importance of a Dress Code for Professionalism

You've seen old pictures of offices where ladies wear dresses and skirts that are perfectly fitted, and men wear hats and sharply tailored suits with pocket squares. There are also images of contemporary tech workspaces that appear to have no restrictions on attire. The optimal option is situated in the middle. Just as options for appropriate clothing have many facets, so too does the significance of a dress code for professionalism.

- **Creating Cohesion:** A company's dress code establishes a standard for visual coherence. This fosters a sense of unity among the workforce and makes them feel as though they are all working toward the same goal. It's also true that there will be awkwardness if one person dresses like it's a beach barbecue and another person wears a suit and tie. Employees, of course, have the freedom to express themselves through what they wear, but workplaces also have the right to declare how they wish their establishment to appear. Whether on purpose or not, our wardrobe conveys a message. Employees are responsible for making sure that their appearance communicates that they are a part of the organization.
- **Creating Imagery:** Workers serve as ambassadors for their employers. The people the company hires represent its objectives and visions. Different industries have different expectations when it comes to professional attire, so each location is free to set its own guidelines. It is generally accepted that everyone should dress as though their clients could walk through the door at any time, even if they work in an office setting where there is little opportunity for face-to-face interaction. You never know who you might run into that could have an influence on business negotiations. People naturally form opinions based on visual cues, so the way you choose to dress

influences how people remember you and your business, either favorably or unfavorably.

- **How to Dress for Professionalism?** Comfort: It's best to never wear clothing that fits poorly, whether it's too tight, too loose, or inappropriate for your body type. It will be a truly miserable workday if you are uncomfortable. Find a fit for both your inner and outer self. When in doubt, show modesty by hiding. As general guidelines, wear closed-toe shoes, skirts or dresses that fall to the knee, avoid shorts, wear sleeves that reach the wrists, and cover your shoulders. It pays to err on the side of caution, even if that sounds harsh. Basically, you should probably avoid wearing something in an office setting if you would wear it on a beach vacation. This gets more complicated when it comes to hair, makeup, and accessories. Certain companies take concern over facial piercings but not over a purple mohawk. Take note of the attire worn by current employees of your company, and confirm with others if necessary. One cannot stress how crucial a dress code is to professionalism. There should be a balance between respecting the company's policies and expressing oneself. Respecting the dress code at work is an essential part of being a true professional, just as much as respecting your expertise in the field.

8.1.4. Examples of Professionalism

Owners of businesses desire a staff full of qualified and experienced workers. However, for certain employees, the term "professionalism" may be unclear. Establishing professional standards for the workplace and educating staff members on how to uphold them will benefit employers. There are numerous instances of professionalism (Noordegraaf, 2007).

- **Overall Punctuality:** One of the first indications of professionalism is punctuality. When someone is punctual, they earn the respect of their coworkers and managers. Being punctual, though, entails more than just arriving at work on time. It involves getting ready for work at your desk. A person should arrive at work a few minutes early if they arrive on time but still need to use the restroom, make coffee, and talk to coworkers. Attending staff and client meetings on time is another illustration of punctuality. Meeting deadlines is regarded by managers as a sign of professionalism. Clients regard timely and conscientious individuals more than those who arrive late on a regular basis.
- **Work Attire and Appearance:** Your professional demeanor is conveyed through your attire. Although each person has their own personal style, most work environments have certain guidelines. In order to present a professional image, if a uniform is required, it should be clean and ironed. Suits should fit well and ties should be knotted correctly in a professional setting. Workers who choose to wear skirts should be aware of their length. Another facet of professionalism is grooming. Makeup and hairstyles must be appropriate for the workplace. Standards are typically more lenient in a highly creative studio than they are in a legal office.

- **Loyalty to the Team:** Business executives look for employees with loyalty because they have to trust them to represent the company well. Being loyal involves more than just carrying out the duties given to you after a long day at work. It entails acting as a positive representative for the business, refraining from challenging management in front of other employees, and never spreading rumors about it. When an issue arises, devoted team members know that management is concerned about the long-term prosperity of the business and each individual worker.
- **Supporting Co-Workers:** Being proactive in supporting colleagues is one aspect of professionalism. Employees are willing to assist those in need when they feel secure in their roles and as members of a team. They know that when one person helps another, the team becomes stronger and everyone wins. A customer service agent might, for instance, go over phone scripts and role-playing with a recent hire. Supervisors value cooperative employees and frequently try to advance them into leadership roles.
- **Being Honest:** Life is full of mistakes and miscommunications, and business is no exception. Sincere workers admit their errors instead of trying to hide the truth or assign blame to others. Sincere laborers have confidence in their skills. When a customer order is placed incorrectly, honest staff members not only acknowledge the issue but also try to find a solution. Additionally, sincere workers are more likely to request time off rather than calling in unexpectedly sick, which allows managers to cover shift gaps. This is considerate of all people.
- **Working at Work:** There are lots of distractions at work. In the break room, people linger longer than necessary while sipping coffee and chatting with coworkers. During the day, employees become distracted by personal calls and texts or by browsing the internet. Professional staff members are aware of when to get to work, but some business owners do permit a certain amount of personal time during work. It's not the same as texting a friend for an hour about your weekend plans and receiving a text from your spouse about being late. Professionalism is exhibited in restraint and completing tasks on time.

8.1.5. Audit Professionalism

Clearly defined standards are necessary for internal auditing, and this helps to foster the growth of expert audit services. The Global Institute of Internal Auditors aims to represent an international perspective despite the challenge of securing a truly international dimension to internal auditing. This intriguing development might have a significant effect on the industry. Prior to examining the different internal auditing standards, the following are the key components of a professional discipline:

- Training program
- Common body of knowledge
- Code of ethics
- Sanctions
- Control over services
- Qualified practitioners

- Morality
- Technical difficulty
- Examinations
- Journals
- Professional body
- Compliance with rules
- Service to society

All of the requirements are met by internal auditing, which is now firmly established as a professional discipline. This is a significant accomplishment because it was unheard of ten or twenty years ago. With its newly acquired high profile placing it firmly on the boardroom agenda, the internal audit community can plan for the future and track the way it needs to progress by having a strong professional base.

8.2. PROFESSIONAL CARE

The internal auditor is facing an increasingly demanding requirement to exercise caution during the audit process. A compelling example of the idea of due professional care is the firing of two internal auditors by Allied Irish Bank's US subsidiary (All first) following the actions of rogue trader John Rusnak. Attribute Standard 1220 (Due Professional Care), which mandates that internal auditors exercise the care and skill expected of a reasonably prudent and competent internal auditor, serves as further evidence of the importance of exercising caution. Adequate expert care does not imply perfectibility. One possible approach to quickly identify the guiding principles of an audit would be to create a model similar to the one shown in Figure 8.1. For an audit to be deemed acceptable in quality, each audit must satisfy a set of baseline requirements; consequently, the previously mentioned elements must be firmly established. In the event that this is not the case, there is a compelling case to be made for improper audit performance.

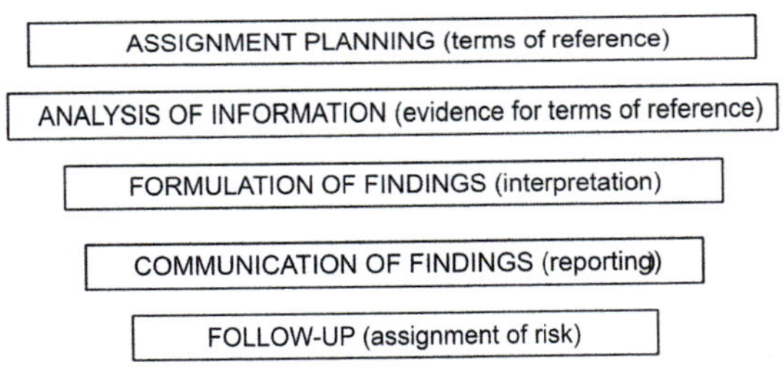

Figure 8.1. *Model of baseline standards.*

Source: https://d3i71xaburhd42.cloudfront.net/b332fb5b95d8a06b1b210dcca2334a4701b84a15/158-Figure6.1-1.png.

8.2.1. Professional Consulting Services

It is evident from the definition that internal auditing is an activity that involves assurance and consulting. An objective review of the available data with the aim of independently evaluating the organization's risk management, control, or governance procedures is what the IIA defines as an assurance service. Due diligence engagements in the areas of finance, compliance, systems security, and security may be examples. On the other hand, consulting services are described as "related client service activities and advice, the nature and extent of which are decided upon with the client and which are meant to add value and enhance an organization's operations." A few instances are guidance, recommendations, facilitation, process design, and instruction. In an assurance project, the client, the auditor, and the third party receiving the assurance are the main participants; in a consulting project, it's just the client and the auditor. The internal audit community understands assurance work well, and over the years, there has been "creeping consulting," which typically takes the form of information and advice provided upon request from line managers. An official consulting service centered on the aspects of corporate governance, risk management, and control has never been offered before. Many auditors merely propose increasing their consulting work; however, it may not be appreciated that there is a whole industry in this field with established standards and procedures, many of which are comparable to internal auditing practices.

- **What is Management Consulting?** The process of offering advice or direction to a company in order to boost performance is known as management consulting. A company that believes it has reached the limits of its capabilities may seek the counsel and assistance of a management consulting firm, whose expertise may enable it to reach new markets. For instance, a management consultant might be engaged to examine the issue from a cost perspective if a company's profits have decreased. After that, the consultant offers a company one or more options for fixing the issue. Any business's normal objective is to boost profits. This can be accomplished in a number of ways, including by reducing salaries, improving production efficiency, reducing waste, and introducing new goods and services. Occasionally, an external viewpoint is required to accurately assess how well a company is performing in these domains. A management consulting firm might be engaged in this situation, and in an ideal world, they would provide a solution based on years of experience assisting other clients in achieving the same or comparable objectives. Outside experience can be a tremendous benefit to a company, particularly for small or expanding enterprises. Independent contractors or major corporations with hundreds of staff members and locations can operate as management consultants. They can also be employed by a company and paid for, or they could just be an unpaid friend, relative, or coworker with a highly skilled skill set who gives business owners advice.

Typically, management consulting is charged on an hourly basis or by the project. However, a creative company owner may bargain for a contract that bases payment on the consultant's performance. For instance, if cutting expenses is the main objective, a management consultant might get paid a portion of the savings that are made by putting the suggested ideas into practice. An individual can receive training in a business subject from any of the many business courses offered in colleges, but management consultants are typically employed and compensated according to their performance and experience. As a management consultant, it is challenging to get started without years of practical experience and/or a diverse clientele. Working for a sizable consulting firm is the best way for someone to begin their career in management consulting. Cost analysis, employee benefit plan streamlining, and implementing new waste control procedures are typical areas of management consulting. Other areas include introducing new technology and modernizing computer systems. A management consultant will typically only offer recommendations for the most effective ways to boost performance; the onus of putting those suggestions into practice rests with the organization. Almost everyone who practices management consulting fits into one of these categories, despite the imprecise nature of these classifications.

The categories are:

1. **Strategy Consulting:** Most of the attention on this website is directed toward strategy management consulting firms. These companies offer senior management advice on broad issues pertaining to important strategic issues in all industries. Booz & Co., the Boston Consulting Group, Bain & Company, and McKinsey and Company are some of the leading management consulting firms that specialize in strategy consulting. These companies are at the top of the prestige hierarchy because they frequently hire from prestigious business schools and undergraduate institutions. To justify the high cost of strategy consulting—often more than $500,000 per month for a team of five—consulting firms must take on high-value assignments at the CEO or senior executive level. Some of the queries a strategy consulting company might address are:

- How do we respond to a new competitive threat?
- Which manufacturing plants should we shut down?
- How can we increase our profit margin?
- How can we increase our market share?
- How do we go about launching this new product?

A typical strategy consulting firm consulting resume might look something like this: Assisted redesign of merchandising and planning functions for a Fortune 100 retailer by working with client VPs to estimate savings under various scenarios and create new job descriptions." Since then, the client has realized annual savings of over $50 million. Since this variety of experiences can offer a nice overview of the business world, new hires into strategy consulting firms typically enjoy the wide range of business questions and industries. Most candidates then quit consulting after two to five years to begin or progress in their chosen careers. A case interview question is typically asked during the consulting interview process for strategy consulting firms. Following this, the candidate and the interviewer work through a business problem that may be similar to one another's prior engagements. A question like this from a consulting interview might be, our client is a $2 billion manufacturer of household appliances. Although margin has decreased, sales have been stagnant recently. You must figure out how to raise the margin for them.

2. **Accounting Firms:** The big audit companies frequently offer their clients consulting services as well. Price Waterhouse Coopers (PWC), KPMG, Ernst and Young, and Deloitte Touche Tohmatsu are some of these significant players. Compared to the elite strategy management consulting firms, these companies typically hire bright accounting and business talent from a larger pool of universities. There are a lot of similarities between consulting and accounting (e.g., both provide senior management advice), both call for an understanding of business mathematics, and there is a significant risk of conflict of

interest. Following the Enron/ Andersen scandal, new laws like Sarbanes-Oxley set forth precise guidelines for how the audit and consulting functions must be kept apart. Accounting firm consultants may answer the following queries:

- What financial tracking and reporting processes are inefficient?
- How can we improve our compliance rates?
- How might we improve cash flow by optimizing our billing or payment processes and policies?

Even though the questions seem to be closely related to accounting, these companies may also have extensive knowledge in other fields. For instance, the Human Capital Advisory practice at Deloitte focuses mostly on change management and human resources issues. Resuming a career as a consultant in an accounting firm could include the following: thoroughly examined the invoice-to-cash cycle to find any obstacles impeding payments. Since then, the client's day's receivable metrics have increased by more than 20%. In an accounting firm, a consulting interview may consist of a series of behavioral questions as well as a test of your accounting knowledge.

3. **IT Specialists:** Given the complexity of IT consulting and the size of the major players in the industry, it makes sense to create a separate category for IT specialists. Accenture, IBM, Hitachi Consulting, Computer Sciences Corp., CGI Group, and iGATE Patni are important participants in this market. (Remember, though, that these classifications are not overly strict. There is a smaller strategy consulting division within Accenture. Even though IBM is thought to employ 100,000 IT consultants, the company also depends heavily on sales of its products. Compared to accounting firms, IT firms hire even more widely and frequently value specific coding knowledge, class rank, or GPA. These businesses frequently assist corporate CTOs or their direct reports.

IT specialists would tackle questions such as:

- How can we automate this antiquated paper system?
- How should we go about fine-tuning and articulating our specific requirements to receive bids from different IT vendors?
- How should we go about implementing a company-wide ERP (Enterprise Resource Planning) software system or CRM (Customer Relationship Management) system? (Examples of such platforms include SAP, Oracle, or Salesforce.)
- What new system should we update our old "green screens" to?
- How can we ensure our important data is encrypted, backed up, accessible, and secure?

An IT professional's consultant resume might look something like this: accelerated online sales process by choosing, customizing, and testing a CRM solution that reduced manual labor and shortened shipping times by twenty percent. An IT specialist may be asked to walk a prospective client through the steps he would take to implement a specific IT upgrade during a consulting interview.

4. **Boutique Consultants:** The category for boutique consulting firms is a bit nebulous. These companies

typically have a distinct focus on one or both of the following: a particular industry or practice area. Boutique businesses have countless options when it comes to specialization. For instance, ZS Associates' primary business is providing pharmaceutical companies with sales and marketing consulting. Hewitt, Mercer, Towers Watson, and the Hay Group concentrate on matters related to human resources. Boutique companies occasionally have the ability to focus only on compensation and benefits, moving beyond human resources. Within the creative innovation consulting niche are two boutique firms: IDEO and Kuczmarksi and Associates. There is no end to the list. But don't be misled by the name of the boutique. Numerous of these businesses employ thousands of people and are global in scope. Their approaches to hiring and the issues they address differ greatly. There are also significant differences in boutique firms' name recognition, selectivity, and prestige.

5. **Internal Consultants:** Employers are the one and only client of many management consultants. It's not unusual for many businesses to have an internal team that serves as a consulting team, taking on worthwhile internal improvement opportunities. An organization's strategy group is frequently referred to as its internal consulting team. Employing an internal consulting team has several advantages for corporations. Internal consultants can frequently progress into other important leadership roles within the organization, have a deeper understanding of the business, and are less expensive than external consultants. The greatest college talent is sought after by many companies for internal consulting or rotational positions; however, stars frequently select strategy management consulting firms over industry picks.

Questions internal consultants might tackle include:

- Why do we have such variation in cost in different parts of our business? What opportunities exist for us to identify best practices and disseminate them worldwide?
- What businesses would make appealing acquisition targets for us?
- What's the competition doing with regard to this particular issue?
- How would we continue our business if the union organized a strike at a key plant?

Employers are the one and only client of many management consultants. It's not unusual for many businesses to have an internal team that serves as a consulting team, taking on worthwhile internal improvement opportunities. An organization's strategy group is frequently referred to as its internal consulting team. Employing an internal consulting team has several advantages for corporations. Internal consultants can frequently progress into other important leadership roles within the organization, have a deeper understanding of the business, and are less expensive than external consultants. The greatest college talent is sought after by many companies for internal consulting or rotational positions; however, stars frequently select strategy management consulting firms over industry picks.

6. **Independent Consultants:** The independent consultants are even more dispersed than the internal and boutique consulting firms. Not even a big company's logo appears on the work of these consultants. These enterprising spirits frequently operate alone or in small teams consisting of two to six individuals. Independent consultants frequently possess deep expertise as a result of years of working on a specific kind of business challenge (e.g., waste minimization in production facilities). These individuals could be young people seeking greater freedom and flexibility in their lifestyle, newlywed parents seeking a decrease in their weekly workload, or semi-retired veterans who find themselves drawn back into new projects. One-off projects, speaking engagements, and executive coaching are common ways for independent consultants to supplement their income. These broad classifications can be a helpful place to start when looking into career options in management consulting. Which is the best depends entirely on your goals and background. Aim for a strategy management consulting company if you're a driven individual with exceptional academic credentials who wants to work for a Fortune 500 company someday as a CEO. The accounting firms will value it most if you are pursuing a CPA certification. If you're fascinated by coding, computers, and process optimization, working in IT consulting might be the most interesting place for you. Select a boutique firm that specializes in the area of knowledge you wish to continue developing on a daily basis. Internal management consulting positions are the best option if you're looking for the long-term stability of an established company.

8.3. THE QUALITY CONCEPT

The CAE should create and maintain a quality assurance and improvement program that covers every facet of internal auditing and regularly assesses its efficacy, according to IIA Attribute Standard 1300 (Quality Assurance and Improvement Program). The program included continuous monitoring as well as periodic internal and external quality assessments. Every component of the program ought to be created with the intention of assisting internal auditing in adding value, enhancing organizational operations, and guaranteeing that internal auditing complies with the Standards and the Code of Ethics.

There is a lot being said about quality assurance, as this appears to be one of the standard management buzzwords. Quality is about:

- Knowing your business.
- Knowing your customers and understanding how they see your business.
- Looking for and dealing with problems.
- Having a way of finding out what stakeholders think of the service.
- Relating all problems to systems that need to be improved. In other words risks to success should be identified, assessed and managed.
- Being very concerned about the section's reputation and overall standing in the organization.
- A clear focus on value for money.
- Resourcing the drive for quality.
- Having efficient and effective procedures.
- Having the quality role built into all staff and ensuring audit managers review and supervise work with this in mind.
- Developing assessment models that can be used to judge whether quality standards are being met.
- Adopting a culture of getting things right and continually improving.
- Several Attribute Standards address the quality concept:
- 1310: The internal audit activity should adopt a process to monitor and assess the overall effectiveness of the quality program. The process should include both internal and external assessments.
- 1311: Internal assessments should include:

- Ongoing reviews of the performance of the internal audit activity; and
- Periodic reviews performed through self-assessment or by other persons within the organization, with knowledge of internal auditing practices and the Standards.
- 1312: External assessments, such as quality assurance reviews, should be conducted at least once every five years by a qualified, independent reviewer or review team from outside the organization.
- 1320: The CAE should communicate the results of external assessments to the board.

8.3.1. Defining the Client

Providing the client with what they need and want is the essence of professionalism and quality. Because internal auditors provide both assurance and consulting services, as well as multiple stakeholders, this straightforward idea becomes more complex for them. Those who obtained audit services were referred to as audits in the past. But, things have changed since then, and opinions on the precise manner in which we provide the audit service differ. First, as many observers have pointed out, internal audit has moved away from being a "them and us" battleground. The new chief internal auditor of Abbey National shares with Neil Hodge what he considers to be an indispensable audit function. It is imperative that internal audit function as a sort of "controls consultant." No matter how well-founded their criticism may be, internal audit cannot continue to just stand by and criticize management plans. Internal audit should explicitly state that they should collaborate with management rather than against it in their interactions with the board. After acknowledging that almost every member of the organization was a customer of internal auditing, we were ready to start a survey process to find out how well we were meeting their needs. We discovered that our audit procedure could be boiled down to five fundamental areas that would interest our clients:

- Audit planning
- Performance of audits
- The reporting of results
- Our response to ad hoc requests for assistance
- Auditor professionalism

8.3.2. Internal Review

Clear standards and efficient oversight to guarantee that they are followed and understood throughout the audit shop can both help to promote quality. It is recommended that the CAE implement an internal assessment system to verify that all is in order. According to the IIA's Attribute Standard 1311, the CAE must provide an internal assessment that must include the following: regular reviews conducted by the CAE or by other organization members who are knowledgeable about internal auditing procedures and the Standards; and ongoing evaluations of the performance of the internal audit activity. The internal review will take into account a number of recent audit-related factors, such as the procedures followed and the standards that were used.

8.3.3. External Review

"External assessments, such as quality assurance reviews, should be conducted at least once every five years by a qualified, independent reviewer or review team from outside the organization," according to IIA Attribute Standard 1312. There are several ways to commission this comprehensive review: The CAE should make use of the external review's findings to formulate a plan for enhancing the audit function and creating a high-quality program. Whatever is specified in the agreed-upon terms of reference—which, as mentioned, might originate from a risk workshop—will be examined by the review. It might, nevertheless, cover a few of the following areas:

- Audit charter—mission and vision and buy-in from staff and stakeholders.
- Organizational status.
- Independence.
- Codes of conduct and internal disciplinary mechanisms.
- Mix between assurance and consulting activity.
- Audit strategy and whether it fits with corporate strategy of organization.
- Relations with the board, senior manager and general reputation.
- Interface with audit committee and whether best practice measures used to keep the audit committee informed.
- Links with external audit and internal review teams.
- Performance measurement system and whether this makes sense—also links with performance reporting systems.
- Communications and participation between auditors and also with external parties—whether use is made of web-based material.
- Mix of specialist such as fraud, IT, projects, contract and other areas.
- Complaints procedure and whether this picks up all significant problems.
- Structure and flexibility—in response to changes and strategies.
- Staff competence, qualification and CPD.
- Morale levels among auditors, and remuneration and retention rates—why do people leave internal audit? Policies on secondment, career auditors and short-term placements.
- Formal training programs.
- Research into developing best practice and links with professional bodies, local universities, conferences, and international developments. Does the audit staff keep themselves up to date?
- Planning systems and the annual audit plan.
- Budgets and budgetary control also cost per audit day.
- Extent to which audit is accomplishing its objectives.
- Planning and control of audit assignments and supervision arrangements.
- Working papers, standards and compliance (also extent of automation, protection, security, retention, back-up and confidentiality).
- Level of equipment such as laptops, communication links, etc.
- Balance work–life issues and use of flexible approaches such as working from home.
- Measures to encourage diversity among staff.
- Quality assurance systems and whether internal with considering outcomes of recent internal reviews.
- Due professional care and measures taken to ensure professionalism and

consistency including the use of the audit manual

- Compliance mechanisms to ensure laws and regulations are adhered to.

The value-add proposition that was chosen and if it is being fulfilled. In a way, the list is unrestricted because it truly depends on the risks that serve as the foundation for the review's terms of reference. When a problem related to non-compliance is discovered through the three-pronged approach of supervision, internal, and/or external review, it must be addressed. Where this affects the overall scope or operation of internal audit, including the absence of an external assessment, senior management and the board must be notified. Any internal audit review of quality and compliance should report its findings back to the original requester, and a suitable action should be formulated based on the recommendations and findings. The CAE is in charge of carrying out this action plan.

8.4. MARKETING THE AUDIT ROLE

Internal audit must demonstrate its value to an organization in order to maintain its standing, as stated in the IIA distance learning manuals: "No function has the right to exist in the modern world." Each must be able to show how it benefits the company and be prepared for frequent inquiries regarding its function and impact. Even though its primary role is review, internal audit is becoming more and more scrutinized like every other department within a company, so it needs to be able to defend its continued existence. Some contend that the special quality of the internal audit function, which has to do with its independence, implies that the delivery of services does not necessarily need to take a market-based approach. They might continue by saying that internal auditors become little more than consultants if managers set the standards for how internal audits are conducted.

While there are certain factors that affect a purist view of marketing, this viewpoint is flawed because it ignores the fact that internal audit serves the organization, not just itself. Applying the basic acid test is a helpful way to determine whether our marketing efforts have impeded our ability to reach the appropriate levels of independence. Purists would argue that a negative response to this question would further the idea that the audit services are independent of operations. From a marketing perspective, the problem is that this exposes the audit role and reduces it to the status of a disposable good. Since there is an inherent conflict between the marketing concept and the independence test that the CAE must acknowledge and manage when considering the marketing mix, this issue deserves more investigation.

- *The Product:* Here we consider whether the audit work that is being provided fits with the requirements of the organization.
- *The Price:* The costs of the audit work should be subject to ongoing review so as to work to an optimum profile.
- *Promotion:* This may be seen more as being built into the public relations function as a way of selling the audit image and underlying services.
- **The Audit Budget:** For example, a quarterly fee charging system is used by clients to pay for audit services, and it is crucial that the charges are connected to the audit budget. The primary annual cost components are displayed below, and we must recoup all expenses incurred in providing the audit service.

We can calculate a recovery hourly rate by dividing the total annual costs by the anticipated number of chargeable audit hours for the year. We may be able to attain a trading surplus by raising this hourly rate, which would go toward non-recoverable time and purchases like computer equipment. Each auditor grade will have a different hourly charge-out rate, and the time monitoring system will account for this. As an alternative, the hourly rate can be roughly estimated using the following formula:

Item	£
Salaries	
Staff expenses	
Office accommodation	
General admin overheads	
Equipment	
Other expenses	
Total cost	

$$\frac{\text{Annual salary } (\times 1.5)}{\text{Chargeable hours for the year}} = \text{Hourly rate}$$

The time charging system will enable audit management to track how well the planned income is being generated; audit management will receive a quarterly report on this. In addition to its general oversight responsibilities, the audit committee may ask for specific reviews and will be paid for them. Regarding any required corporate reviews, the audit committee is likely to receive advice from the CAE. It should be noted that management cannot usually refuse a scheduled audit review; however, in situations where there are adequate audit resources available, they may bargain for a different timeframe or request more work. Managers can also ask for specifics regarding the planning, risk assessment, and time billing procedures for audits.

8.4.1. Creating the Audit Image

Audit needs to formulate and maintain an appropriate image and one auditor who breach professional behavior may tarnish the reputation of the whole department. The audit image is based around the standards set out in the audit manual and the auditor code of conduct. In addition, it requires the following features of the internal auditor:

- Politeness, having regard to the need to respect fellow officers at whatever grade.
- Being positive by building constructive working relations with management.
- Sensitivity to management's needs.
- Respect for confidentiality with an understanding of the damage that idle gossip can do.
- A team-based audit approach working with and alongside management.
- A hard-working attitude with a constant mission to encourage management to promote good controls.
- A desire to explain the role of audit and promote the audit service wherever possible.
- It may be an idea to organize a series of seminars (or a slot at the corporate annual conference) and deliver the new-look internal audit approach.

8.4.2. Audit Feedback Questionnaire

One way of achieving a degree of feedback from the client is to obtain a response to a formal questionnaire that makes enquiries about the audit service. The purpose of the survey should be explained in a covering memo from the CAE, the main objectives being:

- To obtain the client's view on the benefits secured from the audit.
- To isolate any communication problems that may have been experienced by the client.
- To assess whether the client's perceived needs have been met.

CASE STUDY

INTERNAL AUDIT ACTIVITY CHARTER

Internal Auditing is an independent and objective assurance and consulting activity that is guided by a philosophy of adding value to improve the operations of the organization. It assists organization in accomplishing its objectives by bringing a systematic and disciplined approach to evaluate and improve the effectiveness of the organization's governance, risk management, internal control.

Role

The internal audit activity is established by the Board of Directors, Audit Committee, or highest level of governing body (hereafter referred to as the Board). The internal audit activity's responsibilities are defined by the Board as part of their oversight role.

Professionalism

The internal audit activity will govern itself by adherence to The Institute of Internal Auditors' mandatory guidance including the Definition of

Internal Auditing, the Code of Ethics, and the International Standards for the Professional Practice of Internal Auditing (Standards). This mandatory guidance constitutes principles of the fundamental requirements for the professional practice of internal auditing and for evaluating the effectiveness of the internal audit activity's performance. The Institute of Internal Auditors' Practice Advisories, Practice Guides, and Position Papers will also be adhered to as applicable to guide operations. In addition, the internal audit activity will adhere to <organization> relevant policies and procedures and the internal audit activity's standard operating procedures manual.

Authority

The internal audit activity, with strict accountability for confidentiality and safeguarding records and information, is authorized full, free, and unrestricted access to any and all of <organization> records, physical properties, and personnel pertinent to carrying out any engagement. All employees are requested to assist the internal audit activity in fulfilling its roles and responsibilities. The internal audit activity will also have free and unrestricted access to the Board.

Organization

The Chief Audit Executive will report functionally to the Board and administratively (i.e. day to day operations) to the Chief Executive Officer.

The Board will

- Approve the internal audit charter.
- Approve the risk based internal audit plan.
- Approve the internal audit budget and resource plan.
- Receive communications from the Chief Audit Executive on the internal audit activity's performance relative to its plan and other matters.
- Approve decisions regarding the appointment and removal of the Chief Audit Executive.
- Approve the remuneration of the Chief Audit Executive.
- Make appropriate inquiries of management and the Chief Audit Executive to determine whether there is inappropriate scope or resource limitations.

The Chief Audit Executive will communicate and interact directly with the Board, including in executive sessions and between Board meetings as appropriate.

Independence and Objectivity

The internal audit activity will remain free from interference by any element in the organization, including matters of audit selection, scope, procedures, frequency, timing, or report content to permit maintenance of a necessary independent and objective mental attitude. Internal auditors will have no direct operational responsibility or authority over any of the activities audited. Accordingly, they will not implement internal controls, develop procedures, install systems, prepare records, or engage in any other activity that may impair internal auditor's judgment.

Internal auditors will exhibit the highest level of professional objectivity in gathering, evaluating, and communicating information about the activity or process being examined. Internal auditors will make a balanced assessment of all the relevant circumstances and not be unduly influenced by their own interests or by others in forming judgments. The Chief Audit Executive will confirm to the board, at least annually, the organizational independence of the internal audit activity.

Responsibility

The scope of internal auditing encompasses, but is not limited to, the examination and evaluation of the adequacy and effectiveness of the organization's governance, risk management, and internal controls as well as the quality of performance in carrying out assigned responsibilities to achieve the organization's stated goals and objectives. This includes:

- Evaluating risk exposure relating to achievement of the organization's strategic objectives.
- Evaluating the reliability and integrity of information and the means used to identify measure, classify, and report such information.

- Evaluating the systems established to ensure compliance with those policies, plans, procedures, laws, and regulations which could have a significant impact on the organization.
- Evaluating the means of safeguarding assets and, as appropriate, verifying the existence of such assets.
- Evaluating the effectiveness and efficiency with which resources are employed.
- Monitoring and evaluating governance processes.
- Monitoring and evaluating the effectiveness of the organization's risk management processes.
- Evaluating the quality of performance of external auditors and the degree of coordination with internal audit.
- Performing consulting and advisory services related to governance, risk management and control as appropriate for the organization.

Reporting and Monitoring

A written report will be prepared and issued by the Chief Audit Executive or designee following the conclusion of each internal audit engagement and will be distributed as appropriate. Internal audit results will also be communicated to the Board. The internal audit report may include management's response and corrective action taken or to be taken in regard to the specific findings and recommendations. Management's response, whether included within the original audit report or provided thereafter (i.e. within thirty days) by management of the audited area should include a timetable for anticipated completion of action to be taken and an explanation for any corrective action that will not be implemented.

Quality Assurance and Improvement Program

The internal audit activity will maintain a quality assurance and improvement program that covers all aspects of the internal audit activity. The program will include an evaluation of the internal audit activity's conformance with the Definition of Internal Auditing and the Standards and an evaluation of whether internal auditors apply the Code of Ethics. The program also assesses the efficiency and effectiveness of the internal audit activity and identifies opportunities for improvement.

SUMMARY

- Professionalism has undergone change and these changes have been seen as part of a governmental project to promote commercialized and organizational forms of professionalism.
- Professional workplace behavior is necessary for the long-term success of a business, whether it's a big corporation or small business.
- Internal auditing needs defined standards and this contributes to the development of professional audit services.
- Taking care during the audit process is becoming an increasingly onerous requirement for the internal auditor.
- Strategy management consulting firms receive the majority of this website's attention. These firms advise senior management across all industries on broad questions related to major strategic questions.
- The major audit firms also often provide consulting work to their clients. These major players include Price Waterhouse Coopers (PWC), KPMG, Ernst & Young, and Deloitte Touche Tohmatsu.
- The complexity of IT consulting, combined with the sheer market size of the key players, warrants giving the IT specialists their own category.
- Even more scattered than the boutique consulting firms and the internal consultants are the independent consultants.
- Quality can be promoted by clear standards and effective supervision to ensure these standards are understood and employed throughout the audit shop.
- Clients pay for audit services through for example, a quarterly fee charging system, and it is essential that the charges are linked into the audit budget.
- Audit needs to formulate and maintain an appropriate image and one auditor who breach professional behavior may tarnish the reputation of the whole department.
- One way of achieving a degree of feedback from the client is to obtain a response to a formal questionnaire that makes enquiries about the audit service.

REVIEW QUESTIONS

1. Why is professionalism important in business?
2. Discuss the audit professionalism.
3. Define the role of professional consulting services.
4. Explain the creating the audit image.
5. Discuss the audit feedback questionnaire.

REFERENCES

1. Adler, P., Kwon, S., & Heckscher, C. (2008). Professional work: The emergence of collaborative community. *Organization Science, 19*(2), 359–376.
2. Bolton, S. C. (2005). "Making up" managers: The case of NHS nurses. *Work, Employment and Society, 19*(1).
3. Bourgeault, I. L., & Benoit, C. (2009). Comparative perspectives on the sociology of professions. *Groups, 57*(4).
4. Dubar, C. (2000). *La crise des identités: L'interprétation d'une mutation*. Paris: Presses Universitaires de France.
5. Gewirtz, S., Mahony, P., Hextall, I., & Cribb, A. (2009). *Changing Teacher Professionalism: International Trends, Challenges and Ways Forward*. London: Routledge.
6. Kuhlmann, E. (2006). *Modernising Health Care: Reinventing Professions, The State and The Public*. Bristol: The Policy Press.
7. Langer, A. (2008). Academic qualification programmes for professional management: Managerial expertise as one facet of a new professionalism. Paper presented at the interim meeting of the ESA Research Network on 'Sociology of Professions', Aarhus, Denmark.
8. Morgan, N. A., Clark, B. H., & Gooner, R. (2002). Marketing productivity, marketing audits, and systems for marketing performance assessment–Integrating multiple perspectives. *Journal of Business Research, 55*(5), 363–375.
9. Mylonakis, J. (2003). Functions and responsibilities of marketing auditors in measuring organizational performance. *International Journal of Technology Management, 25*(8).
10. Noordegraaf, M. (2007). From pure to hybrid professionalism: Present-day professionalism in ambiguous public domains. *Administration and Society, 39*(6), 761–785.
11. Ruiz Ben, E. (2009). Professionalism patterns in the internationalization of information work. Paper presented at the ESA conference.
12. Schepers, R. (2006). Regulation and trust in action: The subtle balance between doctors and management in two Belgian hospitals. *Sage Journal, 54*(4).
13. Sciulli, D. (2005). Continental sociology of professions today: Conceptual contributions. *Current Sociology, 53*(6).
14. Svensson, L., & Evetts, J. (2010). *Sociology of Professions: Continental and Anglo-Saxon Traditions*. Goteborg: Daidalos.
15. Taghian, M., & Shaw, R. N. (2008). The marketing audit and organizational performance: An empirical profiling. *The Journal of Marketing Theory and Practice, 16*(4), 341–350.
16. Verpraet, G. (2009). Knowledge professions between market professionalism and professional autonomy: The adequation of sociological typologies. Paper presented at the ESA conference, Lisbon, RN19.

CHAPTER

9 Accounting and Internal Control manual

LEARNING OBJECTIVES

After studying this chapter, you will be able to:

- Demonstrate proficiency in categorizing financial transactions using chart of accounts entries
- Evaluate the components necessary for an effective accounting manual, including policies, procedures, and controls
- Implement strategies for designing and evaluating effective internal control systems.

KEY TERMS FROM THIS CHAPTER

Accounting journals
Chart of accounts
Inventory system
Search engine optimization
Business expands
Financial recording
Sale system
Social media engagement

INTRODUCTION

A journal is a document that lists transactions in reverse chronological order. Journalizing is the process of entering transactions into a journal. The accounting equation could be used to record transactions. However, by keeping a journal of transactions, the majority of businesses hope to produce a more enduring record. Every company uses the type of journal that best suits its needs. The type of journal to be used depends on the type of business and the quantity of transactions to be documented. The Latin diurnalis, which means daily, is where the word journal originates. Most companies deal with customers on a daily basis. Every day, the businesses will make entries in their accounting journals to avoid becoming overwhelmed.

There are two general systems that you can use for inventory accounting in order to journalize the transactions for financial recording. The perpetual inventory system continuously updates its database over time with data on inventory availability and quantities. Typically, this is accomplished by integrating an order entry system or a retail point of sale system with an inventory system. The perpetual inventory system updates the inventory system continuously, whereas the periodic inventory system updates the inventory system only occasionally, typically at the conclusion of each accounting year. This is the other common inventory system.

9.1. PREPARE CHART OF ACCOUNTS

All of the accounts in the general ledger are listed in the chart of accounts, each with a reference number. The different accounts that the company will use must first be defined before a chart of accounts can be set up. Every account ought to be uniquely identified by a number. Three digits may be all that is needed for an account number for very small businesses, though having more digits is preferable so that additional accounts can be added as the business expands. It is possible to add new accounts while keeping the logical order if there are more digits. With thousands of accounts, complex businesses might need longer account reference numbers. It is important to consider the account numbers and adhere to any industry-specific guidelines when allocating them logically.

An example of how the digits might be coded is shown in this list:

1000 - 1999: Asset Accounts

2000 - 2999: Liability Accounts

3000 - 3999: Equity Accounts

4000 - 4999: Revenue Accounts

5000 - 5999: Cost of Goods Sold

6000 - 6999: Expense Accounts

7000 - 7999: Other Revenue (for example, interest income)

8000 - 8999: Other Expense (for example, income taxes)

Numerous new accounts can be added between any two while preserving the logical order by dividing each account by a few digits. Making a list of the accounts that relate to your business is all that is needed to set up a Chart of Accounts for it. There is no secret to doing this. If you are unable to think of every possible account type for your business, do not panic. Adding to the Chart of Accounts at any time is a very simple process. Remind staff members who use this list to enter transactions into the bookkeeping system to give them the updated list whenever you add accounts to a Chart of Accounts. If staff members aren't directly handling bookkeeping but need to code invoices or other transactions and specify which account those transactions belong in, they'll require a copy of the Chart of Accounts.

9.1.1. Nature of Business Based on Client Information

Information is essential for any business to succeed. The background information required to assess present performance and plan for future advancement can be found through a combination of internal and external business information resources. Companies can make more effective plans for gathering, evaluating, and utilizing information by understanding the kinds of information resources that are most important to their operations.

Businesses should use the information they already have as their primary source of information. All businesses will be able to collect data regarding their customers, sales, and employees. Business owners can track, trend, analyze, and take action on business information that provides them with hints about issues like what motivates employee satisfaction, the most popular products, and areas of customer and employee satisfaction and dissatisfaction by putting in place systems and processes for obtaining the necessary data.

Any company can think of itself as a member of one or more industries. Additionally, associations related to each industry can be a valuable resource for business intelligence. Businesses can visit the website weddles com to learn more about the associations that support their sector. Acquiring knowledge about industry trends, best practices, and resources can be facilitated for businesses by becoming members of the relevant trade and professional associations.

There is competition for every business, so learning about them is essential. Fortunately, with the development of the Internet, this is now simpler than ever. Through social media engagement on platforms like Facebook, LinkedIn, and Twitter, as well as search engine optimization, businesses can obtain competitive intelligence regarding their competitors' actions.

May include but are not limited to:

1. **Nature of Business:** Business refers to any activity that one engages in to keep oneself occupied and the state of being busy. However, the term "business" in economics refers to the labor, initiatives, and deeds of individuals engaged in the process of creating wealth. A business is the culmination of all activities related to the production, acquisition, and sale of goods and services, with the primary goal being financial gain. Man is a creature of constant desire. When intact, he is an insatiable being with a vast array of desires. He puts in a lot of effort to fulfill his desires by making the most of the limited resources at his disposal. Economic activity is defined as maximizing the utilization of limited resources to satisfy human needs. Therefore, economic activities pertain to earning a living and subsisting. To achieve this, each of us follows a profession based on our aptitude, expertise, knowledge, and training. As a result, one has three options: start a business that creates wealth, seek employment (undertaking to work for others under terms and conditions set for the purpose), or pursue a profession that involves providing specialized, expert, and personal service. Information access and provision to clients is the domain of manufacturing, trading, and product services.

The following are the ten important characteristics of a business:

i. *Economic Activity:* The economic activity of producing and distributing goods and services is known as business. It offers job opportunities in a variety of industries and sectors, including banking, insurance, trade, transportation, and industries. It is an economic endeavor that is rife with the production of utilities to satiate human desires. It gives society a means of subsistence. Enterprise activity generates job opportunities, which in turn propels economic growth. It contributes to the nation's industrial and economic growth.

ii. *Buying and Selling:* Trading is the foundational activity of any business. Purchasing raw materials, stationary, machinery, plants, and other items is part of the business. Conversely, it sells the final goods to retailers, wholesalers, and consumers. Businesses provide a range of products and services to the various societal segments.

iii. *Continuous Process:* Business is a continuous process. The process of producing and distributing goods and services never stops. A single trade transaction is insufficient to qualify as a business. To expand and generate consistent profits, a business must be run on a regular basis. To obtain a competitive edge, businesses should consistently engage in research and development initiatives. A strategy of continuous improvement aids in raising the company's profitability.

iv. *Profit Motive:* Profit is a sign of a business's success or failure. It is the difference between the business's revenue and expenses. A business's main objective is typically to maximize profits through the creation and distribution of goods and services. It's an investment return. The motivation behind all business endeavors is profit.

v. *Risk and Uncertainties:* Risk is characterized as the impact of arising uncertainty on the business's objectives. Every business involves some level of risk. Two categories of risk are present in business: insured and non-insurable. Risk that is insured is predictable.

Predictable factors are controllable to some extent, such as:

- Taxes
- Change in the volume of expected sales
- Cost of supplies and equipment
- Overhead costs
- Salaries
- Cost of goods and services offered

Unpredictable factors include:

- Changes in trends and tastes of customers.
- Impact of the local economy on customer base.
- Any unexpected action taken by your competitors.

A company's ability to calculate and manage risk is essential to its success. Risk management and insurance contribute to reducing the risk that a business faces.

vi. *Creative and Dynamic:* The nature of modern business is creative and dynamic. To produce and distribute goods and services, businesses need to come up with innovative ideas, methods, and concepts. It means to present things in an original, creative, and novel way.

Because the business operates in a constantly changing economic, social, and technological environment, one must be innovative. Companies should also release new goods to meet the expanding demands of their clientele.

vii. *Customer Satisfaction:* The business phase has shifted from a traditional to a modern concept. Businesses today take a customer-focused stance. Achieving customer satisfaction is the ultimate goal of all business endeavors. In order to satisfy customers, modern businesses strive to provide high-quality goods at competitive prices. It places equal emphasis on customer satisfaction and profit. Only when they receive genuine value for their purchase are customers satisfied. Creating and keeping customers is the aim of the business. The key to a successful business is having the ability to recognize and satisfy customers.

viii. *Social Activity:* One type of socioeconomic activity is business. Society and business are intertwined. Social responsibility is a major aspect of modern business operations. Due to its social responsibilities, business depends on the backing of a variety of social groups, including creditors, customers, employees, and investors. Business fulfills a crucial social role and satisfies needs by providing goods to different segments of society. For business to operate properly, it needs the support of various societal segments.

ix. *Government Control:* Government regulation applies to business organizations. The government has enacted rules and regulations that they must abide by. By enacting and periodically amending laws and regulations, the government maintains effective supervision and control over the business to ensure that it is conducted for the benefit of society.

Some important acts framed by the government include:

- The Competition Act, 2002
- Foreign Exchange Management Act, 1999
- The Environment Act, 1986
- Indian Companies Act, 1956
- Consumer protection Act

x. *Optimum Utilization of Resources:* Business promotes economic advancement and the best use of a nation's material and non-material resources. In order to concentrate economic wealth and meet customer needs and desires, the limited resources are used to their utmost potential.

2. **Forms of Organization**: In the United States, corporations, partnerships, and sole proprietorships are the three main types of business organization. The main distinctions between them are in the way the business is taxed, its ownership structure, and its legal standing.

i. *Single or Sole Proprietorship*: A business that has just one owner is known as a sole proprietorship. The owner is the company, and the company is the owner; there is no legal distinction between the two. Any and all debts of the business are owed by the owner personally. The owner's personal income is deemed to include all profit, which needs to be declared on their individual income tax return. This type of business organization has the benefit of simplicity: there are no corporate formalities to complete or partnership agreements to sign. A sole proprietorship is an unincorporated business that is owned (and frequently run) by one person. Small retail establishments, auto repair shops, and even musicians or inventors looking to sell their creations online can all fall under this category. A sole proprietorship can be formed quite easily, and maintaining one is not too difficult either. A sole proprietorship, however, is not able to raise capital by selling shares in the company, and the owner bears full liability for all debts and lawsuits brought against the company.

ii. *Partnership*: A company with two or more owners is called a partnership. General and limited partnerships are the two main categories. Each partner in a general partnership is personally responsible for paying off the company's debts. Within a limited partnership, certain partners have full liability while others have limited liability, meaning they can only lose the money they invested in the company. Income taxes are not paid by partnerships; instead, the owners report the business's profits as personal income based on their ownership stake in the business. Compared to a sole proprietorship, a partnership requires more paperwork, including a formal partnership agreement. With the exception of having multiple participants, a partnership is comparable to a sole proprietorship. A group of individuals collaborate to work at a particular company and split the gains (or losses) made by the company. A partnership does not have to pay the same taxes as larger corporations and is similarly simple to set up as a sole proprietorship. However, partnerships based on unwritten agreements may encounter interpersonal issues when the business falters. The partners bear personal responsibility for business losses and liabilities.

iii. *Corporation*: Legally, a corporation is an individual. It exists as a separate legal entity from its stockholder owners. All of the company's debts are its own responsibility. The money that the shareholders have contributed to the business may be lost, but not more. Like individuals, corporations are required to pay income taxes on their profits directly. Only when corporate profits are paid to shareholders in the form of dividends do they become subject to taxation. One benefit of a corporate structure is that shareholders have limited liability and can raise funds through the sale of stock. The fact that corporate profits may be taxed twice—once as income to the business and again when paid out as dividends—and that increased state and federal regulation are drawbacks. A corporation is an organization that is governed by a group of shareholders who own shares in the business. The owners of the stock control who manages the company and how it operates, and they get paid according to the number of shares they own. Compared to partnerships and sole proprietorships, corporations are more easily able to raise capital and frequently have access to larger initial capital. They are independent of the individuals who work for them, so the owners are not exposed to personal liability risks, and the business will continue long after the founders have retired. Nevertheless, corporations have to follow certain organizational rules, like holding annual shareholder meetings, and they need input from a large number of people, which frequently causes them to act slowly. They also frequently pay comparable fines and higher taxes.

9.1.2. Prepare List of Asset, Liability, Equity, Income, and Expense Account Titles

A list of all the accounts used in an organization's general ledger is called the chart of accounts. The accounting software compiles data into an entity's financial statements using the chart. To make it easier to find specific accounts, the chart is typically arranged by account number. Although they can also be alphabetic or alphanumeric, the accounts are typically numeric. Typically, accounts are listed from the balance sheet to the income statement in the order that they appear in the financial statements. As a result, cash is at the top of the chart of accounts, followed by liabilities and shareholders' equity, revenues, and finally expenses. A company's concept for the chart of accounts can be enhanced by the following points:

a. *Consistency*: To compare the results in the same account over a period of years, it is important to first create a chart of accounts that is unlikely to change for a number of years. Getting comparable financial data for more than the last year gets harder if you begin with fewer accounts and then progressively increase the number of accounts over time.

b. *Lock Down*: Allowing subsidiaries to alter the standard chart of accounts without a valid reason will make it more challenging to combine the business's results because there will be multiple versions in use.

c. *Size Reduction*: Check the list of accounts periodically to see if any have amounts that are comparatively insignificant. In that case, close these accounts and combine the stored data into a bigger account if this information is not required for any unique reports. By doing this on a regular basis, the number of accounts is kept to a reasonable amount.

Typical accounts found in the chart of accounts are:

1. **Assets**: The assets that a business uses for operations or investment. Everything that makes a business successful (anything with value). The treats consists of: money, receivables, investments, real estate, buildings, machinery, cars, etc. Any financial resource that can be easily turned into cash is considered an asset. These assets can be used to guarantee a person's or company's financial capacity to carry out day-to-day operations because they frequently maintain high levels of liquidity. For accounting purposes, assets are typically categorized as current assets, though the terms are not quite the same. Typically, assets are meant to be turned into cash in a single operating cycle, which lasts around a year. The requirement that assets be convertible into cash in three months or less sets them apart from current assets. Treasury bills, money market funds, commercial papers, and other assets that are readily convertible into cash are examples of such assets. Any other deposit or financial investment with a maturity date of no more than three months is also considered an asset. While they may be included in financial statements, property, equipment, and other investments with maturities longer than three months are not regarded as liquid

assets. Moreover, intellectual property like copyrights, trademarks, and patents is not regarded as liquid.

The type of assets are include in business, such as:

- Cash and Cash Equivalents
- Receivables
- Inventories
- Prepayments
- Property, plant and equipment
- Other Assets

2. **Liabilities:** An obligation is referred to as a liability. It can refer to funds that are needed to finish a transaction, unpaid debt, or paid-for goods or services that have not yet been provided. These categories of liability can be broadly divided into two groups: long-term and short-term. Debt paid out over a period of more than a year is referred to as long-term, whereas debt paid out in less than a year is referred to as short-term. Other instances of liabilities include sums of money that have not yet been disbursed, like settlement money or life insurance policy benefits, both of which pose a risk to the insurance company. A company's liabilities also include any savings or retirement fund, as well as an employee's pension. Liabilities for the consumer could be a car payment, line of credit, first or second mortgage, lien of any kind, or any combination of these. Of course, each item usually represents an asset for the organization to which these funds are owed. Liability, in its broadest sense, is the term used to describe any kind of duty or obligation. It stands for unpaid bills, unfulfilled orders for goods or services, or an admission of guilt and the payment of damages brought about by carelessness or other actions.

There are some type of liabilities use in business, it may include:

- Accounts payables
- Loans payables
- Notes payables
- Income tax payables
- Accrued Expenses
- Other Liabilities

3. **Equity:** Possession and use are two of the many aspects of ownership that are covered by the law. Even though a lot of people own cars and homes, they haven't paid for them in full. The Roman goddess of honest traders and fair trade is the source of the word equity. Its foundation is the idea of true value. The actual value of an ownership interest is described by the contemporary definition of equity. Depending on the exact situation, equity can have multiple meanings. Equity typically refers to the ownership value of a certain asset or company. The total market value less any mortgages, debts, liens, liabilities, or other encumbrances is the amount of equity. As the majority of business leaders and homeowners are aware, equity can be leveraged and accessed in addition to serving as a passive store of value. Banks will occasionally offer credit lines backed by a homeowner's equity, with the house serving as collateral. Companies that have sold their equity to the public market in order to raise money for operations

are known as publicly traded companies.

May include but are not limited to:

i. *Capital:* In real-life contexts, financial terms can appear cryptic and challenging to grasp. Two such terms that are crucial to comprehend completely are capital and equity, which can be somewhat perplexing when used in legal and financial documents. Capital is wealth, which includes cash and other assets with intrinsic value that can be turned into cash or pledged as security for loans. This includes money, land, machinery, buildings, and other possessions. Something is considered capitalized when it is paid in full because it is no longer considered a liability but an asset. It turns into a capital item.

ii. *Drawing:* This kind of account's objective is to display the amount of money spent by those associated with a business. A partnership is one type of business that makes use of drawing accounts. For small service businesses and other limited-scale business types, partnerships are a common business setup. Each partner in a partnership may have a capital or drawing account from which they can withdraw funds. More investments will result in a credit to a partner's capital account. Even sole proprietorships, which are relatively small businesses, may find value in drawing or capital accounts. One person may be primarily responsible for taking money out of the business account in a sole proprietorship. For accounting purposes, the drawing accounts are still useful in demonstrating the amount of money that has been taken out at the end of a year or other time period. This will assist the owner or proprietor in handling accounting responsibilities like tax accounting.

iii. *Retained Earnings:* Those who invest in companies as shareholders may be familiar with retained earnings, and any company with shareholders will undoubtedly be familiar with them. The term "earnings" in this definition refers to company profits rather than employee earnings. While the company may typically distribute these as dividends to investors, it is not out of the ordinary for them to be retained or withheld. Companies retain these payouts for a variety of reasons. In theory, businesses reinvest retained earnings primarily back into the company. The expectation behind this reinvestment is that businesses will expand and generate even more revenue down the road. A portion of this will be kept for further investment, and the remainder will be distributed as dividends.

4. **Expenses:** The standard practice for revenue and expense accounts is to start with the items that are most directly or closely related to the business's operations. Prior to revenue or income from non-operating sources, the revenues (sales) from regular operations are reported. Similarly, the list of expenses and costs that are directly related to the business's operations comes before the list of non-operating expenses. The cost of sales appears on the list first, then operating and non-operating expenses. Frequently,

selling expenses and general and administrative expenses are grouped together with the operating expenses. The order in which operating expenses are listed within a category is not strictly regulated. Any expense that a business may have, such as payroll or infrastructure, is considered an expense. While expenses can change at any time, they are primarily within a company's direct control. By making cuts in one or more areas, costs can be decreased. Most companies try to match their costs to their income in order to keep costs within reasonable bounds and avoid going overboard.

May include but are not limited to:

- Salaries/wages
- Rent expense
- Utilities expense
- Depreciation
- Supplies
- Repairs and maintenance
- Transportation

9.2. PREPARE ACCOUNTING MANUAL

An accounting manual, which outlines all accounting policies, guidelines, procedures, and standards for a company's accounts, is typically created by business organizations. The accounting manual contains organization-specific regulations, a summary of accounting rules, and a classification of accounts. Accounting manuals differ from company to company based on the type of business entity, but they all generally accomplish the same thing and even use comparable outlines. The aim of this is to guarantee precision and uniformity in the accounting techniques applied by each employee in the company managing accounting-related duties and processes. To cover every facet of the accounting function, the manual usually consists of multiple sections. An accounting manual will typically open with a summary of its goals, an explanation of its contents, and a statement of the duties expected of those who peruse it. This will usually include an explanation of management's role and responsibility in ensuring adherence to the manual, along with a list of exceptions to the rules contained within. These sections typically function as the manual's introduction. The structure of the finance and accounting departments is typically discussed next, giving workers and contractors a comprehensive grasp of the different positions within the organization. This section also includes an outline and specification of each department's responsibilities. The following sections will typically provide an explanation of management accounting reporting procedures, methods, and policies.

The sections on management accounting and reporting are typically followed by a focus on the core elements of accounting. The following sections discuss the organization's framework for accounting policy and procedure, including the planning process, related responsibilities, necessary communications, and authorized authorities. Systems used in the accounting process, internal controls, audit procedures, security, documentation, cost accounting, and transactions are frequently covered additional topics. The final few sections of an accounting manual typically cover a wide variety of accounting procedures, wrapping it up. Cash accounting, asset and inventory accounting, revenue accounting, purchase accounting, and administrative accounting processes are frequently covered. The requirements for resource management, accounting resource provisioning, accounting infrastructure, and the anticipated work environment are typically included in the final sections. Furthermore, a section on human resources is often included in accounting manuals. This section outlines the expectations for different roles within the accounting function as well as the necessary human capital. Many organizations view coverage of the human resources component as essential to ensuring that the accounting function is adequately staffed with qualified personnel.

9.2.1. Analyze Documents

Accounting is a comprehensive business process used by organizations to track, summarize, and evaluate financial transactions. For external business stakeholders, this data frequently offers support for management and investment decisions. Documentation is usually needed for accounting information in order to create accounting reports and statements. This supporting documentation gives an individual additional documents or figures to evaluate the report with. It also validates the accounting information. The tangible foundation for recording business transactions is provided by documents. Usually, source documents are kept on file in case an auditor needs to confirm that transactions really happened after reviewing the financial statements of the company.

They usually contain the following information:

- A description of a business transaction
- The date of the transaction
- A specific amount of money
- An authorizing signature

An approval stamp is applied to a number of source documents, which can also be used to note the date, the accounts to be used to record the underlying transaction, or even an indication of approval. The following are some instances of source documents and the associated business transactions that show up in the financial records:

- *Bank Statement:* This contains a number of adjustments to a company's book balance of cash on hand that the company should reference to bring its records into alignment with those of the bank.
- *Cash Register Tape:* This can be used as evidence of cash sales, which supports the recordation of a sale transaction.
- *Credit Card Receipt:* This can be used as evidence for a disbursement of funds from petty cash.
- *Lockbox Check Images:* These images support the recordation of cash receipts from customers.
- *Packing Slip:* This describes the items shipped to a customer, and so supports the recordation of a sale transaction.
- *Sales Order:* This document, when coupled with a bill of lading and/or packing list, can be used to invoice a customer, which in turn generates a sale transaction.
- *Supplier Invoice:* This is a source document that supports the issuance of a cash, check, or electronic payment to a supplier. A supplier invoice also supports the recordation of an expense, inventory item, or fixed asset.
- *Time Card:* This supports the issuance of a paycheck or electronic payment to an employee. If employee hours are being billed to customers, then it also supports the creation of customer invoices.

One company operates in the consulting industry, for instance. It compiles data on hours worked from employee timesheets, which is subsequently added to customer invoices, resulting in the creation of a transaction for sales and accounts receivable. The timesheet is the source document for a sale transaction in this case. Several potential controls can be implemented to lower the possibility that source documents are not accurately entered into an accounting system. Pre-numbering documents is a popular control that makes it simpler to locate missing documents. Reconciling the account balances with the corresponding source documents is an additional control measure that determines whether certain documents are missing from the record or whether certain transactions that are recorded in the accounts don't seem to have any supporting documentation. Certain source documents must be kept on file for a certain amount of time, per a number of regulations. Keeping these records may also be wise, even if it's just to have them around for better customer service or as proof in case you get sued. Due to these factors, a business ought to implement a document destruction policy that tightly restricts the shredding or removal of source documents until a predetermined amount of years has elapsed.

9.2.2. Gathers and Checks Documents Verification and Validation processes

Documents are used by a company for analysis, communication, and business transactions. Written documents are crucial because they serve as evidence of an organization's activities and can be consulted for many years to come. Business documents can be anything from quick emails to intricate contracts. While some documents are created by company owners and employees, others are created by experts from outside the organization, like accountants and attorneys. The following types of processes are involved in the organization document when it comes to document collection and verification.

- **Sales Invoice:** A sales invoice is a document that lists several transactional details and is given by the seller of goods or services to the buyer of those goods or services. The names of the buyer and seller, the good or service being bought, and the total amount paid for the transaction are usually included in this kind of document. In addition, a sales invoice may include the addresses of one or both of the parties, a breakdown of the costs and services offered, and guidelines for how and when payments are to be made. A sales invoice is sometimes just called an invoice, but it is usually identified as such by the company or individual that is supplying the goods or services. Since the buyer in this kind of transaction is the person or business making the purchase, they frequently refer to the document as a purchase invoice. A single invoice will typically be referred to as a purchase invoice by the buyer and a sales invoice by the seller; this distinction is usually contextual.
- **Vouchers:** An accounting document known as a voucher serves as internal confirmation of a plan to pay an outside party, like a supplier or service provider. Typically, a vendor invoice is received, matched successfully to a purchase order, and then a voucher is generated. A voucher will include a description of the transaction, the payee's specifics, the amount of the payment, and more. A procedure known as a payment run is carried out in accounts payable systems to produce payments in relation to the unpaid vouchers. The company controller or an accounts payable supervisor may then decide to release or retain these payments. The phrase can also be used to refer to a document indicating the intention to make an adjustment to

an account in accounts receivable, as well as to the general ledger when it becomes necessary to make adjustments to accounts within that ledger; in that instance, it is called a journal voucher. A voucher may also refer to any supporting documentation for the entries in the books of accounts that establishes the arithmetic accuracy of the transaction; such documentation could include a trust deed, bill, invoice, receipt, salary and wages sheet, memorandum of association, counterfoil of the paying-in slip, or counterfoil of the check book.

- **Official Receipts:** To maintain accurate accounting records and file taxes at the end of the year, official receipts are essential. Even though receipts show a financial transaction, the date of the transaction and the data they contain differ. Similar to invoices, official receipts are documents that have been printed on business letterhead with a manager's approval. For any business selling products or services for a profit, invoices and receipts are essential documentation. When a business receives official receipts and cash invoices, it enters them into separate general ledger sections. Cash invoices are recorded by the business in the accounts payable or accounts receivable section of the general ledger since they represent an undertaking to pay at a later date. Since official receipts are only generated when money is actually exchanged, the company promptly enters them into the relevant expense account. For instance, upon receiving a receipt for paying $100,000 in cash for a parcel of land, a business immediately deducts the $100,000 expense from its assets.
- **Purchase Invoice:** One document used in business transactions is the purchase invoice. This document's name originates from the inclusion of a purchase order number. After that, this number will be used for the entirety of the transaction. A buyer and seller may be involved in multiple purchase order invoices at any given time. One can use this kind of document for both goods and services. An offer and an acceptance are necessary for a contract to be enforceable. A contract is created when a buyer and supplier exchange goods and money. The buyer indicates a willingness to buy a specific quantity of goods at a specific price, so in this case, the purchase invoice can be seen as an offer. By completing the order, sending a bill, and getting payment, the supplier confirms acceptance. A purchase invoice typically has a lot of information on it. The buyer's identity and contact information should be made obvious. Additionally, since businesses may have multiple locations, a space is typically provided for the shipping address. A crucial piece of information that is typically located at or close to the top of the document is the purchase number.
- **Transactional Documents:** Documents are used by a business to conduct business with its clients. These documents can be formatted as forms, like order forms, transmittal pages, invoices, or receipts, to save time. The different kinds of transactional documents

that are used depends on the type of business. A lender uses loan applications and mortgage documents, whereas an insurance agent creates insurance policies and applications. In certain industries, companies sign contracts and agreements with other parties; the company's attorney may draft these documents.

- **Financial Documents:** Financial records are used by businesses to prepare budget proposals, file tax returns, and stay within their allocated spending limits. These records include bank statements, income statements, balance sheets, paid bills, payroll reports, receipt records, and tax reporting forms. The accountant for the business may have created these documents. These records are used by a business owner to assess the company's financial performance and pinpoint ineffective areas. Financial records may be used by a department head to draft a budget proposal.
- **Manuals:** Accounting manuals list the precise guidelines and practices that an organization adheres to when managing financial data. The most recognized accounting standards in the US are generally accepted accounting principles, or GAAP. Since GAAP is based on principles, businesses can apply the principles to their financial data with some degree of flexibility. Nonetheless, company owners and managers usually write a handbook to offer supporting records on the particular techniques they employ when using GAAP. Publicly traded corporations are also required to include this information in their publicly available financial reports.
- **Audit Trail:** In accounting, an audit trail is frequently the most used type of documentation. Information from the audit trail makes it easier for people to understand how the accounting department handles financial and accounting transactions. Since most computerized accounting systems record a time/date stamp outlining the recording of transactions, they have strengthened the audit trail process. The original transaction document, handwritten notes about math checks or other calculations, journal entry copies, and a stamp designating the company's receipt of the transaction or its entry into the accounting ledger are examples of additional audit trail procedures.

9.2.3. Selection of Account Title

The terms "account titles" in accounting refer to the different classifications used to monitor a company's financial status. These accounts are updated for each and every transaction to accurately and consistently reflect what transpired. The general ledger of the company, a running list of all these transactions, has the account titles. The general ledger accounts come together to create the company's financial statements when they are combined by an accountant. Let's take an example where a company purchases new inventory from its suppliers with cash. The cost of that additional inventory is added to the general ledger inventory account by the bookkeeper. This causes the books to be updated to reflect the new inventory that has been acquired and is now owned by the business. The same amount will also be debited (subtracted) by the accountant from the general ledger's cash account. This suggests that the new inventory was paid for with cash, meaning the cost of the new inventory has reduced the company's cash balance. An account's title, for instance, in a bank indicates who owns the account. Apart from listing the owners, the title can also specify who has control over the account, how money is distributed in the event of an owner's death, and how taxes are to be paid.

- *Individual Accounts:* An individual ccount is held and owned by a one person. That person is solely responsible for deposits, withdrawals, credits, debits and taxes due in the account. Generally speaking, upon the death of the owner, the distribution of an individual account will either go to a surviving spouse or be covered in the owner's will.
- *Joint Accounts:* Joint accounts are owned by several people, each of whom has complete access and ownership. This kind of account can be used by an adult to oversee a minor's finances, by a couple to split household expenses, or by the child of an elderly person to assist with money management. The majority of joint accounts are configured with rights of survivorship, which triggers an automatic transfer of ownership to the surviving tenant in the event of a tenant's death.
- *Custodial Accounts:* Typically, a parent or other family member opens a custodial account on behalf of a minor. These accounts are frequently used to save money for college. The custodian has control over the account until the minor reaches adulthood, even though the funds belong to him. When the minor reaches adulthood—defined as, depending on the state, 18 or 21 years old—they can take over account management.
- *Trust Accounts:* In the event that one or more trustees pass away, trust accounts are formal organizations created to manage assets included in the trust. By designating one or more successor trustees to oversee the administration and distribution of funds, assets, and property, trusts serve as an alternative to the probate process.
- *Sole Proprietorships:* A sole proprietorship is a basic type of business owned by just one person. Generally speaking, a sole proprietorship account is designed to keep records organized by keeping business deposits and expenses apart from personal use. The company files an individual tax return with the deductions and taxable income from the business's operations, using the owner's taxpayer ID.

9.2.4. Prepare Journal Entry

An accounting transaction known as a journal entry adds financial data to a business's accounting ledger. Different journals often comprise accounting ledgers. Among the various kinds of accounting journals are cash receipts and cash disbursements, sales, purchases, and general. All of the company's financial data, including totals from the other journals combined, is kept in the general journal. Every journal entry that the business records typically consists of a debit and a credit because it is based on the widely-used double-entry accounting system. Account numbers, a succinct description of the transaction, the dollar amount, and a specific reference number are typically included in journal entry information. Businesses can keep track of the financial data entered into their various accounting journals with the aid of this comprehensive data. Journal entries typically list all of the debits first, then all of the credits. The financial data included in the entry is presented in an understandable manner thanks to this format. Companies may use various types of journal entries. Basic, reversing, recurring, and adjusting entries are some examples of journal entries. Basic entries are typically the first time a particular piece of financial data is recorded. These entries can be made at the conclusion of an accounting period or as soon as financial transactions take place. Typically, businesses establish an account policy that specifies when fundamental journal entries must be made.

The quantity of entries, the size of the business, and the urgency with which financial data must be recorded by companies all influence the recording of basic journal entries. Reversing entries can be used to fix basic entries that an accountant entered incorrectly. Additionally, accruals or deferrals that must be reverted at a later date may be set up with this kind of entry. According to accounting rules, businesses may accrue or postpone income, expenses, or other financial data. Businesses that use automated accounting software frequently use the time delay feature of the program to set up reversing entries.

Every month, recurring journal entries typically capture the same data in an organization's accounting system. A standard template that contains the account numbers and other pertinent details for each month's entry can be used to set up these entries. The financial figures are the only data that is updated in a recurring journal entry. The financial figures or ledger accounts used in the basic journal entry are corrected using adjusting entries. These entries can also be used to fix information that needs to be updated at a later time after the initial journal entry has been made, or they can be used to correct journal entries that accountants made in the incorrect journal.

- Journals are prepared in accordance with industry practice and generally accepted accounting principles/ Philippine Financial Reporting Standards for transactions and events.
- Debit account titles are determined in accordance with chart of accounts
- Credit account titles are determined in accordance with chart of accounts
- Explanation to journal entry is prepared in accordance with the nature of transaction
- Journal entries are prepared with 100% accuracy

1. **Financial Reporting Standards for Transactions and Events:** Small businesses can choose to use either the tax accounting method or the financial accounting method; large corporations and publicly traded companies are required to follow the financial accounting method. The timing of when sales and purchases are recorded using accrual or cash accounting differs between the two methods. The majority of small enterprises favor cash-based tax accounting. Different accounting strategies can affect tax returns and business in different ways.

May include but are not limited to:

- Routine/daily transactions
- End of the month transaction to update the books of accounts
- End of the accounting year transactions to close the books of accounts

Accrual-based accounting is the most common name for financial accounting. Regardless of whether sales proceeds have been collected or purchase invoices have been paid, businesses that use the accrual method record sales revenues and purchase expenses as they are incurred. Companies must determine whether a sale or purchase is complete in order to determine the date of the transaction for recording. Partially receiving a purchase and incomplete deliveries of goods or services do not count as earned revenue or incurred expenses. The sale or purchase orders must be completed before any recording can begin. A small business may be affected differently by cash-based tax accounting and accrual-based financial accounting. Financial accounting does not display a company's actual cash reserve situations, even though it can accurately track business transactions as they happen. If clients haven't paid yet, a small business that uses the accrual method may have a healthy amount of revenue recorded in its accounting records but little cash on hand in its bank account. With cash-based tax accounting, a small business can keep a closer eye on its cash flow. On the other hand, if clients pay their bills all at once, leading to a spike in cash receipts, the cash-based approach could provide false information about a company's profitability.

A small business will be impacted tax-wise by the choice of accounting method for financial reporting and business recording because the same accounting method is frequently utilized for tax return preparation. A small business may pay more or less in taxes for the current tax year, depending on the time of year a business transaction takes place and when the money settlement happens. For instance, under cash accounting, a small business would pay more taxes for the current tax year if it delayed paying cash for a purchase made during the current year until the following year. This is because the business would not be able to claim a tax deduction for the purchase expense.

2. **Determine Debit Account Titles:** An accounting entry that lowers a liability or equity account or increases an asset or expense account is called a debit. In an accounting entry, it is located on the left. An accounting entry that credits an asset or expense account, or decreases an equity or liability account, is called a credit.

Debit account titles may include:

- Cash
- Receivables
- Expenses
- Inventories
- Property, Plant and Equipment

3. **Determine Credit Account Titles:** Credit account is an account which a customer has with a shop which allows him or her to buy goods and pay for them later.

Credit account titles may include:

- Sales
- Loans payables
- Interest income
- Cash

9.2.5. Explanation of Journal Entry According to Nature of Transaction

You have to be meticulous with your journal entries in addition to managing your business funds. You can continuously monitor your financial status by recording the debits and credits for supplies, business expenses, insurance, cash, revenue, bank charges, and any other type of monetary exchange. The journal entry is the first part of your monitoring system.

Note the time and date of the entry in the first column, including the year. Dating your entries facilitates finding a particular entry at a later time. Provide a list of the accounts used in the transaction. Take note of the source of the exchange: sales, cash, insurance, business costs, or another kind of account. Use account nicknames and abbreviations to keep this brief. Provide a clear list of all potential accounts for the reader to refer to on a different page. Make a note of the type of transaction: credit or debit. A debit shows that funds were removed from the account to settle a debt. A credit denotes the addition of funds to the account as payment. Put the transaction's amount in writing. This is just the total amount of money that was exchanged in this entry, expressed in dollars. To indicate positive and negative amounts, think about employing plus and minus signs, color coding, or placing debits in parenthesis. Provide any details, like the vendor's name or a delivery modification, that are necessary to comprehend the transaction. Please be brief when providing this information. The additional information should be clear enough for the reader to understand without having to read a ton of words.

The process of entering an accounting transaction into a company's accounting records is called an accounting journal entry. The journal entries can be recorded in multiple sub-ledgers and then combined into the general ledger, or the accounting records can be combined into one. The financial statements as of the conclusion of a reporting period are then created using this data. A journal entry can have as few as two line items, but there is no maximum limit to the number of line items that can be included. A journal entry with two lines is referred to as a simple journal entry; an entry with more line items is referred to as a compound journal entry. It is preferable to use more simple journal entries than fewer compound journal entries when a company uses a lot of them in a single accounting period, as this helps to make the purpose of the entries more clear. This comes in handy when journal entries need to be investigated later on, particularly when auditors are reviewing them. A debit entry is made against one account and a credit entry is made against the other, meaning that whenever you create an accounting transaction, at least two accounts are involved. An accounting transaction is always considered to be in balance if the totals of the debits and credits for the transaction always equal each other. The creation of financial statements would not be feasible if a transaction was out of balance. Therefore, the most crucial of all controls over accounting accuracy is the use of debits and credits in a two-column transaction recording format. Journal entries may be recorded by the bookkeeper in a smaller accounting setting. A general ledger accountant usually has some control over the process of recording journal entries in a larger company because they are usually in charge of doing so.

1. *Format of the Journal Entry:* At a minimum, an accounting journal entry should include the following:

- The accounts into which the debits and credits are to be recorded
- The date of the entry
- The accounting period in which the journal entry should be recorded
- The name of the person recording the entry
- Any managerial authorization(s)
- A unique number to identify the journal entry

- Whether the entry is a one-time entry, a recurring entry, or a reversing entry.
- It may be necessary to attach extensive documentation to the journal entry, to prove why it is being recorded; at a minimum, provide a brief description of the journal entry.

2. *Special Types of Accounting Journal Entries:*

- A reversing journal entry is one that is either reversed manually in the following accounting period, or which is automatically reversed by the accounting software in the following accounting period.
- A recurring journal entry is one that repeats in every successive accounting period, until a termination date is reached. This can be done manually, or can be set up to run automatically in an accounting software system.

3. *Accounting Journal Entry Examples*: Arnold Corporation sells a product to a customer for $1,000 in cash. This results in revenue of $1,000 and cash of $1,000. Arnold must record an increase of the cash (asset) account with a debit, and an increase of the revenue account with a credit. The entry is:

	Debit	Credit
Cash	1,000	
Revenue		1,000

Arnold Corporation also buys a machine for $15,000 on credit. This results in an addition to the Machinery fixed assets account with a debit, and an increase in the accounts payable (liability) account with a credit. The entry is:

	Debit	Credit
Machinery - Fixed Assets	15,000	
Account Payable		15,000

4. *Unbalanced Journal Entry:* An unbalanced journal entry is one that is made when the totals of the debit and credit are different. An unbalanced journal entry will probably be rejected by the software's error-checking controls if you try to enter it into a computer accounting system. In a manual accounting system, on the other hand, an unbalanced trial balance will lead to an unbalanced balance sheet if you make an unbalanced journal entry. The following journal entry is out of balance; the total amount of debit exceeds the total amount of credit. Under such circumstances, financial statements cannot be released until the underlying unbalanced journal entry has been corrected.

	Debit	Credit
Machinery - Fixed Assets	10,000	
Account Payable		15,000

5. *Journal Entry Fraud:* Using journal entries to commit fraud is far more common among accountants than using routine tasks like creating and recording invoices for customers and suppliers. The rationale is that a system of controls built up around these more frequent transactions is intended to identify a range of problems. On the other hand, journal entries are subject to less regulation, which facilitates the creation of fraudulent transactions. If the recorded amount is deemed insignificant, these transactions become even more difficult to identify, making it unlikely that auditors will notice the infractions.

9.3. USE OF INTERNAL CONTROLS

Internal controls, taken broadly, include those that support working efficacy and adherence to management policies, establish the reliability of financial data and records, safeguard organizational assets, and protect the plan. Departmental independence and lines of vicarious duty and authority are the two main classifications for internal control. It is crucial that these internal controls use control total techniques, sanctions and approvals, contrasts, and other tests of data accuracy to confirm the dependability and accuracy of the data supporting all transactions. Management needs solid accounting data to make decisions based on before it can decide how to optimize a company's long-term profit. This information must be accurate, timely, comprehensive, and trustworthy. A strong accounting system should have adequate internal control mechanisms to safeguard the company's assets from theft, robbery, neglecting to take advantage of discounts, insufficiency, and unwarranted credit delays. Since the management of large companies typically does not personally supervise its employees, these controls are required to ensure that the agreed procedures and orders are followed. Controls therefore increase the accuracy of accounting and financial data. In order to provide a system of authorization and sanction and to establish a suitable level of safety over these assets, liabilities, revenues, and expenses, internal controls are essential. The implementation of sound practices in the execution of organizational duties and the assignment of suitably qualified individuals to specific roles are two more essential and proper functions of internal controls in any system.

Corporate governance, which is the framework that management uses to oversee the operations of the company, and an entity's internal control system are closely related concepts. Effective corporate governance should make it easier for the board and management to monitor activities that are in the best interests of the business and its shareholders. This will encourage businesses to use their resources more wisely. Thus, the Board of Directors bears responsibility for senior management's governance, supervision, and oversight as well as for ensuring that an appropriate and functional internal control system is in place, which guarantees the achievement of predictable goals. The link between the business and its external environment is financial reporting. The internal control system put in place around the disclosure of information to stakeholders is one of the key elements that contributed to these failures. Even in the presence of numerous other control components, it appeared that failing to achieve the goal of an effective internal control system over financial reporting demoralizes a company's standing and makes it difficult or impossible for it to be a dependable player in the market, to be able to secure funding, and to be credible to stakeholders and shareholders in general.

9.3.1. Importance of Internal Controls

A company's internal controls, including its corporate governance and accounting procedures, are assessed by internal audits. Accurate and timely financial reporting, data collection, and compliance with laws and regulations can all be guaranteed by these internal controls. They assist in preserving operational effectiveness by spotting issues and fixing mistakes before an outside audit finds them. Ever since the Sarbanes-Oxley Act of 2002 held managers legally accountable for the accuracy of the company's financial statements, internal audits have become indispensable to a business's operations and corporate governance. Although no two internal control systems are the same, many fundamental ideas about accounting and financial integrity have been adopted as best practices for management. Effectively implemented internal controls can help prevent fraud, improve operational efficiency, and streamline processes, even though they can be costly. An auditor should make sure that the business unit they are working on complies with certain policies and guidelines, even though management is ultimately in charge of maintaining an effective internal control system. Since he lacks the authority to impose such guidelines and procedures, the Auditor can only assist or guide management upon request. The effectiveness of an organization's internal control system determines how dependent on it is, so in order to prepare his audit program, the auditor should examine and assess it.

Internal control system should be reviewed by the Auditor before star audit as described below –

- Reviewing the system of accounting entries, whether recorded as per accounting standard or not.
- To frame audit program according to present circumstances.
- Frauds, errors and mistakes are likely to be located or not.
- To review existence of internal audit program and to check the efficiency of internal control system.
- To review the reliability of reports, records and certificates as presented by the management.
- To check if there is any possibility of improvement in existing internal control system.

9.3.2. Components of Internal Controls

A company's internal controls system should include the following components:

- **Control Environment**: Every employee is taught the value of integrity and the necessity of uncovering and eliminating irregularities, including fraud, in a control environment. This atmosphere is established by the management and the board of directors, who set an example. To support the objectives of internal controls, management must implement the necessary internal systems and staff.
- **Risk Assessment:** A business needs to routinely evaluate and determine whether risk or loss is present or possible. The results of these evaluations may lead to the implementation of increased levels of control and focus in order to guarantee risk containment or to monitor risk in related areas.
- **Monitor:** A company must monitor its system of internal controls for ongoing viability. Doing so can ensure, whether through system

updates, adding employees, or necessary employee training, the continued ability of internal controls to function as needed.

- **Information/Communication:** It's critical to communicate consistently and with quality information from two perspectives. First, effective internal controls can be facilitated by roles and purposes being clearly defined. Second, encouraging employees to comprehend and commit to actions can help them perform their jobs as efficiently as possible.
- **Control Activities:** These pertain to the processes, policies, and other courses of action that maintain the integrity of internal controls and regulatory compliance. They involve preventative and detective activities.
- **Compliance with Laws and Regulations**: The financial operations of an organization must abide by all applicable laws, rules, and guidelines. This entails staying informed about modifications to financial regulations and putting policies in place to guarantee adherence.
- **Separation of Duties**: Distributing responsibilities among different people reduces the risk of error or inappropriate actions. This includes separating authorization, custody, and record-keeping roles to prevent fraud and errors.
- **Physical Controls**: A business must implement security measures to protect its assets, including cash, inventory, and equipment. This could involve secure storage facilities, access controls, and surveillance systems.

9.3.3. Top-Down Approach for Audit of Internal Controls

When choosing which internal controls to test for financial reporting, the auditor should employ a top-down methodology. The financial statement level and the auditor's comprehension of the overall risks to internal control over financial reporting are where a top-down approach starts. After that, the auditor works down to major accounts, disclosures, and the pertinent assertions associated with them, concentrating on entity-level controls. With this method, the auditor focuses on statements, accounts, and disclosures that raise the possibility of a material misstatement of the financial statements and related disclosures. The auditor then confirms that they have a clear understanding of the risks associated with the business's procedures and chooses which controls to test in order to adequately address the risk of misstatement to each pertinent assertion. The implementation of the top-down approach has various benefits. Firstly, it is a useful method for organizing auditing tasks since it directs auditor attention to the areas where a material misstatement is most likely to occur. Since auditors can forego testing in areas where controls have already shown to be reliable, it also improves auditor efficiency. To put it briefly, the top-down method is a useful tool for focusing auditor attention on audit areas that are most likely to have issues that could lead to a material misstatement.

9.3.4. Establishing and Maintaining Strong Internal Control

The management of an organization, those in charge of its governance, and other staff members create and implement internal controls to offer a reasonable level of assurance regarding the accomplishment of goals. Furthermore, internal control pertains to a procedure whereby the organization's information system, authority, and organizational structure are crafted to facilitate the attainment of the organization's goals and objectives. When it comes to how management fulfills its agency or stewardship duties, internal control is crucial. To protect bank assets, limit or control risks, and accomplish a bank's goals, for instance, the systems, policies, procedures, and processes implemented by the board of directors, management, and other staff members constitute internal control for a bank. Robust internal control measures can aid an organization in accomplishing its targets and goals while preserving a profitable and well-run business. Effective internal control can assist a bank in achieving its goals and preventing surprises.

Let's examine the management's motivations for creating and preserving effective internal control after we have a better understanding of internal control. There aren't many management incentives available, like protecting company property and records, improving operational effectiveness and efficiency, preventing and detecting fraud and errors, adhering to applicable laws and regulations, preventing resource waste, having effective risk management systems, and lowering the possibility of reputational harm to the business.

Initially, the management has a strong incentive to create and preserve internal controls so that company assets and records can be appropriately protected. Strong internal controls help guarantee that assets are not stolen and that company records, such as certificates, are kept up to date. Then, since the records won't be easily altered, a proper safeguard of the company's assets and records can produce accurate information for the business. In addition, trustworthy data is required by management to guarantee the equity of the financial report. It may lessen the issue arising from the principal-agent relationship. What does it mean to be a principal and an agent? Well, a principal is an absentee owner, like a shareholder, and an agent is a manager employed by the company. Information asymmetry and inter-personal conflicts of interest are the issue. This is so that the manager, rather than the shareholder, is better informed about the "true" financial position. Additionally, there may be conflicts of interest because they have divergent goals at times. For instance, a shareholder's objective is to increase their dividend payments from the company in which they invest. Nonetheless, the manager's objective is to maximize the business's profit. As a result, there will be conflicts over how to use excess earnings to maximize dividends for each shareholder or to grow their market share through increased advertising. It will cause a conflict between the manager and the shareholder because the latter was unsure if the manager had made a wise or profitable choice. They were therefore unaware of any errors or fraud in the financial statement. Strong internal controls, on the other hand, can guarantee the protection of the business's assets and records and boost the organization's credibility. Reduce the issue between the principals and the agent after that. In addition, trustworthy information is necessary for a company to make an informed decision. Management might find it difficult to act quickly and decisively when it comes to decisions like product pricing, profit margins, and production costs if the information system is unreliable in providing its data. Since the top management depends on this information to make crucial decisions, it is imperative that accurate information be generated for them. Therefore, in order to make financial information transparent and available to managers or decision makers, a robust internal control is required.

The establishment and maintenance of robust internal control systems is motivated by the management's desire to ensure the effectiveness and efficiency of the company's operations. The effectiveness of internal controls ensures that all tasks are carried out in accordance with guidelines and that all quotas are fulfilled. Nonetheless, achieving a sustainable competitive advantage and optimizing profitability depend heavily on the effectiveness of internal control. Effective internal controls of efficiency include performance reviews, best practices, and operational procedures. Strong internal controls lower the risk of asset loss, improve operational effectiveness and efficiency, and aid in ensuring legal and regulatory compliance (Ingram, eHow Contributing Writer). Third, preventing and identifying fraud and errors within the company is the management's motivation for putting in place and keeping up strong internal controls. Unintentional misstatements made by employees or managers, such as errors in the collection or processing of financial data used to create financial statements, are referred to as errors. Fraud, on the other hand, refers to deliberate misrepresentations made by employees or managers, such as through the manipulation, falsification, or alteration of accounting records or supplementary materials used to create financial statements. Thus, error and fraud can be prevented and detected by a robust internal control. For instance, segregation duties between physical inventory calculations and record shipping inventories can stop inventory theft. Additionally, a suitable accounting information system can stop fraud or errors. For example, it can restrict access to the data about sales and account receivables so that only sales clerks can access and input it. Therefore, in order to create a fake customer, the sales clerk cannot access the cash account. Additionally, a monthly bank reconciliation can be used to verify the working paper's mathematical accuracy and align the balance between the books and the general ledger in order to identify any errors or bank account fraud.

The management is also motivated to create and uphold effective internal control in order to comply with relevant laws and regulations. Adhering to government laws and regulations demands significant financial outlays, particularly in terms of time. Therefore, by adhering to rules and regulations, a strong internal control is required to avoid legal ramifications. In other words, it can lessen or prevent expenses that might arise from the company breaking the law. The management is therefore motivated to create and uphold robust internal control in order to prevent resource waste. In addition to improving efficiency, a robust internal control system can assist a business in preventing the waste of important resources. This is due to the fact that one efficient method of increasing profits or income is through resource utilization. Robust internal controls are essential for preventing resource waste. For example, an efficient accounting information system can guarantee the accuracy and suitability of the data, preventing inefficient decisions and wasted company assets like cash or needless debt for unproductive investments. The management is motivated to create and uphold robust internal control in order to maximize the effectiveness of risk management systems. An entity's method for locating, assessing, and handling identified business risks is known as its risk assessment process. For instance, a major factor in the constant business risk faced by mobile phone companies like Nokia is not just their competitive environment but also the speed at which technology is developing. Nokia is facing business risks in order to adapt to customer preferences and trends. One such risk is the constant need to invest in the Research and Development Department in order to design new models and quickly upgrade existing products. But not every mobile phone that Nokia produces will be a financial success and a customer favorite, so evaluating business risk and bringing it down to a manageable level requires effective internal controls.

The last management's motivation for putting in place and upholding robust internal control was a lower chance of reputational harm to the association. The reason for this is that robust internal controls can result in a trustworthy financial statement, improve the efficacy and efficiency of operating procedures, stop and identify errors or fraud, and ensure compliance with relevant laws and regulations. As a result, there will be less chance of reputational harm to the association and greater credibility for the financial report. Last but not least, a company's ability to accomplish its goals—like protecting assets and records or enhancing operational effectiveness and efficiency—depends greatly on its ability to maintain strong internal controls. Consequently, one of the elements that guarantees the company's success is a robust internal control.

CASE STUDY

THE LESSONS FROM ENRON: THE IMPORTANCE OF PROPER INTERNAL CONTROLS

The events were finally resulting the filing for bankruptcy in December 2001, started way much before fraud at Enron could be even suspected. Andersen played a major role in the collapse of Enron. Andersen failed two times regarding audit issues just a few years short time before the collapse of Enron, at Waste Management in 1996 and at Sunbeam in 1997. The two audit failures mentioned above should have been huge warning signs for Andersen to protect itself against another client failure but what they had to face regarding Enron was worse than they ever had. Some internal memos at Andersen made it clear that several conflicts existed between the auditors and the audit committee of Enron. These memos contained several e-mails as well which expressed concerns about accounting practices used by Enron. David B. Duncan as the leading partner on the audit tipped over these concern. There is proof that Duncan's team wrote memos fraudulently stating that the professional standards group approved of the accounting practices of Enron that hid debts and pumped up earnings. Andersen's independence is also highly questionable due to the relationship between audit and non-audit fees. The person who first spotted in 2001 that there wasn't even any chance for Enron to make profit was Jim Chanos, the head of Kynikos Associates. He said that parent company had technically become nothing more than a hedging entity for all of its subsidiaries and affiliates. In 2001 the operating margin of Enron went down significantly to 2% from the previous year's figure of 5% which is more than interesting because this kind of a decrease in one year is unheard of in the utilities industry. Chanos also pointed out that Enron was still aggressively selling stocks, despite there was hardly any capital to back up the shares they were selling. To be professional and effective, auditors must be independent of management and evaluate the financial representations of management for all users of financial statements. Less than 30% of the fees that Andersen received from Enron came from auditing, with the balance of fees coming from consulting. Andersen acted as Enron's external auditor and as its internal auditor. Andersen's work as a consultant raises several questions. It appears that Andersen's audit team, when faced with accounting issues, chose to ignore them, acquiesced in silence to unsound accounting, or embraced accounting schemes as an advocate for its client. Auditors assess the internal controls of a client to determine the extent to which they can rely on a client's accounting system. Enron had too many internal control weaknesses to be given here. Two serious weaknesses were that the CFO was exempted from a conflicts of interest policy, and internal controls over SPEs were a sham, existing in form but not in substance. Many financial officials lacked the background for their jobs, and assets, notably foreign assets, were not physically secured. The tracking of daily cash was lax, debt maturities were not scheduled, off balance sheet debt was ignored although the obligation remained, and company-wide risk was disregarded. Internal controls were inadequate; contingent liabilities were not disclosed; and, Andersen ignored all of these weaknesses. Auditors focus on material misrepresentations. A misrepresentation is material if knowledge of the misrepresentation would change the decisions of the user of financial statements. When Enron began to restate its financial statements and investors began to grasp its misrepresentations, the response of the market is indisputable as to materiality. Many errors were known, but were dismissed by Andersen as immaterial. Other errors may not have been known, but should have been known if reasonable inquiry would have revealed them. At Enron and at Andersen, the business model and the organizational culture were changing. Enron was moving to a new business model dominated by intangible assets, the rights to buy and sell commodities. This change in assets was driven by a new organizational culture which then aggressively cultivated its own growth. As auditors moved to become part of a consulting industry, their business model and organizational culture were changing too. It is likely that both the changes at Enron and at Andersen were increasing risks for investors. Enron's movement away from the dominance of fixed assets to the dominance of intangible assets was likely to increase volatility, and this prospect was compounded by the use of mark-to-market accounting. Also, Andersen's movement away from the professionalization of auditing to the commercialization of consulting was likely to weaken auditors as monitors of management. Into the mix of changing business models and cultures, add people who were not equipped for the changes. The young trading executives at Enron chased the deal for earnings, while failing to grasp the risks attached to the intangibles that were driving growth in earnings. Likewise, young auditors at Andersen embraced consulting, while failing to understand the risk of audit failure. Many accounting firms and independent CPAs reacted to these events and implemented changes in procedure voluntarily. The biggest change that accounting firms made was a move made by the four remaining members of the big five, KPMG, Ernst and Young, Deloitte Touche Tohmatsu, and PricewaterhouseCoopers. These four companies decided to break all ties with Andersen in an attempt to avoid being dragged down with the selling controversy surrounding the Enron scandal. This distancing was also due to the major changes mandated to Andersen as a way to get back on their feet after the scandal broke, and the other firms were afraid that these changes would be forced on them as well. The government reacted aggressively when they became aware of the Enron scandal, and a flurry of legislation and proposals emanated from Congress and the SEC about how best to deal with this situation. President Bush even announced one post-Enron plan. This plan was to make disclosures in financial statements more informative and in the management's letter of representation. This plan would also include higher levels of financial responsibility for CEOs and accountants. Bush's goal was to be tough, but not to put an undue burden upon the honest accountants in the industry.

By far the biggest change brought about is the Sarbanes-Oxley Act. The Sarbanes-Oxley Act requires companies to revaluate their internal audit procedures and make sure that everything is running up to or exceeding the expectations of the auditors. It also requires higher level employees, like the CEO and CFO to have an understanding of the workings of the companies that they head and to affirm the fact that they don't know of any fraud being committed by the company. Sarbanes-Oxley also brought with it new requirements for disclosures.These requirements included reporting of transactions called reportable transactions.These transactions are broken down into several categories, which impact every aspect of a business. One of these categories is listed transactions-which are by far the worst. They are transactions that are actually written out in a list, each one pertaining to one specific situation. Another is transactions with a book-to-tax difference of more than ten million dollars. There are several others however these two will have the greatest effect. Accompanying these requirements are strict penalties if these transactions are not reported and discovered later. This act will mean significant additional work for accountants over the next several years. For many years the SEC Chairman, then Arthur Levitt Jr., had been calling for the separation of auditing and consulting services within one company. However big firms like Andersen would apply their proverbial weight to attempt to show that consulting did not interfere with an auditor's independence. Since the major concern of Andersen's role in the controversy centres on their independence, and because of the large monetary consulting fees being paid to them by Enron, the push has been started anew by Paul Volcker the former Federal Reserve Chairman. Realistically, few think that the big firms will be able to dissuade the SEC from actually implementing such a rule. Many companies who use auditors believe that this is not the answer, because of the fact that it will cause them to hire one firm to do auditing work, and another to do non-audit work like taxes and other filings. In an attempt to not get damaged by any imminent government action, many business-including Disney and Apple Computer Inc. have already begun splitting their audit and non-audit work between different firms.

CLASS ACTIVITY

Designing and Evaluating Internal Controls

- **Objective:** To demonstrate the principles and importance of internal controls through a practical exercise in designing and evaluating controls for a business process.
- **Materials Needed:** Pen/pencil and paper or whiteboard and markers
- **Instructions:** Introduce the concept of internal controls and their importance in safeguarding assets, ensuring accuracy in financial reporting, and compliance with regulations. Discuss different types of internal controls (preventive, detective, and corrective) and their roles in mitigating risks.
- **Assessment:** Evaluate students based on their participation in group discussions, the creativity and effectiveness of their designed controls, and their ability to articulate the rationale behind each control.
- **Extension:** For advanced students, introduce scenarios involving control testing and monitoring to reinforce the concept of continuous improvement in internal controls.

SUMMARY

- A form for recording transactions in chronological order is called a journal. Recording transactions in a journal is called journalizing. Transactions could be recorded in the accounting equation. However, most companies wish to create a more permanent record by recording transactions in a journal. Each business uses the kind of journal that best fits the needs of that business.
- The chart of accounts is a listing of all the accounts in the general ledger, each account accompanied by a reference number. To set up a chart of accounts, one first needs to define the various accounts to be used by the business. Each account should have a number to identify it. For very small businesses, three digits may suffice for the account number, though more digits are highly desirable in order to allow for new accounts to be added as the business grows.
- Every business needs information to help it succeed. A combination of internal and external business information resources can provide the background necessary to evaluate current performance and plan future progress. Knowing the types of information resources that are most critical to business can help companies plan for capturing, analyzing and using that information most effectively.
- Business denotes business that is the state of being busy any activity in which one keeps himself busy. But the economic term of business refers to work, efforts, and acts of people or human busy in connection with the production of wealth. Business is the sum of total activities which are connected with the production or purchase and sale of goods and services with the main objective to earn profit. Man always wants and wants more. Intact he is a wanting being having insatiable innumerous wants.
- A sole proprietorship is a business owned by one person. Legally, there is no distinction between the business and the owner is the company, and the company is the owner. The owner is personally liable for all of the company's debts. All profit is considered to be the owner's personal income and must be reported on the owner's individual income tax return. The advantage of this form of business organization is simplicity: no partnership agreements to be signed, no corporate formalities to perform.
- A partnership is a business with two or more owners. There are two basic types of partnerships: general and limited. In a general partnership, each partner is personally liable for all of the debts of the business. In a limited partnership, some partners have limited liability -- they can lose what they have put into the business, but no more -- while others have full liability. Partnerships do not pay income taxes; instead, the owners report the company's profits as personal income according to their share of ownership in the company.
- A corporation is a "person," legally speaking. It is a distinct entity separate from its owners -- the shareholders. The company itself is responsible for all of its debts. The shareholders can lose the money they have invested in the company, but no more. A corporation directly pays income taxes on its profits, just like individuals do. Shareholders pay taxes on corporate profits only if

those profits are distributed to them as dividends. The advantages of corporate organization include limited liability for shareholders and the ability to raise money by selling stock.

- The chart of accounts is a listing of all accounts used in the general ledger of an organization. The chart is used by the accounting software to aggregate information into an entity's financial statements. The chart is usually sorted in order by account number, to ease the task of locating specific accounts. The accounts are usually numeric, but can also be alphabetic or alphanumeric.
- Business organizations usually create an accounting manual, which specifies all accounting policies, guidelines, procedures and standards for a company's accounts. Included in the accounting manual is the classification of accounts, an outline of accounting rules to follow, and rules specific to the organization.
- Accounting is a detailed business function wherein companies record, report and analyze financial transactions. This information commonly provides support for management decisions and investment decisions for external business stakeholders. Accounting information typically requires documentation for prepared accounting reports and statements.
- In accounting, account titles are the names given to the various categories used to keep track of a business's finances. For any and every transaction, these accounts are updated to reflect what happened in an organized and consistent manner. The account titles are found on the business' general ledger, which is a running list of all these transactions. When compiled by an accountant, the general ledger accounts combine to form the company's financial statements. For example, let's say a business pays cash to buy new inventory from its suppliers.
- Large corporations and publicly traded companies must follow the financial accounting, small businesses have the choice of using either the financial accounting method or the tax accounting method. The difference between the two accounting methods is in the timing of when sales and purchases are recorded based on either accrual or cash. Most small businesses prefer to use the cash-based tax accounting.

REVIEW QUESTIONS

1. How do you gather and checks documents verification and validation processes?
2. How to analyze documents for business growth?
3. Focus on financial reporting standards for transactions and events.
4. Explain the term 'sole proprietorship.'
5. What do you understand by business transaction?
6. How to prepare journal entry for bookkeeping?

REFERENCES

1. Deloitte. (2008). *Business Combinations and Changes in Ownership Interests*. Retrieved from: http://www.iasplus.com/en-gb/publications/global/guides/pub2690/at_download/file/ (accessed on 30 July 2024).
2. European Securities and Markets Authority (ESMA). (2015). *ESMA Guidelines on Alternative Performance Measures*. Retrieved from: https://www.esma.europa.eu/press-news/esma-news/esma-publishes-final-guidelines-alternativeperformance-measures (accessed on 30 July 2024).
3. International Accounting Standards Board. (2003). IAS 10: Events after the reporting period. In *International Financial Reporting Standards* (2003). Retrieved from: http://eifrs.ifrs.org (accessed on 30 July 2024).
4. Abbott, L. J., S. Parker and G. F. Peters. 2010. Serving two masters: The association between audit committee internal audit oversight and internal audit activities. Accounting Horizons (March): 1-24.
5. Backof, A. G., T. D. Carpenter and J. Thayer. 2018. Auditing complex estimates: How do construal level and evidence formatting impact auditors' consideration of inconsistent evidence? Contemporary Accounting Research 35(4): 1798-1815.
6. Canning, M., Y. Gendron and B. O'Dwyer. 2018. Auditing in a changing environment and the constitution of cross-paradigmatic communications channels. Auditing: A Journal of Practice & Theory 37(2): 165-174.

Index

Q

R

S

Printed and bound by CPI Group (UK) Ltd, Croydon, CR0 4YY

18/09/2026

14965063-0004